Taverns and Drinking in Early America

Taverns and Drinking in Early America

SHARON V. SALINGER

The Johns Hopkins University Press / Baltimore and London

© 2002 The Johns Hopkins University Press
All rights reserved. Published 2002
Printed in the United States of America on acid-free paper
2   4   6   8   9   7   5   3   1

The Johns Hopkins University Press
2715 North Charles Street
Baltimore, Maryland 21218-4363
www.press.jhu.edu

Library of Congress Cataloging-in-Publication Data

Salinger, Sharon V. (Sharon Vineberg)
Taverns and drinking in early America / Sharon V. Salinger.
p.   cm.
Includes bibliographical references and index.
ISBN 0-8018-6878-5 (hardcover : alk. paper)
1. United States—Social life and customs—To 1775.   2. United States—Social
conditions—To 1865.   3. Taverns (Inns)—United States—History—17th century.
4. Taverns (Inns)—United States—History—18th century.   5. Drinking of
alcoholic beverages—Social aspects—United States—History—17th century.
6. Drinking of alcoholic beverages—Social aspects—United States—History—18th
century.   7. Social classes—United States—History—17th century.   8. Social
classes—United States—History—18th century.   I. Title.
E162 .S23 2002   2001002796

A catalog record for this book is available from the British Library.

To Susan

Contents

$\mathcal{A}$cknowledgments

$\mathcal{T}$he size of my debt has grown exponentially with the amount of time I have been working on this book. A host of knowledgeable archivists and librarians assisted me along the way: Laurie Rofini, Barbara Weir, and coresearcher Lucy Simler, Chester County Archives; Diane Rofini, Chester County Historical Society; Linda Stanley, formerly at the Historical Society of Pennsylvania; Peter Drummey, Virginia Smith, and Jennifer Tolpa, Massachusetts Historical Society; Beth Carroll-Horrocks, formerly at the American Philosophical Society; Stephen Nonack, Boston Atheneum; Libba Taylor, Charleston County Public Library; and Alicia Parker and Jean Russo, Historic Annapolis Foundation. Also the staffs at Baker Library, Harvard University; Massachusetts State Archives, Columbia Point; Massachusetts Historical and Genealogical Society; Essex County Historical Society, Salem, Massachusetts; the New-York Historical Society; New York City Archives; Law Library, Columbia University; North Carolina State Archives, Raleigh; Duke University Library; the library at the University of North Carolina, Chapel Hill; South Carolina Historical Society, South Carolina State Archives, South Carolina Historical and Genealogical Society; South Caroliniana Room, University of South Carolina; the Huntington Library, especially Roy Ritchie; the Colonial Williamsburg Foundation library; Swem Library, College of William and Mary; and Virginia State Library, Richmond. It would have been impossible to study early American taverns while living in southern California without the staff at the Tomas Rivera Library, University of California, Riverside, especially Nancy Getty in the reference department and Janet Moores in interlibrary loan.

Some support was financial. I thank the Huntington Library for a Robert Middlekauf summer fellowship, and the Massachusetts Historical Society and the North Caroliniana Society for travel fellowships. Travel and research funds from the Academic Senate of UC Riverside enabled me to employ a talented cadre of research assistants—Diane Dawson, Thomas Thompson, Barbara Wallace, William Johnson, Chris Ontiveros, Lore Kuehnert, Andrea Maestrejuan, and Dawn Marsh. Deans Carlos Vélez-Ibañez and Patricia O'Brien provided funds for a research assistant. For the past five years, Keith Pacholl has worked with exceptional diligence and enthusiasm.

Friends scattered along the eastern seaboard helped the grant money stretch farther by providing me places to stay while I was on research missions: Cheryl Logan, Jim and Claudia Svara (in North Carolina); Don and Arlene Matzkin, and Linda Stanley and Terry Snyder (in Philadelphia); Nina Dayton (in Connecticut); and Bridget Murnane (in Boston).

Friends and colleagues graciously read and commented on all or portions of the manuscript in various stages of draftiness: Nina Dayton, Barry Joyce, Dale Kent, Monte Kugel, Peter Mancall, Gary Nash, Carla Pestana, Carole Shammas, Sarah Stage, and Michael Zuckerman. I had the pleasure of meeting Andrew Sandoval-Strausz in the Boston archives. He has been a valuable intellectual asset, sharing generously of his work on the hotel. We seek any chance we can to engage in our own reenactment drama of the bar. Ruth Herndon, Jim Merrell, Neal Salisbury, Billy G. Smith, Jack Marietta, and Peter Mancall corresponded with me through cyberspace and shared their insights and materials from their own work. I benefited enormously from conversations and correspondence with Peter Thompson, whose book on Philadelphia taverns I greatly admire. Peter Hoffer and an anonymous reader for Johns Hopkins University Press provided useful criticism. I also thank Christopher Langevin of Langevin Geographic for the maps.

Colleagues and friends who endured without complaint my tavern-related outbursts include Lynda Bell, Philip Brett, Sue-Ellen Case, Judy Coffin, Susan Foster, Arch Getty, Nancy Getty, Ann Goldberg, George Haggerty, Randy Head, Ray Kea, Brian Lloyd, Marcus Rediker, Marta Savigliano, Carole Shammas, Sarah Stage, and Jeff Tobin. Clare Johnson in the UC Riverside History Department office provided more than her share of computer and other assistance.

I am extremely grateful to the hardworking staff at Johns Hopkins University Press especially Robert J. Brugger, Anne M. Whitmore, and Melody Herr. Bob and Anne gave generously of their time and support.

My son, Aaron, left home for college midway through this project. On each return visit, he listened, with good cheer, to endless tavern talk. Long ago he helped me recognize what is truly important in my life. I owe the largest debt to Susan Rose. She applied her choreographic skills to awkward and static prose, and she has participated in ways that have made writing a far less solitary endeavor.

Taverns and Drinking in Early America

Introduction

*T*averns in early America ran the gamut from the elegant to the mean and nasty, from those that catered to every need of society's elites to those that the locals and travelers who used them could only hope to survive. In the urban taverns that served a middle-class and elite clientele, men gathered on a regular basis to transact business, argue over issues of local politics, or share a convivial pint with friends. Visitors staying at such an establishment in Pennsylvania might witness a heated argument about the price of wheat or in Boston a discussion about the inspirational quality of the minister's sermon. The laboring classes engaged in their own entertainments, exchanged news of the day, plotted political action, or just enjoyed drinking with their co-workers and friends. Rural taverns beckoned to a mixed company. If these inns were well situated on a main road, the patrons included local residents as well as travelers who needed a night's lodging, a warm fire in winter, and a cool drink in summer.[1]

Early Americans drank heavily and shared their views about the practice well before the better-known nineteenth-century debate over the evils of alcohol. When Increase Mather penned "Wo to Drunkards" (1673), he expressed a common ambivalence about the value of alcoholic beverages—wine is from God but the drunkard is from the devil. Drinking was not thought to be intrinsically bad, only its excesses. Mather later found an unlikely supporter in Benjamin Franklin. "I doubt not that *moderate Drinking* has been improv'd for the Diffusion of Knowledge among the ingenious Part of Mankind . . . drinking does not *improve* our Faculties, but it enables us to *use* them."[2] Almost one hundred years later, the eminent physician Benjamin Rush acknowledged the important functions that alcohol served in society. In a letter to John Adams in 1808, Rush reported on a remarkable dream. He had been elected president of the United States and as his first act persuaded Congress to pass a law prohibiting the importation and consumption of "ardent spirits." To Rush's horror, the citizenry violently opposed the law. One petitioner argued that all productivity would cease, farmers and artisans would lack the strength to work, ministers and lawyers would lose their ability to preach and plead, and women would become "peevish and quarrelsome" from lack of brandy in their tea.[3]

Rush's description of Americans' appetite for alcohol reflects the reality. Colonists of every rank, size, and age, including children, drank often and in quantity. By the early decades of the eighteenth century, the beverages of choice were varieties of distilled liquors, referred to as spirits—whiskey, rum, gin, and brandy. The alcoholic content averaged 45 percent, or in distillers' terms 90 proof. Colonial leaders were alarmed and visitors amazed by the volume of potent liquids consumed. During the colonial period, according to one authority, the "annual per capita consumption of hard liquor alone, mostly rum, approached four gallons a head." These amounts alone would have provided the drinking public with ample quantities, but spirituous liquors constituted only one form of the alcohol beverages consumed. Colonists also drank fermented brews: beer, hard cider, and wine. Beer consumption lagged behind other choices, except for "small beer," which contained only 1 percent alcohol and was brewed at home. Hard cider, on the other hand, with an alcoholic content of 10 percent, enjoyed extreme popularity. It is likely that most of the alcohol coursing through colonists' veins came from cider. Wine was rarely the colonists' drink of choice; in the period just before the Revolution, Americans consumed an average of only one-tenth of a gallon per year.[4]

The most eminent Americans offered commentary on the consequences of this prodigious appetite for spirituous beverages. George Washington, an active whiskey distiller, was nonetheless convinced that alcohol was "the ruin of the workmen in this Country." John Adams found nothing contradictory in beginning each day with a tankard of hard cider as he ruminated whether it was "not mortifying . . . that we, Americans, should exceed all other . . . people in the world in this degrading, beastly vice of intemperance?" Thomas Jefferson noted with alarm that cheap distilled spirits were "spreading through the mass of our citizens," yet he is credited with inventing the presidential cocktail party. Foreign and domestic travelers commented with surprise at Americans' drinking habits, especially in light of the relative lack of public drunkenness. They judged colonists as "seasoned" drinkers, who could imbibe heavily without the appearance of intoxication.[5]

Alcoholic beverages appealed in part because water was considered an unsafe beverage: it was popularly believed that drinking water endangered one's health. The common distrust of water may have been founded in part on Scripture. The apostle Paul, in his First Epistle to Timothy, cautioned, "Drink no longer water, but use a little wine for thy stomach's sake and thine oft infirmities." Governor William Bradford of Plymouth Colony enumerated the enemies to health and the causes of disease as "chaing of aeir, famine, or unholsome foode, much drinking of water, sorrows & troubls, etc." More than a century later, the *Pennsylvania Gazette* reported on a series of disasters that had befallen individuals as a result of drinking water. One of these water drinkers, a laborer, "was thought would have died, had not a Person present forced a Quantity of rum down his Throat, by which Means he soon recovered." Colonists regarded water as "lowly and common," a drink better suited to barnyard animals than humans. As a result, colonists avoided water as much as possible and quenched their thirst with a variety of alcoholic beverages.[6]

Alcoholic refreshments did not simply substitute for water, however. They fulfilled a number of specific functions. Seventeenth- and eighteenth-century Americans, along with their counterparts in England and Europe, believed that spirituous liquors were nutritious and healthful. Rum, gin, and brandy did not simply accompany a meal but were regarded as food, and supplemented "limited and monotonous diets." Ardent spirits were credited with medicinal faculties as well, able to cure "colds, fevers, snakebites, frosted toes, and broken legs." Then as now they were thought of as "relaxants that would relieve depression, reduce tension, and enable hardworking laborers to enjoy a moment of happy, frivolous, camaraderie." A traveler through Virginia witnessed "the vile Practice of giving children, as well as those of all other ages, Rum in the morning as soon as they rise . . . & the Parents encourage it reckoning it wholesome." Some colonists were convinced that beer and fermented juices contributed to the prevention of certain diseases, like scurvy and dysentery. Mixing medicines with virtually any alcoholic beverage enhanced their potency far more than if combined with water. Midwives prepared a "caudle" for women in labor; a drink made with ale or wine mixed with spices. The Puritans believed so deeply in the health benefits derived from strong drink that they permitted imbibing on the Lord's day "in the case of nesseitie for the releife of those that are sicke or faint or the like for theire refreshing."[7]

Nicholas Cresswell, an Englishman who traveled throughout the colonies just before the American Revolution, divulged yet another benefit to be gained from drinking. Early on in his journey he became extremely ill with a violent headache. After the worst of it had passed his doctor prescribed some "physic" to clear his body and further his recovery and a prescription to prevent a reoccurrence: drink more rum. The doctor believed that Cresswell brought the sickness upon himself by drinking water and too little alcohol. Cresswell recalled the doctor's advice—avoid the water and substitute rum—when he offered it as an explanation of the New Year's Day behavior of the local parson, who had been too drunk to "perform the duties of his office."[8] Given the variety and perceived inherent beneficial qualities of alcoholic beverages, it is no wonder that early Americans imbibed and felt duty bound to do so.

Clearly colonists drank. Until recently students of colonial America have been reluctant to explore the obvious and obscure purposes that alcohol served in colonial society. This hesitation is surprising, since taverns and drinking in early modern Europe and England provide a guide to the nature of public culture, to the articulation of classes, and to the locus of political action. Drinking houses played a central role in the fabric of life.[9] The neglect of the subject is also remarkable because unlike Europe and England, most colonial towns and villages boasted only two types of public buildings—churches and taverns—and public drinking houses were far more common than public houses of worship.

Two recent exceptions in this dearth of research carve a particular niche for the colonial tavern and confer a central place for the public house in Massachusetts and Philadelphia. David Conroy explains that Puritans imported their drinking habits from England to Massachusetts. Old World drinking patterns inculcated shared values and ideals, but in the New World, ministers and provincial elite identified collective drinking as a threat to their control and as an attack on an orderly society. As a result, they worked to regulate tavern culture and to limit the number of public houses. In spite of these actions, taverns functioned as public theater in which colonists "resisted, initiated, and addressed changes within their society," and the citizenry and colonial authorities redefined their relationship. Peter Thompson reveals that taverns operated quite differently in Philadelphia. Public houses there did not sustain tradition so much as they marked change, especially in the choices men made about where and with whom to drink. During most of the colonial period in the port city, the rich drank along-side the poor and Congregationalists imbibed with Anglicans. In the second half of the eighteenth century, a distinctive stratification and specialization of tavern culture gradually emerged. Men drank and conversed only with those from the same socioeconomic stratum; particular taverns became associated with specific political values, which in turn informed the revolutionary politics in the city.[10] In Massachusetts, the tavern, as an important public space, served as the center of socializing and communication and provided space for political debates. Taverns there were secularizing and modernizing institutions that expanded in influence over the course of the colonial period. In Philadelphia, taverngoers from all social and economic layers gathered inside, often with incompatible agendas. The notion of the public sphere was inoperative in the city's taverns, because no agreement existed within groups and no group dominated the space.[11]

This book seeks to provide entree into these sites of social and political life, by exploring the place of public houses and drinking in colonists' lives. The emphasis here highlights the ways the tavern preserved traditional culture, rather than identifying the public house as a site implicated in the transformation of society. This focus also underscores the tavern's exclusionary nature, instead of envisioning the space as essentially inclusive.[12]

We gain a more complete understanding of the role of the tavern in early America if we examine the public house throughout the mainland British colonies rather than within a smaller geographic area. What were the similarities and differences in the role of drinking and tavern life in New England, the upper mid-Atlantic, the Chesapeake, and the South; in cities, towns, and agricultural regions; in Anglican, Quaker, and Puritan communities? In what ways were gender and class implicated in the use of tavern spaces, and what relationship did drinking and the tavern have in the lives of American Indians and blacks? Finally, what does it mean to identify the tavern as a public space?[13]

The tavern operated within dual contexts: the institutional, from the perspective of the law and courts, and the social, from the inside. Legislators required each jurisdiction to have a public house to accommodate travelers. As a result, each colony guided the behavior of drinkers and proprietors with a body of law. The discussion opens on the eastern side of the Atlantic with an overview of general drinking patterns and customs in the Netherlands and England, two cultural legacies that helped shape early American attitudes toward alcohol and taverns. We then step inside the public house to see who the patrons were, how they entertained themselves, where they slept, and the role of drinking in daily life. The text then examines colonial laws related to the tavern and drinking, analyzing the regulatory tactics adopted by colonial leaders and how subsequent statutes were crafted to make existing law more effective.[14] Since the law yields little direct information about behavior, court records help us to understand enforcement practices in cases of tavern- and alcohol-related crimes. The frequency and nature of the infractions reveal which tavern and drinking violations colonial authorities deemed worthy of prosecution. By analyzing whom colonial lawmakers deemed worthy of a license and contrasting this ideal against the reality of who actually received one, we gain further insight into the cultural space taverns occupied. Licensing records also permit analyses of tavern densities, contrasting cities with towns, ports with agricultural regions, as well as gauging change over time. Were there fewer taverns in the seventeenth century than the eighteenth or in new communities than established ones? What might this reveal about the traditional place of taverns within society?

The physical space where this social drama was acted out defies easy description, for it existed in many forms. Although *tavern* was the term most commonly employed; *ordinary, inn,* and *public house* were used interchangeably. Some sold wine and beer, others sold spirits as well. Most offered meals. All were supposed to have nighttime accommodations for people and horses. Some owners constructed their establishments specifically to be public houses; others tacked a sign on the door of their houses and opened for business. Some tavern keepers operated successful enterprises, while others ran much more on hope than profit. Some taverns catered primarily to society's elite, while most invited a multitude and mixture of people. However, the precise form did not alter the fundamental role of the tavern—to provide a place where individuals or groups could gather to eat and drink, talk, sing, argue, conduct business, play games of chance, or while away the hours. As a historian of public drinking in Paris noted, the tavern's most important function was to sell space and "the freedom to use it within broad constraints."[15]

The writings of seventeenth- and eighteenth-century diarists provide a social perspective into the space. Their recollections about their time spent in the local tavern or during stops along the road permit the reader to follow the patrons inside, meet the proprietors and other clientele, eavesdrop on conversations, discover what people read, overhear their arguments, and record the purposes and frequency of their meetings. These first-hand accounts identify a far greater role than simply a place where colonists gathered to socialize. The public house was what a theorist of social relations called a space in which "the informal logic of actual life" can be discovered and reconstructed. Let us open the doors of colonial taverns.[16]

Dutch and English Origins:
For the "receiving and refreshment
of travaillers and strangers"

I was resolved in my own mind to have rested this night at Southerns, but
on my approach to the House it was no more than a mere Hut, full of rude
mean people, and tho' some of their countenances were not quite so un-
promising as those I left at Roans, they were attended with this additional
discouragement to me, that they were every one, as well as the Landlord,
inflamed with liquor and exceeding turbulent and noisy.[1]

*T*hus did Daniel Fisher, the author of this complaint, express his disap-
pointment with the accommodations that greeted him at Southern's tavern, at Southern Ferry on the south side of the Rappahannock River, during his
journey from his home in Williamsburg, Virginia, to Philadelphia in 1755. After
a long day in the saddle, he longed for some rest, tasty food, ample drink, and
agreeable companionship. Instead, Fisher confronted coarse and rude people
who were sloppily drunk. And he doubted he would find any comfort in a structure that was little more than a hut. Although it was late in the day, Fisher elected
to cross the river and search farther for decent lodging. Colonial lawmakers, regarding it as the primary obligation of taverns to provide adequately for travelers and their horses, crafted laws specifying minimum requirements, presumably
so that travelers like Fisher would not have to put up with inferior services.

The legal and cultural context of American colonial drinking and taverns derives from those in the Netherlands and England. A body of early American law developed that designed the basic services tavern customers like Daniel Fisher might expect. But is that what customers actually found? American laws governing taverns also designated who could and who could not patronize public houses or receive credit from them. By defining tavern access legally, colonial authorities limited it to particular groups within society and articulated that this was a peculiar public space.

In the Old World

A glance at the Amsterdam Tun, which for visitors was a curious site, suggests the appeal of nontraditional drinking establishments in attracting patrons. The Amsterdam Tun was a colossal empty cask with a table, two benches, and seating for thirty-two. The Dutch created various types of settings in which to drink. The justifications for their consumption of large amounts of alcohol included that strong drink protected them from the diseases associated with foul water and rank vapors, which there were plenty of in the Low Countries. Writers like English visitor Fynes Moryson ascribed certain of the Dutch personality attributes to their devoted drinking. "These United parts are seated in the wildest of seas and waters and use excesse of drinking, so they commonly are flegmatick complections and beget more females than males." Another visitor, Thomas Coryate, marveled at how long they could perch on their bar stools with unwavering interest in a single mug: "They use to take a tin tankard of beer in their hands and sit by it an hour together, yea sometimes two whole hours."[2]

Contemporary reports linked Dutch drunkenness to wild extremes of behavior—raucousness, for example, punctuated by bursts of sudden hilarity. William Brereton, who traveled in Holland, described with disdain the schutters' annual feast at Dordrecht: "I do not believe scarce a sober man to be found amongst them, nor was it safe for a sober man to trust himself amongst them, they did shout so and sing, roar, skip and leap." A few years later an observer in the same town, Robert Bargrave, became quite alarmed when he noticed the table beginning to revolve in the 'burghers' common tavern. He was relieved to discover that the spinning was not the result of too much wine. Rather an extraordinary mechanical device moved the company as they sat around the table. The commentator, however, did believe that the quantity of wine consumed would have been sufficient "to turn their brains." Some critics implied that the Dutch found their courage through drink. It was reported at Oxford in 1675 that a famous admiral, Cornelis Tromp, owed his intrepid attitude toward the ocean to his frequent tavern visits. The magnitude of his drinking, perhaps designed to prepare him for his next voyage, is indicated by a contemporary account: on one occasion a porter was summoned to transport the sodden admiral in a wheelbarrow from the tavern to his lodgings.[3]

Interpreting these vivid observations presents a thorny problem. They could very well be the product of intense "Hollandophobia." In the case of the painter Isaac Cruikshank it might be just that. It is difficult to attribute simple satire to his quite nasty painting, *Opening the Sluices, or Holland's Last Shift*, in which a long line of half-squatting, full-figured Dutch women is positioned at the edge of the ocean. Gin is being poured into their mouths and flows through them into the sea. Cruikshank paints these women as receptive to the gin while also totally vulnerable to an enemy's invasion.[4]

The proportion of people to taverns and the amounts of alcohol swallowed suggest that the sodden reputation of the Dutch may well have been deserved. In 1613, Amsterdam boasted as many as 518 licensed alehouses, a ratio of one for every two hundred men, women, and children. At the end of the sixteenth century, in Haarlem, city residents consumed prodigious quantities of beer, some in pubs but most at home.[5] Administrators held out no hope that they could curb Sunday drinking; they were accused of infringing on their constituents desire to drink and interfering with the lucrative trade and production of alcoholic beverages. When Mr. Peters, a religious burgomaster, attempted to reform the profanation of the Sabbath by imposing and collecting a fine from anyone who traded or worked on that day, "the brewers (whereof are abundance in this town) made a head, came into the Statehouse, and in a mutinous manner told the burgomaister that they would not be subject unto his new laws; and hereby all quashed formerly effected, and the hoped for reformation came to nothing." William Brereton conveyed the impression that drinking occurred in virtually any context. While touring the "famous and orthodox synod of Dorth," the group climbed up to a high room "wherein we drank two cans of wine." Brereton found it quite odd that a house designated for making business deals included a tap house. He recounted a scene in which three men acted as judges to resolve any disputes during the process of buying and selling. The "judges" sat in high seats near the fire surrounded by the parties and their witnesses. Everyone drank copiously and abided by the judges' order.[6] Almost all social settings, religious or secular, business or pleasure, involved copious quantities of alcohol.

Officials exerted little effort to control drinking behavior. What few laws existed were less about prohibition than about the collection of revenue. In the first half of the seventeenth century, the city of Amsterdam passed approximately thirty ordinances to ensure that drink sellers were licensed. The proceeds from the tariff went to the maintenance of the women's house of correction. The only exception was a 1629 ordinance passed in response to a public riot prohibiting taverns in portions of the city. Anyone found to be operating a tavern in these particular neighborhoods would be fined three guilders "for every day of a violation." Officials knew better than to interfere with the production and trade in beer; it was big business. The Dutch bestowed universal qualities upon beer, giving it an almost sacred status, and competition over its production was seen as healthy and worth supporting.[7]

Although the Dutch were clearly devoted to alcoholic beverages, it does seem curious that a people with a strong Calvinist tradition and an established institutional structure to support it would be so soft on alcohol and its abuses. The church did catalog excesses in drinking along with other sins, but alcohol was too deeply embedded in the culture for the church to have much effect. One historian of the Dutch claims that the church successfully cataloged alcohol along with tobacco as the "devil's food" but did not go so far as to stigmatize its use with the label of moral uncleanness. Church elders were perturbed by the common tendency to reduce alcoholic beverages to just another form of food. Cookbooks, for example, provided multiple variations for home brewing. Before the use of coffee was widespread, farmers breakfasted on beer and eggs and those with stronger stomachs dined on a concoction of eggs, sugar, warm beer, and ample amounts of brandywine. Daily rounds of work were punctuated by drinking. Farmers and buyers, merchants and captains secured their deals over a shared drink in the tavern. This practice was so common that some towns passed ordinances nullifying any business transaction finalized in a tavern unless a notary was present. Smoking and drinking, instead of being placed in categories that portended self-destruction, were characterized as part of the national culture.[8]

FIGURE 1. The Lawes of Drinking, 1617. Gentlemanly taverngoers who revel in the Muses and in their intellects (*top*) contrast with the plebian drinkers in a far more modest house (*bottom*). Both settings depict order. Artist unknown. Reproduced from Peter Clark, *The English Alehouse: A Social History, 1200–1830* (London: Longman, 1983).

In preindustrial England, alehouses were more numerous than any other retail or public-meeting place. The paintings *The Lawes of Drinking* and *The Gin Drinkers* afford an opportunity to enter three different taverns, to locate the changing perception of English drinking houses over time and to understand how lawmakers responded to these shifts. In *The Lawes of Drinking* (Figure 1), the painter invites our gaze into two early-seventeenth-century alehouses. In the top panel society's elites have gathered to drink the wine of conviviality, representing the model of decorum. Finely clad gentlemen are seated around a table smoking pipes, drinking, and engaging in erudite conversation. Lest the observer miss the message, the drinkers are framed by classical columns that evoke a civilized and learned society. Scattered above their heads are various inscriptions: "Hellicon," from which descends the muse, presumably alcohol, appears at the top. Flowing from the left is "Nectar yt Ingenium," or the nectar of intellect. Genius resides in the beverages consumed; those assembled drink to enhance their cerebral prowess. The bottom picture presents a corresponding alehouse. Decorum continues to mark the gathering but these are ordinary folks. Their dress is plain. They are seated around a table; one person is dancing while another plays music. While the top panel conjures pretentiousness and drink as the tool of enhanced intellect, the bottom panel depicts the simple virtues of the plebian space. Both symbolize the sober enjoyment and conviviality of drinking.[9]

By the middle of the eighteenth century, the view inside the plebeian alehouse had changed. Instead of simple sober virtue the scene had transformed into one of debauchery and sexual license. In Hogarth's 1736 print, *The Gin Drinkers* (Figure 2), the London dram-shop is the opposite of order. The space appears unkempt, drunkards are scattered throughout, and adults are carrying naked children. Spirituous liquors are no longer being celebrated nor are they seen to contribute to civilization and the life of the mind. Patrons continue to worship the god that emerges from the barrels of gin, but the deity has no redeeming qualities.[10] The efforts in England to regulate the trade in alcoholic beverages paralleled these changing realities of the public house.

Attempts to control the alehouse in England had medieval precedents. Fines were established for anyone selling ale at an excessive rate or for brewing inferior drink. By the Late Middle Ages an informal system of licensing developed in scattered areas. As the number of alehouses increased, toward the end of the

FIGURE 2. The Gin Drinkers, 1736. This print depicts the squalor popularly associated with the drinking of gin. Attributed to Hogarth. Reproduced from Peter Clark, *The English Alehouse: A Social History, 1200–1830* (London: Longman, 1983).

Middle Ages, regulation kept pace. The 1495 Beggars Act authorized two justices to "suppress ale-selling where necessary and to bind alehouse-keepers to good behavior." By 1552, Parliament introduced statutory licensing. Lamenting the proliferation of popular drinking places, justices of the peace required alehouse keepers to obtain a license and pay a bond for good behavior. Those who failed to take these steps were escorted to jail. The purpose of this law was to control the number of alehouses, "daily growing and increasing" in the realm.[11]

These attempts to control the alehouse inspired little official response. While the law required that there be no tippling or disorder, Parliament failed to define these terms. Some townships, like Chester, tried to fill the void. Early in Elizabeth's reign, Chester passed a series of measures that required alehouses to post signs to control the sale of drink, to assure good order, and to restrict who could imbibe. The license helped govern where alehouses were located, their hours of operation, services offered, including the number of beds, and the purpose of back entries. No one could drink who abused the privilege or who was new to the area. Mixed in to this ordinance was a requirement that everyone attend church, as if lawmakers sought assurances that tavern attendance and church were not mutually exclusive. In certain regions, admission to a tavern was prohibited for poor working men (except at dinner time), those who received parish alms, and miscreants. However, Chester was unusual. Most locales attempted only feeble controls and little systematic effort was made to license sellers of ale.[12]

The impulse to control the drink trade received an additional boost in the late sixteenth century, as public drinking houses increasingly became divided into categories and segregated by class. Taverns and inns, which by law were required to accommodate travelers, were frequented and owned by individuals from the middling and upper classes. The alehouse occupied a second tier. The proprietors and patrons belonged to the lowest orders of society, and alehouses were strictly forbidden to house migrants. It was the alehouse that provoked England's lawmakers and local magistrates into action.[13]

This segregation of the drink trade was a reflection of the intense poverty evident in England from the late sixteenth century through the early seventeenth century.[14] Lawmakers blamed poverty for escalating levels of crime and disorder and they branded the unlicensed alehouse as a source of these disturbances. Located on the geographic fringes of the towns, alehouses were frequented by the incoming or local poor who sought refuge from their wretched economic conditions at home. They could drown their misery in cheap alcohol. Society's elite recognized that these illicit alehouses acted as the hub of lower-class culture and accused these public houses of enticing the population away from church services. From the perspective of England's wealthier citizens, poor alehouses served as a gathering site of the immoral and irreligious poor and threatened the stability and morality of society.[15] The fear of disorder spawned a flurry of regulation aimed at reducing the number of illegal drinking houses.

When the Privy Council took up the matter of drinking houses in 1604, they determined that the number of alehouses needed to accommodate travelers adequately and provide for the poor. Again the response was uneven. The justices of the peace in some counties fixed the hours of nightly closing, forbade any trade on Sundays (except for travelers), and limited the individual drinker's visit to the tavern to a single hour. The Privy Council returned to the problem annually until 1607, but their actions merely tinkered with the 1552 Act or gave approval to local practices already in place.[16] The dedication to controlling the alehouse escalated during the second decade of the seventeenth century. In 1618, licensing procedures were systematized and followed in the early 1620s by acts that tightened various loopholes. Life for the unlicensed alehouse keeper was made extremely difficult.[17]

During the early decades of the seventeenth century, English lawmakers continued their lament that alehouses "made many beggars" and that the poor spent all their relief on drink, "whereby they starve their children." John Taylor, in his book describing his travels from London to Salisbury, supplied a somewhat sympathetic explanation for this phenomenon: "The meanest beggar dares to spend all he hath at the Alehouse . . . for the poore man drinks stifly to drive care away, and hath nothing to lose." The alehouse tempted the poor and turned a bad situation into a worse one.[18] Regulation was unsystematic and its rare effectiveness took place on the local level, as disorderly drinking was increasingly identified as the peculiar problem of the lower orders of society. For society's elite, just the existence of the alehouse threatened the social order, for the poor not only gathered among themselves for their entertainments but squandered their meager resources on drink.

By the mid-eighteenth century, the position of the alehouse in English society began to shift, becoming more respectable. In part, this was because the English economy improved, lessening the numbers of tramping poor and the fears associated with their gatherings. In addition, the alehouse began to attract its clientele from all ranks of society. It was no longer the exclusive site of the poor; now master craftsmen, farmers, parsons, dons, and government officials could be found drinking along side the laboring classes. Victualing houses also attracted a more prominent clientele, and they added to their traditional range of alcohol and food a more varied and sophisticated range of services and facilities. An increasing number of establishments offered guest rooms rather than sleeping accommodations on tables or benches or rooms crammed with twenty or more persons of both sexes.[19]

Although the alehouse no longer presented the same threat to society that it had when it was the refuge for society's poor, the shift did not spell an end to the legal struggle to control public houses. Political, social, and religious groups continued to lament the ill effects of drinking. Secular leaders argued that drunkenness made it impossible for individuals to work diligently and regularly at their work. Religious leaders, primarily Methodists and older dissenting sects, were caught up in a religious fervor and aimed part of their arsenal at public drinking houses and their alleged threat to political and social stability. Although the membership of the chorus was varied, they began to sing a common song. The public houses were the meeting places of England's radicals.

The laws that appeared in the middle and late eighteenth century were not new. The goal remained to limit the number of public houses and enforce licensing. Lawmakers ordained closer supervision of drinking habits and closing times and continued to restrict Sunday hours. In an attempt to protect workers' wages, they directed their efforts toward prohibiting public houses from allowing traveling entertainment and sporting events. The rhetoric may have seemed new, but no legal innovations emerged. The legal controls over the alehouse looked much as they had before the Civil War.[20]

The earliest English tavern laws, designed to control abuses in drinking, were vague and inconsistently enforced. Successful regulation was rare and when it did occur prevailed on the local level. By the seventeenth century, drinking laws reflected society's class stratification. These ordinances were not designed to apply to all levels of the social hierarchy; the upper classes were exempt, because drunkenness, as a member of the House of Commons explained, was a vice of "the woorst and inferior sort of people." Lawmakers designed laws to punish individuals who drank to excess in alehouses in their own towns, while exempting travelers.[21] Local magistrates sought to control the number of public houses by enforcing licensing regulations, setting the opening and closing times, limiting the number of hours individuals could linger, and prohibiting the poor from entering the alehouse altogether, so that they would not waste what little money they had. This power over the tavern and the behavior of individuals kept the public coffers full from the fees and bonds paid by tavern keepers and the imposition of an excise on liquor, which served to promote local manufacture and to contribute additional revenue to the public pot.[22]

The Dutch and English legacies to the North American colonies in their cultures of drinking and their efforts to regulate public drinking houses were founded and sustained by a series of ironic themes. Appearing in the colonies were the familiar cries deploring the proliferation in the number of alehouses and the fears prompted by the increasing numbers of drunkards, yet an accompanying strain rejoiced in the amount of revenue collected from licensing fees, bonds, and the excise. Familiar too was the assumption that the laws preventing people from overindulging in drink or spending too much time in the tavern were not intended for all levels of society and were thus not enforced uniformly within the social hierarchy. Just as with the Dutch, Calvinist leanings barely mitigated the influence of the tavern. Initially the impulses of the godly and the profane were at odds, but through compromise and negotiation the church and the tavern coexisted.[23] Finally, in North America just as in England, tavern and drinking laws focused on locals, exempting travelers from the same restrictions.

Not surprisingly, the laws in colonial America were similar to those that regulated the tavern trade in England. Colonial lawmakers aspired to reach the same twin ends: to curb the potential abuses caused by overindulging in drink and to use the tavern trade to raise revenue. These two goals appear contradictory. Proper suppression of drinking and limiting the number of taverns might reduce colonial revenue. However, just as in England, colonial governors collected money in a variety of ways: licensing fees for tavern proprietors, bonds to insure their good behavior, and excise taxes on liquor. Official coffers were also fattened through a system of fines that penalized those who violated the law.

Over the course of the colonial period, the prerevolutionary tavern and the drink trade in early America paralleled another English trend. Most public houses, until the early decades of the eighteenth century, entertained a clientele that was mixed in terms of social rank. However, gradually and especially in the major urban centers, tavern patrons gathered together based upon their shared characteristics, such as ethnicity, status, or occupation. A few taverns emerged that drew their customers exclusively from the ranks of the elite.[24]

Tavern Services

Unlike in England, in the colonies the terms *ordinary, tavern,* and *inn* remained synonymous throughout most of the eighteenth century; these institutions were licensed to provide entertainment "for all persons" including strangers and their horses.[25] The North Carolina statute was typical: taverns were required to have "good Wholesome, and cleanly Lodging and Dyet for Travellers and Stable, Fodder, and Corn, or Pasturage and Corn . . . for their horses." Massachusetts lawmakers concurred. Public houses were to be established principally for the "receiving and refreshment of travaillers and strangers, and to serve the public occasions of such town or precinct." Massachusetts magistrates were prepared to punish any tavern keeper whose provisions were insufficient for travelers and their horses.[26]

Tavern services and fare often differed dramatically over the landscape, local tastes deciding what was served and what amenities were desirable. A number of counties in New York ordered that taverns be equipped with "three good spare beds, two to be feather beds with good and sufficient sheeting and covering." In addition, New York taverns had to be prepared to accommodate a minimum of six horses "or other cattle."[27] In contrast with New York, Virginia lawmakers did not require tavern keepers to furnish their houses with a specific number of beds. John Hamilton, a Norfolk tavern proprietor, kept a well-furnished house that had six beds, but if travelers intended to sleep on sheets in his house, they had best arrive early. Hamilton's inventory revealed that he owned four pairs of sheets for the six beds.[28] Maryland's lawmakers were not the least self-conscious about their motivations when insisting that tavern keepers furnish their houses with at least "four good feather beds for the Entertainment of customers and four good flock beds." Maryland's magistrates were guaranteeing themelves a comfortable night's rest as they traveled to the circuit courts, which often convened in taverns.[29] Virginia lawmakers expected ordinary keepers to "secure all horses that they have charge of from running away or being stolen upon the penalty of paying the charge for finding the horse or horses or paying for them if lost." Virginia lawmakers were looking out for themselves. Only the gentry in Virginia had the wealth to enable them to own a horse, and they traveled great distances, usually on horseback, when the government assembled or courts met.[30]

The homegrown nature of tavern beverages and services dictated that some colonial laws would be different from those in England. Local leaders determined what forms of alcoholic beverages were to be sold by which establishment. Pennsylvania, for example, designated some public houses for the sale of wine and beer while others could offer the whole range of alcoholic beverages. In addition, a "take out" trade developed that allowed retail establishments to sell larger quantities to be consumed off the tavern premises. In Pennsylvania, if beer or ale was imbibed in the tavern, it was sold by wine measure. If carried home, the cost was based on beer measure.[31] In Massachusetts, retailers could sell beverages "out of doors" or at the purchaser's home. In the seventeenth century, all licenses specified what beverages could be sold. Most establishments retailed beer and cider, while some had permission to sell wine. The Bay Colony drew the finest distinctions. Richard Knot, for example, was granted a license to sell "strongwater at retail only to his own fishermen." In the first decades of the eighteenth century, as demands for particular drinks altered, some Boston tavern keepers stocked rum exclusively. Massachusetts magistrates also stipulated how distilled liquors were to be produced, in an effort to protect the colony's citizens from potentially lethal drink. In 1723–24 it was unlawful to distill rum or other strong liquors in lead pipes, because it was "judged on good grounds to be unwholesome and hurtful."[32]

All colonies set prices on provisions for horses and for food, drink, and lodging for humans, making it a crime to charge above the rates.[33] Certain localities created very detailed price lists. Overnight rates in Hampshire County, Massachusetts, varied depending upon whether the traveler insisted upon clean sheets. A number of price schedules were determined by whether a lodger was willing to share a bed and, if so, with how many people. In Edgecomb County, North Carolina, sharing a bed with one other person was half the rate of having one's own bed.[34] In Rowan County, North Carolina, additional savings were possible if travelers were willing to share the bed "with 2 or more" persons. It appears as if Hampshire County, Massachusetts, lawmakers merely toyed with this idea; they crossed out the line "with 2 or more in the same bed each person."[35] Magistrates in Craven County, North Carolina, and Hampshire County, Massachusetts, priced meals differently depending upon whether the food was hot or cold and served with or without beer or cider. Hampshire County offered a special "Servant's Diet," a cold meal without beverage.[36] Maryland's lawmakers agonized over their inability to enforce tavern rates because "no rate certain can be set upon merchants goods from whom the ordinary keepers must purchase their liquors." Thus, each customer was required to negotiate prices on liquor. The law established costs for other services, like lodging, diet, beer, and horse feed.[37]

Gradually, in an attempt to protect the patrons, all colonies required that tavern keepers display the rates "in the common entertaining room."[38]

Lawmakers in Virginia responded to the manner of tidewater development by stipulating how plantation owners should accommodate travelers.[39] Since towns and taverns were few and far between, it was assumed that planters would offer hospitality to all who asked for it. A 1663 law codified this relationship. Unless the house owner and guest settled on a prearranged price for food and shelter, visitors could not be forced to pay, no matter what the duration of the visit. Although the law does not spell out how these negotiations were to take place, what we know about the culture of the Chesapeake suggests that the gentry may have been very reluctant to have conversations about payment for lodging. The planter elite worked extremely hard to situate themselves above such lowly and mundane cash exchanges.[40] It was possible, as Francis Louis Michel reported on his trip through Virginia in 1701–1702, "to travel through the whole country without money, except when ferrying across a river."[41] Even Massachusetts magistrates, the colonial group dedicated to creating and implementing the most restrictive tavern laws, made allowances for the "want of fit places of intertainment." Anyone living in a town during unusual times, when for example great assemblies met or ships arrived, could, when these events took place legally, provide "lodging & dyot at reasonable rates." The law warned, however, that this was not to be interpreted as permission to provide these services on a regular basis.[42]

Public officials did not limit their oversight of tavern services to the obvious ones. The Boston selectmen were shocked by an advertisement in their local newspaper announcing that a Richard Venables had "opened a Dancing School at the Green Dragon Tavern." Wasting no time, the selectmen demanded that the tavern keeper, a Mr. Williston, appear in their chamber. Dancing schools were not permitted in Boston, they informed Williston, and he was to act accordingly.[43]

Access to Taverns and Alcohol

The laws restricting access to taverns offer some of the clearest indicators that taverns were peculiar as public spaces. By setting limits on who was permitted inside, these laws defined who constituted the public, reinforcing the cultural assumptions about the place of dependent laborers, about hierarchical status, and about the separation of the races. The legislators created the legal limitations, but the laws reflected the idiosyncracies of the moment in which they were passed. In Virginia, for example, the General Assembly would not allow tavern keepers to entertain anyone working on construction of the state capitol building. The legislators suspected that workmen who combined drink with labor would be difficult to manage. The assemblymen may also have had their own safety in mind; they were to occupy this new building, and inebriated builders did not inspire confidence. Students at William and Mary were also forbidden to "frequent" the tavern, "except at the request of relatives or close friends." Surely the college administrators sought to prevent any disruptions caused by drunken students and to ensure students' diligence. In Massachusetts, tavern and alehouse keepers were prohibited from allowing traveling salesmen to lodge or receive entertainment. The tavern served the ambulant vendor in many ways, providing him food and lodging, a place to display his wares, an accessible address at which he could be contacted, and potential consumers in those who were also lodging in the public house. This law served multiple purposes. It protected local shopkeepers from having to compete with traveling salesmen, by removing the latter's base of operation. By denying the traveling salesman access to the space, the law protected the livelihood and property of those who were permanent members of the community. Lawmakers placed these peripatetic vendors in a separate category from other travelers. They were more motivated to support local residents than to abide by the stricture that strangers constituted the tavern's primary clientele. This law may also have provided a defense against the illegal trade associated with taverns; an anonymous traveling salesman would have been the ideal fence for stolen property.[44]

Very significant were laws that singled out certain classes of the population for whom the tavern was off limits. Toward the end of the seventeenth century, Massachusetts law lumped servants, slaves, and apprentices into a single group and forbade anyone to sell liquor to them unless given permission by their masters. The low penalty, set at ten shillings for each offense, suggests a minimal concern over this offense. When the law was revised, it was broadened to include free minors, and the fine for any violation was augmented to four pounds. The city of Boston went further. Selling liquor to "any Indian, Negro or Molatto Servant or Slave, unless sent by his master" promised the perpetrator a stiff fine or three months in jail and the loss of one's license to retail liquor. City leaders considered this a serious breach of the law and a threat to good order.[45]

New York City lawmakers initially allowed Indians and blacks access to taverns. The subsequent refusal in 1680 to serve African and Native American slaves in New York City taverns appears to have been based upon a common, stereotypical assumption that money or goods used to pay for these beverages or services was, according to the councilors, "Pilfered purloined and Stolen from their Several Masters." It was also necessary to restrict slaves' access to alcoholic beverages, because New Yorkers feared that drunken slaves would commit crimes. New York lawmakers set the penalty for violating this law at five pounds, a clear sign that they took this issue very seriously.[46] After the New York City slave conspiracy of 1712, the pressure to prevent slaves from entering taverns in New York City emerged from a different impulse. City authorities identified taverns as seedbeds of anti-white conspiracies by blacks. Virginia lawmakers provided a slightly different explanation for restricting tavern access to unfree laborers and minors, as well as to sailors. These people, they contended, could not be held legally responsible for their own actions nor could they be sued in court for debts or misbehavior. Making access dependent upon permission of their masters placed responsibility with the person who was legally accountable.[47]

Because married women, a group that included most women in early America, were defined legally as dependent and could not be held responsible for their debts, it seems logical that they too would have been prohibited from participating in tavern services or have had their access to the tavern restricted.[48] To bar women from the public house would also have been consistent with society's insistence that "good wives" fulfill their duties to their husbands and children by remaining at their labors rather than squandering their time drinking. However, the laws governing tavern and drinking behavior rarely mentioned women at all. Pennsylvania was a minor exception. Although no Pennsylvania laws restricted women's access to taverns, the language placed in the laws to discourage and punish drunkenness makes it clear that both men and women were warned not to over drink: any person "abusing him or herself with excessive drinking" could expect to be punished.[49] Clauses in the other colonies' legislation to promote sobriety and punish drunkenness or to prosecute a tavern keeper operating without a license were gender blind, as were the ordinances that pointed toward the enforced abstinence of servants and slaves.

Although no laws prohibited women from patronizing taverns, they were implicated in the laws aimed toward preventing individuals from meeting at taverns or at houses of ill repute to engage in illicit sex. In Virginia, for example, lawmakers lapsed momentarily into poetry as they lamented the proclivity of public house inhabitants for "dissolute and ill lives and conversation many time in their houses women of ill names and reputation." These women were allegedly maintained by the men who were their frequent visitors. Anyone caught harboring, entertaining, or providing for the maintenance of these women or who spent time in their company after they were once warned, would be punished according to the laws prohibiting adultery. The women would be prosecuted under the same law and subject to the same punishment.[50]

Indians

The Chesapeake and southern colonies expended only feeble efforts to prohibit the trade in alcohol with Indians. According to a historian of Indians and drinking, the laws passed were "short-lived, inconsistent, and ineffective." Maryland's council in 1683 proclaimed that liquor caused Indians to become "drunk and mad" and that the results of this behavior would likely be "a chargeable and expensive Warr." Leaders from local Indian communities had approached the lawmakers periodically complaining about the pernicious effects that the colonists' trade in alcohol was having on their people. Rather than pass a general law that might address the problem broadly, the councilors had responded by prohibiting the sale of liquor to specific Indian groups. A more comprehensive law was passed in 1687 but apparently had minimal effect. The General Assembly passed one final law later in the seventeenth century, but again the lawmakers settled for a bill that was limited in scope with short duration. They passed no permanent legislation.[51]

Virginia legislators as well devoted minimal energy to preventing the sale of liquor to Indians. Not a single act was passed relating to this trade for almost one hundred years after the founding of Jamestown. Finally a 1705 law made it illegal to sell rum and brandy on any lands belonging to Indians. Just as in Maryland, the law yielded little result. After the law was implemented, representatives from the Pamunkey Indians complained to the colony's council about how easy it was for them to purchase hard liquor. Lawmakers responded by banning the sale of alcohol "in any Indian Town within this Government," and later, in 1712, they enlarged the act by proclaiming it unlawful to sell rum "within the precincts allotted to the Tributary Indians." An act passed in 1744 reveals how ambivalent Virginia authorities were in their attitudes toward the liquor trade with Indians. In that year the council noted that Nottoways and Nansemonds were abusing liquor and that shady traders were taking advantage of them, selling liquor on credit. The council did not seek to solve the problem by outlawing the trade; rather they decreed that alcohol could be obtained only with cash. Anyone who sold liquor to Indians on credit would be fined. Clearly the monetary advantages to the trade outweighed its deleterious effects on the Indians or the desire to stop unethical traders. It was not until acts passed in 1757 and 1765 that lawmakers outlawed the liquor trade with Indians.[52]

South Carolina confronted the issue of Indians and liquor with a series of laws beginning in 1691. The first of these acts prohibited the sale of alcohol to Indians on their own lands. Four years later, in a comprehensive act to limit the points of friction between "White Man and Indian, and Indian and Indian," lawmakers reiterated the ban on the sale of "rum, brandy or any sorte of spirits." When the relationship of Indians to alcohol was revisited in 1707, the restriction on the sale of liquor to Indians was included in a law devoted to regulating the Indian trade and "Making it Safe to the Publick."[53]

The legislative attempt to forbid Indians' access to spirituous liquors extended over a mere twenty years in South Carolina's history. This brevity of effort most likely reflects the colonists' utter disregard for the law. Even government officials seemed prepared to ignore the law. When Indians demanded liquor, the governor "felt compelled to give it to them." Colonial laws also had no effect in curbing the intertribal exchange in alcohol. John Lawson, a successful Indian trader, chronicled how in the early eighteenth century some Tuscarora and their neighbors supplied the "westward Indians" with liquor. In Lawson's account, some of these Indians who were reselling liquor consumed portions of their stores before reaching their trading partners, and, taking lessons from white traders, topped off the barrels with water so that they were trading the proper quantity but not quality. The Tuscarora were not the only Indian purveyors of liquor in South Carolina. In 1752, an unnamed agent in Coweta Town witnessed the Savannah Indians bringing three or four kegs of rum for distribution to the Indians and colonists.[54]

Although the record of intertribal trade in alcohol is sparse, many examples exist of shady colonial traders using liquor to their advantage. Colonial traders presented the largest obstacle in the effective enforcement of the laws prohibiting the liquor trade with Indians. In 1669, a liquor seller named John Lederer offered a pamphlet containing advice on how to gain the maximum profit from the Indian trade. "Sometimes you may with Brandy or Strong liquor dispose them [Indians] to an humour of giving you ten times the value of your commodity."[55] The trader James Kenny admitted in his journal that traders and settlers totally ignored the laws that prohibited their supplying Indians with rum and that the continuing trade had a debilitating effect on Indians. Kenny discovered that a Mr. Levy's business success depended upon distributing liquor to Indians. In order to maintain this trade relationship, Levy would reassure his Indian purchasers that if they traded with him on a regular basis he could promise them a dependable supply of rum. Kenny was troubled by the effect of this trade on Indians' lives. He reported that one Indian from Tuscorora Town had claimed that a fellow tribesman and his family, in order to purchase rum, had pawned their possessions, including their clothing. Kenny seemed quite stunned by the lengths to which Indians would go to procure alcohol. He was approached by a Delaware "call'd Davy" who asked if he would be willing to give him some rum in exchange for "a White Boy Taken at Tuscorara."[56] Davy's need for rum may have brought him to the brink of poverty; he may have had been reduced to his last economic asset, a white boy, whom he was willing to exchange for strong drink.

Although it is unclear why Indians should be expected to heed the colonizers' laws, the Indians took considerable interest in the laws attempting to control the trade. In a report to the Grand Council of South Carolina in 1692, representatives from the Savannah Indians requested that "noe person whatsoever presume to carry any Rumme or other Spirits to ye: Savanoes or any other Indians whatsoever." They were concerned with the ways alcohol might "cause a difference between the English & the Indians."[57] Although laws appeared to protect Indians from alcohol, the acts apparently did not affect practice.

North Carolina officials never passed a specific law preventing the sale of alcohol to Indians, although they occasionally expressed a desire to implement such a ban.[58] Indians were well aware of the deleterious effects of alcohol. At a treaty conference held in August 1754 between commissioners from North Carolina and headmen from the Catawba people, one of the issues before those gathered was two related killings in which one of the Indian perpetrators was drunk. A headman named Hagler blamed the colonists.

> You Rot Your grain in tubs, out of which you take and make Strong Spirits You sell it to our young men, and give it them, many times; they get very Drunk with it this is the Very Cause that they oftentimes Commit those Crimes that is offencive to You and us and all thro' the Effect of that Drink it is also very bad for our people; for it Rots their guts and Causes our men to get very sick and many of our people has Lately Died by the Effects of that strong Drink, and I heartily wish You would do something to prevent Your People from Dareing to Sell or give themm any of that Strong Drink.

Hagler identified the source of the liquor and noted that if "White people make strong drink let them sell it to one another or drink it in their own families." He asked colonial officials to do something about the problem. While his impassioned plea did compel the governor to respond with a proposal to ban the sale of liquor to Indians, no laws were actually passed to protect the Catawba from alcohol.[59]

The leaders of New Netherland waged a losing battle against the sale of alcohol to Indians. The first ordinance "against selling intoxicating liquors to Indians," issued in 1643, was renewed regularly until the Dutch relinquished control of the area.[60] Authorities claimed that laws were required to redress an untenable situation, because selling alcohol to Indians had "caused great difficulties to the country." The director general and council determined that to prevent further occurrences "all tapsters and other inhabitants [were] henceforth [forbidden] to sell any wine, beer or strong liquors to the savages [*sic*]." Anyone convicted of violating the law would pay a fine and be financially responsible for any resulting damage from too much drink. Less than a year later, complaining that "drunken Indians" were a "daily" sight, they reiterated the prohibition on selling, bartering, or giving any drink to Indians. The stakes had increased, because now the perpetrator would receive "arbitrary corporal" punishment in addition to the monetary punishment. The director general and council further tightened the law in 1655 by adding prohibitions against selling any liquors "along the river by yachts, barks, scows, ships and canoes, going up or down." The penalties for violating this law continued to escalate; the following year, the fine increased, the corporal punishment remained, and now perpetrators were banished from the colony.[61]

Even these laws did little to discourage colonists from trading alcoholic beverages to Indians. In March 1656, the burgomasters of New Amsterdam requested increased vigilance in the fight to prevent the sale of alcohol to Indians. The motivation for this law is rooted in the September 1655 attack on New Amsterdam by representatives from ten local Indian groups. The burgomasters equated insolent Indian behavior, and thus invasions of their territory, with excessive drinking by Indians and reminded residents about the prohibitions on the sale of alcohol.[62]

In 1657, the magistrates implored Director Stuyvesant to visit Fort Orange, so that he might see first hand the disorders which resulted from the sale of beer and other liquors to the Indians. The magistrates hoped that after Stuyvesant had witnessed personally the effects of alcohol on Indians he would appoint a new commissary and the sale of liquor to Indians would cease. In the 1660s, colonial leaders took a slightly different tack and engaged the local Indian chiefs to assist them. First they empowered Oratan and Mattano "to seize any brandy found in their country, and all persons peddling the same." They were to bring these wrongdoers to New Amsterdam so that the courts could deal with them. Secondly, an ordinance was passed to empower inferior courts to make local laws "for the prevention of the sale of spirituous liquors to Indians."[63]

The English colonizers in New York City followed their sectarian neighbors and initially did not prevent Indians from entering taverns. The councilors closed tavern doors to Indians with a 1680 law, because they assumed that any money used to pay for service there was by definition stolen. Indians' other means of legal access to alcohol lasted until the end of the first decade of the eighteenth century, at which point the concern was apparently related to the threat of violence. The preamble to the 1709 law on the subject states this motivation explicitly: "it hath been found by Experience that the Selling or giving rum to the

Indians hath been very Prejudicial in time of War." The colony's leaders wished to prevent this possibility, so they instituted a three-pound fine for anyone who sold liquor to Indians. The act was revived regularly through 1716. Then, a hiatus in the attention to this law occurred until 1755, when the specter of war, no doubt, rekindled interest.[64]

The Pilgrims legislated against the sale of alcohol to Indians in their first laws governing taverns and drinking behavior. In 1636, they made it illegal to sell wine or "strong water" to any Indian unless "in case of sicknesse or faintnes & then onely with the foreknowledge & consent" of a magistrate or other official. Even if all parties satisfied these requirements, the sale was limited to a small quantity. Plymouth leaders expressed little actual concern about Indians' access to alcohol, but this law remained in place and unchanged for more than twenty-five years. When the law was amended in 1662, lawmakers revealed that it had been ineffectual and Indians had had little difficulty obtaining strong drink. The new law was directed not at the sellers but at Indians. If any were found drunk anywhere in the colony, they were to be placed in the stocks. Indians were exempt if they could demonstrate that they had received the liquor with the full knowledge of the court. The concern over drunken Indians was sufficiently great that anyone was authorized to act as a constable. It was "lawful for any man to seize any Indian found drunke."[65]

The tone of the colony's ordinances expanded slightly and reaffirmed the perception that Indians with alcohol posed a considerable threat. In 1664, the law reiterated that it was illegal to sell liquor to Indians; thus, if any Indian had strong drink he or she had, by definition, acquired it illegally. This meant that any "man either English or Indian shall find any Indians having or carrying any liquors," they may apprehend the Indian and confiscate the drink and treat it as if it were stolen. Again, Indians could demonstrate that someone had allowed them the alcohol; if not, the informer shared in the spoils of the fine and confiscated goods. In 1667, the lawmakers felt it necessary to clarify that cider was to be included on the list of illegal beverages, although Indians who were traveling and staying at an inn were exempted from this prohibition. By 1677, lawmakers in Plymouth elaborated on why they considered alcohol and Indians such a threat: drunk Indians fomented considerable disorder and offended those who were sober. Whipping was introduced as the proper method of punishment. With the 1685 restructuring, lawmakers lamented their failure to prevent Indians from obtaining alcohol. The practice "still doth abound." They were clearly fearful of Indian aggression and found it far easier to place the blame for the hostilities on alcohol than on how Indians were treated at the hands of the colonists. The Indians who obtained alcohol, and their providers, risked fines and whipping, unless of course the alcohol was given to an Indian who was ill. Even so, it was not to exceed a dram or two.[66]

The Bay Colony's record demonstrates the same ambivalence in its move to prevent Indians from having access to "strong waters." In 1633, the Court of Assistants ruled that it was forbidden, even in the course of trade, to sell alcoholic beverages to Indians.[67] However, this law was modified in 1644. The Puritan leaders experienced mild pangs of conscience. "It is not fit," they argued, "to deprive the Indians of any lawful comfort which God alloweth to all men." As a result the law was modified to allow Indians "so much as may be fit for their needful use or refreshing." Reversing themselves four years later, Puritan wisdom concluded that the sale of liquor should be restricted to a single Indian trader, William Phillips. This was expanded in 1654 to be enforced throughout Massachusetts Bay. One agent per district could trade alcohol with Indians as long as the agent used discretion and as long as he did not sell more than one pint of liquor to natives at a time.[68] Three years later, lawmakers completed the circle and returned to their original position. The House of Deputies expressed its belief that Indians were incapable of drinking in moderation. In an attempt to discourage drunkenness, "the fruits whereof are murther & other outrages," it was unlawful to "sell, truck, barter, or give any strong liquors to any Indian" and all licenses that had previously allowed traders to sell to Indians were revoked. Lawmakers made it clear that they did not intend "to restrayne any person from any charitable act in relieveinge any Indian, bona fide in case of suddaine extreamitie by sicknes or fayntinge which cals for such help, not exceedinge one dramm," nor discourage any physician from treating an Indian with strong drink. The prohibition on the alcohol trade with Native Americans lasted well beyond the end of the colonial period.[69]

Rhode Island's lawmakers tinkered with the laws throughout the colonial period. In 1649 Roger Williams was granted permission to "sell a little wine or stronge water to some natives in theare sickness." A 1654 law specified that no liquor could be sold to Indians under penalty of a fine, and a 1655 ordinance, designed to prevent Indian drunkenness, forbade ordinary keepers from selling "any sort of strong drink, either to English or Indians by retaile; that is to say, under a gallon." Ordinary keepers were also prohibited from selling to Indians more than a quarter of a pint of liquor or wine per person. The law cautioned that if an Indian was found drunk, the keeper would be fined twenty shillings and the Indian ten shillings or be whipped. By 1659, however, it was illegal to sell liquor to Indians in any quantity and stiff fines were imposed for those who violated the law—forty shillings for the first offense, five pounds for the second. This law also stipulated that any informant who might "spie an Indian convayinge or havinge of liguors" would receive half the fine for his trouble. The one exception to the prohibition on Indians having liquor was designed to treat Indian workers in the same manner as other free laborers. It enabled anyone who hired an Indian to give "him a dram, if he can make it apeare he is his hyred servant."[70] The value of a laborer appears to have mitigated against the lower status of Indians.

The Rhode Island Assembly was unable to effect a successful policy to suppress Indian drinking. In 1666 tavern keepers were ordered to refrain from selling liquor to Indians on the First Day, that is, Sunday. Seven years later no liquor could be sold to anyone on Sunday. However, the issue of Indians and alcohol still troubled the magistrates, and a series of committees were formed, beginning in 1673, "concerninge the Indians drunkenness." A few years later the governor and council determined that Indians should not be allowed to set up wigwams on colony property. The colonists feared that if Indians were allowed to meet in this way they would get drunk and take the opportunity "to plot anew, mischiefe to our great damage." Again all colonists were encouraged to intervene and to confiscate any liquor they found in Indians' possession.[71] Most of the concern over Indians drinking during this period appears directly related to the fear of war.

An element in the Rhode Island laws was directed toward protecting Indians from unscrupulous colonists. In 1718, it became unlawful to sue Indians for debt. The lawmakers recognized that greedy colonists often drew Indians into debt and took "advantage of their inordinate love of rum, and other strong liquors, by selling the same to them." These actions impoverished Indians.[72]

The laws that pertained to Indians and alcohol represented many sides of a complex relationship. Like their sectarian contemporaries, Rhode Islanders feared that inebriated Indians engaged in hostile behaviors. The law's ambivalence combined with an unwillingness to outlaw completely Indians' access to liquor suggest that Rhode Islanders grappled with the contradictions inherent in expecting Indians to maintain one standard while they adhered to another.

A 1729 Rhode Island law related to Indians contained a unique provision. Rhode Island towns were to regulate Indian dancing. The assembly argued that the dances were very "prejudicial to the adjacent inhabitants, by their excessive drinking and fighting, and wounding each other; and many servants are enticed to out-stay their time at such dances and run away from their masters." Dancing did offer a moral challenge to the Puritan hegemony. The problem lay mainly in the possibility that dancing might "promote sin and sloth." Puritans passed no statute forbidding dancing, but they did have local restrictions on particular forms of dancing. The most dangerous dances involved men and women touching or holding each other. Increase Mather was willing to permit the dancing and leaping associated with expressions of joy. The problem, however, was that innocent dancing often led into "gynecandrical dancing or that which is commonly called mixt or promiscuous dancing, of men and women." God would condemn such actions as the "Devil's Procession." Mather no doubt represented the extreme, a position without much support in Rhode Island. However, it is possible that while not all Puritans shared his contempt for dancing among themselves, they may have been willing to support his notion that dancing was invented by the devil, especially the dancing practiced by Indians.[73]

The 1729 law linked Indian dancing and drinking with the need to prevent servants, be they Indian or black or white, from abandoning their labors; but without doubt, Rhode Islanders feared that more than servants would be susceptible to the lure of the dancing. We do not know what Indians were wearing when they danced and if that offended colonists' sensibilities, nor do we know if the dances were mixed or segregated by sex. Colonists may have feared the presence of the devil in a style of bodily movement that was far more evocative and sexually liberated than their own. If whites were so easily captivated by the emotional and sexual displays of Indians, this law appears to be less about protecting Indians from drinking and dancing than ensuring that colonists did not see them.[74]

The colony of Rhode Island differed from their sectarian brethren in that none of its laws prevented African Americans access to drinking or taverns until the early eighteenth century. In 1703, the assembly passed an act prohibiting any tavern keeper from entertaining "men's servants, either negroes or Indians, without leave of their masters or to whom they do belong." The law was amended five years later because the original act had failed to authorize corporal punishment for those convicted but who were without funds for the fine.[75]

East Jersey and Pennsylvania also, like Rhode Island, initially opened ordinaries to Indians. East Jersey formalized two constraints on imbibing by Indians. Anyone who sold an Indian sufficient alcohol to cause intoxication would be fined ten pounds, and Indians could not be granted credit for drink. It was further declared that if any Indian emerged from a house intoxicated, the proprietor was *ipso facto* guilty of breaking the law. This law remained in effect until 1692, when the East Jersey lawmakers reconsidered the situation and declared failure—it seemed that Indians would not drink in moderation. The new law therefore forbade altogether the sale of alcoholic beverages to Indians and substituted corporal punishment for the fine. Offenders received five lashes for the first conviction; for subsequent misconduct the penalty increased to twenty lashes. This solution also failed to satisfy the lawmakers and, in the following year, the ten-pound fine was restored.[76] The motivation behind reinstating the fine is unclear. However, if few Indians had access to colonial currency or pounds sterling, a fine might have been a sure route to forcing Indians into indebtedness.

William Penn pursued legalizing the sale of rum to Indians. The members of the Provincial Council, however, did not share his inclination. While their Jersey neighbors revealed an ambivalence in their attitudes toward Indians and drinking, Pennsylvania lawmakers demonstrated consistency. Discussion of the policy appears to have been inspired by at least two not necessarily contradictory impulses. The first originated in the Quakers' desire to deal fairly with their native neighbors. The second is related and emerges from the Quaker leaders' paternalistic attitudes toward Indians.

One goal is evident from the Provincial Assembly's first meeting in 1682. They approved a law that prohibited the "selling or Exchanging of Rum, Brandy or other Strong liquors, to Indians." However, in 1684, Governor Penn informed the Provincial Council that he had called a meeting with the Indians and proposed "to Let them have rum" if they would be willing to abide by the colonists' laws and be punished accordingly. The Indians who assembled agreed, provided that "ye Law of not Selling them Rum be abolished." Penn apparently saw no reason to deny Indians' access to rum as long as they modeled their drinking behavior on the English. If they failed to emulate the English, they would be subject to colonial law. Penn failed to convince the Provincial Council or the Assembly. Each body considered the motion but "answered in the Negative."[77]

Pennsylvania's policy on Indians and alcohol betrays other impulses as well. The legislators acted from a position of paternalism, the belief that Indians required protection. Authorities outlawed the sale of "rum and other strong liquors to Indians" to shield them from the pernicious effects of drinking because when Indians were drunk, colonists could cheat them more easily and Indians would be "reduced to great poverty and want." At times, colonists argued, intemperance caused Indians to hurt each other. Colonial leaders also acted out of fear. The behavior of drunken Indians terrified their Euro-American neighbors.[78] A subsequent law invoked the founder's hope that the Indians and colonists could live in tranquility with good understanding between them and identified that the "fatal breaches" in the neighboring colonies were the work of colonists who traveled into the woods and traded "promiscuously" with the Indians as they returned from their hunt. They "debauch the native with great quantities of rum and strong spirits, and then cheat them of their peltry." Hoping to put an end to these practices, Pennsylvania lawmakers increased the penalties for selling liquor to the Indians.[79]

Alcohol, like many of the trade goods adopted by Indians, was gradually incorporated into familiar cultural traditions. The Iroquois embraced alcohol for its access to the spiritual world and its power to limit personal responsibility. Individual Iroquois also drank to achieve a state of intoxication that enabled them to release aggression, which under normal circumstances was to be suppressed. Because the Iroquois equated drunkenness with possession by a spiritual force, individuals were not held responsible for any actions committed during this state. A French observer of the Seneca concluded that they displayed their aggressiveness against their enemies while drunk "so as to be able to say afterward that they committed the wicked act when they were not in their senses."[80]

Indians living in the eastern woodlands of North America incorporated alcohol into their culture in a variety of ways. Some integrated liquor into hospitality or religious rituals. Others valued the power imparted by drunkenness, while still others relied on liquor during mourning ceremonies. In the societies of the southeast, certain drinks were associated with specific practices. "Creek men swallowed black drink in public rituals to establish or maintain political and social ties, both within the village and with visitors." Other drinks had particular qualities that went beyond inebriation and were involved with rites of purification. John Smith described such an event in the 1620s. Each spring the Indians drank the juice of the root *Wighasacan* mixed with water, "whereof they powre [pour] so great a quantitie, that it purgeth them in a very violent manner."[81] Alcohol offered a means to achieve traditional ceremonial states like trances, "quests for vision, and searches for external sources of spiritual power." Indians found little or nothing attractive in the concept of moderate social drinking.[82] Unlike their white counterparts, Indians sought drunkenness for its transformative power.

Were the drinking styles of Indians and white colonists strikingly different? No and yes. Historians have justifiably questioned the motivations behind contemporary accounts of Indians' drinking behavior, while taking at face value the description of colonial whites' habits and patterns. Members of both groups, Indians and Euro-Americans, drank to get drunk. For Indians, a drunken state was the articulated goal, it was the means to achieve the next plane of altered consciousness. Colonists, however, required lofty disguises to mask their desire to drink large quantities of alcohol, especially those who were guided by religious principles; Cotton Mather's dictum, the wine was from god but the drunkard from the devil, resonated loudly. So, although inebriation was often the desired result of white male sociability, when white men engaged in rituals of toasting, interpretations of a text, arguments over politics, or just gathered together, the settings sanctioned the heavy drinking. Ironically, some Indian observers articulated the contradiction between white men's stated ideals and their practice. Jasper, in his conversation with Danckaerts, pointed out that the Christians taught them drinking was wrong but also supplied them with the alcohol and "drink themselves drunk." On a trip from Pennsylvania to Onondaga in 1743, the naturalist John Bartram observed that both Indians and whites drank to intoxication but they reacted differently when inebriated. "An Englishman when very drunk will fall fast asleep for the most part, but an Indian, when merry, falls to dancing, running, and shouting."[83]

Upper status colonists wagged their fingers at what they claimed were Indians' incomprehensible and at times repellent drinking styles, to rationalize their reluctance to drink with them.[84] In 1736, James Logan reported being disturbed to see a group of Indians wandering through the streets of Philadelphia drunkenly, having obtained their liquor at a low-end establishment. Logan's agitation was not provoked by the Indians' drinking, per se. Rather, he was critical of the manner in which they imbibed. They broke open the casks of rum and drank very quickly. Those genteel souls of Logan's station established the model of drinking behavior that was in opposition to Indians. Logan's drinking companions "can every day have as much rum of their own to drink as they please . . . at least not one man will on any account be drunk." Logan did not wish to prohibit Indian drinking. "They show very good sense in other things," he lamented, why in their manner of their drinking could they not "act like us?"[85] James Kenny, a trader and normally sympathetic observer of Indian life, disparaged the behavior of "Levy ye Jew & Crafford ye Trader," by noting that they were "like so many Drunken Indians."[86] James Logan could tolerate inebriation if the state was attained slowly and by white men. John Bartram was dubious about the demonstration of emotion and behaviors that might reach an unpredictable, frenzied state. In the stereotype evoked by James Kenny to criticize the behavior of traders, it is possible that on some hierarchical scale Indians were placed higher than Jews. All three of these observers of Indian drinking failed to confront the consequences of whites' drinking, preferring to promote the fiction that only Indians were vulnerable to drunkenness and to unpredictable behaviors as a result.

Colonists proved able to forgo their lofty prose and ignore their disgust over Indian drinking practices when their own purposes were well served by shared drinking. Colonial traders and officials who negotiated treaties joined with Indians in the ritual of toasting. When a group of Iroquois arrived at the post at Oswego in June 1745 to meet with colonial officials, they were greeted with "a Dram round." After this first drinking session, the Indians wanted more, and asked first to drink to the king's health and then another round to the governor of New York. On the following day, Conrad Weiser gave them a supply of rum to take with them "to drink the King of Great Britain's health in Montreal after their Arrival." Later, in the Ohio Country, Weiser raised the English flag, and "treated all the Company with a Dram of Rum; The King's Health was drank by Indians and white men." James Kenny remarked that an Indian agent who refused to drink to the king's health, "would be looked upon like Treason & ye Man . . . not very fit to be Trusted as an Indn Agent." This practice of using food and alcohol to cement a bond between whites and Indians was evident in southern transactions as well. When the Cherokee met with agents from the colony of North Carolina in 1755, they were "treated with meet and liquor for several days."[87]

Indians mastered the protocols of treaty negotiation including those portions designed by colonials to use alcohol to their advantage. Witham Marshe, who represented the colony of Maryland at the treaty of Lancaster in 1744, reinforced the stereotype of Indians as heavy drinkers. However, he also noted their shrewdness in the course of bargaining. "Whenever they renew old treaties of friendship or make any bargain about lands they sell to the English," Marsh wrote, "they take great care to abstain from intoxicating drink for fear of being overreached; but when they have finished this business then some of them will drink without measure."[88]

In the eyes of colonists, considerable legitimacy was imparted to Indians when they practiced the drinking rituals of whites. An article in the *Pennsylvania Gazette* glorified the meeting of Catawba and Cherokee in 1757 near Williamsburg, Virginia. "After smoking a pipe round, the Head Warrior of the Cherokees desired the Head Warrior of the Catawbas to give him an Account of their late Rout, which being done, they called for Liquor, drank King George's Health, and the Head Warriors of each Nation, and then proceeding to dancing." Who is to say what the intentions were of these toasts or whether the white reporter had any clue as to their meaning. Whatever the answer, readers of the *Gazette* no doubt nodded their heads approvingly at this example of Indians' civil behavior.[89]

The negotiation of treaties and other official business also afforded Indians access to taverns. Tavern keepers were encouraged by provincial governments to offer services to Indians engaged in such business. In a 1732 proclamation issued by Governor Patrick Gordon of Pennsylvania, he asked tavern proprietors to provide the Indians traveling to and from treaty meetings with "Meal Drink & other Accomodations & Conveniences in their Journey . . . the charges whereof will be defrayed by the Government." In 1736 Indians could apparently get alcoholic drinks in Philadelphia, and we know that the proprietor of the Rose tavern in Bethlehem, Pennsylvania, served Indians, because there is record of an unpaid bill for services to a Jacob Volck, a Levi Jung, and three unnamed Indians, who ate, drank, and fed their horses on a mission to confer about captives.[90]

Southern taverns offered the same hospitality to Indians engaged in official business. In South Carolina, tavern keepers presented the Commons House of Assembly a bill for services provided for Indians' lodging and other expenses. A Mrs. Russell operated a tavern on a convenient route known as the Cherokee Path in South Carolina. Her bills to the provincial government listed three separate occasions, from 1742 to 1750, when she entertained Cherokees and Catawbas who were visiting the governor. Sugar, punch, and drams constituted the largest items on the tab. In a report to the Commons House, a committee complained that the expenses incurred by Indians at taverns were unnecessary. Previously, the committee observed, when Indians entered the city of Charleston they were supplied with "a little Corn, or Rice and Beef, at any Planters living near the Road." In the contemporary practice, they argued, traders accompanied the Indians into town, stopping at each tavern along the way at a great cost for the government. These needless expenses could be avoided by discouraging Indian access to taverns.[91]

Mariners

The law consigned mariners to a separate category with regard to their access to the tavern. Restricting mariners' use of taverns appears to run counter to the image of the eighteenth-century seaman as the "free and mobile worker in an expansive international economy" and odd in light of their substantial presence in colonial America. They constituted between one-tenth and one-quarter of the adult male population in colonial seaports. Tavern law recognized a difference between mariners who were under contract to a ship and those who were currently at liberty. The Virginia law is representative. For the purpose of regulating mariners' access to taverns, Virginia distinguished between those "in actual pay on board any ship" and those who could prove that they had been discharged and were not currently in service. The former could not be served without "license from their respective masters." The latter could partake of the tavern fare.

The law was consistent with the tendency of tavern law to limit the unfree consumer.[92]

South Carolina also controlled mariners' access to the tavern and, like Virginia, directed the restrictions at seamen who were attached to ships. In 1695–96, a law established a twenty-shilling fine for any tavern keeper who was found entertaining mariners "belonging to any ship or Vessel," after eight o'clock on a winter night or nine o'clock in the summer without permission from their masters. In 1703, South Carolina lawmakers enacted a unique variation to control excessive drinking among mariners and sailors during times of emergency. The law opens with the wish to marshal the assistance of sailors and mariners "in Time of Alarms." When the guns fired and the drums beat, captains and their men were ordered to come on shore and obey the orders of those in command, creating a corps of "volunteers." Any tavern or punch house keeper discovered selling strong drink in the time of the alarm, "after the Beat of the *Taptow* until the Beat of the *Revellie*" risked a twenty-shilling fine. If this fine failed to deter public house keepers from selling liquor during these times and authorities found people inside taverns when they should have been participating in the main guard or other public duty, the publicans risked imprisonment.

South Carolina lawmakers also directed an act toward persons who gave credit to mariners or seamen. The preamble to the law explains that when mariners and sailors were unable to pay their debts, their search for the funds delayed the ship's departure and greatly inconvenienced their employers. In order to solve this problem, lawmakers resolved that employed mariners were limited to five shillings of credit unless their master or commander explicitly permitted a different amount. The law contained a fairly common exception: a justice of the peace could allow a "Master or Mistress of any Publick House or Ordinary" to trust a seaman who was ill for the cost of his care until he was restored to good health. Some legislators attempted to broaden this law to cover "trusting Labourers, Handicraftsmen, or Artificers for more than a certain Sum," but it never received enough support in the House. The motivation for this act is left unsaid but might reside in the desire to prevent alcohol-induced rioting during times of chaos.[93]

Half a century later, South Carolina legislators resorted to yet another justification for a law that restricted mariners' and seamen's access to taverns. This

1751 law recognized that the temptations of taverns and punch houses lured these men. After weeks at sea, mariners stumbled into the first tavern they saw, eager for their first dram, the company of women, and food that had not been stored aboard ship. The new legislation made it unlawful for tavern keepers to entertain any mariner or seaman for more than one hour in twenty-four or to provide him food or strong drink valued at more than ten shillings.[94]

Credit

Forbidding tavern access to particular groups of people helped define the social order in early America. Setting limits on the credit particular patrons would receive reinforced this effect. The laws protected the tavern keeper from trusting individuals from whom he or she could not collect a debt and prevented patrons from drinking up their family's resources. Maryland's assembly took a unique position with its first credit law, passed in 1662; it protected tavern keepers by specifying that any bills or accounts were payable and that the sheriff or a person selected by the ordinary keeper could be appointed to collect the debt. It did not expressly protect the customer. In 1676, however, when tavern keeper Christopher Andrews sued John Wright for 742 pounds of tobacco owed for services at his ordinary, the Kent County Court threw out the case. The ruling specified that the debt was an "amount greater than might under the act be legally charged a free man who was not a freeholder." Maryland's law was atypical. Most laws regulating credit reflected the dual concern that tavern keepers not jeopardize their incomes and that customers not indulge beyond what their personal resources could allow. North Carolina produced a unique statute as well. Legislators set the credit limit at five pounds unless the customer signed his or her name in a book acknowledging the debt. If not, the tavern keeper could lose the entire amount. This requirement that the debt be acknowledged in writing suggests that debt obligations in the colonies were primarily oral and thus difficult to collect or prove.[95]

Most of the colonial legislatures established a credit limit based on an amount they thought reasonable. Massachusetts tavern keepers, retailers, and victualers were permitted to sell food and drink on credit for ten shillings or less. Above ten shillings was considered not recoverable. For Pennsylvania tavern keepers, it was unlawful to trust anyone for more than twenty shillings. New Yorkers passed a law that prevented tavern keepers from extending "large Credit to others"; they were not allowed to trust anyone, except travelers, for more than "six shillings current money of this colony . . . for any Sorts of Strong Liquors or other Tavern Expenses." Otherwise, they would forfeit the debt.[96]

Virginia lawmakers' struggle to settle on a proper law to define credit limits for alcohol purchases reflects the attempt to locate the balance between encouraging tavern keepers to ply their trade and discouraging individuals from overindulging in drink. Having acknowledged the relationship between drunkenness and the tavern, the oscillation in the credit law suggests that lawmakers were seeking the most effective means to control the amount of drinking. Yet, taverns were necessary. While they might lead many to sin, they played important roles in society. These public spaces provided tavern keepers with an income, offered magistrates a place to which to retire after their day's work, and served as one of the focal points of community social life. Lawmakers achieved an important balance by extending credit to individuals of a particular economic status. In this way, tavern patrons with ample resources could drink on credit. However, individuals who needed protection from their weaknesses and were tempted to squander their meager resources on drink had to pay ready cash.

The Virginia House of Burgesses continued to search for a policy on credit that would balance the various functions of the tavern. In 1643, lawmakers determined that tavern keepers could recover no debts "made for wines or strong waters." However, they repealed the act the following year and ruled that all debts had to be paid. Two years later, the burgesses reversed themselves again. They determined that for the welfare of the colony no debts on wine or liquor would be allowed, nor could the creditor use the debts as a plea. In 1666, the language of the law that established the rates tavern keepers could charge for certain beverages softened somewhat. Tavern keepers would be encouraged to charge the correct rates, it was argued, because if they did, they would be "admitted to plead their accounts and recover judgments." By the early eighteenth century, the rules flip-flopped once more, although the following law remained in force throughout the colonial period: Virginia tavern keepers could extend an annual credit of three hundred pounds of tobacco to anyone who owned two servants or who owned property valued at fifty pounds sterling or more. The credit limit was tightened significantly in 1734 and was reduced to twenty shillings annually. Clearly these laws were directed at those least able to pay and were not intended to inconvenience Virginia gentry; the regulations were suspended in Williamsburg during times when the colony's leaders gathered for the general court or assembly.[97]

Although the laws that established the ceiling on credit attempted to locate the middle ground between the needs of patrons and those of proprietors, Virginia tavern keepers found the laws onerous. In a letter to the *Virginia Gazette,* William Dixon, a Suffolk tavern keeper, charged that the Reverend Patrick Lunan had stayed in his house for four days and during that time treated anyone willing to drink with him. His account totaled two pounds, fourteen shillings and ten pence. However, when Dixon demanded payment, the good reverend refused. Dixon petitioned the county court, but Lunan was protected under the act of assembly that limited the amount of credit that a publican could extend to twenty shillings. Dixon hoped that the public exposure would embarrass Lunan into paying. He also wished to inform the public that by upholding his part of the licensing bargain, by providing the best entertainments to his patron, he was being punished, since he could not collect his due.[98]

Dixon was not the only keeper to complain. Between 1744 and 1765, the House of Burgesses received numerous petitions protesting the twenty-shilling limit on credit. In 1744, innkeepers from Yorktown and Williamsburg asked that the 1734 law be repealed because it occasioned "great Inconveniences, as well as manifest Losses in their Way of busines." Williamsburg tavern keepers complained again in 1746. They wished to extend unlimited credit throughout the year not just at public times. Finally, in 1762, the law was amended. Virginia tavern keepers could extend as much credit to travelers as they wished. Local residents were still restricted, in an attempt to prevent loitering at the tavern or drinking so much that they might mortgage their family's economic well-being. Unsatisfied, the inn holders of Williamsburg, Norfolk, Hampton, Yorktown, and Gloucester presented a united petition in 1765 trying to remove the barriers to credit for local residents. They were successful in 1774.[99]

According to some, public house keepers ignored the law on credit with regularity, an action that gave them enormous discretion. Although Pennsylvania lawmakers limited credit to twenty shillings, 98 of the 251 individuals (39%) who had an outstanding debt with Philadelphia tavern keeper Martin Kryder at his death, owed him more than the legal amount. This was not unusual for upper-end establishments. When James Connor, of Sadsbury Township in Chester County, Pennsylvania, died in 1742, the debt to his estate totaled more than five hundred pounds from his tavern business. Similarly, when William Wirt, the proprietor of one of the best taverns in Prince George's County, Maryland, died in 1772 more than seven hundred patrons owed him money.[100]

Because of their pervasiveness in colonial taverns and their ambiguous status as laborers, portions of the credit law were directed specifically at mariners. Some jurisdictions restricted mariners' access to taverns, but even in places like New York City, where this was not the case, lawmakers limited the amount of credit mariners could receive. New York City leaders distinguished between mariners in and out of service, as their contemporaries in Virginia and South Carolina did in regulating access. However, whereas seamen in service had less access to taverns in some ports than did seamen not under contract, when it came to debt, those in service were considered the better risk. A tavern keeper could extend a credit of up to six shillings to a mariner who was attached to a ship, but if unemployed, mariners could receive only a twelve-pence credit. The law also mandated that mariners would owe a six-pence fine if found guilty of receiving too much credit, a stiff penalty; six pence would buy two quarts of double beer or three nights of lodging. By extending considerably more credit to a mariner in service than to an unemployed seaman, New York City magistrates signaled their understanding that mariners with work were more likely to have the resources to cover their debts. In the matter of credit, the law treated in-service seamen more like free than unfree labor.[101]

While slow to limit the credit of sailors, Virginia too eventually legislated this policy. In the early days of the colony, the lawmakers vacillated. The first laws made it impossible for tavern keepers to plead on behalf of any outstanding accounts. In 1663, if the tavern keeper abided by the established rates, "all persons keeping ordinaries and selling at those rates shall be admitted to plead their accounts and recover judgments for the same . . . Provided the party drinking know the price he must pay, be alive and be impleaded within a year after the debt accrues due." By 1691, the law had changed and ordinary keepers were prohibited from giving any credit to seamen. The preamble to the law states specifically why the controls over issuing credit had to be more strict: "Forasmuch as the unlimited credit given by the ordinaries and tippling houses, within this their majesties country and dominion of Virginia, to the seamen and others, where they spend not only their ready money, but their wages and other goods, which should be for the support of themselves and families, is found very prejudicial, and occasions many persons newly free to run away to the neighboring plantations to the great disadvantage to this country." The penalties for the keeper were set high. If convicted, the proprietor lost his or her tavern license, and therefore most likely the family livelihood, and forfeited "double the sum of such obligation, so covenously taken."[102]

Clues to untangling why seamen were singled out by the laws on credit and included in the body of law that refused to allow the unfree access to the tavern are found in the nature of mariners' work, their ethos, and the legacy of English contract labor.[103] Part of the explanation lies in the nature of the sea trades and the merchant seaman's inherent vulnerability, stemming from his lowly position in the hierarchy of trans-Atlantic labor. Seamen would search for work along the waterfront, spy a likely vessel, inquire of a mate where the ship was bound, and ask whether the captain was hiring. If workers were needed and the seaman was interested, a wage contract was signed. The contract established the relations between the owners and the crew, the length of the voyage and the wages, seamen's labors while in port, and often included an oath of loyalty and obedience to the captain. The most common form of payment was a monthly wage distributed in two or more installments: "first at the second port of delivery and at every second port thereafter; and finally, upon the completion of the voyage in the home port." While the vice-admiralty courts had as a large part of their charge the resolution of "seafaring wage disputes" and while judges recognized the indispensability of the seaman to commerce, an unmistakable downside was visible as well. The court's primary responsibility was "to uphold and protect the interests of the owner, merchant, and captain of the shipping industry." As a result, many legal provisions stipulated that the seaman's wages were susceptible to forfeiture. If a sailor should be "mutinous, disobedient, or desert the ship," if he should "purloin or embezzle any of the goods," or if he were responsible for faulty storage of goods that were subsequently damaged, he would lose all or a portion of his wages. Thus, as Marcus Rediker explains, the seaman could find himself anchored in port without "ready money," cheated out of his wages, "docked" for a wide variety of reasons, or due only a portion of the wage, having "paid" the captain for basic necessities. Finally, while contracts specified wage rates in pounds sterling, seamen were often forced to take deflated colonial currencies. The profits of a voyage could be greatly enhanced by paying the crew in currencies valued at 25–50 percent less than sterling.[104]

By limiting mariners' access to taverns and credit, colonial lawmakers protected colonial commerce and mariners' meager earnings. Seamen had earned the reputation of being loose and careless with their money, squandering in a matter of days what had taken them many months to earn. Mariners were among the poorest of the colonial urban class. They were the largest single group in the bottom 30 percent of Boston's probated decedents.[105] These data reflect the nature of their work, their low pay, and the zeal of their search for entertainment upon landing in port after months of confinement at sea. Their constant movement accounts, in part, for how difficult it was for creditors to collect any debts from the merchant seaman.

Mariners also subscribed to an ethic of nonaccumulation: "Never mind the main chance," meaning, "Don't worry about old age" or "Never let us want when we have it and when we have it not too." An example would be Hugh Everard, who took control of a slave ship in 1739 after the captain, first mate, and second mate had died, landed the ship in port, sold the cargo, and "spent all of the said Mony in drinking and Extravagant Living."[106] The preamble to the South Carolina law on the subject points to a conventional image of seamen, that once in port, they often absented themselves from their responsibilities to the ship, tempted perhaps by the wiles of drink and the companionship of tavern life.

The nature of English contract labor in the seventeenth century provides the final thread in an understanding of the relationship of mariners and tavern law. For one historian of labor, "the nearly universal form of consensual manual labor was not free labor but unfree labor." Hired servants who did not fulfill their contracts were subject to criminal penalties. Servants needed to provide proof that they had completed their previous obligations before they could be hired by another employer. Any violation in the contract was punishable by imprisonment. Labor relations derived less from antiquated medieval assumptions than from the idea that "individuals owned themselves and were free to dispose of their energies in the marketplace." A free individual could sell the property "he held in his own energies" to someone else for a particular purpose or term. The property then became the employer's.[107] Measured by this yardstick, mariners were free laborers only in name, a distinction not lost on lawmakers designing the codes for the tavern.

A certain irony exists in the mariners' position. Merchant seamen appear to have been caught in a web that was one part new political economy and another part old labor system. On the one hand, they lived a nonacquisitive ideology, one that enabled them to spend whatever ready cash they had, at a time when acquisitiveness was emerging as the guiding light to an increasingly capitalist economic mode. The lawmakers, who fashioned the law to control seamen's movements in the tavern and elsewhere, were involved in ushering in the new economic order. On the other hand, while under contract to a ship, the relationship between the seamen and their captains harkened back to English labor relations of the early seventeenth century when "free" labor was merely an illusion. Although increasingly paid a monthly wage and therefore part of the emerging wage labor system, mariners were obligated by a labor contract that bound their labor for a specified period of time to a ship captain. At a time when free wage labor increasingly characterized labor practice in the North American colonies, seamen were trapped by the vestiges of the old labor order. Taverns, and the laws governing their operation and governing drinking behavior, reinforced the mariners' marginal position within society.

❖　❖　❖

THE INSTITUTIONAL STRUCTURE of the colonial American tavern owed an undeniable debt to the legal and cultural heritage of the English and the Dutch. Early American lawmakers designated the range of services patrons could expect and clarified that the primary responsibility of the public house was to accommodate travelers. However, colonial statutes gradually included portions not found in Old World law. Although the timing of these laws varied from colony to colony, by the eighteenth century statutes in each colony denied particular groups within society access to the tavern and to alcohol. The early American tavern was off limits for the unfree and free people of color. Lawmakers crafted specific language limiting mariners' access to public houses and to credit, indicating that seafaring laborers fell into a kind of limbo between free and unfree. And while women were not legally barred from the tavern, those from the middling and elite strata patronized the tavern only rarely, since doing so risked damaging their reputations. As colonial leaders refined the laws pertaining to tavern services and access, they defined the colonial tavern as a particular public space. Lawmakers reinforced this image of the tavern as exclusive rather than inclusive by the legal framework they designed to control the behavior of tavern keepers and their clientele and by holding only a particular stratum of the population culpable for breaches of the law.

Inside the Tavern:
"Knots of Men Rightly Sorted"

With . . . reflections I entertained myself upon the road; and about two of the clock I reached Captain Marshal's house, which is half way between Boston and Salem. Here I stayed to refresh nature with a pint of sack and a good fowl. Captain Marshal is a hearty old Gentleman, formerly one of Oliver's Soldiers, upon which he very much values himself. . . . if I would have stayed as long as would have talked, he would have spoiled my ramble to Salem.

About six of the clock in the afternoon I came to Salem. . . . The first person I went to visit was Mr. Herrick. How kindly he received a poor Traveller whose life he had saved at sea. . . . From his house we went to take a glass, and talk over our Sea-voyage. . . . When we were at the Tavern, among other things, I renewed my acknowledgments for his former favours; and drank a kind remembrance in wine.

*J*ohn Dunton, a bookseller from London traveling in Massachusetts, stopped midday, in April 1686, at a Captain Marshal's house, on his way to Salem. Dunton suffered through Captain Marshal's long, detailed reminiscences of his participation in the English Civil War by washing down a fowl with a pint of sack. Refreshed, Dunton continued on to Salem, where, by prior arrangement, he joined Mr. Herrick, a merchant, at the local tavern. Dunton felt obligated to Herrick, whom he credited with saving his life at sea. Wine helped them both relive their past exploits. Dunton toasted Herrick, "to the bottle of water that saved my life at sea," and the captain and crew of Herrick's ship, and Herrick returned the ritual by toasting Dunton's wife; "I believe we drank her health five times in an hour's sitting," Dunton wrote in his journal.[1]

John Dunton punctuated his travel with steady drinking. He endured Captain Marshall's bragging with a pint of wine and he expressed his indebtedness to Mr. Herrick through an evening of toasts. Dunton's reminiscences capture the essence of the tavern experience—lots of alcohol, shared drinking rituals, and companions from his stratum of society. By observing Dunton and other colonial drinkers inside the tavern, we can reconstruct how early Americans used the public house, what activities they engaged in there, and how the institution fit within the fabric of their lives.

Although taverns were not exclusively distinguished by class until the eighteenth century, colonists had always ranked them by their level of respectability. Only four years after the settling of Pennsylvania, its founder, William Penn, began to complain about the disorders rising from the taverns located in the caves along the Delaware. These establishments were attracting a particular and rather rowdy class of patron. Penn perceived that the existence of these caves and the behavior inside them were a threat to good order. Because the city had so few taverns during the seventeenth century, the genteel Philadelphian was forced to drink inside these noisy, dissolute establishments, side-by-side with his laboring brethren.[2]

The status of patrons and proprietors differentiated taverns in seventeenth-century Massachusetts as well. Of twenty licensed taverns in Boston in 1673, only four were allowed to dispense wine and brandy as well as beer and cider. These more exclusive inns were operated by men, of course, two of whom derived further elevated status from their militia titles. When the magistrates of the Essex County Quarterly Courts met, they preferred John Sparke's tavern in Ipswich, because his house was a model of elegance and decorum, especially when contrasted with Perkins's tavern. In Haverhill township, which had allowed only two licensed taverns, proprietor Daniel Ela frequently violated the law while John Johnson ran a quiet, decorous ordinary. Seventeenth-century licensing and adjudicating magistrates were keenly suspicious of certain drinking establishments and their clientele, particularly those clustered by the waterfront. They contrasted these rougher establishments, where a landlord might set out a bench with a few mugs and open for business, with the more elegant houses that were virtually private clubs.[3]

By the eighteenth century the better taverns in the major seaport towns, those that catered to a more exclusive clientele, had moved away from the waterfront, increasingly being found toward the city center.[4] When Benjamin Franklin first arrived in Philadelphia, residents steered him away from the Three Mariners, because it was "where they receive strangers, but it is not . . . reputable." They recommended that he go to the Crooked Billet in Water Street, "a better one."[5]

Throughout the eighteenth century—earlier in Boston than in New York or Philadelphia—drinking establishments emerged that were designed for the exclusive use of the social elite. Although most taverns drew a mixed clientele, they were distinguishable from each other based on their reputation and character, their level of noise and smoke, the degree of raucousness allowed, and their quality of service. Men involved in the sea trades had their regular haunts; carpenters and builders had theirs. What laboring-class taverns shared with their elite counterparts was segregation by sex. Women rarely entered as patrons. Only those ordinaries usually identified by local officials as disorderly catered to mixtures of gender and race. These taverns often remained clustered along the waterfronts in the major seaports and growing sea villages, although they were scattered throughout cities.[6]

In laboring-class taverns, patrons were embroiled in their own distinctive culture, and colonial officials commented frequently on their activities. Essentially, patrons and proprietors of lower-class establishments paid little heed to what colonial elites thought constituted a proper tavern environment. Constables and magistrates were summoned to these ordinaries when the activities inside became too loud, continued too late into the night, or when the patrons were suspected to be engaged in plotting against those in power. Local officials often found such establishments in defiance of good order because their clientele included both men and women, whites and blacks, free and unfree. At the very least, the proprietors were in violation of the law that prohibited servants and slaves from being entertained without express permission from their masters.

About the turn of the eighteenth century, a shift occurred in popular drinking patterns. As the supply of distilled spirits, especially rum, increased and the price dropped, they became the drink of choice throughout the colonies. The evidence is extensive. Throughout the 1720s rum dominated the liquor bought and sold by Thomas Amory, a Boston wholesaler. Proprietors in all of the colonies, like Jane Cazneau, a Boston innkeeper, purchased far more rum than any other beverage, sometimes to the complete exclusion of other potables. In 1762, Philadelphian Benjamin Mifflin arrived at a tavern in Susquehannah, Pennsylvania, looking to quench his thirst, and discovered that all the tavern had was rum. In John Wilson's tavern in Guilford County, North Carolina, in 1774, of eighty-nine people who carried liquor away, eighty-three bought a form of hard liquor: rum, brandy, whiskey, or spirits. Of 221 customers who drank inside Wilson's tavern that year, 165 ordered rum alone and another forty-one consumed concoctions that included rum—grog or toddies.[7]

It was not that drinkers had failed to achieve the desired level of inebriation with beer or cider; rather, hard liquor enabled drinkers to reach this state more quickly.[8] As these new beverages grew fashionable, officials expressed their consternation over the effects of this burgeoning drink culture and focused their critiques upon hard liquor. What appeared foremost on their minds was alcohol abuse, drunkenness, disorder, and their decreasing control over popular drinking habits. When in 1714 Massachusetts superior court justice Samuel Sewall tried to disperse a riotous group gathered in a tavern, he was forced to confront his diminishing influence. Instead of disbanding on demand, the drunken crowd continued in their revelries. Instead of quieting the disturbance, Sewall endured humiliation. The 1744 Philadelphia grand jury drew an explicit link between the "vast" number of drinking establishments and the beverages being consumed. The grand jury proposed to remedy this condition by diminishing the number of public houses and they turned to the example of London, which, they noted, had experienced the same turmoil due to the number of gin shops.[9]

In two 1751 prints, Hogarth dramatized visually the stark contrasts between beer drinking and gin drinking in London at that time. In "Beer Street" (Figure 3), he presented an orderly London. The men and women are sitting close to each other, their bodies touching. The image is of a connected society that appears calm, in good order. Although most of the figures clutch mugs of beer, the

FIGURE 3. Beer Street, 1751. In the first of two prints, Hogarth cele-
brates the orderly, stable society of beer drinkers. Hogarth. Michael
Rosenthal, *Hogarth* (London: Jupiter Books, 1980).

city's business progresses uninterrupted—the painter remains absorbed by his
canvas, the fish monger is only pausing before continuing her delivery, a number of folks focus their attention on a broadside or pamphlet, and so on. "Gin
Lane," (Figure 4) represents disorder. Society is literally dissolving and death
stalks the city; a mob gathers, corpses lie in the center of the square, and a baby
tumbles headfirst over a railing, having fallen out of the arms of its mother. In
this scene "each main figure withdraws into him- or herself, drunk on gin." In
case his message remained unclear, Hogarth included text:

FIGURE 4. Gin Lane, 1751. The second of two prints illustrates the ravages of gin drinking wrought on London society. The healthy woman in the middle of Beer Street now lies in a coffin. Buildings reveal neglect. Only the pawnbroker thrives by taking the carpenter's tools so the crafts-man can buy more gin. Hogarth. Michael Rosenthal, *Hogarth* (London: Jupiter Books, 1980).

Gin cursed Fiend with Fury fraught,
Makes human Race a Prey;
It enters by a deadly Draught,
And steals our life away.[10]

Colonists also transferred their appetites for alcoholic beverages from beer to gin and rum.

Tavern Fare

Although taverns were licensed to sell alcoholic beverages and were expected to provide lodging for humans and horses, the range of services depended upon their clientele. The City Tavern in Philadelphia, for example, was an elaborate establishment—a two-story-high brick building measuring fifty feet by forty-six feet, made even more fashionable because it was set back a considerable distance from the street. Patrons ascended a stately flight of stone steps to the first floor, which contained the bar and public meeting rooms, each extending for the entire length of the building. In these spaces, patrons could find various colonial and British newspapers. Moveable screens provided flexibility for smaller, more private meetings. On the second floor were two clubrooms that could be altered to be one large space measuring nearly fifty feet in length. The second floor also contained a long room appropriate for gaming; for the more genteel folks opposed to this sort of entertainment, the rooms could be used for meetings. Similarly, the Indian King, a converted Philadelphia mansion, consisted of eighteen rooms, fourteen with fireplaces, and stables for up to one hundred horses. Although Alexander Mackraby does not name the inn in which he stayed, he waxed eloquent about its plush accommodations. He "could hardly find myself out this morning in a most elegant crimson silk damask bed."[11]

These upper-class establishments required experienced, worthy proprietors. One applicant to manage the City Tavern claimed to be qualified because he had kept a tavern in Dublin that "entertained noblemen and gentlemen." Proprietors of such large public houses had a wide range of functions. They cared for the rooms and stables, managed the kitchen, acted as host, greeted new arrivals, assisted with special events, and handled the funds. They also played supervisory roles over a staff, which might have included cooks and waiters, drivers and wood carters. They were also responsible for the quality of the entertainments, which ranged from food and drink to conversation and diversions.[12]

Taverns for lower- and middling-status patrons varied enormously. Proprietors often converted their own houses into ordinaries merely by posting a sign, serving liquor, and setting up additional beds for guests. Interior spaces were undifferentiated; travelers might encounter sleeping accommodations in any room of the house. Benjamin Bullivant, journeying from Massachusetts, spent a sleepless night in a New Jersey tavern because his bed and those of privateers making merry with "theyr girles" all occupied the public room. When the tavern was a single room, all activities took place in the same space. Traveler Waightstill Avery recounted arriving at Powel's tavern, outside Halifax, North Carolina. There he encountered a drunken assembly—the landlord, a neighbor, and two other travelers—eating supper. "There being but one room in the house . . . I watched carefully all night, to keep them from falling over and spewing upon me." Folks who lived in the neighborhood of a tavern gathered there on a regular basis after a day's work, to drink, dance, and talk. Discussions might be of the most innocuous sort or might turn toward the planning of an illegal venture or, as in a famous case in New York City, to a plot to free the city's slaves.[13]

Unlike the majority of society's taverns, women were often present in these low-end establishments, as patrons or as prostitutes. In seventeenth-century Ipswich, Massachusetts, Perkins' inn was imputed to be a place where men could meet local women. Because tavern clients were almost exclusively male, female proprietors worked to maintain reputations that were free from suspicion and to avoid the appearance of operating a disorderly house.[14]

Providing food, drink, and lodging may not have been the only or the primary source of income for the proprietors of some taverns. The tavern run by Robert and Lydia Moulder, located in Chichester Township in Chester County, Pennsylvania, was a "Large and commodious House" with a prime location, facing the Delaware River. The tavern measured forty feet by thirty-two feet and had three rooms on each floor. The lot extended for five hundred feet down to the river and included a wharf and store. The Moulders also had extensive lands of meadow and an orchard with hundreds of trees, "mostly house apples."[15] The wharf and store might not have been related to the tavern business, but travelers' horses probably grazed in the meadow and the Moulders produced cider from their apples. The surplus of apples and drink might have been part of the store's stock.

As the law required, these hosts offered a bed, drink, and the possibility of three meals a day to the weary sojourner plus stabling and oats for his horse. They appeared particularly capable of quenching everyone's thirst and satisfying all tastes. They stocked the ingredients for punch, toddy, and slingers, as well as cider, bitters, grog, beer by the bottle or mug, rum, wines, brandy, and various flavorings, such as cherry and vanilla, which were added to punch or slingers. They kept a supply of Batemans drops on hand—no doubt guaranteed to cure the effects of the previous night's over indulging. At their store they sold beef, butter, eggs, veal, lamb, and beverages in quantity. They had a chair for hire and could arrange day labor to help unload travelers' wares. In addition, like many tavern keepers in the period before credit institutions, the Moulders functioned as a lending agency. Robert Moulder noted "cash lent" on a regular basis, for instance, 13 shillings 8 pence to Rachel Pedrick and 3 shillings 9 pence to Captain Abe Camp, who received the loan after partaking of a night's lodging.[16]

Taverns were the focal point of many and varied activities and ventures. They were a part of the regular stage routes, providing passengers both midday meals and lodging. Taverns also operated as the first post offices; although this system lacked efficiency and precision, it did provide avenues for news and gossip. When Daniel Fisher ventured from Williamsburg, Virginia, to Philadelphia in 1755 and lodged the first night at Chiswell's Ordinary, he noticed that "A letter directed to John Palmer, Esq. at Williamsburg lay upon a Table, which several Persons who were going thither viewed, but neither of them took the trouble of conveying it as directed; a common neglect it seems unless it happens to be an acquaintance, or the person has a mind to see the Inside of the letter, a Practice often complained of."[17]

Taverns could be depended upon to have the local newspaper, and at times it was read aloud. Tavern keepers handled a huge variety of items for sale and provided local residents with a place to advertise lost objects. Anyone in Philadelphia who had information about a lost spotted dog that tilted its head due to an injured ear was asked to report to a Mr. Smith, the proprietor of the City Tavern. Mr. Smith also advertised the sale of a second-hand mail wagon, "not much worse for wear." Sales of real estate or imported goods were held in the public rooms of larger taverns. These might include estate sales, like those held in Boston for Joseph Callender at the Great Britain Coffee House and Peter Blin at the Sign of the White Horse. The Blin estate's was a vendue sale, in which the goods are displayed ahead of time and individuals can bid on items. The sale, consisting of sheets, rugs, quilts, blankets, and more, was to begin at five o'clock, but interested buyers were invited to view the items ahead of time. Such an event could cause problems. A group of Chester County, Pennsylvania, residents petitioned the colonial assembly in 1743 asking that something be done about what they considered a particularly pernicious aspect of vendue sales: because it was the practice to have liquor available, excessive drinking often took place, producing "scandalous" effects, especially causing poor folks to pay "extravagant prices for unnecessary things." Trafficking in human beings also went on in taverns. Advertisements appeared regularly in the Boston newspapers announcing the sale of servants and slaves, most of whom were sold from the city's taverns. In May 1726, an announcement in the local newspaper offered ten slaves—eight men, one woman, and a young girl—for sale at the Salutation. A month later, the proprietor at the Salutation alerted Boston residents that several likely Negro men had recently arrived from the West Indies and could "be seen and sold." Some taverns specialized in certain types of goods. The Royal Exchange Tavern, on King Street in Boston, acted as the headquarters for the sale of sloops and brigantines. Individual purveyors of goods or services sometimes set up shop in a tavern. A notice in the *Boston Newsletter* announced that a room had been "taken up at Mr Busby's in King Street where Gentlemen for a reasonable consideration may be taught geometry." Similarly, Le Chevalier de Pogresay announced in the *Virginia Gazette* that he was lodging at the Raleigh Tavern in Williamsburg and was about to begin classes in the "Art of Fencing, Dancing, and the French Tongue." In 1757, residents of Bethlehem and Nazareth, Pennsylvania, were notified that if they wished to consult Joseph Miller, practitioner of physic, "in the vital matter of venesection," or bleeding, he "would within certain hours on certain days of every month, give audience in the 'great room'" of the Rose Tavern. Traveling artisans stopped at taverns to ply their trades. In 1772, in Bethabara, North Carolina, a silversmith stopped at the "tavern to mend articles which were brought to him."[18]

Taverns offered colonists one of the few sources of secular diversion and amusement in early America. Locals or travelers could attend scholarly lectures, listen to musical entertainers, or gaze upon unusual animals. After consuming a substantial amount of food and drink, a group of men listened to a "Philosophical Lecture on the Eye." A New York tavern treated guests nightly to a violinist who sang while he played and amazed the audience with his animal imitations. A physician and diarist named Alexander Hamilton was "alarmed (not charmed) for half an hour by a man who sung with such a trumpet note that I was afraid he would shake down the walls of the house about us." For just six pence per person at Mr. Alexander Cabran's Sign of the Black Horse on the Boston Common, patrons could view a black moose, "the like perhaps never before seen in this town." The Indian Queen in Philadelphia displayed notable curiosities, including a camel and "the Great Hog's portrait." In Westfield, Massachusetts, Fowler's tavern had a "She Lyon" on exhibit.[19]

Not surprisingly, what constituted acceptable tavern entertainment was very narrowly construed in those colonies where religion exerted a strong influence. In Boston, for example, "a number of Inhabitants" complained to the selectmen that an anonymous person and his mother, while staying at Moulton's tavern, exhibited a wood model they had created of the "City Jerusalem." Their concerns were twofold. These vigilant inhabitants worried about the "considerable sums" of money being collected to view this work. In addition, the citizens, in their newly established role as art critics, determined that this was not a "work of Art & ingenuity, but rather an imposition on the public." The selectmen voted to have the alleged artists warned out of Boston and to inform Mr. Moulton that he should "not suffer any more exhibitions of the same in his House."[20]

Local Use of Taverns

Although the laws stipulated that taverns existed first to cater to the needs of travelers, in practice they primarily served a local clientele. Residents went to their local taverns knowing they would meet the regulars and they could expect to continue an argument or conversation from a previous visit. After Landon Carter, a wealthy Virginia planter and justice, concluded his day in the Richmond County court, he walked the short distance to the ordinary, the same public house he visited after all such days. Many of Carter's tavern visits involved conversations with Dr. Nicholas Flood, with whom he had been quarreling for about four years. On one particular meeting, Carter had convinced himself that he had but a short time to live and he was contemplating working toward a reconciliation with Flood. "Accordingly I drank to this devil and Colo. Peachey, but he would not take notice of me." They alternated drinking a series of toasts. Each feigned inattention to the other until Flood got up and Carter "asked if he would not finish the bottle." Flood refused and "paid his reckoning." Carter eventually left as well but only "after much cheerfulness with 2 or 3 more bottles."[21] In New Amsterdam, Borger Jorissen, while drunk, struck one of his drinking companions, a Mr. Atwater. They appeared in court, Jorissen confessed, he paid Atwater the beaver skins he owed him, and they returned to the scene of the crime to settle matters "with a drink in friendship and harmony."[22]

In towns with multiple drinking establishments, locals who did not patronize their neighborhood tavern selected a public house because they shared attributes with the other patrons, like status or occupation.[23] John Shewbart (also Shubart and Sheubart) operated the London Tavern on Water Street in Philadelphia before moving to Hannover Square. His ledger details the years 1736 to 1743 and logs the assortment of transactions for about 245 customers. Shewbart did not explain the purpose of his ledger, so it is impossible to determine whether it records all of the daily transactions inside his tavern or just those for which he extended credit. Many tavern keepers used a chalkboard to keep track of customers' running tabs. Shewbart may have transferred all of the figures from his chalkboard into his account book, leaving a complete record of the day-to-day activities inside his ordinary, or he may have erased the paid accounts from the board and recorded only the names and amounts for those who owed him money.

All of the customers listed in Shewbart's ledger were men. They came to Shewbart's primarily to drink, although they also borrowed cash, bought "sundries," and purchased beverages to take home. Shewbart's clientele frequented the tavern at various rates. Some were fixtures at his bar while others stopped in only once.[24] Of those listed, 176 came in nine or fewer times (83 were listed as having made a single transaction). Very few names appear in all years. Not quite 30 percent of his customers patronized the tavern ten or more times. In 1737, a Mr. Crofts appeared 110 times. During the year and a half from September 1736 to March 1738, Samuel Carpenter made 117 visits to Shewbart's establishment. He rarely skipped more than two days, and in June of 1737 he sidled up to the bar almost daily. Philip Van Horne was among Shewbart's most loyal patrons. Over three years, Van Horne made 283 appearances, including thirty-two visits to eat and drink with a club, one to lodge, and another to take liquor home. For the remainder, he stopped to drink and/or pick up sundries.

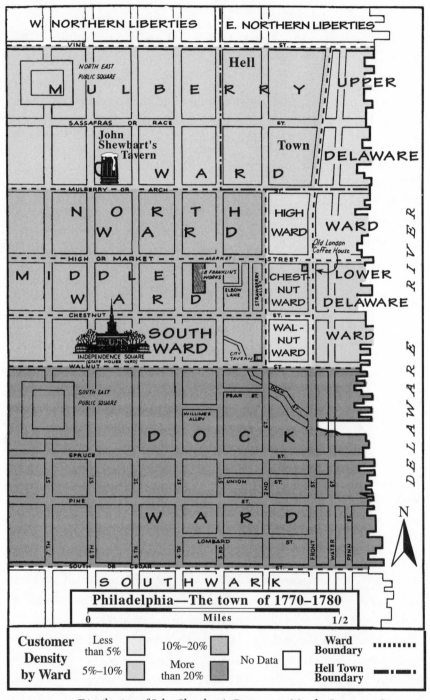

FIGURE 5. Distribution of John Shewbart's Customers. Map by Langevin Geographic.

The title of grand drinking master of the Shewbart tavern, however, belonged to Richard Hudson. He first arrived in November of 1736 and entered the tavern regularly until he disappeared from the journal in July 1741. Over four and one half years, Hudson's name appears 386 times.[25] Shewbart's customers clearly intended to meet there. Hudson, for example, was paired with the same few men over and over as were other regular Shewbart customers.

Shewbart's tavern attracted patrons from all over the city of Philadelphia (Figure 5). Only one-quarter of his customers are listed in the taxpayer rolls of Dock Ward, where the tavern was first situated. However, more than 60 percent lived in the adjacent wards of Chestnut, South, Middle, and Lower Delaware.[26] Perhaps more revealing, Shewbart's London Tavern attracted a high proportion of men from the maritime trades—captains, mariners, sailmakers, shipwrights, blockmakers, ropemakers, ship carpenters, and merchants. Shewbart identified thirty-two of his customers as captains. (These included Charles Cox. It is interesting that the Chestnut Ward tax collector listed Cox in the lower income bracket of "mariner.") Because the London Tavern was convenient to the docks and shipyards, it attracted those who labored in these trades. Shipmasters used it as a temporary office. Samuel Wallace advertised that prospective passengers or anyone wishing to ship goods on his next voyage should meet him at the London Coffee House.[27] Surely Shewbart's customers lived closer to other taverns, but when they appeared at this tavern, his patrons would find their regular drinking companions.

Martin Kreyder's (also Kreider, Krieder, and Kryder) tavern was located in Mulberry Ward. The largest proportion of his customers, patched together from his 1773 inventory of estate, were neighbors residing in the same ward.[28] About one-quarter (23–25%) were on the tax rolls of the wards adjacent to his—High, Upper Delaware, Northern Liberties, and North. (See Figure 6.) Those who came to Kreyder's tavern from elsewhere in the city, like the hatter William Crispin from Walnut Ward or William Dishong from Chestnut Ward, may very well have stopped for a drink after fitting Kreyder with apparel.

The most telling characteristic of Kreyder's patrons is their shared ethnicity. German surnames fill Kreyder's inventory; they include a group that ventured into Philadelphia from Germantown, the township situated ten miles north of the city and containing, as its name implies, a large German population. These

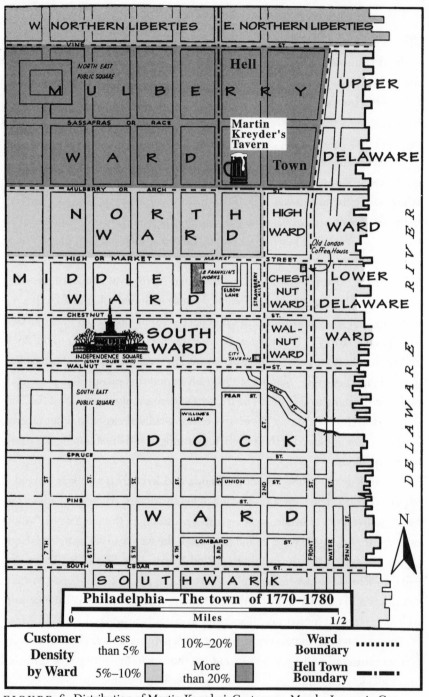

FIGURE 6. Distribution of Martin Kreyder's Customers. Map by Langevin Geographic.

customers selected his establishment when business or pleasure brought them into the port city because they could gather with their kinsmen, reminisce about their homeland, and speak and sing in German. Gottfried Bockius and Gottfried and Jacob Frey met with Lewis Fohrer and Jacob Friss when they ventured in from Germantown. Abraham Recks and Samuel Backman, both farmers, may have stopped at Kreyder's after purchasing supplies in Philadelphia, and the tavern provided them an opportunity to compare their crop yields, talk about seeds, and inquire after the health and welfare of their families. Kreyder's tavern offered the German community of Philadelphia and its environs a comfortable, secure social world.[29]

Noting that taverngoers had their favorite tavern haunts does not imply that the men listed in Shewbart's and Kreyder's account books drank exclusively in those houses. If workers ran an errand or picked up supplies, the resulting dry throat might require a quick drink, and they would quench their thirst at the most convenient place. However, Shewbart and Kreyder's ordinaries had unmistakable identities. In Shewbart's tavern, the men were bound by their labors and shared experiences of the sea. In Kreyder's house the tie was their German ethnicity. These drinkers bypassed ordinaries closer to home in favor of these specific sites. The clientele in Shewbart's and Kreyder's taverns was decidedly mixed by class. The large number of men from the maritime trades included the highest status and the lowest and everything in between, merchants and captains to common mariners. Similarly, since Kreyder attracted a substantial proportion of the German residents from Philadelphia and its environs, they too represented a mixture of status.

In rural areas, great distances separated one tavern from another, and they very likely served anyone who appeared at their door. Benjamin Mifflin, on his 1762 tour south from Philadelphia, expressed his discouragement upon discovering that the only tavern ten miles south of Wilmington, Delaware, had closed because the proprietor had lost his license. Because rural taverns tended to be spaced far apart, he had no idea how to locate lodging and perhaps more importantly, punch or wine.[30] The patrons of John Lowrence's tavern in Rowan County, North Carolina, traveled quite a distance to drink at his bar. Of the account holders who can be identified, almost three-quarters lived within a ten-mile radius, but the length of this distance suggests that many customers combined a trip to Lowrence's public house and other business in the area.[31] John Wilson, in Guilford County, North Carolina, did a substantial, steady business in his store and tavern. During a three-month period in 1774, he handled over 500 transactions for slightly more than 220 individuals. Wilson's store must have been the only one for many miles, and as a result he stocked an assortment of goods that ranged from salt, sugar, and fabrics to nails and imported steel. He also sold many specialty items, which suggests that he placed special orders for whatever his customers needed. Robert Bell, for example, bought a set of hinges for a chest. Wilson also sold liquor, to be consumed on the premises or taken away. The drinkers in his house represented a variety of occupations and places of residence. David Waddle may have been the local tailor. On two of his four visits, he purchased large quantities of thread, buttons, and fabric and then idled over grog before returning to work. James Saunders picked up a substantial amount of nails, which indicates that he worked as a house builder or carpenter. On each visit Saunders took a break from his labors and paused over a bowl of toddy or "sangree." Robert Rollstone may have used his purchase of small amounts of black ribbon as the excuse to toss down some rum.[32] The customers of William Wirt, who operated a tavern in rural Prince George's County, Maryland, similarly did not fit into any obvious categories. What bound his patrons to the tavern was their proximity, since the majority lived in the nearest town or elsewhere nearby. Wirt's tavern drew customers because it was the only tavern within a wide region.[33]

Business in some taverns fluctuated with the seasons. Rural taverns in the northern colonies attracted fewer drinkers during the winter months. Business was the most sparse in the Moulders' tavern in Pennsylvania during January, when one year they served clients on only four days, and in February, that year they were busy only six days. Dry throats accompanied the thaw, however, and activity resumed in March. The Moulders' very best months extended from May through August.[34] The patronage of Arnold Hudson's tavern, another Pennsylvania establishment, followed a similar pattern. This is best illustrated by the behavior of one of Hudson's most regular customers. Jacob Duhadanay averaged just over eight visits per month from May through October. However, from November through March he frequented Hudson's tavern on the average of only once each month. At the time when the cold weather might have slowed his work and a stiff drink would have removed the chill from his bones, getting to the tavern might have been more difficult.[35]

Patterns of use in rural taverns appear related to a combination of labor cycles and weather conditions. In both North Carolina and Pennsylvania, for example, the heaviest burden of labor was during spring and summer. The drinking patterns in North Carolina confirm what we would suspect; when labor demand was low, in late fall and all winter, men had more time to spend in the tavern. The infrequent use of taverns in rural Pennsylvania during the winter months may not reflect their levels of thirst or idleness but the severity of the winter. There were fewer labor demands in January and February, but ice storms and freezing rains may have encouraged drinking at home rather than in the public house.[36]

Shewbart's city patrons seem to have been oblivious to the seasons. No single month or season dominated. The range in his business activity ran only from a high of 10 percent of the year's business in May and again in June to a low of 6.7 percent in September. Neither the winter snows nor summer heat dampened Philadelphians' enthusiasm for their time in Shewbart's bar.[37] Shewbart's customers were overwhelmingly drawn from the maritime trades and while shipping slowed considerably during the winter months, labor at the docks and warehouses did not totally cease. City dwellers gathered in the tavern after their summer labors to drink away their fatigue and wash away the humidity. In the winter, when the cooper could not work outside and the ships lay anchored in the river, one's favorite tavern provided an ideal place to warm hands and find companionship. As in the countryside, the weather impeded the labors of some city workers. Unlike in the rural areas, snow and sleet did not inhibit their ability to get to the tavern. Weather and location were not the only considerations, however. Men were less likely to pay their local tavern a visit without secure wages. When work slowed, so did income. Indeed, the public houses examined here do not appear to have been havens for the unemployed. Rather, money and time were spent in the tavern when jobs were plentiful and incomes more secure.

Taverns were also the sites where locals attended meetings. From November 1746 to through 1750, the Philadelphia County Commissioners alternated their meeting places. They began in Robert's Coffee House and in 1747 shifted to the Widow Jones's Sign of the Three Crowns. In 1748, they left the comfort of the tavern and began holding their meetings in the courthouse. The commissioners complained to the magistrates of the county court that the building was unsuitable. They were referring to the lack of spirits and fireplace but also to the greater perceived risk to their health. They pointed out that "in order that they might be in some measure, more comfortable when they are administering justice," the building needed repairs and to have a stove installed. The commissioners prevailed. Through 1750 they returned to the warmth and comfort of Widow Jones's tavern. In 1749, William Logan, president of the Governor's Council of Pennsylvania, gathered with other members of the Owners of Lamps in Philadelphia at an unspecified tavern to explore better methods of city lighting. Logan was also approached by members of the Dutch Calvinist Church to participate in a panel that would mediate in a disagreement between the minister and the congregation. He was named to head the panel, thus he had to decide where and when the group should meet. He "proposed next day after tomorrow Evening at James's Coffee House." The deliberations took place over many days and all of the meetings continued to be held at the coffee house. In Charleston, South Carolina, justices rented the long room in John Gordon's tavern and held court there. In an attempt to collect a larger rent, Gordon listed the expected expenses, like costs for the room and candles. He then noted that he lost other "public business . . . During the Time of the sitting of the Court" and that more money should therefore be charged. The governor of South Carolina, James Glen, in a letter to the council and assembly in 1750, complained about official functions being conducted in inappropriate places. "The courts are kept in Taverns, and the Prisons in private houses." He asked the legislators to find a remedy for this situation by erecting proper spaces for these specific purposes.[38]

Before the middle of the eighteenth century, few public buildings existed in the colonies, and taverns proved to be remarkably adaptable. Religious as well as secular communities relied on public houses for meeting spaces. Even those religious groups whose beliefs forced them to avoid tavern rituals were involved in the culture of taverns because of a need for the space they offered. English traveler Thomas Story recorded that the Quaker meeting in Newbury, Massachusetts, took place at an inn. When a Swedish pastor, the Rev. Gabriel Nesman, paused in Philadelphia in the winter of 1749, to prepare for his return to Sweden from the Swedish church at Wicaco, Pennsylvania, he contracted several debts. "In order to discharge them," to support his family, and to have sufficient funds for his passage home, he rented some rooms at the Indian King from which to operate a school. He also announced that he would preach a sermon in Swedish from his lodging in the tavern, on the second and third Sundays of each month.[39]

Although tavern rituals had the potential of binding the participants together, they could "divide the company" as well, by "identifying and isolating customers who refused to conform." The interactions between a tavern crowd determined to toast, sing, and dance and those who identified these behaviors as "sinful revelry" produced intense tensions. Elizabeth Ashbridge's husband had moved them out of their Chester County home because he hoped to find a cure for her Quaker leanings. While the Ashbridges lodged temporarily in a Philadelphia tavern, Elizabeth's husband forced her to dance, an effort that served to humiliate his wife and divide the sentiments of those present. Some tavern patrons sympathized with Mr. Ashbridge, who reported a personal loss as a result of Elizabeth's adherence to Quaker beliefs, for she had once been a good dancer and singer. Others thought Mr. Ashbridge had pushed Elizabeth too far.[40]

Drinking

No matter what drew men into the tavern, where they gathered, or during what time period, the consumption of prolific quantities of liquor was the order of the day and night. While visiting New York in 1697 on his journey from his home in Boston to Philadelphia, physician Benjamin Bullivant recorded that after one midday dinner he went down the road to Clapp's "a kind of a pleasure garden, and dranke good cyder & mead." He and his group returned to the city about three o'clock in the afternoon and were invited to take part in an evening treat, but he refused because he "understood itt would scarce breake up before 2 or 3 the next morneing." On the next day, after morning prayers, he returned to Clapp's for his dinner. This elegant feast ended only after several toasts were drunk to the king, the governor, and the neighboring governors.[41]

Most forms of recreation and all celebrations were accompanied by large quantities of alcohol and excessive drinking. The liquor bill from a York County, Virginia, funeral in 1617 totaled twenty-two gallons of cider, twenty-four gallons of beer, and five gallons of brandy sweetened by twelve pounds of sugar. The cost for liquor at such events caused Ralph Langley, also of York County, to contemplate the expense for his own funeral and he cautioned his executors to calculate the amount of alcohol so that they did not spend more than his estate could support. He estimated that about six gallons of an unspecified drink would suffice. The costs for a funeral reception could be significant. The liquor bill for the funeral of planter John Grove amounted to one thousand pounds of tobacco.[42] Ten thousand pounds of tobacco were spent in 1688 to treat the citizens of Rappahannock County when they solemnized the birth of King James II's son. To place the quantity of drink in perspective, the county jail was built two years later at a cost of six thousand pounds.

Continuous drinking and large quantities of alcohol characterized the eighteenth century as well as the previous one. An anonymous traveler from Philadelphia stopped at a tavern about three o'clock and washed an "indifferent" dinner down with a "so called" claret. His supper, down the road a way, was accompanied by both wine from Lisbon, "good," and "Spirits very good." William Black, a resident of Manchester, Virginia, traveled to Philadelphia, in 1744, as the secretary to the commissioners appointed by Governor Gooch to negotiate a treaty with the Iroquois. Before crossing the Schuylkill River into Philadelphia, he and his traveling companions were welcomed by a group of gentlemen, who provided a "Bowl of fine Lemon Punch big enough to have Swimm'd half a dozen of young Geese; after puring four or five Glasses of this down our throats we cross'd the River." While in the port city, he was invited by the governor for a noon meal. Black was enormously impressed by the food, both its quantity and its variety, "substantial as well as curious." After dinner ended, the table was filled with wines and more food. The "Glass went briskly around" passed among the guests, its contents continuously changing, "sometimes with Sparkling Champaign, and sometimes Rich Madeira, Claret, or whatever the Drinker pleas'd." Over the course of one of Black's days in Philadelphia, he consumed bread, cider, and punch for his noonday meal; rum and brandy before supper; punch, madeira, port, and sherry with supper; liqueurs afterwards; and wine and spirits "ad libitum" until bedtime.[43]

Dr. Alexander Hamilton compared the drinking habits in the middle colonies with those of his Chesapeake home and determined that when visiting there he needed to exercise extreme caution. He was with some "polite company" in New York, and "after supper they set in for drinking." Hamilton confessed to his diary his aversion to the practice of drinking all night and his astonishment at such devotion to the quantity of alcohol. Hamilton also intimated that, at least for members of the Hungarian Club, it was good sport to try to get a stranger drunk. After one midday meal, "we tossed about the bumpers so furiously that I was obliged to go home and sleep for three hours."[44]

Charles Woodmason, an Anglican itinerant minister, would have disagreed with Hamilton's perception of regional colonial drinking patterns. In Woodmason's opinion, no group could match the drinking prowess of South Carolinians. He had to compete with their constant states of inebriation when attempting to rally participants for his church services. In one town, he could not locate a private room anywhere and was forced to lodge in a tavern where the the occupants were "continually drunk." Later in his travels he complained that those dispensing drink were more successful than he was in attracting devotees. "All the people round me got drunk so that had but 40 Persons to attend Service." The level of noise generated by the drinkers also interfered with Woodmason's ability to hold his services effectively. "The Company got drunk by 10 oth Clock and we could hear them firing, hooping, and hallowing like Indians."[45] The pervasiveness of heavy drinking in the colonies did not prevent individuals from talking and writing about the prodigious quantities consumed. It was as if colonists doubled their pleasure by reliving the drinking experience through quill and ink.

Hamilton, who had arrived from Scotland in 1738, offered some insight into colonial attitudes toward drunkenness, implying that part of the lure of taverns was to participate in excessive drinking. When he witnessed a drunken group leaving a Maryland tavern, Hamilton was moved to describe the odd position each man assumed on his horse and to recount the garbled speech he heard. Hamilton was clearly amused by what he saw, and as he approached the tavern door, the proprietor sputtered an apology to him about the rowdy, disorderly conduct and assured him that he did not like entertaining unruly crowds in his house. He claimed that he was forced to oblige this group on occasion, because, he confessed, it was the way he earned his "dayly bread."[46]

Indeed for Hamilton, the state of inebriation, whether his own or others, often inspired his writing and provided him with myriad tales worth telling. His diary records that a tavern keeper at Darby, Pennsylvania, was "drunk as a lord;" he recounted of one companion that "the liquor had a strange effect on him, having deprived him of the use of his tongue." At times Hamilton expressed genuine awe at the quantities of alcohol imbibed by his companions. However, he never offered his descriptions as lessons in morality or arguments for temperance.[47]

Drinking enormous quantities of alcohol does appear to have been a requirement of the tavern experience. When Durand of Dauphiné visited Virginia in the 1670s, he noted, as any upstanding Frenchman would, the absence of wine and the large quantities of other alcoholic beverages that were consumed at virtually any time of the day or night. He observed that heavy drinking was a requirement as were the rituals associated with it. Each time a new person joined the party, he had to be toasted. This, he reported, became a burdensome responsibility as the group he was with grew gradually to twenty people. "When they were not intoxicated they usually let me drink in my own way, & generally I just kissed the glass; but when they were drunk they would have me drink at their will." Durand was also moved to report on the amount of alcohol consumed at a wedding he attended. At the event's end, the guests were so drunk, Durand had to select his sleeping arrangements with great care, to keep him out of the way of falling bodies. And when he awoke in the morning, he could "not see one who could stand straight."[48] One hundred years later, the description of a day in the life of Virginia merchant William Gregory confirms that colonials drank throughout the day. At his noon meal in the London Coffee House in Philadelphia, he washed biscuits down with punch. That night at supper, he and his companions consumed two bottles of wine each.[49]

Colonists drank alcoholic beverages in a variety of settings, beginning with any time food was served. Any meal, from breakfast to supper, was washed down with drink. Alcohol flowed liberally at all celebrations and the events were punctuated with appropriate toasts. Demonstrating the ability to consume great quantities of liquor in the company of friends and/or acquaintances also offered one measure of a man's worth. Hamilton and Durand developed techniques to appear as if they were keeping up the pace of consumption. Both felt they lacked the necessary capacity but both understood that if they appeared reluctant to drink, their actions would be interpreted by their gentleman companions as an insult. Their manner of drinking was one of a number of signs that marked them as members of the "better sort."[50]

Gaming

Games of chance are rightfully associated with the colonial tavern. Members of all ranks converged to bet, lacing the entertainment with alcohol.[51] As taverns diverged and catered to individuals according to rank and occupation, tavern keepers provided games and recreation appropriate to their patrons' specific interests. Large urban taverns had multiple rooms, so that the merchants and city officials who frequented them could choose whether to engage in cards or billiards. Richard Neave, a Philadelphia resident, left an account of his activities for the years 1773 and 1774 that included travel. He recorded regularly his "losses [and] gains at the Club."[52] In a letter to the *Pennsylvania Gazette*, Celia Single complained about the vices of Mr. Billiard "who spends more than he earns, at his Green Table."[53] In Philadelphia, even though lawmakers outlawed billiard tables and they enforced the law, anyone wishing to play could find a table with little difficulty. In his 1744 visit to the port city, William Black's June 12th activities included going "with some Company to the Billiards Table, where we spent the Afternoon, and return'd to the Coffee House." A dozen years later, William Gregory likely played at the same table: "went to the Billiard Table, almost a mile out of Town—they are forbid being in the Town—& played till towards bed-time."[54]

Taverns in southern cities offered similar amenities for their patrons. Being equipped with a billiard table worked as a lure to potential customers. An advertisement in the *South Carolina Gazette* reassured its readers that "the Billiard-tables will be continued as usual, the loser paying half a crown each game for the use of the table."[55] Samuel Rowland Fisher, a Philadelphia resident, traveled in the late 1770s to Charleston, South Carolina. He spent a most disagreeable evening in a coffee house: "there are very few there at any time but those who are playing Back Gammon, the noise of which is so great that you can scarce hear anything."[56]

Nicholas Cresswell conveys the ubiquitous quality of gaming in Virginia. He arrived from England in 1774 and traveled throughout the colonies for three years. Upon his arrival in Williamsburg, his search for lodging proved enormously frustrating because the House of Burgesses was in session. He was mollified when he located a room in Mrs. Vaubes's tavern "where all the best people resorted." He was in the tavern only a short time when he met some of the region's most distinguished citizens, including William Byrd. Cresswell soon lamented these new acquaintances, however, and "had reason to repent for they are all professed gamesters, Especially Colonel Burd who is never happy but when he has the box and Dices in hand." According to Cresswell, people scurried back and forth between the Capitol and the taverns throughout the day, "and at night, Carousing and Drinking In one Chamber and box and Dice in another, which Continues till morning Commonly. There is not a publick house in virginia but have their tables all baterd with the boxes."[57]

For one unnamed "young gentleman" on the road in the southern colonies, a game of chance saved the day. He had been forced to swim across a river with his horse. After he dried himself and "began to examine my pockets, I recollected that I had not one farther of money." He had no idea what to do since he would be unable to pay for "ferriage, and horse, lodging and punch." As his good fortune would have it, three country planters approached him when he reached the tavern and "proposed playing a game at whisk, but wanted a fourth to make up a set." The landlord was not at home so they asked him to join them. The game lasted until two in the morning, and by its end, our hero's problem was solved. He was two pounds, seventeen shillings, and six pence richer than when the game started.[58]

Virginians took their gaming seriously. Cresswell claimed that even if taverngoers wished only to drink and converse, they would find themselves involved in gambling. If guests did not care for dice, they had a number of options. Cards were quite common. Whist seemed to be the favorite of the upper classes. It was similar to the game of bridge and required some training and skill. In contrast, "all-fours" appealed more to the lower classes and, according to society's elite, relied less on skill than luck. In his journal, Philip Fithian, a tutor on the Carter plantation, Nomini Hall, in Virginia, referred to all-fours as "that vulgar game fit only for the meanest gamblers."[59] All card games were potential vehicles for betting. Alexander Hamilton encountered some form of gaming in almost every setting and at all times of the day and night during a trip from Maryland to Maine.

On a midday visit to a coffee house in New York he found "some rattling fellows playing att backgammon, and some deeper headed politicians att the game of chess." The very next evening, Hamilton too participated.[60]

Combined with enough alcohol, any event or challenge could turn into an occasion for gambling. These incidents could become loud, rowdy, and often violent. In 1736, Thomas Apty, a Philadelphia plasterer, found his way to the Red Lion in Elbow Lane. He bet that he could drink a gallon of cider royal in the space of an hour and a half. He had no sooner accomplished the feat when he said "I have finished, but he fell down, . . . and then expir'd." A group of heavy drinkers in a tavern in Prince George's County "got to making Sport, . . . with one of their Company, by tripping his Heels, and throwing him down on a Floor, till they gave him a Fall which kill'd him." Roger Addams, an inebriated patron in a Dorchester County, Maryland, tavern, bet that "he could then Drink all the Wine there left in a Decanter, at one Draught. He won the Wager; but Died a few Minutes after."[61]

Taverns were often the sites of popular spectator sports that also afforded the possibility of gambling. Both horse races and cockfights were organized near taverns, where drinking helped participants relive their victories or forget their losses. It appears that the southern and Chesapeake colonies deserve their reputations for having more of these gaming events than the northern colonies. Although cockfights were not exclusively a southern phenomenon, Josiah Quincy's Bostonian sensibilities appear to have been mightily offended by the propensity of "young men of fortune" in Maryland and Virginia to engage in cockfighting and horse racing. "To hear them converse you would think that the grand point of all science was properly to fix a gaff & touch with dexterity the tales of a cock while in combat. He who was at the last match, the last main, or last horse race assumed the airs of a hero or german potentate. The ingenuity of a Locke or the discoveries of a Newton were considered as infinitely inferior to the accomplishments of him who knew when to shoulder a blind cock or start a fleet horse." Quincy was amazed at how much time and effort went into "that vile practice." Two separate groups of men spent "three successive days at this inglorious amusement & as many nights in riot and debauchery."[62]

Anyone eager to participate in the games needed only to watch the advertisements in the local newspaper. A notice in the *Virginia Gazette* alerted all interested parties that "A Cock Match will be fought on the seventh Day of April next" for a purse of sixty pistoles. The winner earned this amount but the side bets could equal or exceed it.[63] Cockfights provided entertainment in rural New Jersey as well. Jonathan Holmes spent a rainy day inside and then gathered two friends and his brother to go see the cocks fight. He lost a penny, "it being as large a wager as any then Layed."[64]

Cockfights were sufficiently embedded in the culture that Virginians attended them for many reasons. They offered one of many venues for gambling. They also provided men with an opportunity to meet and conduct business. John Jerdone arrived in Virginia in 1746 "as part owner of a cargo of goods, and as factor." He contemplated purchasing a crop of tobacco and commented in a letter to his British agents that he would be attending a "grand Cock fight" in New Castle and expected to see many of the gentlemen with whom he would consult about this proposition. While the cockfight served as the site of gaming, men from the region were expected to gather, providing them with another exclusively male context in which to perform.[65]

The tavern also functioned as the focal point for militia training. The day's events might start with militia practice and after the training was concluded, the action might evolve into an impromptu horse race. When horses and men were exhausted, those gathered would drift quite naturally toward the nearest tavern. The actors in one particular such series of events in 1711 included Benjamin Davis and George Wortham, both residents of Middlesex County, Massachusetts, and long-time neighbors. Davis was "a freeholder and occasional minor office holder" who was on a slide toward indebtedness. Wortham was also a freeholder, minor office holder, and the captain of the local militia, whose economic fortunes were moving in the opposite direction.[66] They became embroiled in an argument, which gained momentum slowly. William Matthews, another Middlesex County resident and a former tavern keeper, who had also fallen on hard economic times, was serving time in jail for stealing Wortham's mare. Davis proclaimed that Matthews had not stolen the horse, for he was "an honest man and took his [own] mare where he Could find her" (apparently Matthews's horse was not always easy to locate). The argument escalated, and at one point Wortham raised his cane at Davis, who "struck at the cane with his sheathed sword, then drew the sword from its scabbard and cut at the cane." By the time the fight moved outside the tavern, both had their swords drawn. Davis ran into Wortham's outstretched sword and died from his injuries.[67]

The drama and death involved in this exchange are fathomable by factoring into the equation the differences in Davis's and Wortham's rank in society and economic circumstances and combining this with the quantities of alcohol each had consumed. They were not equals, a reality that must have angered and frustrated Davis. Wortham's star was on the rise while Davis's was on a downward slide. Both of them, and their companions, were apparently thoroughly drunk. A witness at the trial admitted that he could not be sure about his testimony because "he was Something in drink." This must surely have been a gross understatement. "The hard cider had been flowing for at least three hours" and was the flame that ignited the passions.[68]

When horse races were connected with ordinaries, the events started and ended with tavern jaunts. Seventy-one "gentlemen of the turf" organized the Jockey Club in Philadelphia in 1766. They held annual race meetings with entries from many colonies. The local Quaker meeting discouraged the sport, but this opposition did not dampen its appeal or success. Races occurred more than once a year and the stakes were often quite high, like the one hundred–pound purse that went to the winner of the race on October 4, 1768.[69]

Running horses was a common diversion in Virginia. When Philip Fithian was riding to the Richmond courthouse, he encountered a two-horse race with the substantial purse of 500 pounds. He claimed that the side betting was so popular it was impossible to estimate the number of smaller bets. At this event, Virginians could have taken care of their court business, run their race, consulted with Colonel John Taylor, one of the horse owners and among the wealthiest residents of the county, and with Dr. Flood, the owner of the second horse. Dr. Flood apparently combined horse racing with the art of physic.[70]

In these gaming and sporting events, colonial men of all classes participated in contests. Horse races, cockfights, and games like billiards and cards pitted the prowess of one male patron against another. Unlike polite discourse, a pastime in elite taverns, these contests involved men from mixed ranks and, at least momentarily, served to suspend traditional social conventions and boundaries. If the cock that won was owned by a member of the lower class, the event exerted a leveling effect. However real, the effect was short-lived.[71]

Clubs

Elite white men commonly drew together inside the tavern, or on occasion at one of their homes, and formed clubs. Dr. Alexander Hamilton claimed that the male personality contained some innate quality that predisposed it to clubbing. Hamilton's brother, also a physician, whom he had joined in the colonies, prescribed that he join a club when he first arrived in Maryland, as a means of alleviating his homesickness. Clubs provided the assembled company, locals as well as travelers, with some structure, even though their intention was often solely as an excuse for heavy drinking. Tavern keepers encouraged clubs; they were a guarantee of regular clientele. Proprietors supported the activity by offering a club rate, a slightly discounted price for their fare.

The size and composition of the group might ebb and flow, but interested men could arrive at the appointed time with some guarantee that they would be joined by a predictable group. Hamilton noted that some participants had little "talent for that Sort of conversation, that is carried on by Language or speech, or, at least, if they used Speech, it was to no better purpose, than one that says *Bo to a goose,* there whole dialogue consisting in, you've baulk'd your glass—you drink kelty— put about the bowl—fill tother pipe—here's to you—pledge you—and such like short Sentences."[72] Hamilton had no illusions that most of these clubs were dedicated to little but intense drinking, nevertheless, he was so taken with the idea that he organized a club in Annapolis. It met at his house and included eight men, who would gather weekly. It was "designed for humor, and . . . a sort of farcical Drama of Mock Majesty."[73] Such a club is pictured in Figure 7, which may have been drawn by Hamilton.

Clubs existed in many forms. Some were informal, as in James Logan's experience: "spent the Evening at a publick House with several friends of the Young Sort, where we agreed to meet once a week to have a supper." Some were elaborate and formal, like the Governor's Club, "a society of gentlemen that met at a tavern every night and converse on various subjects." They were the embellishment of civilized living: "we meet, converse, laugh, talk, smoke, drink, differ, agree, argue, Philosophize, harangue, pun, sing, dance and fiddle together, nay we are really in fact a Club." A successful club was a homogeneous gather-

FIGURE 7. "The Royalist Club." Gentlemen in colonial towns and cities spent a considerable amount of time together in clubs, meeting at their favorite tavern or in private homes. Elite clubs mixed intellectual exchange with considerable drinking. Here they pass the convivial bowl of punch around the table. Attributed to Maryland physician Alexander Hamilton. *Gentlemen's Progress: Hamilton's Itinerarium of Dr. Alexander Hamilton, 1744,* ed. Carl Bridenbaugh (Chapel Hill: University of North Carolina Press, 1948).

ing of men that restricted its members by status, thereby promoting camaraderie, a sense of belonging, and unity of purpose.[74]

The stated intent of clubs varied. When Josiah Quincy was in the south, he most commonly lodged and was entertained in private homes, mainly in elegant

FIGURE 8. "Mr. Neilson's Battle with the Royalist Club." Gentlemen claimed that their club activities represented the highest levels of decorum and erudition, but the discussions could become quite heated. Attributed to Dr. Alexander Hamilton. *Gentlemen's Progress: Hamilton's Itinerarium of Dr. Alexander Hamilton, 1744,* ed. Carl Bridenbaugh (Chapel Hill: University of North Carolina Press, 1948).

plantations. In Charleston, however, two of his nights were spent with clubs. The first was the Friday Night Club, which included "substantial gentlemen: About 20 or 30 in company." Quincy reported that the conversation wandered greatly and included "negroes, rice, and the necessity of British regular troops to be quartered in Charlestown." The Monday Night Club consisted of "cards, feasting & indifferent wines."[75]

Whatever their stated purpose, because of all the drinking, club meetings could get quite rowdy. (See Figure 8.) Hamilton described one such group: "Just as I dismounted att Tradaway's, I found a drunken club dismissing. . . Their discourse was as oblique as their position; the only thing intelligible in it was oaths and God dammes; the rest was an inarticulate sound like Rabelais' frozen words a thawing, interlaced with hickupings and belchings."[76]

In contrast, the Governor's Club combined eating and drinking and, according to the participants, lively and entertaining conversation. Hamilton, became a member, noted that in his first visit to the Governor's Club the topic for discussion was "the English poets and some of the foreign writers, particularly Cervantes . . . whom we loaded with elogiums due to his character." William Black, while in Philadelphia to discuss policies regarding the Six Nations, joined the Philadelphia Governor's Club. "A Select Number of Gentlemen" met every night at a particular tavern passing the presupper time in "the Pleasures of Conversation and a Cheerful Glass." Black thought the supper, served at about nine o'clock, most genteel, but he was most impressed by the lemon punch and the variety of wines, "of which everyone might take of what he best like'd and what Quantity he Pleas'd." Black returned to the Governor's Club most of the nights he was in Philadelphia.[77]

While in New York City, Hamilton was invited to join the Hungarian Club, which met nightly at Todd's Tavern. The ostensible purpose of their gatherings was learned conversation, and the topics of these events varied greatly. One night's discourse ended with "a piece of criticism upon a poem in the newspaper." A lawyer, Mr. Moore, "showed more learning than judgment in a disquisition he made upon nominatives and verbs."[78] Hamilton was made to feel as if he were part of the group. "They saluted me very civilly, and I, as civilly as I could, returned their compliments in neat short speeches." However, after all was said and done, Hamilton was convinced that the purpose of this club was drinking. "Two or three toapers in the company seemed to be of opinion that a man could not have a more sociable quality or enducement than to be able to pour down seas of liquor and remain unconquered while others sunk under the table. I heard this philosophical maxim but silently dissented to it. I left the company att 10 att night pritty well flushed with my three bumpers and, ruminating on my folly, went to my lodgings."[79]

There were plenty of clubs that engaged in more than drinking. Black was invited by the governor of Pennsylvania to the Tunn Tavern to participate in another club. As Black described it, a "Number of Gentlemen that meet at this house every Saturday to Eat Beef-Stakes, and from that is Call'd the Beef-Stake Clubb." The dinner included about twenty separate dishes.[80] Alexander Mackraby was in a club that met weekly at a Philadelphia tavern, where he purchased a subscription for billiards for 40 shillings even though he had little intention of playing. He did so only because he "like[d] the party so well." Hamilton joined the Physicall Club in Boston, where "Dr. Douglass gave us a physicall harangue upon a late book of surgery published by Heyster, in which he tore the poor author all to pieces." In Newport, Rhode Island, Hamilton was eager to accept an invitation from the Philosophical Club. However, he was disappointed to discover that "no matters of philosophy were brought upon the carpet."[81]

Clubs combined the exclusive with the inclusive. Strangers were invited to participate, but they were expected to prove themselves worthy. Some could qualify more readily than others. John Fontaine, an Irish Huguenot who traveled to the colonies in the early part of the eighteenth century, met the standards of both the Irish Club of New York and the French Club.[82]

When elite men participated in clubs, they were bound together by their shared characteristics. As an historian of English history explained, clubs were "private but very rarely secret." Men met to conduct whatever business they wished, unobserved by their wives or by those beneath them on the socioeconomic ladder. Those not present caught a glimpse of what transpired only through an occasional newspaper story or from gossip on the street. Elites claimed their right to separate themselves from the rest of society and to maintain this private space within the public realm.[83]

The amount of a husband and father's attention consumed by club membership became a public issue when a writer signed "Amy Prudence," in a letter to the *American Weekly Mercury,* complained on behalf of all wives that clubs offered men an excuse to leave work midday for the purpose of drinking in someone's home.

Sir, I must inform you that we are wives to a certain set of men that stile themselves the Meridional club, which they think intitules them to leave their business in the midst . . . so that . . . twenty or more of them can get together over a flowing bowl of fresh limes, which makes them of more fluency by far than we are over a dish of tea; . . . when our rooms are set in decent order to dine in, we are immediately discommoded with a numbers body of twelve o'clock punch drinkers which beloved liquors they pretend is to whet their appetites. This being ended, (the president they call him) makes a long harangue, whose house and family they shall next disoblige, and so departs 'til the next long wish'd for hour . . .[84]

The club men were not "whetting their appetites"; they were spending the afternoon drinking and in the process displaced their wives and families.

The letter evoked a response from "Amicus Curiae," who defended his bruised honor by arguing that the club had a far grander purpose than mere drinking.

Upon reading your last record, I find a scurrilous complaint lodged against a society that meets alternately at each other's houses once a day, to regale themselves for about half an hour over a bowl of punch and thereby to preserve an agreeable unity among themselves, a profitable correspondence in regard to business and a happy decorum in mixt affairs, such as characters, controversies, etc.[85]

"Amy" and "Amicus" were both correct. The Meridional Club was about drinking in a space protected from any and all outsiders. It was also about the unity of those assembled and their "happy decorum" which permitted them to express their shared gentility and cultivate business.

Clubs were not exclusively of the elite. When formed by the laboring classes, however, their activities remain even more obscure, in part because the participants did not leave memoirs chronicling their witticism and erudition, and colonial writers rarely found anything in the activities of these clubs worthy to report. Their interest was peaked only when the actions of laboring-class clubs sent menacing messages or threatened the peace. The Geneva Club, composed of free and enslaved New York City blacks in the mid-1730s, articulated as part of its aim a subversion of class order by mocking the clubs of middling and elite white men. The justices of the New York Supreme Court proclaimed that they were unamused by this "impudence." The Geneva Club adopted the title "free masons." The justices labeled this a "gross affront to the provincial grand master and gentlemen of the fraternity" of the genuine Free Masons.[86] The Geneva Club members performed a burlesque of the rites of the Free Masons. They mocked the supposed wisdom and learnedness of clubs by naming their organization after an increasingly popular alcoholic drink. They proclaimed that rather than erudition and conversation, clubs were mostly about legitimating the regular gathering of white men for the primary purpose of drinking. Finally, the Geneva Club critiqued the issue of privilege, pointing out that by separating themselves from those whose status was beneath them and from women, the club men were creating the rules that would protect their positions of privilege within society.

While elite clubs convened for a variety of purposes—to discuss particular subjects like medicine or natural philosophy, to establish and maintain unity among the members, or to eat and drink—what did not vary was their composition. Elite clubs were composed entirely of white males. Hamilton occasionally referred to an assembled club group as mixed. However, he was not insinuating mixtures of gender or race. Rather, he he was indicating that the group included white men from different religious persuasions: "there were Roman Catholicks, Church men, Presbyterians, Quakers Newlightmen, Methodists, Seventh day men, Moravians, Anabaptists, and one Jew."[87] In the gushing sentiments of an avid contemporary frequenter, clubs consisted of "Knots of men rightly sorted."[88] Their identities were based on this belonging, tied to an exclusive club that prevented access to women, people of color, or men beneath them. The elite white men who participated in the clubs looked around the room in their alcoholic fog at the men gathered together and took pride in their belonging, in their shared entitlement. They could take comfort in knowing that they were protected from those excluded and that their mutual experiences served to reinforce their positions within society.

Three

Preventing Drunkenness and Keeping Good Order in the Seventeenth Century: "A Herd of Planters on the ground / O'er-whelmed with Punch, dead drunk we found"

Thomas Robins and Thomas Woodmans being convicted before John Bristow for drunkenness breach of peace breaking ye great cabin doore and ye head of Samuel Harison mate on board of ye ship[.] Tryall was for ye same called to ye barr butt upon their submission to ye court was ordered to pay 5s with all court charges. . . .

. . . Queens authority presents John Cos of Ridley township for keepeing a disorderly house of entertainment there being lately a revell and men have a busied them selfs to drunkenness and fighting and abused themselves and others to the terrors of the inhabitants thereabouts and therefore dangerous for strangers to goe to the house or pass by.[1]

*I*n 1688, while drunk, Thomas Robins and Thomas Woodmans, of Chester County, Pennsylvania, bashed in the cabin door (as well as the head) of one of their ship mates. They had been drinking at the tavern of John Cos, also of

Chester County, who kept a disorderly house. Cos established no limits on the amount of alcohol his patrons could drink. As a result, his tavern was the scene of drunken revelries. The fighting eventually reached such a frenzy that when neighbors walked in the vicinity they gave the tavern a wide berth for fear they would be drawn into the melee or struck by a hurled object.

Seventeenth-century lawmakers conveyed their dual concerns—for the behavior of both keepers and customers—in their approach to tavern law. Working to prevent drunkenness and the resulting disorders, they also confronted the problem of drink sellers who gouged thirsty colonists by charging huge sums. The discussion treats the sectarian and nonsectarian colonies as separate groups, tracing and comparing the origin and development of colonial law as lawmakers attempted to control tavern operation and the drinking patterns of early Americans. Seventeenth-century lawmakers focused their energies on regulating tavern activities to maintain order, to prevent drunkenness, and to sever any link between drunkenness and the Sabbath, as well as to establish the responsibilities of tavern keepers.

Statute books offer a way to compare what motivated colonists to pass particular legislation. Laws offer insight into which behaviors colonial leaders wished to control and which previous laws were deemed to have been unsuccessful. Each successive amendment of a law reflects the perception of lawmakers that a particular statute was ineffectual and required clearer definition of the limits of behavior. To explore the juncture between the law and behavior, to understand how often these laws were violated or how much effort was expended to enforce them, we must enter the courtroom. An analysis of the prosecution record makes it possible to assess where laws and patterns of behavior diverged and to investigate how the culture of each colony contributed to the creation and enforcement of law.

Despite variations in social arrangements, population, ideologies, institutional development, and economic organization, the North American colonies shared remarkably similar legal systems.[2] They had a layered court structure in which the provincial or colony-level courts usually dealt with the most serious crimes. In Pennsylvania, for example, the provincial court—two justices who traveled the state each spring and fall on a county circuit—heard all appeals of civil and criminal suits, and a special court of oyer and terminer—judges who were sum-

moned to a county—acted in capital cases.[3] Most of the legal labors were handled by the county courts. These courts had jurisdiction over civil matters and
criminal jurisdiction over misdemeanors. They heard most of the misdemeanor
cases involved in liquor-related violations.[4]

What remains somewhat cloudy is precisely how authorities judged whether
particular behaviors were illegal. For example, individuals were commonly
hauled before the magistrates on the charge of drunkenness. However, the definition of drunkenness varied wildly. One historian claims that proceedings were
brought against individuals in Plymouth County, Massachusetts, only when the
courts suspected "sinful, frequent, and Continued following of strong Drink."
From this prescription it appears that colonial magistrates were concerned with
problem drinkers not the occasional binger. Church discipline confirms this view:
members were to talk to perpetrators to ensure that they were reforming their
drinking habits. In one case the church elders noted that "Yet we have no reason to think that he still lives in the practice of it, to the reproach of religion."
They appeared satisfied that this drinker had amended his ways. The church was
concerned with relapses. Mrs. Bozworth, for example, was warned that "if she
falls into this sin again (this being the 2d time of Conviction) they will not
immediately receive her upon a confession, But will Suspend her for some time
to see whether her Conversation be answerable: and so with Respect to other
Relapses."[5]

As clear as these cases seem, others, at least from the perspective of the early
twenty-first century, appear far more blurred. It was, for example, illegal in every
colony to drink to excess. But what constituted legally drunk? Was the meas-
urement of intoxication the same in Virginia as in Massachusetts? Was there any
consistency between counties within the same colony or towns within counties?
When John Hodges was prosecuted for drunkenness in 1637 in Massachusetts,
was it for the same offense as William Chadborne's 1643 crime of "drinking too
much" or Ralph Golthrope's 1643 transgression of "being distempered with
wine?"[6]

The common use of confession as a form of evidence suggests that contemporaries shared an idea of what constituted excessive drinking. However, colonial records are peppered with innumerable and wide-ranging definitions of
drunkenness. One yardstick for determining drunkenness was based on a per-

son's loss of motor control. In 1650 Thomas Cook had consumed so much that when he came out of the tavern "he fell down," and that would have qualified him as drunk; in 1725 John Cavender was judged to be "in drink" because "he realed and staggered." One court was content to find an individual drunk because he was "bereaved of his understanding which appeared both in his speech and behavior." The courts had a difficult time distinguishing what "degree of intoxication should be punished," and they could not always differentiate between the outward symptoms of drunkenness and those of illness. William Busbey was presented before a Cambridge court in 1638 for drunkenness, but the cause of his actions was found to be "the falling sickness."[7]

Other behaviors were used as signs that an individual was drunk. In 1653, the Essex County Court assumed that Thomas Wheeler was drunk because of his "profane and foolish dancing, singing, and wanton speeches." In Plymouth, a drunkard was defined as a person who "lispes or faulters in his spech by reason of overmuch drinke or that stagers in his goeing or that vomits by reason of excessive drinking or cannot follow his calling." Massachusetts law enumerated explicitly the signs of drunkenness: Anyone "bereaved or disabled in the use of his understanding, appearing in his speech or gesture" could be assumed to be drunk.[8] Justice Askham of Maryland denied the claim that he was drunk because "a man is never drunk if he can go out of the carts way when it is coming toward him." Askham may have subscribed to the following definition:

> Not drunk is he who from the floor,
> Can rise again and still drink more,
> But drunk is he who prostrate lies,
> Without the power to drink or rise.

Ebenezer Cook, the bard of Maryland, adopted a similar definition. "A Herd of Planters on the ground, / O'er-whelmed with Punch, dead drunk we found."[9]

Because no reliable yardstick existed with which to measure inebriation, the potential for drunkenness was linked to the amount of time spent inside the tavern. This was the rationale cited when the Provincial Council of Pennsylvania passed a law to ensure good order in taverns, by limiting an individual's stay to one hour. Massachusetts lawmakers also stated explicitly how long a person could remain in an ordinary, but they went even further and indicated how much drink could be consumed before drunkenness would result: they deemed it excessive to serve a patron more than half a pint at a time or to allow individuals to drink for more than half an hour or after nine o'clock at night.[10]

One student of the social behavior connected with drink identifies two categories of deviant behavior that fit the definition of drunkenness in most societies in which alcoholic beverages were regularly consumed—deviant physical comportment, which includes "stumbling, falling, mispronouncing words, and passing out," and deviant social comportment, "illegal immoral, unethical, sinful, or just bad behavior." These describe accurately the range of behaviors that were in varying degrees deemed intolerable by early Americans. In order to compare rates of prosecution, the following analysis assumes consistency across colonies in the definitions of these crimes. Thus, we assume that being drunk involved similar behaviors, as did operating a disorderly house.[11]

An analysis of indictments and resolutions offers the opportunity to determine where society wished to draw the line in terms of drinking and tavern behavior. Those individuals who were prosecuted had crossed into the territory of behavior that society was unwilling to tolerate. By following the cases through the colonial period, analyzing the ways the prosecutions changed, and by placing them alongside activities that escaped prosecution, a litany of what colonists valued emerges, as well as a demonstration of how these attitudes changed over time. In addition, the prosecutorial record reveals the shifts in the types of crimes that drew the courts' attention. To this we can add questions about the gendered and class nature of the criminal process and whether this too changed.[12]

Prosecution records also afford an understanding of those who operated the legal system, a system that was based on the values shared by those whose duty it was to enforce the law and operate the courts. At times, the records of prosecution enable us to see the difference between the values and attitudes of those on the top of the social hierarchy and those on the bottom. At these moments, the tavern becomes the stage upon which the lower orders acted out part of their lives, and in the courtroom their "betters" looked down upon them with fear and loathing.[13] Taverns were implicated in criminal actions beyond violations of drinking and tavern law. They were often the sites of violence.[14] They played, as Cornelia Dayton reports, "a major supporting role in libel cases. . . . words uttered in anger, phrases penned in ridicule," because as the focal points of early American sociability, public houses were where the participants often gathered.[15]

As valuable as court records can be, they do have limitations as sources. In general they provide only cryptic detail, including the charge, the defendant's plea, whether a jury was called, the result, and in cases where the defendant was found guilty, the penalties. If the case was not heard, the records do not articulate why. Although the lapse of time has caused their voices to grow faint, occasionally the men and women involved as defendants or witnesses can be heard. By paying close attention to the testimony of those who appeared in court, events can be reconstructed and pieces of stories fitted together to create the patterns that constituted their lives. On rare moments their words provide an entrée into the tavern.[16]

Although the court records provide a unique and valuable dimension into the tavern and drinking behaviors of early Americans, the nature of early American law renders them incomplete. Much of colonial law, especially in New England and Pennsylvania, was meted out informally by local officials or by the church. Thus, many of the behaviors that violated the law never reached the courts, and some disputes over drinking and taverns were resolved through other means. New Englanders, for example, spent an enormous amount of energy regulating and enforcing the laws of personal conduct and morality.[17] Assemblies authorized constables and magistrates to take the law into their own hands. In Massachusetts and Connecticut, constables were empowered to search their local taverns from time to time to ensure that the laws of order were upheld. If they discovered violations, they could "punish according to the law." North Carolina law stipulated that when the crimes of bastardy, swearing, or drunkenness were detected, the justice of the peace could handle the matter without bringing it to court.[18]

The behavior of Samuel Sewall, one of the justices of the Massachusetts Superior Court of Judicature, and James Logan, secretary to the Pennsylvania proprietor, William Penn, and member of the Assembly, demonstrate this informal policing and adjudicating process. On December 4th, 1687, Sewall met with John Wing, the owner and proprietor of the Castle Tavern. Wing prepared a room in his house with seats, theater style, and proposed to rent the space to a magician so that he could perform. Sewall was a member of a three-man committee whose task it was to help Wing see the error of his ways. They explained to Wing that the magic show was unlawful, and by providing the accommodations for the act he too would be violating the law. Order was restored and a dangerous performance narrowly averted without any formal legal process.[19] Sewall was an unwilling participant in a second tavern confrontation some years later. This event too acts as a cautionary tale in the effort to understand the limits of the court records. In 1714, a neighbor called on Sewall to investigate the "Disorders at the Tavern at the South-end." The following Monday, Sewall provided Henry Howell, a town Constable, with the names of the offenders and directed Howell to collect the fines from as many as would pay. Only if they refused to remit the fine would they be called before the bench for their behavior.[20]

James Logan's engagement in the informal policing of taverns confirms the problematic nature of colonial court records as evidence. In 1750, "in pursuance of the agreement with the overseers, [Logan] visited Thomas Marshall—near Masters's Mill—& dealt closely with him for suffering & Encouraging Gamin in his house & other disorders." Logan was authorized to resolve Marshall's transgression of the law without an official indictment. As a result, a very sketchy record of the event remains, captured by a diarist.[21] Because the law enabled the constables to handle these problems informally, these occasions and countless others like them elude the official historical record.

Curbing drunkenness was deemed a worthy goal, and each colony devised its own methods to deal with problem drinkers. In Massachusetts, the names of repeat offenders were posted over the tavern door. Presumably, this prevented the drinker from entering and it warned the tavern keeper that these individuals should not be served. These handbills also functioned as a form of public humiliation. By broadcasting the names, everyone knew who had failed to resist temptation and exactly how they had violated the principles of the commonwealth. In addition, just as all townspeople were responsible for reporting on their neighbors if they transgressed God's law, they were expected to exclude the perpetrators from the social world of drink. "The fellowship of the tavern" was open to those who "could control themselves."[22] The Quakers in Pennsylvania exerted a similar pressure on members who could not control their drinking. In the period before twelve-step programs and rehabilitation centers, Friends warned alcoholics away from the tavern, reminding them that they risked disownment and in extreme cases banishment.

While keeping in mind that early Americans did not always resort to the formal instruments of the law in order to maintain order, the following analysis examines statute law and prosecution as they pertained to the general operations of the tavern and drinking. Included are only those cases that made it into the official legal record, thus the discussion must be considered only a guide to the magnitude and direction of the legal culture of drinking and the tavern.

Nonsectarian Colonies

Virginia and Maryland

The problem of drunkenness emerged frequently. Even before the settlement of Virginia, its 1606 charter admonished the settlers to "punish all manner of excesse, through drunkenness or otherwise."[23] In 1619, the first Virginia Assembly decreed that any person who was not a colonial official and was found abusing alcohol would be reprimanded privately by the local Anglican minister. However, upon the second occasion, the rebuke would be public. For the third time, the offender would be required to "lye in boltes 12 howers in the House of the Provost Marshall, & to paye his fee." Any continuation of this behavior would result in "suche severe punishment as the Govern & Counsell of Estate shall thinke fitt to be inflicted on him." The impetus for this law may have been the floating taverns that anchored in the James River every summer. These shipboard havens provided Virginians with easy access to alcohol, and planters eagerly traded their tobacco for "strong water."[24]

Although lawmakers focused considerable attention on drunkenness, their first attempt to control the sale of alcoholic beverages was apparently unrelated to problems of consumption. In March 1624, the assembly dictated "that no commander of any plantation do either himself or suffer others to spend powder unnecessarily in drinking or entertainments, &c."[25] The origins of this law are enmeshed in the general scarcity of gunpowder in Virginia and the acknowledgment by those in charge that Virginia would be rendered defenseless if residents habitually celebrated their inebriation by shooting their guns.

Tavern laws addressing drunkenness evolved. In Maryland in 1642, the law simply stipulated the fines for drunkenness; a dozen years later, they added liability to anyone "who shall suffer drunkenness in their house." By 1662, lawmakers had acknowledged that there was "a great necessity of allowing and Keeping Victualling houses." The need emerged because the distances between houses was so great and many people were required to travel to attend court. Without public houses, "divers persons are either exposed to great hazards of their health or much burdensome to particular adjacent Neighbors." Four years later, the General Assembly further aided tavern patrons by penning a law that tried to stop ordinary keepers from overcharging.[26]

While Chesapeake lawmakers were lavishing their attention upon the problem of drunkenness, they also were devoting an enormous effort to maintaining a sober Sabbath. It took almost one hundred years, however, for the Virginia General Assembly to link the two and make it illegal to drink in public on Sunday. Lawmakers passed a steady stream of ordinances insisting that Virginians attend to the Sabbath, refrain from working or traveling on Sunday, even admonishing sheriffs and other officials to desist from making arrests on the Lord's day. It was not until a 1705 law that tavern keepers were constrained from allowing tippling on the Lord's day or any day set apart "by public authority for religious worship."[27] Maryland lawmakers had outlawed drinking on the Sabbath in 1674.[28]

Virginia lawmakers also responded to their belief that everyone, including those in positions of public responsibility, was vulnerable to the temptations of drink. Virginia was the only colony to address explicitly the danger to the public trust when ministers, judges, and members of the assembly drank too much. Ministers were warned to avoid intemperance and instead devote themselves to the hearing or reading of holy scriptures or other "honest studies." In this way they could fulfill their responsibilities and serve as examples of how to "live well and christianlike." Although these leaders were ordered to maintain sobriety, no penalty was specified should they fall victim to temptation.[29]

The House of Burgesses, in acknowledging that too much drinking diminished its members' capacity to fulfill the responsibilities of their office, ordered that if public persons violated the rule of drunkenness, the governor would privately admonish them. For a second infraction they would receive public humiliation in church, and for a third they risked being committed to jail and losing their public position. In 1663, the House of Burgesses was prompted to amend the law in a direction that suggests momentary tolerance of drinking. For a brief period, public officials no longer risked public humiliation and the loss of their positions. Punishment shifted to fines, a more private sanction. A 1663 law imposed a fine of one hundred pounds of tobacco on any member "adjudged by the major part of the house to be disguised with drink." For the second and third offenses, the amount increased to three hundred and one thousand pounds of tobacco, respectively. This was apparently an unsatisfactory solution for in 1677, the punishment was stiffened and the threat of being removed from office renewed. With the third conviction, the justice would part with two thousand pounds of tobacco and lose his position.[30]

By 1668, Virginia lawmakers were grappling with what they identified as the social effects of tavern abuses and were confronting the problem with an analysis and language reminiscent of England. The preamble to the 1668 law lamented the "excessive number of ordinaries," the amount of mischief found within them, their promotion of idleness and debauchery, and their necessary seductiveness, which forced their patrons to "mispend their times in drunkennesse." This law also repeats a familiar refrain—shady tavern proprietors, who knew how devoted Virginians were to drinking, were charging their patrons exorbitant rates for alcoholic beverages. Taverns had the power to transform the most economically solvent customers into hopeless debtors.[31]

In 1691, Virginia's lawmakers expressed for the record their frustration that their attempts to control an entire range of "sins and offences of swearing, cursing, profaineing Gods holy name, Sabbath abusing, drunkenness, and fornication and adultery" had proven ineffective, but they worked only halfheartedly to control tavern behavior.[32] They waited until the middle of the eighteenth century to pass a law limiting the amount of time Virginians could spend inside a tavern drinking, and even then the wording was vague: a 1748 law ordered that no tavern keeper could allow anyone to drink "more than was necessary, on the lord's day, or any other day." From midcentury until the American Revolution, Virginia statutes remained silent on the issue of drunkenness and on the public house as the site where residents might drink to excess.[33] Then Virginia lawmakers began to expend considerable effort in creating a code to enforce sobriety and to control the tavern.

Despite the evidence of abundant drinking, prosecutions in Virginia were infrequent throughout the colonial period. For the decade 1622 to 1632, the Council and General Court heard only thirteen cases in which drinking played any role. In more than half, drunkenness was of secondary concern. Alcohol was involved in two of the more celebrated cases that came before the general court, an accusation of "misconduct" against a woman and a conviction for manslaughter. Committing a crime while drunk did not provide mitigating circumstances, nor was it included in the indictment. Rather, it played more of a role in the drama of the narrative than in the criminal proceedings.[34]

In the first case, which occurred in 1627, Captain William Eppes was accused of "misconduct" with Mrs. Alice Boise, a guest in the tavern. Eppes arrived at the public house of James Slight and Bridges Freeman in Martin's Brandon plantation.[35] He, with half a dozen "divers others," devoted four or five hours to consuming between two and three gallons of wine. One deponent testified that after the drinking ended, Captain Eppes staggered to his feet, asked where he might sleep, "pulled off his cloathes & went into bed." According to the same deposition, Alice Boise asked Captain John Huddleston if he would share the bed with Captain Eppes. He refused to, so "she lay downe upon the bed besides Capt Eppes with her cloathes on." One witness testified that Eppes lay beneath the sheets while Alice Boise lay on top of the covers. The alleged crime of misconduct was committed soon after. Various witnesses who shared the room testified that they "heard a great busselling and juggling of the bed" soon after Alice Boise joined the captain. The activities resumed in the middle of the night and again, two hours before daybreak. The court ruled, "concerning the report of some lewd behavior betweene Capt William Eppes & Mrs. Alice Boise," that the case did not prove that they had "offended the Law." "Being in drink," confirmed by all of the deponents, was either unconvincing or, more likely, inconsequential in terms of the justices' sensibilities.[36]

The second dispute took place in 1628 at the public house of William Parker at Merry Point. Alcohol played a role in the unfolding of the drama but, as in the previous example, not in the final determination. The defendant, Thomas Godby and a small group of other men, settled into after dinner drinking, sharing a "bottle of burnt clarett wine conteyning five pints or thereabouts." Godby consumed about four cups. The excitement began when a small boat ran aground on the shoals against the house and one of the men on board, William Bently, stomped into the house. He was extremely angry because no one in the tavern had been willing to leave their drinking long enough to respond to the boatmen's cries for help. A quarrel ensued, caused by a combination of Godby's inebriation and Bently's anger. The fracas ended when Bently kicked Godby hard while he lay on the floor. Godby rose to his feet, stumbled and fell. Patrons assisted him home but by the next morning, he was dead. A jury found Bently guilty of manslaughter.[37]

These cases underscore the seemingly benign role played by alcohol in the community's legal consciousness. In the first instance the charges may have been dismissed in part because everyone was drunk and could not be held responsible for their actions. In the second case, Godby's state of inebriation had little effect on the proceedings. Bently does not appear to have used Godby's drunkenness as an excuse for his own behavior. Did Godby spew drunken taunts or insults about Bently's skill as a boatman? It is as if Godby's state was so common it was up to that rare sober individual to take proper precautions.

In the remaining eleven cases recorded in the minutes of the Council and General Court, over indulging in drink is most commonly combined with some sort of public spectacle. The one exception was Thomas Wilson who "abused him selfe in drincke" and as a result beat his wife. In addition to his twenty-shilling fine, Wilson was placed in the stocks and had to give bond for his future good behavior. John Radish was fined the same amount and sentenced to "lye neck and heels" in the stocks for plying Robert Sitts with drink and for entertaining the servants of Sir George Yardley and making them drunk. Sitts was fined forty shillings for being so drunk that he could not make it home from the tavern without assistance. Although Sitts paid a larger fine, his behavior concerned the court less than the actions of Wilson and Radish. When judges levied fines, the transactions were kept private between the offender and the authorities. Sitts escaped the public humiliation associated with time in the stocks. In contrast, the court's punishment of Wilson and Radish was designed to humiliate these men publicly and to convey the message, especially to those who took the time out to see them strapped in to the stocks, that their behaviors were intolerable. When Wilson beat his wife, he risked hurting or killing a scarce resource. Very few white women emigrated to Virginia in the first half-century of its existence, and as a result they were in great demand, valued as household laborers, sexual partners, and bearers of children in a colony struggling to maintain a stable population. By supplying servants with alcohol, Radish had threatened their master's livelihood. Success in the first fifty years of Virginia depended to a great extent upon controlling the labor of indentured servants. Drunk servants would not do the work to grow the tobacco that would make their master, Yardley, wealthy; and in their inebriated state, servants might be prone to rebelliousness.[38]

The court did acknowledge that illicit sex was a possible outcome of drunkenness. In 1624, William Couse, a galley slave, testified that he had been forced to lie with a man. The episode took place on a ship anchored in the James River. The master of the ship, Richard Williams, had been drinking most of the day when he asked Couse to put clean sheets on his bed. Couse did so. However, Williams wanted more. He desired that Couse come into the bed with him; Couse testified that when he refused, Williams forced him into the bed where he, "there lay upon him, and kissed him and hugged him, saying that he would love him if he would now and then come and lay with him and so by force he turned him upon his bely and so did put him to pain in the fundament and did wet him and after did call for a napkin which Couse did bring unto him." Couse claimed that Williams would often put his hands in Couse's "codpiece and played and kissed him." Because Couse resisted, he was forced to cook for the entire ship and eat his meals alone. My primary concern here is not an exploration into early American sexuality, but evidence suggests that these sexual behaviors were common but not socially or legally acceptable.[39]

County courts in Virginia also spent very little of their time with accusations of tavern or drinking violations, which reinforces the notion that Virginians were unperturbed by drunkenness. From 1632 to 1645, the Accomack-Northampton County court prosecuted no one for violating drink or tavern law. Similarly, in Northampton County, only twenty-six incidences of drunkenness were reported in the thirty years from 1635 to 1665; twenty-one ended in conviction.[40] A few years later, the court convicted tavern owner John Cole of "selling drinke on the feast day of the Nativity of our Lord," and fined him twenty shillings, ordered him to do community service, including making a new pair of stocks. Almost 20 years later, the court found another tavern keeper guilty of selling liquor on a Sunday. Both of these cases reveal that court officials were undisturbed by acts of drunkenness. Rather than prosecute those who purchased liquor on the

Sabbath or drank on Christmas Day, officials targeted the tavern keepers and held them responsible.[41]

The Northumberland County Court also heard a negligible number of cases related to the abuses of alcohol during this midcentury period. In one case, a defendant's drunken state may have worked in his favor. David Spiller stood accused of defamation as a result of being in drink.[42] The court charged Spiller for saying that "Jane the wife of William Allen was the said Robert Lambson his whore." Spiller professed his sorrow and apologies "for any words that he hath in his drincke or other wyse at any time spoken tending to the defamation of Jane Allen." The charges were dismissed. It was of no consequence to the court that Spiller confessed to being drunk, except that the drunkenness might have caused his words. This outcome is reminiscent of the attitude among Indians, who absolved wrongdoers of responsibility for acts committed while inebriated.[43]

The reverse however, was also possible. Being drunk did not exonerate John Littell; rather, when it was determined that he had committed the crime under the influence of strong drink, the magistrates increased his punishment. In September 1634, Littell was ordered to lie in the stocks, confined at neck and heel, for three hours. He was convicted of "abusinge his house in going to bed to the mayd of the syd Taylors, and the next day the syd Litell being at worke in the ground with a Company of men boasted that the Cooke was up, and the steale down and ready to give fyre." When he admitted that he had been drunk at the time, the court slapped an additional five shillings onto his punishment.[44]

The records from the Charles City County Court confirm what historians have concluded about Chesapeake legal concerns: Virginia's magistrates were most involved with cases of debt, labor, and protecting their own reputations. Controlling taverns or drinking behavior barely entered their consciousness except as it affected these concerns. Even then, drunkenness might be viewed lightly. In 1659, two separate plaintiffs brought suits against Capt. Edward Matthews, apparently for debts resulting from horse racing. The court postponed hearing both cases, because Matthews failed to appear. When he finally arrived at court he was drunk. The bench treated lightly this disregard for its authority and dignity. The judges received his "humble petition," and, since he had confessed his error in appearing before them having had too much to drink, they released him from having to post bond.[45] On the rare instances when drunkenness became a legal matter, the infraction was usually combined with some other public nuisance behavior. Virginians, unlike their Puritan compatriots, spent little time or effort on the private morality of their neighbors. Even if a violation of tavern law infringed on personal morality, it seems to have escaped litigation.[46]

Virginia's neighbor to the north, Maryland, shared this disinterest in prosecuting drinking or tavern related crimes. In Charles, Kent, and Talbot counties, from 1658 to 1676, courts ruled on a total of thirteen cases of drunkenness, and three cases of selling without a license or at the incorrect rate were heard by the court. An equal number of cases were filed by tavern keepers against individuals who had failed to pay their bills; just as in other forms of business in the Chesapeake, debt relations dominated. In 1670, William Nevill appeared before the Charles County Court to defend himself against accusations by tavern keeper Edmond Lensey. Lensey produced an account and claimed that Nevill had received "Divers parcells & quantities of Drink and other ordinary accommodations" in the amount of 498 pounds of tobacco. The jury was convinced and ruled for the plaintiff. Maryland, too, follows the pattern—prosecution was necessary over issues of property not morality.[47]

The Carolinas

Authorities in the southern colonies, like their counterparts in the Chesapeake, created drinking and tavern laws but paid scant attention to anyone transgressing them. It is, however, difficult to determine precisely when taverns were first regulated in South Carolina. There is no written record of a law until 1683, more than a dozen years after the founding of the colony. Then the General Assembly extended, for twenty-three months, the expired "Act to prevent unlicensed Taverns and Punch-Houses, and for ascertaining the Rates and Prices of Wine and other Liquors."[48]

Just as in Virginia, the tavern in South Carolina escaped blame as a site for tempting people away from worship. When, in the 1690s, lawmakers in South Carolina announced their intention to maintain a sober Sabbath, they included no words about the responsibilities of tavern keepers. A 1691 law reminded everyone of their duty to respect and attend divine service and promised to impose a five-shilling fine on anyone found drunk on the Lord's day. A year later, they stiffened the law and moved from the more private penalty of the fine to the more public punishment of jail. Anyone caught drinking during the time of the divine service would be sentenced to twenty-four hours in the clink. When South Carolina leaders revealed an increasing concern with drunkenness in general, they also placed some of the responsibility for maintaining a sober Sabbath on the colony's public house keepers. In the 1712 "Act for the better Observation of the Lord's-Day, commonly called Sunday," entertainment inside a tavern on Sundays was reserved for strangers and lodgers. Both the keeper and the drinker would be fined five shillings for violating this act. In case South Carolinians remained unconvinced of the serious intent of this law, lawmakers established a mechanism to enforce it. The constables and church wardens of Charleston were required, once in the forenoon and again in the afternoon, to walk through the town in search of violators. No one drinking on Sunday would escape; the constables and wardens were empowered to break down any door if they suspected that it sheltered an idle tippler.[49]

North Carolina lawmakers protected the Sabbath from overindulgence in drink in the first laws published in the colony, in 1715. Ordinary keepers were threatened with a fine if they sold "any wine, beer, Punch or other Liquors on the Lord's Day," except for the "necessary occasions, for Lodgers or Sojourners." Any person found drunk on Sunday also risked a fine. Being discovered drunk on any of the other six days of the week would cost the offender half the fine set for Sunday transgressors.[50] This law was supplanted in 1741 by a far softer version cautioning all retailers to ensure that no one should "tipple" on the Lord's day or "drink more than necessary." In 1758, constraints were tightened somewhat. In a refrain heard in almost all of the colonies, the lawmakers conceded that the laws then guiding tavern conduct were ineffectual and specified that it was illegal to sell "immoderate quantities of strong Liquors whereby such a person may be intoxicated on the Lord's Day."[51]

Both North and South Carolina had laws on the books to prevent drunkenness and protect the Sabbath from "unnecessry" drinking, and, in response to continued abuse of drink, constables and wardens were empowered to ferret out anyone violating these laws. However, not a single court case involving drunkenness has been uncovered for seventeenth-century North or South Carolina. While in part this reflects the spotty nature of the records, it also indicates the rarity of prosecutions having to so with drinking- or tavern-related crimes.

New Netherland and New York

The Dutch bequeathed an indelible cultural mark on the region that became New York, although it did not take long for the laws to resemble those of the other North American colonies. Director General and Council noted that quarreling and fighting inevitably occurred when people were drunk and that these events exploded without regard to the Sabbath. It was, they warned, a disgrace and violated their duty to keep "Gods holy laws," and they ordered that no one "tap or draw any wine, beer or strong waters . . . before 2 of the clock in case there is no preaching." If a sermon was preached, drinking could not begin before 4 o'clock. The lawmakers made exceptions for thirsty travelers and for those who did not brew their own beer or cider—"daily customers, fetching the drinks to their own homes."[52]

The Dutch leaders were frustrated by the continued disregard of the Sabbath, and a year later, in 1648, they decreed that a sermon should be preached in the afternoon as well as the forenoon and that all work and tapping must cease.[53] Apparently, keeping the Sabbath sober was a losing battle, though, for the laws were continually amended and the penalties increased from fines to jail time.[54] Although New Netherland renewed and tightened the laws against drinking on the Sabbath, once the Duke of York's troops sailed into the Manhattan harbor in 1664 and claimed New York for England, concern over tippling and the Sabbath appeared to vanish.[55]

Either the city of New York was extraordinarily effective in controlling proper conduct on the Sabbath or, more likely, it was not an issue that commanded much attention. During the last quarter of the seventeenth century, New York lawmakers twice confronted the connection between the tavern, drinking, and the Sabbath. And rather than increase the punishment, they relaxed it. In 1676, New York City's Common Council ordered that no one should "profane the sabbath" either by unlawful "Playing at Cards Dice Tables or any other Unlawful games whatsoever Either in Sermon Time or without." Any sellers of wine, brandy, rum, or beer "who permit any Person upon the Sabbath day to Drink or Game In their houses Gardens or Yards" would be fined for the first and second offenses and for the third offense the tavern keeper would be fined and risked losing his or her license. The City Council had no intention of interfering with the comforts and pleasures of "any Strangers or Travellers Lodging in Inns or Ordinaries" and exempted them from any penalties if they indulged in beer or wine, as long as these beverages were necessary for their refreshment.[56] The huge difference between the fines for proprietors versus indulgers suggests that councilors placed responsibility for these behaviors firmly in the hands of tavern keepers. The nominal ten-guilder fine for violating the drinking laws did not increase with each successive conviction and was surely not intended as a deterrent.

In 1684, the law was again softened considerably. The earliest law had kept the tavern doors closed to the local residents all of Sunday. However, now no tavern keeper was to "suffer their Doors to be kept Open or doe Entertain or Receive, any Company, into their houses and to Them sell Any kind of Wine or other Liquors" during the time of the service or preaching. Travelers and strangers were exempted once more. To enforce this order more effectively and to prevent any violators, the constables were empowered to take turns walking through the streets of the city and to enter "all or Any Public houses Tapphouses or Ordinaries." The fine for each offense was reduced to ten shillings. No change occurred in the fine when the law was repeated for a final time in 1731.[57]

New Netherland boasted a full arsenal of tavern laws, and punishable infractions were varied. However, New Netherlanders' attention to drinking and taverns did not come close to that of their sectarian neighbors. Of the fifty cases tried before the Council through the entire Dutch period, eighteen (36%) involved drunkenness. This charge was handled inconsistently. Intoxication might be the culprit in further wrongdoing or it might mitigate the circumstances. In 1640, when Captain de Vries brought a case of slander against John Wilcock, the defendant pleaded that he was drunk at the time and had no idea what he had said. He begged that the captain forgive him and confessed that he had spoken falsely. Wilcock paid a small fifty-guilder fine and received no other penalty. Maryn Adriaensen sued Hendrick Pietersen because Pietersen had refused to honor his agreement to purchase Adriaensen's house and plantation. Pietersen pleaded that he was drunk at the time that they negotiated the terms. A witness testified that they were both drunk. The Council ruled that the defendant was obliged to rent the place for six years; being drunk did not entirely relieve Pietersen of his contractual obligation. In another case, Jan Hobbesen was accused of stealing a sheet from the city tavern. He testified that he remembered nothing of the event because he had been intoxicated at the time. Unconvinced by his denial, the court ordered Hobbesen "put to the torture, after which he confessed his guilt." They sentenced him to be whipped with rods and to leave New Netherland immediately "on pain, if found again in the country to be put in chains and set to work with the companys negroes."[58]

Using drunkenness as a defense therefore seems to have yielded mixed results. Although Wilcock was found guilty of committing slander, his level of inebriation softened the punishment. Pietersen received no such relief even though both parties admitted to being drunk. Lying to the court was intolerable in New Netherland, and no amount of intoxication would mitigate Hobbeson's liability. The court descended mightily upon him, banishing him from the colony.

The most commonly prosecuted violation of the law in New Netherland, accounting for 40 percent of all of the cases, involved selling alcoholic beverages to Indians. Colonial leaders revealed their concern by continually amending the laws prohibiting this practice, and the court emphasized its seriousness by imposing harsh sentences upon those found guilty of the transgression. When Jan Juriaens Becker was convicted of selling liquor to Indians, he was fined five hundred guilders, removed as clerk of the church, ordered to move away from the South River, and required to pay court costs. Becker petitioned for a pardon, but the mercy of the court was limited to remitting the fine. Michiel Tadens received the same sentence for selling alcohol to Indians, but when he petitioned for reconsideration, the court upheld the fine, imprisoned him until he paid, and then banished him.[59] Magistrates revealed their collective fears about the dangers of Indians' having access to strong drink and their awareness that violations of the law were widespread, by prosecuting infractions with regularity and imposing harsh penalties. Dutch traders engaged in a lucrative trade with Indians, especially with the Iroquois, and the staples of that exchange were alcohol and guns. The combination, according to the colony's leaders, bred potentially deadly violence for both sides.[60]

The prosecution record for New Amsterdam includes offenses found elsewhere in the Dutch colony as well as those peculiar to a seaport. From 1654 to 1664, the New Amsterdam court heard a total of sixty-one cases related to drinking and tavern behavior. The most common were the fifteen cases that had to do with serving liquor during the Sunday service combined with various types of disorderly behavior like gaming or dancing. The next most frequent type of infraction (twelve cases) involved the drinking behaviors of the town's soldiers and sailors. The court summoned Joris Dopzen to answer to complaints that he kept a disorderly house serving liquor to sailors. Captain de Coninck appeared before the court and explained that when tavern keepers entertained his crew, the sailors would "run around here in this city drinking considerably and thus . . . do no work." Finally, city leaders confronted those who sold drink without a license. For New Amsterdam, these cases constituted 18 percent of the tavern related prosecutions (eleven).[61]

The English maintained a tradition of an all-encompassing legal code when they took over the region from the Dutch. New York had laws on its books to cover the entire spectrum of infractions from preventing tippling on the Sabbath, to requiring tavern keepers to be licensed, to outlawing exchanges of goods from servants and slaves. However, it must have been the mere existence of these laws that provided magistrates with solace, because the laws served no other purpose. Only two cases appeared in the Mayor's Court in 1674–75, and both looked like Elizabeth Poole's conviction for selling "drinke and tappes without a Lycence." In 1680, the mayor and aldermen issued a proclamation—a portent of things to come. "Indian and Neger Slaves," it declared, were being served "Wine, Rumm, and other Strong Liquors." Since, according to these leaders, slaves obtained the money to pay for these drinks by stealing, tavern keepers were said to encourage this illegal behavior when they sold them alcohol. Authorities also claimed that the practice of serving slaves inflicted great harm on their owners, because it made slaves less obedient. While prosecutors in seventeenth-century New York ignored the behavior of free individuals who drank too much or refused to heed the restrictions on Sabbath drinking, they paid increasing attention to what they perceived to be a dangerous practice, providing slaves with alcohol. They saw a far greater responsibility in protecting owners' rights to their human property than in policing the behavior of free residents.[62]

Sectarian Colonies

New England

In New England, just as in the Chesapeake and the South, drunkenness constituted one of many possible abuses of the moral code. Three years after the founding of Massachusetts Bay Colony, magistrates formulated the first policies to control taverns and drinking. They were rather permissive with the sellers, decreeing that any persons who wished to sell alcoholic beverages need only ask permission of the governor or deputy governor. Taking a broad view in their strategy to enforce a sober public, the colony's leaders fashioned a law that encouraged residents to consume alcohol exclusively at mealtime.[63] In 1634, lawmakers set the price tavern keepers could charge for meals and a penalty on beer consumed "out of meal time." They were not seeking to end drinking, but they did hope to restrain excessive consumption and to discourage the intemperate drinker, while indicating their understanding that alcoholic beverages constituted an essential dietary supplement. These restrictions apparently failed to have the desired effect, because three years later a new law forbade tavern keepers from selling sack or hard liquor at all. In that same year, legislators worked to fill in all of the loopholes in existing law, and a new law deemed it unlawful for keepers of inns or common victualing houses to sell or have in their houses any wine, beer, or "strong waters" unless they intended to sell it by the quart for customers to take home or they were supplying the needs of travelers.

In 1639, Massachusetts Bay lawmakers reversed their attempts to suppress public drinking, by repealing legal prohibitions of the sale of alcoholic beverages to other than travelers. They also gave up on their efforts to limit residents' access to taverns and instead required that every town have a public house. Town officials were to select an appropriate man to operate the town's ordinary, and the name of the potential proprietor was to be submitted to the General Court. Once approved, the tavern keeper would be allowed to sell wine, spirits, and beer, which he was encouraged to brew himself. Instead of prohibition, tavern keepers were required only ensure moderation in drinking by their patrons. In 1645, magistrates presented their legal formula for enforcing their demands— no "tipling above the space of halfe an hour," no drinking more than half a pint of wine, and doors were to close at nine in the evening. Finally, and ironically in light of their failed movement to quash public drinking, the court lamented the paucity of houses of entertainment; and they reiterated that it was legal for anyone to offer lodging, food, and drink at reasonable rates when the circumstances dictated, even though they could not consider themselves to be ordinary keepers.[64]

Bay Colony leaders did not give up completely their efforts to prevent overindulgence in alcohol, but they adopted a new method, consistent with their approach to social control. They believed that everyone was answerable for the behavior of everyone else. Rather than preventing residents from drinking inside public houses, much of the onus for maintaining good behavior landed on the keeper. If the publican could not prevent illegal activities from taking place inside the tavern, he or she was at the least responsible for reporting infractions. Thus, by the 1680s, when sellers of alcoholic beverages requested the annual license renewal, they needed a unanimous decision of the town selectmen, who approved or disapproved on the basis of the proprietor's record of good conduct by his customers. There was also an assumption that if a citizen of Massachusetts Bay entertained, all eyes would be watching, to ensure that the guests did not step outside the boundaries of decent behavior. Finally, the laws created a further policing mechanism by empowering the constables "from time to time" to enter and "search the taverns, for any disorder" and to ferret out any tavern keeper who might have been selling wine illegally.[65]

Massachusetts lawmakers took very seriously the task of keeping the Sabbath free of drink. In response to the threat of "abuses and misdemeanors committed by divers persons on the Lordsday," in 1658 it became unlawful to frequent the tavern on Sunday. Perhaps for added insurance, to prevent a party on the preceding day from lasting too long or the lingering headache from interfering with church attendance, taverns became off limits on Saturday nights "after the sun is set" as well. A five-shilling penalty was assessed for all who violated this law.[66] When the law was amended at the end of 1692, lawmakers reiterated that the tavern was to be avoided from sundown Saturday night through Sunday, except, of course, for strangers and lodgers. Identifying a potential loophole, lawmakers repeated the clause preventing drinking in houses and added "yards, orchards, or fields" to the places that were off limits for drinking. Drinkers could not legally pick up their drinks, move outside, and continue imbibing.[67]

Plymouth Colony's treatment of tavern and drinking law more closely resembled that of the nonsectarian colonies than of its Puritan neighbors. Taverns and the retailing of strong drink are first addressed in the Plymouth laws of 1636, sixteen years after the colony was founded. Innkeepers and owners of victualing houses were allowed to sell wine, beer, or other strong drinks indoors or out-of-doors, prices were established, and no one was to be allowed to drink to excess. Proprietors of public houses were also cautioned against allowing children or servants access to strong drink, and young men and "other labourers" were forbidden to eat or drink in inns or alehouses in the towns in which they lived. Plymouth authorities insisted that the godly community be interior as well as exterior. No mention was made, however, about how an individual could gain the right to retail strong drink. Later that year, a retailer was defined as someone who drew and sold "a lesser quantity or Caske of wine then 10 gallons"; anyone selling wine, beer, or strong water was required to be licensed.[68]

Over the course of the next few decades, Plymouth magistrates focused their attention on preventing drunkenness, tightening licensing controls, and collecting the excise. With regularity, they sounded warnings against drunkenness and defined it precisely, listing specific indicative behaviors, like slurred speech, loss of motor control, or vomiting. Lawmakers settled on what they thought was a solution: in order to prevent overindulgence, the law limited townsmen's visits to the ordinary to a single hour. This law reminded residents that the tavern was not designated primarily as a local institution; it was intended for the entertainment of strangers and travelers. Residents could evade the law and eat and drink in their local inn only "for such Intents and purposes as to releive the weake and sicke."[69]

Lawmakers in Plymouth Colony can be contrasted with their sectarian neighbors again in their apparent lack of concern with the relationship of the tavern to the Sabbath. In 1662, more than four decades after the colony was founded and almost thirty years after they passed the first law regulating behavior in public houses, they responded to complaints received by the court. Ordinary keepers were allowing people to stay in their houses on the Lord's day. It was not just that taverns were open on Sundays and the meetings inside were taking place during the "times betwixt the exercises." They were concerned about who was drinking, "especially young p[er]sons and such as stand not in need thereof." To protect the young and the colony's servants from having access to drink, tavern keepers could not draw any wine or liquor on the Sabbath "except in case of necessitie for the releife of those that are sicke or faint or the like for theire refreshing." Tavern keepers were to be penalized for violating the law; no penalty, however, was stipulated for those caught drinking on the Lord's day. This law was periodically repeated, virtually unchanged, until 1674, when an amended version required that all ordinary keepers "cleare their houses of all Towne dwellers and strangers that are there (on a drinking accompt) except such as lodge in the house" during daylight hours on Sunday. The problems with defaming the Sabbath must have been minimal in Plymouth; the 1674 law reduced the fine by half from the original law, written a dozen years earlier.[70]

In 1685, when the colony established a more complex and comprehensive legal system and revised the laws, an entire subsection of the new code was devoted to the Sabbath. It delimited a broad range of unacceptable behavior: "unnecessary servile work," "unnecessary traviling by Land or passing by Water," "bearing Burthens," "carrying of Packs," "Buying or Selling," "Sports" and "Recreations." The law reiterated that the tavern was off limits for residents on Sunday; in addition, ordinaries were to be closed on Saturday evening "after the Sun is Set." "Strangers or Sojourners" remained exempt. Although the fine for violating the Sabbath laws stayed at five shillings, the punishment included time in the stocks, not to exceed two hours. The increased attention to the tavern and the Sabbath discloses the broader concerns of Plymouth leaders in the late seventeenth century. They redesigned the structure of an increasingly complex society to shore up the challenge to the Puritan hegemony within the colony and to define clearly the behavior expected from those residing in a Puritan community.[71]

Rhode Island lawmakers were also delayed somewhat in addressing the tavern and drinking, but this was more likely due to the confusion surrounding The Rhode Island Assembly's jurisdiction, rather than a lack of concern for the public house. The assembly included matters relating to taverns and drinking in the laws of 1647, the first comprehensive statutes passed after the colony received its charter. Like lawmakers in the other sectarian colonies, the assembly established licensing procedures, required proprietors to keep good order, and made it illegal for anyone to become drunk. The Rhode Island leaders added a unique twist, however. In order to divert colonists from these idle temptations and to prevent the resulting poverty, legislators recommended that residents substitute archery, because it was "both man-like and profitable." Furthermore, "every person from the age of seventeen yeares, to the age of seventy" was to own a bow and four arrows and practice shooting. If, as the assemblymen feared, the colony ran out of powder and shot, they could "outshoot these natives in their owne bow." This law must have been devised to address Rhode Island's precarious position. Both local Indians and neighboring colonies claimed rights to their lands. Magistrates sought ways to protect the colony and at the same time ensure that its defense was safely in the hands of sober bowmen.[72] When the Rhode Island Assembly amended the law in 1654, they were following a path similar to that of Plymouth and Massachusetts: control over the tavern and drinkers was the responsibility of the tavern keeper.[73]

In the late seventeenth century, the Massachusetts Bay Colony Assembly embarked on a renewed campaign. In an attempt to reduce the number of licensed public houses in the colony, for example, the 1681 law revitalized the effort to legislate temperance. Attempts to prevent drinking at the tavern did not succeed. In 1645 and 1672, legislators passed laws prohibiting the exchange of drink for labor, however, workers continued to expect the provision of drink as part of their employment. Lawmakers also failed to put an end to drinking toasts to each other's health; the law lasted a mere six years before it was repealed. More general laws to prevent excessive drinking were equally ineffective. The preambles to the 1651 and 1682 code explain why—"persons addicted to that vice find out ways to deceive the laws." Edward Ward, an Englishman visiting Boston in 1682, concurred; the laws existed but they were not enforced. "All their Laws look like Scarecrows[;] the worst of the drunkards may find Pot companions enough, for all their pretenses to Sobriety."[74]

The persistent reiteration of the law offers further evidence that the efforts to legislate sobriety failed to solve the perceived problems of drunkenness. From 1693 to 1698, a series of laws either duplicated a previous statute or amended it slightly. Tavern keepers could not permit drunkenness in their houses, licenses were required of all keepers, and patrons could not tarry for more than one hour. A 1704 law targeted Boston, Charlestown, and Salem, claiming that there were too many taverns in these port towns and cautioning that it would breed the over indulgences of seamen and other strangers. In that same year, the assembly warned the colony's selectmen and justices not to approve widows as license holders. A concerted effort by Bay Colony clerical leaders succeeded in convincing lawmakers to further confront the growing number of taverns. As a result, in 1710, the assembly ordered each country town to limit the sale of liquor to one inn holder and one retailer. Exceptions could be made if the town selectmen decreed that more taverns were required to serve the region's travelers.[75]

By the mid 1680s, Plymouth Colony leaders were wrestling with the same set of issues as their neighbors to the north. They expressed their collective concerns about the increasing problems with alcohol abuse and placed the burden for controlling good behavior on the tavern keepers. In the 1685 judicial and legal reorganization, the licensing law was continued and a portion of the law was devoted to an outline of innkeepers' responsibilities. The role of the tavern as a site for visitors rather than locals was reaffirmed. "Town-dwellers" were permitted during "extraordinary" occasions or if the individual was employed in some public capacity.[76] In addition, a series of severe punishments was established for anyone discovered drunk. The law reiterated the physical description of drunkenness but also introduced a new category—the common drunkard—anyone convicted at least four times for the same offense. For these, the government ordered public humiliation; their names were to be posted for all to see. Ordinary keepers were prohibited from serving them.[77]

Plymouth courts prosecuted tavern and drink abuses with slightly more energy than did their counterparts in the nonsectarian colonies, and the justices handled a much wider variety of infractions. From 1633 to 1686, this one small New England area prosecuted 158 people for tavern and drinking related offences, approximately 8.6 cases a year. The entire colony of Virginia averaged just a bit over one case annually.[78] Too much drinking accounted for slightly less than one-half of the cases (75 of 158). Plymouth courts also punished those who sold or distilled liquor without a license, traded liquor to Indians, were responsible for getting Indians drunk, suffered drinking on the Sabbath, or were found in the tavern on Sunday. They prosecuted violators who misspent their time in the tavern, entertained other men's servants, and played at games. They chastised those who appeared in court "distempered in drink."

John Barnes' inability to handle his liquor and his regular visits to the court reveal how the Plymouth magistrates attempted to handle a "problem drinker." Barnes made his first court appearance in 1638 to answer a complaint for "inordinate drinking." However, the evidence was insufficient to charge him. Five years later Barnes "proved to be drunken," both in the Bay and at Scituate; he was fined. In his next appearance before the court, in 1648, Barnes was given permission to brew and sell beer until the court "shall see reason to the contrary." Two years later and again in 1651, he was fined for being drunk. One year later he was back. This time he was presented not only for drunkenness but for appearing in court intoxicated. Barnes's precise penalty for his rude behavior is unclear: he was "sentenced according to order of court and to fund sureties for his good behavior." By 1657, the court expressed its frustration with Barnes's behavior and slapped him with a large fine, five pounds, for "his frequent abusing himselfe in drunkenness, after former punishment and admonition." And, any tavern keeper who entertained him "in a way of drinking," would risk a twenty-shilling fine. Anyone found drinking with him would owe the court two shillings, six pence. The fine for serving Barnes increased to fifty shillings in 1661. Barnes disappears from the records after 1665, but not before he was again presented for "being lately detected of being twice drunk," for which he was fined twenty shillings. In 1672 he was fatally gored by a bull on his own farm. The Plymouth officials do not mention whether this was the result of negligence or the final intoxicated moment in his long drinking career.[79]

The case of Thomas Lucas of Plymouth provides another example of how the courts struggled with the behavior of a problem drinker. Lucas's saga takes place over twenty-one years. He appeared before the court in 1658 "for being taken in drinke" and for retailing strong drink without a license and once in 1659, for being drunk. A year later he was back on four separate occasions, to answer for drunkenness, refusing to take an oath of allegiance to the king, and making threatening speeches against James Cole Senior and Junior. In 1661 he made five court appearances. He was found guilty of being drunk a third time; of being in court drunk; of being in the home of his neighbor Ann Savory without her husband's being present, on a Sunday during the time of the divine service; and probably of drunkenness again, since he lost half of his twenty-pound bond. In 1663 when he was found drunk, the court postponed his sentence and he was warned that he would be whipped should he be "taken drunke the next time." The court kept its promise. In his first of three appearances in 1664, Lucas was whipped for being "fownd drunke againe." He was in court seven times during the next decade, for crimes of drunkenness, swearing, abusing his wife and children, breaking the peace, and "reviling some deceased majestrates." The records then contain no mention of Lucas until 1678, when a jury was called upon to rule on the cause of his death. They found that Lucas had died as a direct consequence of his drinking. "Hee being very ancient & decriped in his limbes, and it being very cold, and haveing drunk some drinke, gott a violent fall into a ditch, in a very dangerous place and could not recover himselfe."[80] In the case of problem drinkers, magistrates appear to have granted a long period of forbearance before cracking down. This would reflect the "local knowledge" of judges, who might remember previous infractions before handing down an indictment.

Unlike in the nonsectarian colonies, drunkenness and violent behavior were not closely related in Plymouth nor were Plymouth residents prone to sexual conflict when inebriated. While half of the prosecutions in Virginia included violent behavior, from quarreling to manslaughter, only two such cases were recorded among the 158 Plymouth indictments. The penalties imposed in these cases— an attempted incest and a white man's sexual advances toward an Indian woman—suggest that the magistrates considered them to be lesser sins than hurling verbal abuse at the magistrates in court. In 1639, James Till was found guilty of getting John Bryan drunk and then slandering his "dame," claiming that he would take her home and "lye with her." Till was sentenced to be whipped. Thomas Atkins, during one drunken night in October of 1660, attempted incest with his daughter Mary. He confessed and was sentenced to a whipping, cleared, and "att liberty to return to his own house." The court imposed no fines nor did they formally caution Atkins to refrain from this behavior in the future. In 1669, the judges rebuked Christopher Blake for his "unseemly carriages in his drunkenness with an Indian woman." They assessed a five-shilling fine and ordered that he spend two hours in the stocks during the next training day at Yarmouth. (The judges maximized the visibility of Blake's punishment by forcing him to serve his time in the stocks while the local militia engaged in its training exercises, an event often witnessed by admiring local townspeople.) If he were to attempt an escape before his punishment could be executed, any constable could whip him publicly.[81]

That slander should be punished more harshly than incest or lying with an Indian woman was consistent with the priorities established in secular colonies. Maintaining a good name was critical. On the practical side, the loss of one's reputation could affect one's livelihood. It was bad for business if a tradesman was accused of doing shoddy work or a shopkeeper was denounced for using inaccurate scales. If a man's wife was slandered, he too might suffer a diminution in his status within the community. One's well-being was dependent upon a positive reputation among one's neighbors and within the community; slander and libel cases consumed a large proportion of the colonial courts' calendars. They were regarded as a far greater threat to the order of society than acts committed against women while drunk.[82]

Suffolk County, Massachusetts, magistrates, like their counterparts in Plymouth, struggled to find ways to control individuals whose drinking bordered on the pathological. William Perkins and Robert Coles presented particularly thorny problems. It appears that, after the court had exhausted more common penalties, like fines, it ordered forms of public humiliation for both men. In 1636, for "drunkenes & other misdemeanors," Perkins was to stand in public view for one hour with a white sheet of paper on his breast "haveing a greate D made upon it."[83] Coles offered the Bay courts one of their greatest challenges. Ordinary penalties for drunkenness did not deter him from drinking. In 1634, Coles was convicted of drunkenness and "intiseing John Shotwell wife to incontinency, & other misdimeanor" and was forced to wear on his back a sign, a sheet of white paper bearing the word *drunkard* in large letters. A few months later, he was found guilty of being drunk in Roxbury. For this, he was sentenced to be disenfranchised and to "weare aboute his necke, & soe to hange upon his outward garment, a D, made of redd claoth, & sett upon white; to contynue this for a yeare, & not to leave it off att any tyme when hee comes amongst company." Coles remained out of court, if not sober, for two months, at which point the court reversed its sentence.[84]

The Boston selectmen considered that part of their duty was to identify residents who abused alcohol. In 1670 and 1671 they named six men who were "required to forbeare the frequentinge of publique houses of entertainment." All represented the lower orders of Boston's society. They included a laborer, a tailor, a cooper, and a blacksmith. In addition, John Hurd and John Matson, whose occupations are unknown, both fought for the province of Massachusetts in King Philip's War in 1676. Their service as common soldiers suggests that Hurd and Matson also belonged to the colony's laboring class.[85] It is unlikely that these six drank more heavily than their more elite contemporaries. However, when the laboring classes abused alcohol, their behavior was seen as especially problematic. Elites feared that laborers, when inebriated, would lose control over their behavior; perpetrators also risked harm to their families by squandering their meager incomes. The sinful behavior of those laboring class drinkers also risked bringing God's retribution into the Bay. The Boston selectmen thus maintained their vigilance.

Puritan magistrates expressed their collective distress about "disorderly houses" as well. Here again the class basis of that concern is clear. These establishments were usually intended to quench the thirst legally and satisfy the sexual needs illegally of Boston's male population. These were the places prostitutes plied their trade.[86] The magistrates betrayed feelings of grave concern when, in January of 1672, they discovered that Alice Thomas was operating a house of prostitution. Widow Thomas requested a jury trial to answer to the accusation that she committed "severall shamefull notorious crimes and high misdemeanors." The lengthy list of her misconduct included abetting those who broke into a warehouse; giving "frequent secret and unseasonable entertainment in her house to lewd lascivious & notorious persons of both sexes, giving them opportunity to commit carnall wickedness;" selling strong drink without a license, entertaining servants and children, and profaning the Lord's day "by selling drinke & entertaining idle persons." The jury brought in a verdict of guilty and the court imposed an extreme sentence. Fines totaled more than one hundred pounds— more than sixty-six pounds to replace the goods she helped to steal and fifty-five pounds in fees and court costs. Thomas was also to spend some time in prison. The magistrates however, were not finished with her. She was to be carried to the gallows to stand with a rope around her neck for an hour. Afterwards, she would be brought from the prison to her house, stripped to the waist and tied to a cart's tail, to be whipped through the streets of Boston in a route that would lead them back to the prison where she was to receive "not under thirty nine stripes." Thomas was to remain in prison "during the pleasure of this court."[87]

The magistrates called upon two forms of public shaming to demonstrate to the citizens of Boston the range of their powers and the horrors that would befall those who followed a similarly crooked path into sin. Criminals, who were forced to stand on the gallows with a rope around their neck, were expected to contemplate the wages of their transgression while being humbled before the eyes of their neighbors who might parade by for a look. As a legal historian observed, the courts used the penalty only rarely, primarily for offenders of the code of sexual morality. Being stripped to the waist and tied to the cart's tail also placed

Thomas in a novel category. This form of painful, public humiliation was traditionally reserved for two classes of offender—Quakers and prostitutes. The Puritans created innovative punishments. Public humiliation engaged the offender in the process of repudiation, to acknowledge the error of her ways before the eyes of God. It was also intended to deter others from stumbling and in effect pointed a collective finger at the accused "by setting of the offender from respectable society and from the approval of his fellows."[88]

The court's judgment of Alice Thomas was severe because her behavior challenged the order of Boston society. She crossed class lines, entertained and served both free and unfree persons, and she provided the setting for sexual liaisons among these groups. In a society that worked hard to preserve status hierarchies, Thomas flaunted her disregard for these arrangements. She further defied the status quo by being involved in an underground economic network. Although this would become a more common and more threatening urban practice during the eighteenth century, Thomas's connection with the warehouse theft, as the agent who fenced stolen goods, may not have been an isolated incident. Servants and the laboring poor may have called upon her with regularity as part of a network of stealing that served to supplement their incomes. These enterprises transgressed the law and crossed class and gender lines. They were intolerable to local officials because they subverted the natural hierarchy of society. Punishing such behavior was part of what the Puritans saw as their responsibility to defend God's ordained order.

The case of Alice Thomas must have served as an inspiration to the General Court. One year after her trial, they passed a law codifying the sentence they had imposed upon her. The court expressed alarm at the "bold and audacious presumption of some to erect a stews, whore-house, or brothel house." It decreed that all "vile persons" convicted of establishing these houses, were to be whipped at the carts tail "through the streets where such offence or offences hath been committed, with thirty stripes" and be committed to the house of correction "to be kept with hard fare and hard labour." They would be required, at least once a week, "in hair frocks and blew caps by the executioner to be fastened to a hand cart and forced along to draw all the filth laid up in the cart, through the streets to the sea side."[89]

As offended as they appeared to be by Thomas, Boston's leaders displayed no consistency in their treatment of houses of ill repute. They failed, for example, to close at least one bawdy house, even though they had ample evidence about its character. Provided Midwinter, an apt name for someone sheltering lost souls during the frigid winter months, appeared before the court on two separate occasions for operating a disorderly house. At each appearance, in 1707 and 1710, Midwinter was discharged because of insufficient evidence. When she was first presented to the court, the magistrates decreed that because Midwinter was a "person of ill fame," she was to pay ten pounds to insure her good behavior and she was forbidden to entertain Richard Ellis and the Widow Faulkner, persons known to have frequented her house.[90]

In light of the Puritans' desire to identify and suppress sin, magistrates' unwillingness to put Midwinter out of business is curious. The evidence was clear. Elizabeth Faulkner was "seen in the very act of uncleanness" with Doctor Hewes.[91] Faulkner was required to give security and was forbidden to frequent Midwinter's house. The magistrates may have kept their hands off Midwinter's house because they or other Boston elites were among her clientele. Cotton Mather expressed his distress over the numbers of houses of pleasure. "I am informed," he wrote in 1713, "of several Houses in this Town, where there are young Women of a very debauched character," and a large number of young men who frequent their services. Mather wanted these houses permanently closed, and he requested a list of all of Boston's whorehouses with the names of their clientele. Mather was not successful. Perhaps because his contemporaries did not share his views, Midwinter's house remained open for business. Sixty years later, John Peebles, a British officer who visited Newport in the early years of the Revolution, reported on an encounter he had with a prostitute and commented about her reputation. She (unnamed in the diary) had kept a "house of pleasure" for many years and "is Spoke of by every body in Town in a favourable manner for one of her Profession." Peebles surmised that the attitude was shaped at a time when houses of prostitution were publicly allowed "and the Manners of the People by no means rigid when subjects of that sort become family conversation." If Peebles characterized eighteenth-century New England accurately, Mather may have been in the minority in the vehemence of his opposition to Midwinter's business. It remained open because she had a clientele willing to protect it.[92]

The records of prosecution display leniency toward houses of pleasure. Women like Midwinter rarely appeared in court on tavern-related offenses in New England. Even in Suffolk County, which had the largest number of prosecutions and where almost all of the cases (85.5%) involved Boston residents, only 27 (11%) of the 240 cases heard in the early eighteenth century involved disorderly houses. Of these 27 defendants, the court convicted 8 women (30%). Women were most often found guilty of selling liquor without a license. Almost all of those prosecuted were widows (36%) or the wives of mariners (61.5%). These data suggest that the illegal trade in alcohol was the strategy chosen by the most economically marginal women in the port city to provide themselves with some income. Women who lived on their own were among the most economically vulnerable members of the early American population. Mariners' wives were forced to find ways to survive while their seafaring husbands were absent and their incomes nonexistent. With the death of her husband, a middling- or laboring-class woman often lost her only economic support. Widows would hang a sign on their front door inviting customers in for food or drink, until the authorities noticed and charged them for selling liquor without a license.

Pennsylvania

In Pennsylvania, just as in the other sectarian colonies, the tavern and drinking laws expose the ambiguous status of the tavern as both necessary and potentially evil. While Quaker beliefs and practices contrasted dramatically with those of the Puritans on a wide range of issues, they differed little in the matters of tavern regulation and drinking. William Penn hoped initially that his holy experiment would prosper without taverns, and in an early draft of his Fundamental Constitution he stipulated that there be "no Taverns, nor alehouses, . . . nor any Playhouses nor morris dances, nor Games as dice, Cards, Board Tables, Lotteries, Bowling greens, Horse races, Bear Baiting, bull Baiting, and such like Sports." Penn eventually backed away from this position, resigned to the necessity of taverns, and he proposed an elaborate series of regulations to govern their operation. He cataloged two types of punishable behaviors, one for tavern patrons, the other for the proprietors of public houses. Patrons were forbidden to swear, over drink, spread false news, or defame someone's character. Tavern keepers had to obtain a license, charge specific rates for food and beer, and be equipped with stable and a supply of hay for four horses. Penn's fears about taverns were apparently confirmed. In the first month of 1683, the Provincial Council of Pennsylvania entertained a complaint about the many disorders in public houses. They appointed two assistants to the justices of the peace and requested that they, along with the constables, visit taverns to "see good orders kept." A year later, the council passed bills stipulating that any "Bargains made when People are in Drinke" would be null and void.[93]

Early on, lawmakers singled out city taverns for special treatment. They adopted a fee schedule in which Philadelphia tavern keepers paid larger amounts than their rural or small-town counterparts, which suggests that the colony's lawmakers took into consideration that city taverns had a greater potential for profits and greater possibilities for disorder. Penn determined that city taverns were, for instance, more likely to be involved with illegal trade; this prompted the council to require that all keepers provide magistrates with the names of all the strangers they entertained. Penn's concerns about the negative influence of too many taverns operating in the port city were addressed by limiting Philadelphia residents to a one-hour stay unless they were involved in conducting business and requiring an 8:00 P.M. closing time. Not only did these rules separate city and rural taverns, but authorities imposed a two-tiered system within the city, based on class. Taverns in which the patrons were not engaged in business could legally operate for only a few evening hours before the doors were to be shut. For public houses where merchants or town officials conducted business, the rules were nullified; patrons could remain as long and as late as they wished.[94]

Pennsylvania lawmakers were unambiguous, however, in their desire to prevent Sabbath drinking. A law enacted in 1706 was intended to provide greater freedom for individuals to devote themselves to "religious and pious exercise." Toward that end everyone found drinking in a public house on the first day of the week was to be punished. The law made it very clear that it was not meant to interfere with the refreshment of "travelers, inmates, lodgers or others."[95]

Prosecution rates for alcohol and tavern related offences were extremely low in seventeenth-century Pennsylvania. Philadelphia's leaders, like those in New York, were more fearful of the disorders that might emanate from unlicensed houses than the problems of individuals distempered in drink. The Provincial Council, from 1683 to 1700, heard six complaints related to drinking and the tavern. Of these, two individuals had their licenses revoked for improper behavior. In the first case, it remains unclear what precipitated the loss of the license. However, the council gave the proprietor, Joseph Knight, three months to sell the stores of drink and provisions in his house and then search for "some other way for a Lively hood." The council also rescinded John Richardson's license, because he "behaved himself so violently and Inhumanely towards his wife, that it is much feared he may be her Death." He was bound over to answer the charges and while no record exists of the proceedings, the council, two and a half months later, ordered that his license be voided due to his "Ill Character." Mary Lichfield was the only ordinary keeper denied a license renewal during the February session in 1685. The council allowed her to maintain her tavern for four months, an amount of time they felt would permit her to collect any outstanding debts owed to her and to find some other way of earning a living. She had been presented for adultery, accused of living with Thomas Lichfield and pretending to be his wife.[96] These cases reveal that Pennsylvania's leaders had limited tolerance for tavern keepers with questionable characters, because publicans carried the greater responsibility for upholding drinking and tavern law.

Of the six cases that came before the Provincial Council from the founding of the Pennsylvania to the end of the seventeenth century, the councilors admonished only two people for overindulging in drink. In 1683, John Richardson and the following year Timothy Metcalf were presented for being "disordered in drink." One year after hearing the case against Metcalf, the councilors, aware of wider ramifications that might arise when individuals drank too much, introduced and passed a bill "against Bargains made when People are in Drinke."[97] The colony's economy, especially that of Philadelphia, depended upon commercial success, and this bill protected all transactions contracted. The council was preparing for a problem that did not materialize in the Quaker colony, or at least required no further court involvement.

The final two cases decided upon by the Provincial Council during this earliest period of Pennsylvania's history involved the illegal sale of alcohol to Indians. Unlike the matter of individuals' drinking problems, selling liquor to Indians did become an important issue early. In 1684, Robert Terrill was accused of selling rum to Indians and "Entertaining other person's servants." Jesper Farmer's servants were accused of making Indians drunk, "lying with their Wives, and of . . .

beeting both men and their wives." A date was set to resolve the issue but no record exists of the outcome.⁹⁸ Selling drink to Indians not only violated the law but threatened the fragile peace between native peoples and colonists. Prosecutions for transgressing these laws, while minimal in the early decades after settlement, took on more import in the eighteenth century.

Prosecutors heard small numbers of tavern- and drink-related cases outside the city as well. The Bucks County court, in the period 1684 to 1700, considered only nine tavern- or alcohol-related cases. Most were involved with illegal selling, as in the case of Gilbert Wheeler, who was found guilty of selling rum to the Indians and yet, ten years later, was issued a license to operate a tavern. Cases of drunkenness invariably involved other unlawful activities as well. It may have been impossible for the justices to avoid prosecuting Thomas Coverdale when he appeared in court drunk. Philip Conway's conviction involved threatening Jane Coverdale, swearing several oaths, and cursing the Quakers.⁹⁹ Authorities in Chester County engaged slightly more in ferreting out violators. The court indicted and convicted fifty-four individuals from 1681 through 1710. Their time was almost equally divided between tavern keepers and tavern patrons. Most of the proprietors (27) had sold without a license or allowed individuals to get drunk in their houses. Twenty-two men were convicted of drunkenness, including three who indulged in a three-day binge and one who showed up in court inebriated. Chester County courts deviated somewhat from Bucks County and the city of Philadelphia; rather than placing the bulk of the responsibility on the proprietor, Chester County prosecuted both tavern keeper and the person found drunk.¹⁰⁰

❖ ❖ ❖

THE ENGLISH LEGACY came across the ocean virtually intact. Although colonial legislators adopted specific laws to address their own needs and the timing and emphasis of the earliest laws varied by region, by the late seventeenth century it was virtually impossible to distinguish the legal framework of New England from that of the Chesapeake or to identify differences between the laws of New York and those of South Carolina. Underlying legislation on both sides of the Atlantic was the assumption that alcoholic beverages were a natural part of nourishment and that humans required them. Moderate drinking was therefore an acceptable practice. Colonists also shared with England their attitude toward diversions; the time spent in the tavern was not necessarily pernicious. As a seventeenth-century Virginian observed, "Diversions which have no immoral Tendency, when purchased by those who can well afford it, unbend the Mind from severer Applications, promote a social Temper, and diffuse a general Satisfaction through the Ranks of Life."[101]

The statutory record reveals much more than colonial magistrates struggling to control drinking abuses. It confirms the persistence of English "social customs and criminal precepts," despite that colonists prided themselves on creating a new social order. Colonists boasted that in contrast to their former homes in England and Europe, they participated more fully and exercised more power over their own lives in New England. The colonies provided new economic opportunities for those who possessed skills, some resources, and luck. Nevertheless, while colonists celebrated the opportunities and control over their lives in the New World, they also maintained their loyalties to much that was English—social and economic customs and especially law and embedded them in the legal code in early America.[102]

The history of tavern law also belies the notion that the fundamental principles and attitudes toward drinking and the tavern were incompatible among the North American colonies. The body of law suggests that by the late seventeenth century the nonsectarian colonies shared with the sectarian ones a commitment to punish anyone who violated proper drinking or tavern behavior. While it might come as some surprise that Virginia's legal code was as involved with the regulation of personal behavior as was the law in New England, morality and law were closely entwined throughout early America. Devising laws to regulate morals did not depend upon the existence of a vigorous established church. Even if the theological tenets of Puritanism were not shared by all colonies, most colonists did subscribe to a moral ideal as a way of life.[103] The laws were created by an upper class that had internalized a responsibility for the morality of the lower orders. An intact moral order helped to ensure a stable class system. Laws that prohibited the dependent classes from overindulging in drink and from staying too long in the tavern fit into the class of law aimed at social control.[104]

While the laws appear uniform, the seventeenth-century prosecution records of tavern and drinking law highlight differences between the sectarian and nonsectarian colonies. Throughout the seventeenth century, Virginia, Maryland, North Carolina, South Carolina, and New York had laws on the books to control individual morality with regard to drinking and the tavern, but no one paid much attention if they encountered drunk individuals or groups. At particular moments, Virginians complained about their leaders being so inebriated that they could not perform their offices, but, in general, they remained oblivious if their neighbors drank to excess or sold liquor illegally. The court paid attention if the abuse of alcohol was implicated in other, usually more serious infractions, like assault or murder. In contrast, New England leaders demonstrated their collective desire to regulate personal morality by enforcing the law. Among the colonies, they hauled the highest proportion of individuals before the magistrate and prosecuted the largest number of crimes. A member of the laboring classes in Boston who drank to intoxication or sold alcohol to an Indian would be called upon to answer for his or her behavior. Pennsylvanians deviated somewhat from this pattern; they paid little heed to individual transgression but attended to policing taverns.

Eighteenth-Century Legislation
and Prosecution:
"Lest a Flood of Rum do Overwhelm
all good Order among us"

Mr. Robert Routlidge, a merchant of Prince Edward County, in this colony, a worthy blunt man, of strict honesty and sincerity, a man incapable of fraud or hypocrisy, spent the greatest part of the day in Benjamin Mosby's tavern at Cumberland courthouse, with several gentlemen of his acquaintance, and was joined in the evening by Col. John Chiswell. After some time had passed, Col. Chiswell was talking in an important manner, . . . upon which, Mr. Routlidge . . . signified his disapprobation, with less politeness perhaps than was due to a man of Col. Chiswell's figure. Upon this Col. Chiswell was extremely abusive, and after calling Routlidge a fugitive rebel, a villain who came to Virginia to cheat and defraud men of their property, and a Presbyterian fellow, Routlidge, who was then drunk, was provoked to throw wine out of his glass at Col. Chiswell's face, some small part of which did touch him. This was an indignity which perhaps men of honor ought to resent from any one, unless from . . . a man intoxicated with liquor. Col. Chiswell . . . then attempted to throw a bowl of toddy at Mr. Routlidge, but was prevented by some of the company; then he attempted to throw a candlestick at him, but was prevented also in that; and then he tried to strike him with a pair of tongs, but he was likewise prevented in that. Upon which he ordered his servant to bring his sword.

*T*he *Virginia Gazette*, in July 1766, ran a lengthy account of a disagreement between Robert Routlidge and Col. John Chiswell, which took place in Mosby's tavern. Routlidge had spent most of the day at the tavern drinking, and, according to the newspaper story, by the time Chiswell arrived, Routlidge was drunk. Routlidge objected to Chiswell's use of language, too liberal a sprinkling of oaths, likely swearing, and he informed Chiswell of his disapproval. Chiswell countered with name calling and accused Routlidge of being a crook and "a Presbyterian fellow," an epithet that was meant to carry a special sting in the largely Anglican society of colonial Virginia. The two men then resorted to throwing things at each other.[1]

The argument escalated when Chiswell called for his sword, ordered Routlidge to leave the room, and threatened to kill him if he did not. Routlidge had no intention of giving up his tavern seat and, through his hiccups, explained to Chiswell that he did not believe he would really try to do him harm. The two men began to chase each other around the inside of the tavern. Their movements were so complicated that the author of the newspaper article felt compelled to include a diagram to enable readers to follow them as they moved through the space and among the patrons. The fracas ended when Chiswell drew his sword and stabbed Routlidge "through the heart." Routlidge collapsed in the arms of a Mr. Carrington, a tavern patron, and "instantly expired, without uttering one word, or showing the least emotion." Chiswell commanded his servant to clean his sword, while he sat down, ordered a bowl of toddy, and waited for the authorities to arrive.[2]

This tale exposes the fragile relationship among the tavern, drinking behavior, and the law. The laws concerning taverns and drinking were directed toward controlling colonists' cravings for drink.[3] Lawmakers set limits on the amount of time individuals could spend inside a tavern. When colonial leaders crafted the legal framework to prevent over indulging or when they concerned themselves with how folks spent their time, their attention was focused primarily on the lower orders, who, they believed, lacked restraint. They were not intending to interfere with Routlidge's tavern behavior or with others of his status. It was understood that elite men knew how to drink; their tavern visits did not require monitoring. By the late seventeenth century, lawmakers adjusted the laws to provide constant vigilance, lest too much drink threaten the stability of their families and the general ordering of society. Routlidge could while away an entire day inside the tavern, in defiance of the law, confident that his behavior was beyond reproach.

Throughout the seventeenth century, legislators in each of the North American colonies attempted to solve these dilemmas with virtually identical arrays of law. The similarity among the bodies of law resulted in part from their Dutch or English legal heritage. Conspicuous differences emerged, though, in how colonial jurisdictions prosecuted violators of tavern and drinking law. Although all jurisdictions in the seventeenth-century focused attention on policing individual morality, the sectarian colonies prosecuted with more vigor. Through the eighteenth century, the emphasis shifted; authorities devoted their energies to maintaining the social order that elites feared was threatened by new styles of drinking. Authorities responded by creating a category of citizen labeled "problem drinker," by controlling access to taverns, by forbidding particular kinds of activities like gaming from taking place inside the tavern, and by restricting the amount of credit patrons could receive. Certain classes and groups of individuals would abuse the tavern, drink too much, waste their time, behave in an unruly fashion, and consciously act to subvert order. By stipulating how individuals should drink and who could not partake of tavern services or receive credit, lawmakers created a blueprint for maintaining the social order.

Nonsectarian Colonies

Virginia

The eighteenth century saw no noticeable increase in prosecutions for tavern or drinking violations in Virginia. The lone tavern-related business conducted by the Fairfax County court was to issue licenses.[4] The Richmond County courts, while not totally inactive, convicted fewer than fifty individuals in a forty-year period. Most (38), like Robert Rooker and John Heyles, combined a few swear words with their drinking and were hauled before the court as much for cursing as for intemperate drinking.[5] The record on prosecutions for drinking is equally silent in King and Queen County; no one appeared before the court for violating drinking or tavern law. Alcohol is mentioned in three instances: John Redwood received seventeen pints of rum as his payment for guarding a prisoner. Colonel Leigh's fall from his horse, which resulted in his death, was attributed to his having been drunk. And finally, in the debate over the recall of Governor Nicholson, William Beverly offered a long litany of the governor's sins. Included was that he lived in a "little low wooden House worse than many Overseers in the Country . . . besides at the end of it there is kept an ordinary or tipling house."[6] Either Virginians were a sober lot or, more likely, magistrates did not place drunkenness high on their list of offenses warranting prosecution.

While cases involving excessive drinking played a minimal role in the courts, Virginians most assuredly were not abstinent. Alcohol was integrated into all layers of Virginia society. Indeed there appears to have been an inverse relationship between prosecution and drunkenness. Residents accused judges of administering justice while under the pernicious effects of alcohol. A 1704 petition before the governor and council from residents of Middlesex County complained that "diverse irregular Proceedings" took place in their court. The dispute between the people of Middlesex County and the justices, which was complicated, included the accusation that Mathew Kemp dispensed justice while drunk. Kemp did not deny the charge but he reassured his constituents that all matters before the court received "his due Attention." A further remonstration, presented a month later, carried the signatures of virtually all of the county's freeholders. This time the men who petitioned the governor and council reiterated their charge that the court proceeded with irregularities and also demanded that construction of the courthouse stop, since the placement of the building constituted another grievance. The governor and council concurred, and they halted construction until the General Assembly could act on the matter. A third petition received no response, perhaps because the council decided not "to meddle further" in the business.[7]

Prominent planter and political figure William Byrd confirmed that the absence of alcohol-related prosecutions should not imply that acts of drunkenness were a rarity in Virginia society. The skimpy legal record most likely reflects an attitude of tolerance toward the state of inebriation, or at the very least an unwillingness to prosecute violators. Byrd's accounts show that, whether on the road or at home, with peers or slaves, men or women, he met or dined with people who had already had too much to drink or were about to overindulge. He reported on a doctor who arrived at the Byrd plantation, Westover, during the midday meal drunk. Byrd also recorded the story of Mr. Blackamore, headmaster of the College of William and Mary. Blackamore never called at the Byrd plantation alone because, according to Byrd, "he did not dare to come by himself, for I had reprimanded him for his being drunk." The governors of the college dismissed Blackamore from his post because of his drinking. When he submitted a petition to be reinstated claiming that he "would for the time to come, mend his conduct," they reversed their decision and agreed to let him remain. Byrd described admonishing his slaves John and George for being drunk. After one of his regular stays in Williamsburg, Byrd recounted that he and his companions had drunk "some of Will Robinson's cider till we were very merry and then went to the coffeehouse and pulled poor colonel Churchill out of bed." A few evenings later, after a night of cards, he and his drinking companions again became "merry and in that condition went to the coffeehouse and again disturbed Colonel Churchill."[8]

Byrd's contact with heavy drinking extended beyond his own circle of companions and laborers. On a spring evening in Williamsburg, Byrd took a walk and "saw several drunk people in the churchyard." During that day, "some people came to court and got drunk in defiance of the sickness and the bad weather." Byrd strolled to the courthouse one summer night to retrieve mail, "where the people were most of them drunk." And he reported on a restless sleep because "there was a great noise of people drunk in the street a good part of the night." William Byrd understood that these behaviors contradicted the law, but he summed up the situation accurately when he noted that "several people drunk" in the churchyard commanded no legal attention, despite a recent law aimed at restraining "tippling houses and other disorderly places."[9]

When Daniel Fisher visited Philadelphia from Virginia, he commented upon what he considered a most unusual practice—tavern keepers serving gentlemen of his status actually abided by tavern law. While Fisher was impressed by the quality of service provided him at the Indian King, he appeared taken aback by the custom of early closing hours: "For whom remains here after Eleven of the

Clock in the Evening is very civilly acquainted with the time by a servant, and that after that hour, it is invariable custom of the house to serve no more liquor that night to any Body, and this Custom I am told never is infringed." In Virginia especially, the laws of the tavern were rarely enforced for those of Fisher's status and culture. He had no experience with authorities interfering with his time inside the tavern.[10]

Most occasions in Virginia could not be celebrated without enormous amounts of alcohol. Byrd recorded that on a militia muster, he supplied an entire hogshead of punch, which "entertained all the people and made them drunk and fighting all the evening, but without mischief."[11] No harm came from this particular drunken brawl among militiamen; however, it was not always the case that armed drunken celebrants behaved in a safe manner. Virginia funerals required prodigious quantities of alcohol and gun powder, at least until such merriment was outlawed. The mixture of drinking and gun firing resulted in so many accidents that the Lower Norfolk County Court ordered that firearms could not be discharged at funerals unless an officer was present to regulate the event.[12] It is unclear why the presence of an officer would ensure a safe environment. The supply of liquor to soothe the thirst and sorrow of assembled mourners often amounted to a substantial proportion of the funeral's costs.

Court days also required heavy drinking. These monthly events were almost exclusively gatherings of men—a time when men who were geographically isolated from each other could assemble, socialize, lament the price of tobacco, and generally catch up on the news of old friends. The Northampton County Court provided local folks with a convenient location in which to gather so that they could get drunk. They had no other business to transact, and the court expected the quarreling and fighting that inevitably resulted. If the drunken group entered the court room and impugned the reputation of the justices, the matter became serious. In one case the men were punished and the local tavern keeper who supplied them with the liquor was warned that future drunkenness and quarreling would result in the loss of his license.[13]

Where were female Virginians in this picture? Not a single case has been found in eighteenth-century Virginia court records in which a woman was accused of an alcohol-related offense. Women did drink, and at times to excess, but they consumed alcohol in private, rather than public, settings. William Byrd described calling on James Blair, founder of the College of William and Mary, and finding Mrs. Blair drunk. According to Byrd, this was an increasingly common occurrence.[14] An inebriated woman was a private affair, if her state concerned anyone at all. That every defendant in Virginia was male provides loud testimony to the separation of the cultures of women and men. As in all colonies, the public culture was male. Men in Virginia gathered at each other's homes, assembled on court days, or met in a Williamsburg tavern when the House of Burgesses was in session. Yet for all of the drinking that took place, like the two to three gallons of wine that six people consumed in in one evening at Martin's Brandon plantation, and with a set of laws designed to control these behaviors, individuals rarely appeared in court.

Eighteenth-century Virginia records are also conspicuously silent about the sale of alcohol without a license and the trading of alcohol with Indians. Also absent are any cases accusing tavern keepers of allowing unlawful behavior in their houses. All of this suggests that drinking and the trade in alcoholic beverages were firmly enmeshed in the fabric of Virginia. Prosecuting drunkenness would have required a full-time effort. Drunkenness became serious enough to warrant the attention of the court when it was combined with another breach of the law, disturbed the peace of the community, or involved a marginal member of society.[15]

The Carolinas

The North Carolina courts responded to breaches of drinking and tavern law much as did their neighbors to the north.[16] Beginning in 1709 until the Revolution, the courts prosecuted only a very small number of cases. The ten individuals indicted for drunkenness usually combined their drinking with some other activities. The court found Joseph Young's behavior to be the most egregious. In his drunken state he swore at and cursed the grand jury. Mathew Bryant confessed that at the time he took a lamb belonging to Thomas Mathews he was drunk. Bryant admitted that he could not remember the event, owing either to his degree of inebriation or "being very aged." The people convicted of selling liquor without a license—there were sixteen prosecutions for the entire prerevolutionary period—were apparently responding to the absence of taverns in the colony. In 1724, six men, all planters residing in Bertie County, appeared before the court because they had retailed strong liquors at their homes. They likely argued, in their defense, that neighbors and those passing by called upon them for drink. They were only carrying out their responsibilities as good neighbors. The courts accused six individuals of operating disorderly houses, an infraction defined more broadly in this rural county than in port cities, where it implied unruly behavior or even prostitution. Hugh Campbell was found to have a disorderly house because he failed to have proper provisions. The law required tavern keepers to stock food for humans and horses, and Campbell apparently had neither. The record indicates that his house lacked "fodder, corn or other entertainments."[17]

Although South Carolina lawmakers tinkered with the laws up until the middle of the eighteenth century and the grand jury in Charleston complained regularly that the existence of too many licensed houses corrupted the morals of all inhabitants, authorities prosecuted very few cases involving violations of tavern or drinking law. During the seven years prior to the Revolution, the most common offense in Charleston, as in the northern port cities, was operating a disorderly house (14 of 23 cases). The attorney general was ordered to prosecute Mary Grant for harboring loose and idle women in her Church Street house. William Wayne and William Holliday corrupted the youth by serving them in their disorderly houses and allowing them to game. As in the other colonial cities, tavern keepers were also prosecuted for receiving stolen goods, evidence that in Charleston as well, tavern keepers participated in a second economy. They received and fenced stolen property.[18]

New York

Prosecutions involving taverns and drinking in eighteenth-century New York were concentrated within a narrow range that spoke to the fears of the city's officials and residents. Not a single defendant was hauled before the court accused of drunkenness. One historian of early New York legal history speculated that the lack of cases might be an artifact of extant documents. Records for the lower courts are incomplete and, as elsewhere, authorities relied on informal procedures. The support for this view is mainly anecdotal. New Yorkers maintained that drunkenness was a common offense, blamed in part on their proclivity to drink large quantities of alcohol due to the lack of potable water in the city.

The case of "Montonny's negro man" corroborates the sense revealed by the records that those few individuals who were prosecuted came from a particular stratum of society. In 1772 "Montonny's negro man" was found guilty of drunkenness and sentenced to jail. He died the night he arrived to start his sentence, after receiving the "usual punishment in such cases . . . a plentiful dose of warm water (three quarts) and salt enough to operate as an emetic; with a portion of lamp oil to act as a purge." The penalty this slave suffered never appeared again in the records, even though the contemporary account describes it as usual. In New York as elsewhere in colonial North America, while drunkenness was common and prosecution rare, those individuals who were charged with drunkenness were likely to be among the most vulnerable members of society. If servants or slaves gained access to alcohol, they and the supplier were violating the law, and authorities were eager to uphold the laws that helped control the city's servile classes.[19]

City magistrates also rarely prosecuted houses of prostitution, despite observations from contemporaries that they were common in eighteenth-century New York. One charge that was brought, heard on December 13, 1700, by a special session of the quarterly court, was based on information from Charles Oliver, one of the lieutenants in charge of the British army garrison. On the previous night, Oliver had discovered that several soldiers were missing from the barracks. They were found in Jannica Inmin's house, in bed with women of "Evil Name and fame and wicked lifes & Conversations." As the patrol entered the bedrooms, the women fled. Elizabeth Stoaks and Isabell Aggot, who "had been in bed . . . got from thence into the Cellar without Shoes or Stockings." Residents of New York were well acquainted with Inmin's house. Indeed, it appears that Oliver knew precisely where he would find his missing men. Although the women were ordered to be tied to a cart and marched through the city, no corporal punishment was involved and they were discharged after paying fees. It was punishment by humiliation and public spectacle but the effort was without much potency. The complaint had not stemmed from a citywide vigilance to uphold a moral code. Rather, the court had been prodded into action by an army officer whose men were not abiding by military rules. The records do not reveal what happened to the soldiers; most likely, any discipline was left to the military.[20]

The city undertook what appears to have been a sweep of its brothels in July

1753, but town officials generated very little enthusiasm for the effort, and as a result, most of the city's prostitutes were only slightly disturbed. Constables rounded up twenty-two "ladies of pleasure" and committed them to the workhouse. Five of them, who gave "but a poor Account of themselves," were sentenced to fifteen lashes. According to the local newspaper, the punishment took place at the whipping post, in front of a large number of spectators. Afterwards, the five women were given forty-eight hours to depart the city or be imprisoned. All of the remaining women were dismissed, having lost one night's work.[21]

A British visitor, in 1774, confirmed the sense that New Yorkers appeared undisturbed by the existence of brothels. Patrick M'Roberts compared the situation of prostitutes in New York City with what he had seen at home. Referring to a section of New York known as St. Paul's, named for the church that owned the land, he claimed: "above 500 ladies of pleasure keep lodgings contiguous within the consecrated liberties of St. Paul's. This part of the city belongs to the church, and has thence obtained the name of the *Holy Ground*. Here all the prostitutes reside, among whom are many fine well dressed women, and it is remarkable that they live in much greater cordiality one with another than any nests of that kind do in Britain or Ireland."[22] For all of their visibility, the New York prostitutes and disorderly houses that catered to a white middle-class or elite clientele failed to capture the attention or raise the ire of the city's legal establishment, but some residents objected. One complained, in 1765, that he had witnessed two women standing in the pillory for an hour "for keeping bawdyhouses." He lamented that this sight was all too rare and if the city would enforce the laws, the doors of the houses of ill repute could be shut forever. An anonymous writer in a local newspaper, in 1766, whined that officials essentially sanctioned the existence of these houses, because nothing was done to punish the proprietors, the women, or their patrons, and these brothels existed "as so many receptacles for loose and disorderly people."[23]

Eighteenth-century courts did, however, energetically uphold a particular portion of tavern law. Virtually all of the cases involved proprietors who sold liquor and provided entertainment to black slaves. In New York City from 1683 to 1772, fifty-eight individuals were required to appear before the General Quarter Sessions Court, all but three of whom answered to the charge of operating a disorderly house and specifically "entertaining sundry Negro slaves." Some cases, like that against John Roome in 1702, involved entertaining and selling drink "to Negroes upon the Sabbath Day." The court found John Gardner's behavior more serious; "on the Fourth Day of April [1706] . . . and diverse other days and times as well before as afterward" he had entertained "sundry Negro slaves." He had given them rum and other strong liquors without the knowledge of their masters. For this, the court revoked Gardner's tavern license.[24] There were inequities in the penalties for this offense. In 1715, Thomas Noble, a white man, was convicted of selling liquor to slaves and entertaining them in his house. His fine was a meager one shilling. However, the alarm bells sounded when women or blacks perpetrated this action. In the same year as Noble's conviction, the Quarter Sessions court tried Peter, "a Negro . . . laborer" who in his dwelling house in East Ward did "deceitfully receive, harbour & entertain" other men's slaves. Peter received a ten-pound fine, twice the penalty of any other person found guilty of violating this act.[25]

New York leaders worked most diligently to prosecute women who operated public houses that offered entertainment to black patrons. Judith Peters appeared before the New York General Quarter Sessions court in 1723 to answer to charges of "keeping a disorderly house & selling strong liquors to Negroes." In a very similar case in 1728, the Grand Jury summoned Susannah Hutchins, "a single woman of evil behavior and conversation [who] received entertained harboured and supported diverse Negro slaves." The court fined both women. Indeed the tavern-related crime in which women were most often implicated was operating a disorderly house, and in virtually every instance, the court focused most of its attention on the presence of blacks or slaves inside these public houses.[26]

Tavern keepers who served and entertained slaves or free blacks touched a raw nerve in colonial New York. The case against Ann Butler divulges precisely what New Yorkers feared would be the result from disorderly houses that served black clientele. According to the court, Butler lived a lewd life based upon her association with slaves and more specifically that she tried to seduce a slave into running away. The court needed very little time to determine that the city could not tolerate Butler's presence in the province. Even Butler's protests that she was "weakly in body and constitution," barely softened the court's resolve. The justices permitted her to go to Connecticut where "she pretended she had friends

& moneys, owing unto her." Butler made the mistake of testing the court's resolve and when she reappeared in New York, the judges ordered that she be "re-
transported out of the city and county" and be whipped as a vagrant.[27]

The authorities also responded with indictments and convictions of patrons
and proprietors when the clientele inside the bawdy or disorderly house was eth-
nically mixed. The court's scrutiny was fueled by fear of the city's multiethnic
population. The social geography of Manhattan included more ethnic diversity
than any other city in the early modern world. Although English and Dutch residents predominated, Scots-Irish, Irish, Germans, French, Jews, and Africans,
both free and unfree, resided there as well.[28]

As in the other major port cities by this time, New York's white population
contained a narrow band of elites and a large middle class. Those in the upper
stratum flaunted their wealth by riding around in fancy carriages, driven and
maintained by their slaves. They met with each other in taverns to discuss business, make political decisions, and exchange toasts. The large middle class of
artisans and shopkeepers also socialized in taverns and might in fact recognize
a judge or wealthy merchant at a table nearby. Those in the bottom tier of society, primarily unskilled laborers, rendezvoused in the taverns and dram shops
that dotted the waterfront. After the work day ended, groups of laborers, soldiers, and sailors, servants, and slaves gathered at these "vile" and "disorderly"
houses "to drink drams, punch and other strong liquors," often staying until "two
or three o'clock in the morning." They told stories, perhaps embellishing upon
the details of the 1712 slave conspiracy or criticizing their local leaders. They
danced and sang. According to the city's authorities, the public disturbances aris-
ing from these taverns required vigilance in order to quash any threat to the public order.[29]

The tavern keepers who catered to the city's laboring classes violated the laws
on a number of levels. They encouraged servants, apprentices, and slaves to
gather in their houses, sold them liquor, provided them other entertainments,
and extended credit to them. A New York grand jury in 1735 called Henry Hyck,
a "south ward tavern keeper," to appear before them to answer to the charge that
he entertained servants and apprentices. In one sideline to the 1741 New York
Conspiracy trial, Justice Philipse asked the grand jury to inquire into the number of persons "who sell rum, and other strong liquor to negroes. It must be ob-

vious to every one, that there are too many of them in this city." These sales occurred without permission from their masters, which the law required.[30]

New York tavern keepers' involvement with the city's black population went far deeper than providing the site for socializing and drinking. They acted as factors in the city's second economy by fencing stolen goods and supplying arms. Some of these transactions were random, small-scale exchanges. One witness at the 1741 conspiracy trial testified that while he was drinking and playing dice at Hughson's, "Wyncoop's negro" was observed in possession of a silver spoon that had been hammered down and which obervers assumed was stolen. Other activities were larger and more organized, involving theft rings like the best-known Geneva Club. The group earned its name, in 1735 or '36, from some Geneva gin they stole from a tavern cellar. Two of the men hanged in 1741 as a result of the conspiracy trial, Ceasar and Prince, had been leaders of this organization and had previously been "chastised at the public whipping-post" for their participation in the theft that gave the group its name. The two tavern keepers implicated in the 1741 conspiracy, Hughson and Romme, were identified as fences for disposing of stolen goods. Witnesses at the trial testified that Romme had received a variety of goods, including "fifty or sixty firkins of butter," and a cloth coat and cape that Romme wore.[31] This trade with black slaves was so extensive that it prompted an amendment to the existing law, doubling the amount of the fine or promised jail time for the offending tavern keepers.[32]

This extensive underground economy centered on the tavern, but it was the particular history of New York that made this interracial, working class network particularly menacing. In 1712 and again in 1741, New York had the distinction of being the only North American city faced with organized rebellions against the institution of slavery. Fears of slave revolts were confounded by the reality that slaves and free blacks did not act alone. While they planned and executed the plot, slaves and free blacks depended upon tavern keepers for assistance. They offered blacks a place "to resort, and be entertained privately (in defiance of the law) at all hours." They also received goods stolen from masters.[33] Although the law denied blacks access to public houses, they engaged in a busy tavern culture, engaging in a host of activities that white society deemed unlawful. Laws prevented their assembly and imposed a curfew, but blacks circulated in groups through the city without the passes the law required that they carry.

The record of prosecution in New York City exposes a fault line in society, embedded in the concept of race. All colonies prosecuted those who kept disorderly houses, but the infraction included a range of activities from selling liquor without a license to operating a brothel. New York's version of the practice was unique; it was synonymous with multiracialness. Authorities identified disorderly houses as conspirators in a range of behaviors they abhorred. It was not just that taverns provided free blacks and slaves with places to eat, drink, and socialize, although this subverted an orderly society. Gatherings of slaves were dangerous. Memories of the New York City slave conspiracy of 1712 were firmly etched in New Yorkers' collective psyche. In 1741, when white New Yorkers discovered that a group of black Spaniards had been enslaved in the city and that they were outspoken and angry, rumors circulated that these new arrivals were working to convince New York blacks to join with them to fight their common white enemy. They promised Spanish reinforcements to aid the cause. Hughson's house as well as other waterfront establishments provided the settings for poor whites and blacks to hear the stories of laboring class insurrections elsewhere and to form their own plan for New York, "a design," according to one justice, that "was conceived to destroy this city by fire and massacre its inhabitants."[34]

White New Yorkers imparted great meaning to the activities inside the disorderly house, especially their place in fomenting rebellion. On some level, New Yorkers wished to believe that slave conspiracies were designed and carried out by blacks alone. This view helped maintain the fiction that the races lived separately, which they viewed as a necessary element of an orderly society. But overwhelming evidence supported the notion that waterfront taverns harbored a culture in which laboring-class whites mixed freely with blacks and assisted slaves in their plot. New Yorkers also seemed wedded to the belief that slaves were fundamentally happy, accepting their station in life, and were far better off than they would have been had they remained in their African homelands. The institution of slavery was perceived as an agency of civilization, "uplifting blacks from the natural backwardness of the 'Dark Continent.'" According to a New York supreme court judge, slavery enabled slaves to live in close proximity to civilized society and surely, he assumed, some of it would rub off. And even with their lowly status, laws protected them; "none can hurt them with impunity." The evidence from the conspiracy contradicted this image because the major players were the slaves of the New York elite—the Roosevelts, DeLanceys, Courtlands, Jays, Livingstons, and Philipses—slaveowners who perceived themselves and others like them as ideal masters. How could well treated, "happy" slaves foment rebellion?[35]

Another dimension of the scene of the contented slave was provided by the assumption that blacks lacked the intellect necessary to design and implement a plot. "It cannot be imagined" thundered the New York attorney general, "that these silly unthinking creatures could of themselves have contrived and carried on so deep, so direful and destructive a scheme, as that we have seen with our eyes and have heard fully proved." The attorney general offered his theory. The slaves had had ample assistance. He claimed that "Hughson's black guard," his sarcastic name for the slaves who called regularly at Hughson's tavern, were "stupid wretches," who had been "seduced by the instigation of the devil, and Hughson his agent."[36] Justice Horsmanden shared this view, perhaps not literally; but he believed that the plot was conceived jointly by whites and blacks. The title he gave to the first edition of his monograph on the subject displays his understanding of the events: *A Journal of the Proceedings in The Detection of the Conspiracy formed by Some White People, in Conjunction with Negro and other Slaves, for burning the City of New-York in America, And Murdering the Inhabitants* . . . Apparently this view was widely shared. Mr. Smith, a court clerk who provided a summary of evidence, issued a report early in the trial. On May 29th he recorded, "Great numbers of persons have been concerned in the plot; some whites, and many blacks."[37]

When blacks and whites met together, they challenged the city's racial hierarchy. Frederick Philipse, the second justice, passed judgment against the Hughson family on June 8th, chastising them for behavior unbecoming those living in a Christian nation. Their most egregious transgressions against society were "not only of making negro slaves their equals, but even their superiors, by waiting upon, keeping with, and entertaining them with meat, drink, and lodging." They also joined with them to conspire, "to burn this city, and to kill and destroy us all." The court had little choice but to close the disorderly house. The behaviors inside challenged the city at its core. When white tavern keepers served blacks inside a public house, that act worked to invert the ideology of inferior to superior. When whites and blacks plotted to overthrow the institution of slavery, it served to provide the city's blacks with a sense of autonomy. These houses offered evidence to the court that the mixing of social classes foretold an end to the divisions within society.[38]

Sectarian Colonies

Massachusetts

During the latter decades of the seventeenth century and early decades of the eighteenth, New England lawmakers devoted increasing attention to alcohol consumption, in response to what they considered to be a new problem, the growing availability and popularity of distilled liquors. In an attempt to stanch the flow, a 1712 Massachusetts law forbade the sale of rum in taverns. When New England's ministers exhorted their listeners to change their ways or expect God's wrath, they included in the list of sins alcohol and its abuses. Ministers were not blaming excessive drinking for all of their problems; but it was their responsibility to punish "all the vices which disturb the good order and repose of human society." Drunkenness and idleness were high on the list.[39]

The fear that New England was drowning in a sea of alcohol coincided with other crises in the Puritan world. From 1686 to 1694, events in Massachusetts left little doubt in the minds of ministers that the Puritan way of life was under siege. The colony lost its charter when the king imposed the Dominion of New England. To make matters worse, Sir Edmond Andros, the man selected to govern the Dominion, was hostile to Puritanism. And while New Englanders celebrated when Andros was ousted from power, the colony remained without a charter, leaving its future uncertain. The ministers' dire warnings were not, as it turned out, idle threats. The 1691 charter dissolved the link between franchise and church membership and marked the end of the Puritan way. Representatives to the provincial assembly were to be elected by all of the white adult males with estates valued at a minimum of twenty-four pounds sterling or a freehold of at least forty shillings per year. The Puritan authority of the colony had been stripped away.[40]

Before the wide-scale introduction of rum and other distilled liquors, Puritan authorities viewed drinking as a rather benign activity, monitored to a certain extent by the upper classes. Ministers were aware that drink could be abused, but before the popularity of rum, they were more sanguine about alcoholic beverages and their use. The arrival of rum altered drinking styles, and, according to religious leaders, public drunkenness increased, along with crime and disorder. Just at the moment when the power of ministers and secular leaders in the colony was decaying, the pervasive use of rum was further eroding their control over the behavior of the laboring classes.[41]

Heightened ministerial and secular panic can be traced through their writings. In 1673, Increase Mather had written that drink was the "good creature of God." This gift was to be received but not abused. Mather cautioned that man should not "drink a Cup of Wine more then is good for him."[42] Slightly more than a decade later, just as rum was becoming increasingly common, Mather expressed his fear that the poor could procure rum at a very cheap rate and "make themselves drunk." What was worse, they "were addicted to this vice" and were thus incapable of temperance.[43]

In 1708, Cotton Mather applied his father's early teaching to rum—rum also was "a Creature of God." He reiterated that spirituous liquors had medicinal and nutritional qualities and when taken in moderation enabled the drinker to gain strength. He was deeply troubled, however, by the specter of drunkenness. He reminded his listeners that God had often in the past sent various pests to destroy sinful towns. "Would it not be a surprize" he asked, "to hear of a Country destroy'd by a Bottel of RUM?" Cotton Mather equated inebriation with "social unrest, as a sign of divine affliction, and as a warning of eternal damnation." He was especially distressed "lest a Flood of RUM do Overwhelm all good Order among us." While distressed about increases in gaming, whoring, pauperism, and crime, Mather was most alarmed by the pernicious effect rum was having on the class structure of New England society. These effects forewarned the demise of the existing hierarchy; "It threatens a Confusion to all Societies." Drink was highly valued in early American society and "its use was limited only by how much people could afford." Much to Mather's horror, rum had become cheap enough for everyone.[44]

The drinking habits of society's more wealthy citizens, according to Mather, had dire consequences for the social order. Mather assumed that, since they could most easily afford the price of spirits, the elite were most likely to overindulge. "The Votaries of Strong Drink, will grow so numerous, that they

will make a Party, against every thing that is Holy, and Just, and Good." The authority of the righteous would not stand a chance for those who abuse drink "will
be too Strong, for wiser and better men, and carry all before them." Ministers'
efforts to persuade them otherwise would fail in the same way that strong drink
had interfered with "the Evangelical Work of Christianizing the Indians." With
a sodden upper class, society would turn upside down. The tavern would replace
the church and the tavern keeper would assume the authority of the minister.
Families would become ill nurtured, "the Wife be a Mistress of a Bottle" and
children would "ask for it." The maintenance of good order had the best chance
of success if the elite were a model for the rest of society. "Let persons of the
Best Sort, be Exemplary for this piece of Abstinance."[45]

Boston minister Benjamin Wadsworth concurred that rum deserved considerable blame for the evil behaviors he witnessed. In his 1710 "Essay to Do Good,"
Wadsworth adopted a calm tone in an attempt to dissuade "tavern-haunting, and
excessive drinking." Taverns, he admitted, were appropriate places for people to
gather especially when they were engaged in business. Drinking rum, he reassured his readers, was lawful and at times convenient. Wadsworth linked the
abuse of drink to the many problems encountered by the Bay Colony. "God is in
various ways contending with us" by inflicting a war and by sending a drought.
The behavior of all citizens required reformation, so that order might be restored.[46]

Almost two decades later, Wadsworth's tone turned more shrill and he sounded
an alarm about drink and its abuses. In "Vicious Courses" he condemned all
those who stayed in taverns, with the exception of travelers, and questioned why
it was so important to "tempt and prompt others to drink to excess." In the course
of his denunciation, Wadsworth described with great precision what he termed
vile practices, the central place of drink in colonial society. Why was it, he grumbled, that all who "[enter into] a bargain, make up accounts, pay or receive a little
money, but that they must needs go to a tavern, and solemnize the matter as it
were by swallowing strong drink?" Similarly, he complained, "[Why] can't tradesmen finish or bring home a piece of work, but must almost think themselves
wronged, if they are not treated with strong drink?"[47] In a sense, Wadsworth answered his own questions. He well understood how embedded the tavern and
drink were in society. The addition and dependence upon cheap, plentiful hard
liquor made the change in drinking behaviors he advocated all the more unlikely.

In 1724, an anonymous, witty, and satirical pamphlet responded to the ministers' sermons on drinking by demonstrating the central place rum had attained within colonial society. In the sketch, Sir Richard Rum was placed on trial at a court held at Punch-Hall. The presiding "Chief Judges of the Courts of Justice constituted by King Bacchus" were Nathan Standsoft and Solomon Stiffrump. The clerk of the court read the indictment. Richard Rum, the country's most potent and popular drink, was being tried for having "knocked down, killed, maimed, and despoiled many of the good people of *America;*" for a "traiterous-conspiracy with Mr. *Punch,* and Mr. *Flip*" to intoxicate and impoverish the good people of this country.[48]

The witnesses agreed that Richard Rum was responsible for a slew of transgressions against individuals and for colonywide distress. John Vulcan, a blacksmith, attested to his close personal relationship with the defendant. The heat from his trade created an "unquenchable spark in my throat." Other beverages like beer or cider might have worked. "But happening to be acquainted with the prisoner, I became a lover of his company, and when I am once got into his company, he scarce ever parts with me till he has catcht me fast by the noddle, tript up my heels, and laid me fast on my back, so that I have not been able to get up to go to work for two or three days." Vulcan had little doubt that Rum should be punished. Other witnesses conveyed similar tales of woe. William Shuttle, the weaver, claimed that this wicked companion prevented him from working at his loom. Rum lured him to the tavern and kept him there, preventing him from returning to his home. He too supported punishment for Rum. Mr. Snip, the tailor, and Mr. Wheat, the baker, joined the chorus of those testifying against Rum and wished that he be harshly punished for his deeds. Finally, the colonies were called to the witness stand, and they too laid a litany of complaints upon rum— it was responsible for the financial distress of the citizens of Boston, for consuming their labor, and for draining their currency.[49]

Sir Richard Rum mounted a feeble defense. He did not deny his popularity but he informed the court that no one was forced "to keep company" with him. He appeared only when invited. He charged the colonies and cities with hypocrisy, since he was indispensable to their economies. The excise to import rum was a dependable means of revenue. In Barbados and the Islands, rum was the best "branch of trade." It enabled New England to trade its horses, fish, and lumber, and New York, New Jersey, and Pennsylvania to sell their bread, beer, and other provisions.[50]

In the opinion of the jurors, whose names betray their fondness for drink—Benjamin Bumper, Edward Emptypurse, Edward Thirsty, Jonathan Lovedram, John Neversober, Giles Toper, and so on—Richard Rum was not guilty. It was not that the accusations against rum were false or that the ministers had imagined the problems associated with its use. Rather, the jury voted acquittal because it "had become one of the most popular items for purchase by the colonists." Rum had taken its place as the preferred alcoholic beverage in a society in which drinking continued to play a central role. Rum was incorporated into the rituals of the tavern, in displays of respect and sociability, and for the conduct of business. As soon as Sir Richard "got his liberty," he retired "with some friends to a convenient place," most likely a tavern, and summed up the lessons of his trial in song.

There's scarce a tradesman in the land,
    that when from work is come,
But takes a touch (sometimes too much)
    of Brandy or of Rum.

Therefore all honest tradesmen,
    a good word for me give,
And pray that good Sir Richard Rum
    may always with you live.[51]

The debate that echoed loudly from the pulpit and linked concerns about the general health of the Puritan colony to the popularity of rum in public houses culminated in the 1712 law forbidding the sale of rum in taverns. With the increased use of hard liquor by the New England population, religious and civil leaders had lost control over the style and nature of popular drinking. The law was an attempt to regain some of that control, without which total ruin was surely in the not too distant future. The law failed; rum was here to stay. By passing such a law, however, the legislators conveyed the depth of their collective concern and their struggle to return to a more benign drinking past.[52]

Massachusetts superior court justice Samuel Sewall came face to face with his diminished authority when he entered William Wallis's tavern in Boston's South End on a winter's night in 1714. The constable had summoned Sewall to deal with the disorders inside. Those assembled had been inside the tavern all night toasting the queen's health in honor of her birthday, and their merriment continued until well after the official closing time. When Sewall commanded them to disband, the crowd responded by ordering more drinks and by trying to lure him into their revelries. The group hurled insults at Sewall and the provincial government, which, they claimed, had not created a single worthy law. The drama in the tavern, along with Sewall's frustration and embarrassment, illustrate the level of conflict between the laboring classes and provincial authorities. The group of drinkers resented the imposition of law on their gathering, and they expressed their contempt for Sewall's interference. Sewall felt both frustration and rage that the authority he represented no longer commanded an automatic response to his demands.[53]

New England leaders feared that the increased consumption of distilled spirits would result in individuals' careening down the path of sin with no perceivable end, but these concerns did not translate into increased civil prosecutions for drinking- or tavern-related crimes. On the contrary, the overall rate of prosecutions in New England declined in the eighteenth century as compared with the century before. Rather than enlarge their efforts to haul perpetrators of tavern crimes into court, New England authorities focused their attention on particular groups—the problem drinker and members of the laboring or lower classes—and just as in the seventeenth century, churches continued to discipline congregants who drank too much. As a result, these cases never reached the civil courts.

In Plymouth, after its absorption by Massachusetts, the overall rate of prosecution for tavern-related infractions dropped dramatically. Over a ninety-year period, 1686 to 1775, the county court handled only 104 cases, barely one case per year, approximately half of the annual rate for Plymouth Colony, even though the population had increased steadily.[54] Similarly, rates of prosecution in Suffolk County and especially in Boston during the first three decades of the eighteenth century confirm that for all of the ministerial concern with the potential for overindulgence in drink, civil authorities remained unconvinced that the citizenry would drown in a sea of rum. The Suffolk County Court heard a wide variety of infractions, but they prosecuted a smaller number of transgressors than they had in the seventeenth century. The crimes committed included "suffering persons in houses on the Lord's Day," entertaining other men's servants, entertaining men and women in a "suspicious manner," and "haunting" alehouses and "misspending" time.[55]

Courts intervened less often in drink-related cases in part because the abuse of alcohol was defined more narrowly, and the efforts of both civil and church hearings were aimed at persistent drinkers. Members of the church in Halifax, Plymouth County, examined Mrs. Bozworth because they thought her guilty of "sinful frequent and continual following of strong drink." They sought some recourse in case she continued to drink. The ministers warned her that if she fell into the sin of drunkenness again, "this being the 2d time of Conviction," the church would suspend her for some time, to see whether she could avoid further relapses. Sometimes clergy themselves were subject to this failing. Thomas Palmer, who served as the minister of Center Church in Middleboro until 1718, struggled with his attachment to drink. He was removed from his ministry "and suspended from communion at the Lord's table for his scandalous immoralities"—drunkenness. He apparently recovered his reputation, at least somewhat, for he later worked as the town physician. It remains unclear if he regained his place at the Lord's table or if he stopped drinking.[56]

Suffolk County magistrates expressed their concern about drinking styles and the accessibility of hard liquor by trying to control the drinking behavior of those they identified as problem drinkers from a particular stratum of society. The seventeen men who in 1727 were labeled "Drunckard and Comon Tiplers" represented occupations that placed them on the bottom of the urban economic ladder—four shoemakers, three porters, two turners, two laborers, and one each a brick maker, card maker, rope maker, butcher, tanner, and oar maker. We will likely never know if they overindulged together. Perhaps they had gathered in the house of William Thornton, mariner, and his wife Hannah, who in the same month and year entertained people during the divine service and allowed profane cursing, swearing, quarreling, and fighting to occur in their house.[57]

The Boston escapades of Capt. Francis Goelet testify to the latitude allowed taverngoers if they were white men who belonged to the middling or upper classes. Goelet violated tavern laws by engaging in heavy drinking and late-night frolicking, yet no officials came forward to squelch his activities. From 1746 to 1750 Goelet's ship sailed the Atlantic, docking in London and various North American ports. During his days, he took care of business, meeting with merchants, arranging for cargo to be off loaded and loaded, and procuring crew. He reserved his nights for diversion, frequently ending his nightly escapades in the wee hours of the morning.[58]

Goelet's frenetic nighttime activities may have been related to his occupation, a need to maximize his social life on land since he would soon be confined on board his ship. His diary entries read as if his impending departure inspired him. Before one trip he wrote, "Being almost ready to Sale, I determined to Pay my way in time, which I accordingly did at Mrs. Graces at the Request of Mr. Heylegher and the Other Gentlemen Gave them a Good Supper with Wine and Arack Punch Galore, where Exceeding Merry Drinkg Toasts Singing Roareing &c. Untill Morning when Could Scarce see One another being Blinded by the Wine arack &c. We were in all abt 20 in Compy."[59]

In seventeenth-century New England, when individuals of any class remained too long in the tavern, stayed long after closing hours, were found dancing or singing, they risked being called before the court to account for their actions. The legacy of prosecution for drinking- and tavern-related crimes in New England through the eighteenth century reveals a focus on the behavior of the laboring and lower classes. Civil and church authorities believed that it was necessary to monitor the drinking patterns of these classes, to mitigate the effects of hard liquor. No one interfered with Goelet and company, even though his activities took place over many nights and constituted a flagrant violation of the law. Boston's authorities must have been aware of Goelet and his nighttime revelries. On some nights he changed location several times and traveled in the company of many folks. In mid-eighteenth-century New England, middling and upper-class white men had no need to account for their drinking habits or tavern behaviors. This selective application of the law protected Goelet from prosecution.[60]

Rhode Island

The evidence from eighteenth-century Rhode Island towns confirms these trends. From midcentury until the Revolution, magistrates in the larger port towns acted most vigorously against the disorderly house whereas the smaller towns devoted their attention to curbing the appetites of the problem drinker. In both Providence and Charlestown, town councils summoned tavern keepers, like Thomas Addams, who was accused of operating a disorderly house because he allowed Indians "to resort together." The council denied Addams residency and ordered him to leave the town. An Indian council also appeared before the town leaders, claiming that Isaac Dick, "a Molato Fellow," together with his wife and children, kept a disorderly house and entertained Indians and "people's Servants." Few jurisdictions bothered white middle- and upper-class men who violated drinking and tavern laws, but when people of color or unfree people gathered to drink in the tavern, authorities expressed their concerns that the social order might become unhinged. Following the pattern of smaller municipalities, the Gloucester town council brought no action against tavern keepers who failed to maintain order or who illegally served Indians and servants; they did, however, ferret out problem drinkers. In March 1773, the council posted the names of ten "common drunkards" who spent "too much time and money in taverns." Tavern keepers were enlisted in the effort to control problem drinkers. In October 1764 in Cumberland, a Daniel Wetherhead was called to answer the charge that he spent too much time and money in the tavern, risking ruin to himself and his family. All of the town's retailers were warned against selling liquor to him. Similarly, the town of East Greenwich posted the names of four individuals, warning all publicans that they were not to be served.[61]

Pennsylvania

In Pennsylvania, although the rates of prosecution increased during the eighteenth century, the overall incidence of tavern-related crimes remained negligible. From 1695 to the beginning of the American Revolution, Philadelphia city courts found 201 individuals guilty of violating tavern laws. All were involved with operating a disorderly or tippling house, or selling liquor without a license. The Philadelphia Court of Quarter Sessions found 310 individuals guilty in the third quarter of the eighteenth century.[62] The courts in Pennsylvania focused their energies on unlicensed houses. In 1720, tavern keepers in Philadelphia launched a complaint against the unfair competition they endured from the city's unlicensed houses and dramshops. Benjamin Franklin, as chair of the 1744

Philadelphia grand jury, expressed their collective concern about the "vast number of tippling houses within this city." These nurseries of "vice and debauchery," the report claimed, were homes of "profane language, horrid oaths, and imprecations." The grand jury recommended that some method be found to diminish the number of public houses.[63]

Because the Quarter Sessions court interpreted the grand jury's pronouncements as an attack on its licensing procedures and by extension on its authority, the grand jury felt compelled to elaborate. Their alarm was triggered specifically by the increase in the number of public houses and the fact that the establishments were clustering in particular neighborhoods.

"the Grand Jury do . . . still think it their duty to complain of the enormous increase of public houses in Philadelphia, especially since now it appears by the Constable's returns that there are upward of one hundred that have licenses, which, with the retailers, make the houses which sell strong drink, by our compilation, near a tenth part of the city, a proportion which appears to us much too great, since by their number they impoverish one another as well as the neighborhoods they live in, and for want of better customers, nay through necessity, be under greater temptation to entertain apprentices, servants, and even negroes."[64]

These fears may also have come from the accurate perception of what transpired inside disorderly houses. These dens contained all the worst in tavern behavior—drunkenness, brawling, and prostitution. Another side to the fear was that many of these illegal houses were operated by women, who ran a substantial proportion of Philadelphia taverns, both licensed and unlicensed. Thirteen women were indicted between 1720 and 1776 for operating disorderly houses—implicated as brothels or houses of prostitution—or for operating taverns without licenses. A Margaret Cook appeared in court twice. In 1741 she was accused of entertaining and receiving "Whores, Vagabonds, and divers Idle Men of a suspected bad conversation and continually did keep bad order and Government." She seems not to have reformed, for she returned to court almost twenty years later to answer to the charge of keeping a disorderly house. Philadelphia tried but was unable to rid itself of these less respectable public houses.[65]

While Philadelphia courts did prosecute operators of disorderly houses and individuals selling liquor without a license, they did not hear a single case against an individual accused of drunkenness unless the inebriation was combined with some other illegal activity. Sailor Charles Goss was charged with abusing John Wilkinson by "words and blows" at Richard Kee's public house. Goss's defense was that he was "in drink" and therefore did not know what he was doing.[66] Evidence indicates that city elders realized that excessive drinking posed a problem and was getting worse. In 1744, the Philadelphia Grand Jury identified the source of the evil. "The profane oaths and imprecations grown of late so common in our streets, so shocking to the ears of the sober inhabitants tending to destroy in the mind of our youth, all sense of the fear of God and the religion of the oath, owes its increase in great measure to those disorderly houses."[67]

In Philadelphia, problem drinking was handled by the formal mechanism of the Quaker meeting instead of the civil courts.[68] From 1684 through 1776, the three quarterly meetings, at Bucks, Chester and Philadelphia, dealt with 1,037 cases of drunkenness. According to a historian of Quakers, drunkenness was "the most common error in the sectarian category," accounting for almost one-quarter of the meetings' delinquencies. Quakers feared that drunkenness was a stepping stone to other evil behaviors, and sure enough, half of the Friends accused of drunkenness had violated some other church discipline. One drunk Friend passed out in the public highway. One woman was "seen with a young man acting such things as are a shame for a woman to be found doing." Of those disciplined before the meeting, about 3 percent were women.[69]

Pennsylvania Friends considered to have serious problems with alcohol were treated with sympathy by their brethren. When "D.E." of Philadelphia was visited officially by some Friends, he professed his desire to improve; but four months later, in April of 1760, he was ordered by the meeting "to putt out his children" into other Quaker homes, because he had failed to reform. Over the next six months he tried to convince the meeting that he had recovered. However, he relapsed and would have been disowned except that he "begged for forebearance." This pattern continued over the next three years; he improved, then regressed, then improved again. Late in 1763, he was no longer under the scrutiny of the meeting, because he had remained sober. While he recovered his business, no record indicates whether his children returned to him.[70]

When Philadelphia leaders worked to close disorderly houses they were responding to the same set of issues confronting authorities in Boston and New York. Disorderly or tippling houses were synonymous with the existence of "brawling, drunkenness, and prostitution." The alehouses and dramhouses found on the waterfront and in the laboring-class areas of cities were dens of vice and sin and a threat to the social order.[71] In addition, lower-class taverns defied the laws of propriety. By the middle of the eighteenth century, some Philadelphians who lived on the economic margins participated in tavern activities in which the free and the unfree, whites and blacks exchanged stolen goods in an underground economy and participated in illegal sexual activities. The city's watchmen, who patroled the streets and who were charged with keeping order in their wards, forced those responsible for these taverns and those who patronized them to answer for their behavior in court.[72]

Hannah Gooding's story provides a glimpse into the economic network located in Philadelphia's poor waterfront taverns. The Philadelphia Mayor's Court indicted Gooding for selling liquor without a license. She defended herself with the claim that she had a license to sell penny pots of beer. She asked the court for mercy, arguing that if they prevented her from selling beer she would lose her primary means of earning her livelihood, and she would be reduced to begging for public support. The court was unmoved by her plea and refused to renew her license. The decision was based, in part, on her having previously exceeded the limits of her license. However, the court was also paying attention to a more troublesome allegation against Gooding. She and her adult son were known to entertain other men's servants in their waterfront dwelling and to encourage them to "purloin" their masters' goods.[73] By pulling her license to sell alcohol, the court was probably hoping to end her involvement in the underground economy of illicit trade with the city's servant class.

The trade in stolen goods was flourishing in the winter of 1750. The citizenry of Philadelphia were "alarmed by the unusual Frequency of Robberies, Thefts and burglaries." Stores and houses were broken into. Clothing, jewelry, handkerchiefs, silver spoons, a tea chest, and many other items of value were disappearing. The night watch conducted a search in the neighborhood in which those suspected of the crimes lived, but they found nothing. Over a period of time, however, the suspects were rounded up, charged, and taken off to jail to await trial. The court was serious about halting such illegal activity, and the penalties were impressive. While one of the culprits was sentenced to be "burnt in the Hand and his Goods being forfeited were seiz'd by the Sheriff," three men and one woman received sentences of death. Another woman was exonerated, the judge suspecting that she was too weak to act on her own and must have been coerced by her husband.[74]

The records of prosecution for the more rural Chester County confirm that the Quaker colony was not overly concerned with tavern-related offenses, and it substantiates that the problems associated with lower-class taverns were an urban affair. The court records for Chester County are almost continuous from 1681 until the Revolution, and yet only eighty-seven tavern-related cases are recorded. Consistent with the pattern, half of the cases prosecuted involved unlicensed houses or selling liquor without a license in this rural area as compared with 86 percent of the court activity in Philadelphia.[75]

✿ ✿ ✿

BY THE MIDDLE of the eighteenth century, the litany of laws pertaining to the tavern and drinking exhibited a remarkable consistency throughout the North American colonies. Drunkards were accused of misspending their time, and ministers reminded them that overindulging "waste[d] of the good creatures of God."[76] Spending too much money on drink threatened the family's economic well-being. Like their English counterparts, colonial authorities feared that the abuse of drink would have serious social consequences, like crime, riot, disorderly behavior, poverty, and the "overthrow of many good acts and manuall trades." Thus, the authorities who crafted and enforced tavern laws—against drunkenness, Sabbath breaking, and the Indian trade—or who attempted to prevent servants, slaves, minors, and apprentices from being served and limited sailors' access to the tavern and to credit, were legislating against vice.[77]

Rates of prosecution had varied among the colonies during the seventeenth century; authorities in the sectarian colonies litigated with more frequency. During the eighteenth century, the distinctions between the sectarian and nonsectarian colonies softened; the rates of prosecution for crimes related to the tavern and drinking diminished in both. Patterns emerged that reflected the location of the infraction. If a tavern-related crime was committed in an urban area, the likelihood of prosecution was greater than in more rural regions of the

colonies. Indeed, in cases of drunkenness and other violations of personal morality, prosecution rates in New England declined, approaching the levels of the
Chesapeake and southern colonies. Critics in both Virginia and Maryland complained that the laws against immorality were going unenforced, a plea that resembled the wails from their New England counterparts. In Maryland, for example, the governor closed the 1696 session of the colonial legislature with the
admonition that laws were ineffectual if they were unenforced. He charged them
to "put in Execution all the good lawes against Sabbath-breaking, Prophane Cur-
sine and Swearing, Adultery, fornication, etc." No evidence suggests that anyone
was listening or that any action was taken. Rates of prosecution reveal no effect.[78]
The patterns in Pennsylvania mirrored those of the seventeenth century; rather
than prosecute the infractions of individuals, like drunkenness, magistrates confined their attention to controlling the activities inside the tavern. Officials in
New York City, Philadelphia, and Boston feared the disorderly house for the
havoc it wreaked on the ordering of society. Officials passed and revised the laws,
they whined about the debauched behaviors inside taverns, and they shuddered
at the sinister plots contrived by those on society's margins. Fears of urban disorder far outweighed the lingering desire to police individual morality.

The overall decline during the eighteenth century in the rates of prosecution
is linked to a number of impulses. Although the original settlers had embraced
the collective ideal to enforce morality and had passed laws with that intent,
these tendencies had softened by the eighteenth century. Colonial courts devoted their attentions to cases that reflected the emerging capitalism, and civil
authorities abandoned to the churches the responsibility for upholding morality.[79] Those prosecuted in the eighteenth century represented an increasingly
narrow class base. If a violator was a member of the elite or served an elite clientele he or she was less likely to be penalized for an infraction. Magistrates se-
lectively determined which bawdy house needed to be suppressed. If proprietors
allowed a mixture of races and classes to congregate and if they were fencing
stolen goods, the heavy hand of the law descended. If the clientele of the house
represented the "better sort," the house remained, its future secure. Operating
a disorderly house was the most commonly prosecuted violation of tavern law
in the port cities of Boston, New York, and Philadelphia. These taverns offered
their services to individuals on the margins of colonial society, free white men

and women of the laboring classes, the unfree of any race, and persons of color free or unfree. Colonial authorities could not risk mixtures of classes and races, because this threatened to subvert racial and status hierarchies. It was in these disorderly houses that whites and blacks fomented rebellion and participated in the economic anarchy of illegal trade.

That the intent of the courts was social control helps to account for variations in punishments as well. Courts had enormous discretion in their administration of the law.[80] Colonial magistrates could maintain order by controlling the drinking patterns of the laboring classes and preventing unfree persons and persons of color from gathering inside. In these ways, the legal culture of the tavern reinforced gender, racial, and status hierarchies within the colonies.

Licensing Criteria and Law
in the Eighteenth Century:
"Sobriety, honesty and discretion
in the . . . masters of such houses"

William Hartley . . . your petitioner not long ago took a house . . . called
Charles Town house in the county of Chester in order to keep a store of
dry goods and to live privately but has since found that said house being
lately a tavern and many miles distance from any taverns or public houses
is continually infested with travellers who call for and demand [drink] . . .
he has been at great charges in supplying them with bedding and their
horses with proper provender without any consideration or payments. . . .

   Mary Moore . . . widow and relict of William Moore late of Willistown,
your petitioner having these several years lived at a noted stage formerly
and commonly known by the name of the harrow at which place your petitioners husband followed the trade of hatter and having the misfortune
of receiving a wound in his legg by [which] he had his thigh cutt off and
then dying your poor petitioner is reduced very much considering her
present condition and a large sum to the doctor.[1]

*I*n the summer of 1740, William Hartley and Mary Moore, like aspiring public house proprietors throughout the colonies, petitioned the justices of their local court for a license to operate a tavern. They aimed to convince the magistrates that their personal situations warranted a license. William Hartley employed subtle persuasion by claiming that he had little interest in a license and wished to live a private life but that travelers stopped at his house and demanded drink, forcing him, by the laws of hospitality, to provide refreshments and bedding for themselves and their horses. Mary Moore wrote about a different predicament. She had struggled through the injury and then death of her husband and was requesting a license so that she might have the means to support herself. In determining whether to issue William Hartley and Mary Moore licenses, the justices applied a series of criteria. Could these petitioners be trusted to provide food and provisions for persons and their horses? Would they be able to strike a balance between serving ample quantities of alcohol while preventing their clientele from overindulging? Could they ensure good order inside their house?

During the seventeenth century, official sentiment throughout the colonies had expressed a similar ideal about the license to sell alcohol. Officials were to issue licenses to the most qualified, sober individuals, because proprietors were the first line of defense against the possibility that tavern gatherings might degenerate into unlawful behavior and disturb the public peace. Keepers of public houses were to maintain an awareness of persons known to be problem drinkers and prevent them from entering their establishments. They needed knowledge of the law so that they might enforce proper hours of operation, control the length of an individual drinker's stay, deny access to the unfree, refuse credit to sailors and mariners, and prevent rowdy and debauched behavior. Only men could be relied upon to carry out these responsibilities. Women, it was assumed, were too weak to enforce closing times and incapable of refusing service to known drunkards. Licenses were to be dispensed only to those who could be trusted to defend order.

An investigation into licensing laws and procedures throughout the colonies provides clues to the gendered nature of tavern keeping. Three interrelated factors put pressure on those administering the licensing process—a requirement by the crown that colonial leaders collect revenue, a need to issue tavern licenses only to individuals who were deemed qualified to be proprietors, and a desire to control tavern density.

Licensing Procedures, Revenue, and Density

As in England, operating a tavern in any of the North American colonies required a license. The process to obtain a license varied somewhat from colony to colony but in the seventeenth century was usually initiated by petitioning the office of the governor or a provincial level agency. The hopeful applicant stated why he or she was a suitable candidate for selling alcoholic beverages and assured the governor or assembly that his or her house was well equipped to tend to the needs of travelers. By the eighteenth century, the licensing procedures had moved from the provincial level exclusively to a local jurisdiction, the town or county. For example, a Bostonian petitioning for a license would apply to the local selectmen, who made their recommendations to the Court of General Sessions of the Peace. The court then gave final approval. Committees appointed by this court annually visited "the taverns and houses of retailers" in Suffolk County, surrounding Boston, to assess the quality of accommodations, furnishings, and provisions. They also determined whether the current tavern keepers were suited to the employment and ascertained whether any of the towns might be in need of more taverns.[2] Based on this annual tour, the selectmen presented various recommendations. They identified towns that required taverns and listed tavern licenses to be renewed or canceled. Similarly, the first Philadelphia residents desiring to operate a tavern would petition the Provincial Council. William Penn, the colonial proprietor, decided that, beginning in 1697, hopeful publicans would request their licenses from the justices of the Court of Quarter Sessions, who passed on their recommendations to the governor.[3]

Most jurisdictions licensed tavern keepers for an entire year. Rhode Island towns varied this practice. Town councils licensed individuals for discrete purposes and for shorter periods of time. For example, James Rogers of Cumberland was licensed to retail liquor to his workmen in May 1751. A few weeks later the town council clarified that Rogers could not retail liquor to any other persons. John Fisk, also of Cumberland, received a license for two days in May 1763, because a lottery was to be drawn at his house and this event demanded strong

drink. Nathan Staples was allowed to retail liquor on a single day for the celebration of the minister's ordination in October 1771. The town of Exeter issued
Simeon Fowler a license in December 1772 "for Twelve Days at Cristmus." In
the town of Hopkinton, Captain Edward Wells, Jr., was given the liberty of retailing liquor when the militia training occurred at his house. If he ordered the
training to take place at someone else's house, the license was transferred to the
owner of that residence. Attendees at ordinations or militia training expected
generous liquor supplies. The leniency with which towns bestowed licenses for
short-term special events suggests that the restrictions on retailing liquor relaxed
through the eighteenth century even though authorities expressed heightened
concern with problem drinkers.[4]

In its very first year, the Pennsylvania Assembly ordered that anyone keeping an ordinary be required to have a license. As in other colonies, this first law
was intended to check the amount of potential disorder both inside the tavern
and outside on the streets. If tavern keepers did not control their patrons, they
risked losing their licenses and thus their means of securing a living. Pennsylvania lawmakers also responded to a particular concern stemming from the city's
convenient access to the sea and the number of taverns situated near the docks.
Authorities deputized tavern keepers in an attempt to prevent pirates and sea
robbers from committing crimes. Anyone who kept a public house was required
to report to the magistrate the name of "suspected persons coming to their house
to lodge" and to provide a description of the people and their horses.[5]

Although South Carolina lawmakers, as part of their earliest legislation, required licenses for anyone who wished to retail liquor, the statutory record conveys the same tension evident in English law. The tavern and drinking occupy
one side and licensing and bond fees the other. Tavern keepers posted a bond as
a guarantee that their patrons would be well behaved. In 1693, the governor of
South Carolina fretted about "Diverse persons in this province Especially in
CharlesTowne" who kept disorderly houses and retailed strong liquors. This disturbed all of the inhabitants but involved "many poor laboring people especially
seamen" as well as "Great numbers of Negros," who knew that in these houses
they could procure drink with money or whatever else they could bring and no
one would question how they had obtained the payment.[6] The first act to regulate public houses in South Carolina, passed in 1694, may have been in direct re-

sponse to the governor's warning. The preamble to the law lamented the "unlimited number of Taverns, Tapp Houses, and Punch Houses," which resulted in a lack of "sobriety, honesty and discretion in the owners or masters of such houses" and caused an encouragement of drunkenness. It is unclear, however, how the law addressed these particular concerns. In order to prevent these disorders, lawmakers reiterated that drink sellers were required to have a license and to renew the license annually and that any planter who lived outside of the city of Charleston could sell liquor to his neighbors and his laborers, but they could not consume the beverages inside the planter's house.[7]

On the three separate occasions, in 1703, 1710, and 1711, when the laws were reenacted, legislators lamented the "unlimited number of taverns, tap houses and punch houses" and the resulting encouragement of the vices usually associated with drinking and idleness, and so they renewed the requirement that all persons wishing to operate a public house or sell "wine, syder, beer, brandy, rum punch or any strong drink whatsoever" be licensed. In order to prevent, suppress, and punish any misbehavior within the tavern, the governor, any one of the Lord Proprietor's deputies, or any two justices of the peace were empowered to enforce the tavern laws. Drink sellers were to pay a fee for the license and a bond to insure good behavior in their houses. Planters continued selling liquor to their neighbors provided it was consumed at the buyer's residence. Finally, the law noted that several persons "used boats and canoes to carry liquors from plantation to plantation"; this practice, it declared, should cease, since it impoverished "the otherwise sober planters."[8]

While public houses were potential sites for disorders in society, and civil authorities were concerned about this, the governor was understandably reluctant to limit their numbers, because the licensing fees provided him with a reliable income.[9] When the legislators debated the licensing issue in 1711, they disclosed the apparent conflict between limiting the number of taverns and financing the governor. The governor's desire to pocket the money from licensing fees encroached upon what they saw as the greater need to limit the number of public houses. Since the licensing powers rested exclusively with the governor, he was inclined to license as many drink sellers as possible, in order to maximize the fees colleted.[10] The resulting law threatened a stiff fine for anyone who sold "any strong Drink whatsoever, under the Quantity of one Gallon at one Draught" without first obtaining a license. Stiff penalties were also imposed on the Public Receiver, the person who collected the license fee, if it was discovered that any "unfit or unqualified" person had been granted a license to retail liquor. In order to disrupt the relationship between the number of taverns and the revenue, the legislators changed the revenue disbursement so that the governor would no longer receive all of the money collected. Instead, he would be awarded a set sum and the remainder would be deposited into the public treasury. The revised law also required that licenses be issued by the Public Receiver of the Province, but only in consultation with the commissioners, three men who were to oversee all licensing decisions and deny licenses to anyone they thought unfit.[11]

Three decades later, when the South Carolina legislators again revisited the laws that regulated taverns and punch houses, the conditions the law was devised to address had worsened. To add to their difficulties, the legislators figured out that the 1711 law required the consent of three particular commissioners by name, Col. William Rhett, Col. Hugh Grange, and Mr. Ralph Izard or "any two of them"; all had long since died, leaving no one overseeing the issuing of licenses. Even the commissioners' attempts to prevent unfit and unqualified persons from obtaining licenses had, according the legislators, failed; and the province was riddled with taverns, punch houses, and tippling houses, a situation that was proving hurtful to the "common good and welfare" of the colony.[12]

As revised in 1741, the law reorganized the licensing system. The deceased commissioners were not replaced; tavern licenses were to be issued by two justices of the peace, who were to meet twice a year for this purpose. The colony's treasurer could no longer grant licenses without approval by the justices. If the order form for a license did not include a precise location of the public house, the application would be voided. This law included a new twist. The justices of the peace could deny a license to any person who had practiced the "trade of carpenter, joiner, bricklayer, plaisterer, shipwright, wheel-wright, smith, shoemaker, taylor, tanner, cabinet maker, or cooper" and who was capable of working at these employments and earning a proper livelihood.[13] This provision appears to have been aimed at limiting the number of people eligible for licenses while protecting those for whom tavern keeping was the only means of procuring a living. By denying licenses to the city's artisans, the law also hints at the potential problems associated with drinking establishments that catered to laborers. Perhaps the specter of tailors and tanners drinking and talking together raised the collective eyebrows of the provincial leaders. Those gathered might organize an action against those in power or decide that their rates and fees should be raised.

Although no further amendments were added to tavern regulations before the Revolution, the South Carolina Assembly continued their debate on how best to disburse license fees and bonds and expressed their collective concern over the number of public houses. Governor James Glen, who sparred with the colony's elected officials through the duration of his term, asked the legislative body, in 1748, to reconsider the amount the governor received from licensing fees. He noted that inflation had reduced the annual payment to the governor to a mere pittance, and he requested that the fees be set and disbursed in such fashion that he would earn six hundred pounds.[14] Although the record does not make clear whether the governor's share was increased, Governor Glen was granted the powers necessary to regulate the number of taverns and punch houses.[15]

Maryland and Virginia lawmakers waited for almost four decades after settlement to establish a licensing system. The Maryland Assembly, prompted by its need to control proprietors' misbehavior, in 1674 empowered the governor to license taverns.[16] By 1678, lawmakers had moved even further from their initial position. They no longer passively accepted the need for taverns to provide services to travelers, and they worked to limit the number of taverns. Maryland's leaders grew increasingly disturbed by their inability to control various abuses. They specified where taverns could be located and increased the bond for licensees.[17]

The pressures to create a licensing system were similar in Virginia. Legislators were trying to protect the colony's financially vulnerable planters from squandering their resources on alcohol or being price-gouged by greedy tavern keepers.[18] In addition, the sparsely settled landscape of the Chesapeake and its southern neighbors ensured that taverns were never plentiful and, as a result, they appear to have offered a less obvious site of debauchery than they did in the more densely settled Puritan north or the Quaker communities. It was not until the March 1660–61 session that the members of the Virginia General Assembly articulated the relationship between the tavern and liquor abuse. This law explicitly reveals the dual purposes of control and revenue; it instituted a licensing fee of 350 pounds of tobacco.[19]

Colonial governors depended upon various kinds of licensing fees as a source of revenue. The governor of Pennsylvania in 1704 stated it most baldly: "Whereas, ye assembly had not made any manner of Provision for ye Support of ye govmt, and there is a necessity that money be raised for Defraying its incident Charges, by all such just & reasonable wayes as ye Law will allow of, & ye Licensing of Publick Houses in all Govmts in Am'ca., being a perquisite belonging wholly to ye Governs, of wch some Profit is usually made. It was, therefore, Proposed to ye Board to consider what might be reasonable to take for every such License."[20] The governor was asking the Provincial Council to determine what amounts could reasonably be collected from fees for licensing public houses. The council responded by creating a licensing fee schedule. Tavern keepers who sold only wine paid the governor five pounds, only beer fifty shillings; and "for every well customed Ordinary, that keeps not stables & sel's no wine, four pounds." During the final session of 1710, the Provincial Council amended the licensing law. The cost of a license continued to be based on what alcoholic beverages were sold and which services were rendered, but now graduated fees took into account where the tavern was located. A license to operate a tavern cost more in Philadelphia than in the outlying towns of the colony.[21]

Charles Thomson, a Philadelphia merchant, accused the governor of Pennsylvania of being far more concerned with his "handsome fixed annual Salary" from tavern licenses than with regulating the tavern trade. In a letter addressed to Benjamin Franklin in 1764, Thomson reported that on the first day of his journey he traveled for thirty-two miles up the Lancaster Road and lodged "at the 19th Tavern." He admitted that the road was heavily traveled and that that "in some measure excused" the number of taverns. However, he complained, less frequented roads were no less endowed with public houses. This plethora of taverns, he claimed, created a population in which people's manners were debauched, "their bodies enervated, their time and Money uselessly dissipated." Thomson argued that this situation existed because licensing fees were used to line the governor's pockets rather than regulate public houses.[22]

Again Rhode Island's policies differed from the norm. The individual towns set the licensing fees, not a legislative body or the governor. The Rhode Island Assembly expressed its concern when some towns reported that the amount of the licensing fee, set by the colony, was insufficient to be effective, especially in the case of public houses that had "great trade and custom." The assembly resolved the problem by giving each town council the right "to raise the price or value to be paid by such licensed persons, to such greater sum or sums as they shall think needful, not exceeding ten pounds for each license."[23]

To Approve or Disapprove

Licensing laws were part of the originating legal structure in all of the colonies. The attempt during the seventeenth century to control who operated a public house emerged from the shared ideal that law should enforce individual morality. Tavern keepers acted as an informal police force to control the public's use of alcohol and their behavior inside the tavern. During the eighteenth century, tavern keepers assumed even greater responsibility for maintaining order in their establishments, because courts no longer prosecuted individuals who occasionally drank too much or stayed too long in the tavern. Magistrates directed their legal arsenal at the operation of disorderly houses and the sale of alcohol to Indians. John Adams linked the quality of a public house and the likelihood of decorum within it to the propriety of the publican. He contended that houses run by lower-class proprietors "become the eternal haunt of loose, disorderly people of the same town, which renders them offensive and unfit for the entertainment of a traveller of the least delicacy." Adams included the familiar concern that these public houses debauched the youth, but he added new fears. Strangers, he claimed, "are apt to infer the character of a place from that of the taverns and the people they see there. But the very worst effect of all, and which ought to make every man who has the least sense of his privileges tremble, these houses are become in many places the nurseries of our legislators." These officials, Adams claimed, were guaranteed the votes of tavern keepers and retailers by approving their licenses and could count on the support of "the rabble" by making sure they had ample establishments in which to drink. Adams did recommend a solution: if a tavern was run by a proper individual, it would appeal to an appropriate clientele and the roots of disorder would disappear.[24]

One purpose of licensing the proprietors of taverns was to ensure that only those "deemed of suitable character" could retail spirituous liquors. Exactly what this meant was ordinarily left vague and subjective but implied that only sober and honest individuals were to be trusted with selling intoxicating beverages and tending to the needs of travelers. Since colonial officials presumably renewed the licenses of tavern keepers who ran orderly, law-abiding establishments and refused renewal to those who did not, it was in the proprietor's best interest to ensure that customers behaved themselves. Licensing only "qualified" persons did not, however, result in a coherent enforcement of policy.

In a few selected moments, lawmakers specified whom they deemed un-qualified to operate a tavern. In 1685, the Common Council of New York City determined that "noe Jew ought to Sell by Retaile." The councilors did not elaborate about why a Jew could not be a trustworthy purveyor of alcohol nor did they record why in the case of Saule Browne, they were willing to compromise and recommend him if the governor agreed. Browne was not entitled to a full license but was allowed to sell liquor wholesale. A 1749 North Carolina law specified that "no person keeping ordinary be recommended to the governor to be appointed sheriff for any county." Lawmakers must have been attempting to redress some perceived conflict when sheriffs doubled as tavern proprietors. Perhaps they suspected that order and decorum would be of secondary interest to profits and sales. In any case, the law apparently had little effect. Deputy sheriff Robert Love, a resident of Cumberland County, North Carolina, was granted a license in 1756 that was renewed annually until 1762. In addition, Neil McNeil, who was a constable and William Dawson, Hector McNeil, and Stephen Phillips, who were justices, were licensed during this same period. Searching for proprietors that would maintain order was apparently not an essential quality: Robert Bennerman's petition for a tavern license was rejected twice in 1763 because he kept "bad rules and unlawful gaming in his house." However, three months later the court relented and Bennerman received his license.[25]

Virginia lawmakers prohibited proprietors of taverns from being jurors. Their motivation is unclear. Perhaps it was that courts required access to taverns while in session and tavern keepers needed to be available and vigilant to fulfilling the magistrates' needs. Or, lawmakers may have feared that the tavern keepers, because they offered the community drink and sociability, might have been capable of exerting undo pressure on their peers by threatening to withhold their services if they failed to return a particular verdict. A tobacco inspector was also forbidden to keep a tavern "at or near the warehouse where he is an inspector."

Lawmakers must have anticipated a conflict of interest between the roles of inspector and seller of drink. The inspector might be unable to carry out his tasks with objectivity and fairness, or his clients might feel obligated to drink exclusively in his establishment.[26]

Licensing Women

The gendered nature of tavern licensing in early America followed a pattern similar to that of England. In the early fourteenth century, selling ale was a common practice in English towns and countryside and the great majority of the sellers were women. The socioeconomic position of these women was mixed—a significant proportion came from the upper stratum of society; slightly fewer were from lower-class families. Significantly, although large numbers of people dispensed ale—in some towns as many as half of the population was engaged in this activity—only a small proportion did so from a building identified as a tavern or inn. Most commonly, individuals brewed and sold small quantities from a variety of sites. They dispensed pails full of ale from their houses; their customers carried them home. Or, they set up in make-shift stalls in the market or placed themselves near a town's annual fair. During the time when ale selling was on a small scale and intermittent, women dominated the trade.[27]

As the trade began to acquire a more organized basis and alehouses "became more formalised," women's dominance faded. Drinking continued to take place outside the tavern, but the public house developed into an increasingly important site of sociability. By 1500, the great majority of licensed drink sellers in England were male. While the transition took place more quickly in cities and towns, it happened everywhere. Young or single women who sold drink on their own became morally suspect and their attempts to sell legitimately were quashed. Town leaders in Chester, for example, while acknowledging that young women had in the past sold drink, in 1540 passed an ordinance that explicitly banned women aged 14 to 40 from participating in the trade.[28]

Although English officials preferred that men operate public houses, they willingly issued licenses to women in some instances. Widows, for example, were likely to be granted the right to sell liquor. With their husband's death, women often lost their economic base, and their struggle would have been compounded if they had to care for small children. In these cases administrators looked more favorably upon women as candidates for licenses, because on balance it was more prudent to issue a license than to have to support them. Similarly in 1594, the Privy Council added the honest, sober elderly to their list of likely female proprietors. Although magistrates preferred that women and the poor refrain from running alehouses, their distaste for licensing them was more than offset by the advantage gained by keeping them off the poor roles.[29]

This informal policy continued in Tudor-Stuart England; officials favored men as the proprietors of public houses. Women played a role in their day-to-day operation, and popular lore maintained that successful businesses depended upon women's labors. At times, the alehouse was a family's second business. Men officially held the license, and their wives were charged with running the enterprise while their spouses pursued their trades. Sometimes both the husband and wife participated; ballads extolled just how economically valuable an attractive wife could be for business. "She welcomed guests, plied them with liquor and kept them happy with smiles, kisses and sometimes more intimate favors." Wives also developed reputations as shrewd business people: one tough, no nonsense wife confiscated a male customer's possessions, including his clothes, and refused to return them until he settled the bill. Some female publicans displayed formidable personalities: in Norfolk, Margaret Molle, was reputed to have kept a lover in the house despite protests from her husband. But operation of an English alehouse was rarely a woman's show. A woman primarily served at the whim of her husband or master, and the drudgery of the labor and the likely abuse from customers were her most common accompaniments.[30]

In the colonies, as in England, women were more likely to be the proprietors of taverns in cities, especially port cities, than in smaller towns or the countryside. Despite a declared preference for authorizing male tavern keepers, colonial cities issued a substantial portion of the tavern licenses to women (see Table 5.1). Women's significance as proprietors varied little throughout the eighteenth century.[31] Women maintained a notable presence as drink sellers in Philadelphia. In Charleston, South Carolina, in all but one year in the fifteen years before the Revolution, female tavern keepers outnumbered their male counterparts, reaching a numerical apex in 1771, when women accounted for almost two-thirds of Charleston's drink seller licenses.[32]

Beyond the cities, women held an insignificant number of tavern licenses. The records from North Carolina, Pennsylvania, and Massachusetts counties reveal

TABLE 5.1
Women Tavern Keepers in Colonial Port Cities

	Years	Number of Women Licensees	Percentage of Total Licensees
Boston	1690, 1696,		
	1707, 1708, 1718	134	41.2
	1736–37	127	41.9
	1764–65	119	41.6
New York	1759–60	91	15.0
	1763	42	14.7
Philadelphia	1762–63	69	24.4
	1770	45	29.6
Charleston	1762–63	75	48.3
	1767–69	177	53.3
	1771–74	244	55.5

SOURCES: David Conroy, *In Public Houses: Drink and the Revolution of Authority in Colonial Massachusetts* (Chapel Hill, N.C., 1995). New York Mayor's Office, Tavern Keeper's License Book, 1757–1766, New-York Historical Society. Secretary's Office Ledger A; Licenses for Marriages, Taverns, Peddlers; Philadelphia County, Historical Society of Pennsylvania, AM 2014. Charleston: *South Carolina Gazette.*

that even at their height of tavern-keeping women held only 16 percent of the licenses (see Table 5.2).[33] For the period, 1734 to 1736, Worcester County, Massachusetts, licensed only men. The records from Suffolk and Plymouth counties, Massachusetts, confirm how few women received tavern licenses there; through the last decade and a half of the seventeenth century, Plymouth County issued a license to only one woman (1% of applicants). Similarly, during most of the 1670s, Suffolk County magistrates licensed only men. By the eighteenth century, women gradually appear in the records as licensed drink sellers in these non-urban areas; however, they continued to hold a minority of the licenses, never achieving more than 16 percent of the total.[34]

The situation in regions with mixed urban and rural landscapes exemplifies women's relationship to tavern keeping. If Philadelphia County is examined in its entirety, women represented a small proportion of licensees (12%). Within the Northern Liberties and Southwark, however, regions of the county that were becoming increasingly urbanized, the proportion of women tavern keepers (26.7% in 1763) mirrored that of Philadelphia. While women accounted for a small proportion of the tavern keepers in Plymouth County, Massachusetts, almost half of the women licensed during the first three decades of the seventeenth century (6 of 14) resided in Plymouth Township.[35]

The higher proportion of women tavern keepers and drink sellers in urban

TABLE 5.2
Women Tavern Keepers in Rural Areas

	Years	Total Number of Taverns	Number of Women Licensees	Percentage of Total Licensees
MASSACHUSETTS				
Plymouth County	1686–99	104	1	1.0
	1700–45	890	65	7.3
Suffolk County	1737	57	9	15.8
	1762	39	5	12.8
PENNSYLVANIA				
Philadelphia County	1754–74	525	63	12.0
Northern Liberties and				
Southwark, Phila. Co.		203	40	19.7
Chester County	1736–74	591	53	9.0
NORTH CAROLINA				
Craven County	1749–55	22	1	4.5
	1772	20	3	15.0
Cumberland County	1759–64	104	3	2.9
New Hanover County	1759–61			
	1764–65	29	4	13.8
Orange County	1753–66	122	3	2.5

SOURCES: "Names of Persons licensed in the County of Suffolk, James Otis Sr. papers," 1642–1747, box 1; Miscellaneous Bound, Massachusetts Historical Society, vols. 1688–1694, 1695–1698, 1699–1705, 1706–1713, 1714–1718, 1719–1722, 1734–1740, 1741–1748, 1749–1755, 1756–1760, 1761–1765, 1766–1769. Licenses for Marriages, Taverns, Peddlers; Secretary's Office, Ledger A, Philadelphia County, Historical Society of Pennsylvania, AM 2014. North Carolina Court of Common Pleas, North Carolina State Archives, Raleigh, N.C.

areas reflects in part a denser population and a larger number of female-headed households. The General Court of Massachusetts limited the number of taverns and retailers in smaller towns to a single establishment, thus the opportunities for tavern keeping were more circumscribed. Almost invariably these licenses were reserved for prominent male residents, like militia officers or selectmen.[36] No quotas on the number of taverns existed for Boston and the larger seaport towns, so the odds were better for women in the more populous regions. In addition, single women were more likely to reside in cities. The major port cities "contained a disproportionate number . . . of white widows," while they were a negligible presence in rural townships.[37]

Women on their own presented a particular challenge to colonial officials, and it is quite clear that many jurisdictions opted to grant women licenses rather than have them depend upon the city for support. While the law stipulated that only honest and upright, and preferably male, persons were qualified to receive a tavern license, officials did take into account the petitioner's economic position. In the 1680s, Sarah Rowell of Amesbury, Massachusetts, reported to the selectmen that she had been deserted by her husband. They supported her petition for a license to sell strong drink. In 1681, Samuel and Elizabeth Norden petitioned the Suffolk County, Massachusetts, General Court for the privilege of operating a house of entertainment, stressing that they were both ancient and that Samuel was unable otherwise "to worke to procure a subsistance for himself and his family." In the same year, Joseph How asked the court to reconsider its decision not to renew his license, which he had lost, even though no one had ever filed a complaint against him, when the justices denied some licenses in order to reduce the number of public houses in Boston. He had recently suffered severe misfortune, having lost his goods in a fire and having been shot in the hand, disabling him. His entire hope for procuring his own living rested upon having his license reinstated. Another elderly petitioner, Hugh March of Newbury, Massachusetts, claimed that the town had searched for years to find a proper proprietor for its tavern and that numerous townsfolk had urged him to apply for the license and he was persuaded to do so. March noted that it had been "the usual practice of courts and towns to put antient persons in to such places and callings."[38]

Licensing these sorts of persons seems contrary to the moral and business philosophies of the time. Colonists assumed that any impoverished person of either gender who had experienced economic failure suffered from character flaws. Women carried a double burden. Colonial leaders judged them unworthy by virtue of their sex and shortcomings, a condition exacerbated by their financial status. Many women petitioners explained that it was their poverty that compelled them to apply for a license. Officials likely awarded licenses to the elderly, infirm, and poor because it made good economic sense. The license provided them with the means to support themselves so they would be less likely to require public support. The selectmen may also have been genuinely moved by the predicament in which these folks were mired and believed that as civic leaders they had a moral obligation to provide assistance.

Boston officials sought to mitigate what they saw as the negative effects of licensing women by awarding men and women different types of licenses. Of the twenty-three licenses granted in Boston in 1673, thirteen were for public houses of entertainment—providing lodging, meals, and alcohol—and an additional five licenses were awarded for cook shops, effectively restaurants that served wine and beer with the food but offered no lodging. Women held only three of the tavern licenses and two of those for cook shops. Even within this breakdown women were more restricted and were relegated to lesser establishments. Elizabeth Connigrave's cook shop was licensed to serve only "one penny quart beer"; she was subsequently accused of exceeding her license. Jane Barnard had a tavern license but she could serve only coffee and bottled cider. The most elaborate inns in town were operated by men.[39]

Women were increasingly relegated to the less lucrative retail business of selling out-of-doors. Table 5.3 reveals that while the magnitude of the licenses given to women changed little from 1708 to 1736, the proportion of tavern licenses awarded to women became smaller and smaller. In 1735, Ann Lewis petitioned the Court of General Sessions for a license, explaining that her husband had recently died "in a very deplorable manner." She was now left as the sole support of her five children and was truly destitute. She was well situated for operating a tavern; she lived close to several shipyards and mast maker's yards, "where great numbers of labourers are constantly employed" and she claimed that no one was licensed to retail liquor in her neighborhood. Even though the selectmen described Lewis favorably, as a person of "sober conversation," and agreed that she had suitable accommodations, was well situated and could handle this sort of employment, they issued her a license to retail strong liquors only out-of-doors "at the house where she now dwells."[40] Had Lewis been a man, presented the selectmen with the same personal history and character qualities, and offered the same promise of a large clientele, she would likely have been given a tavern license.

Women who did run taverns were responsible for very diverse sorts of public houses. They did not, however, typically manage the best establishments. When the Old London Coffee House opened in Philadelphia in 1754, its owners advertised for a man who had experience running a "good establishment and could entertain his customers well." An applicant for the position of tavern keeper of the newly established City Tavern in Philadelphia, in 1773, explained that he felt qualified for this job, because he had kept a public house in Dublin, Ireland, where he entertained noblemen and gentlemen to their great satisfaction. He also promised letters of recommendation from a number of elite men in Philadelphia, since he had provided them with good service. The taverns in Williamsburg catered to the colony's legislators and gentry and, with the excep-

TABLE 5.3
Drink-Selling Licenses Held by Women in Boston

Year	Number of Tavern	Number of Retail	Total Licenses	Percentage Tavern	Percentage of Total Licenses
1708	15	16	31	48.4	43.1
1718	10	19	29	34.5	35.0
1736	4	52	56	7.1	43.8

SOURCES: Data from David W. Conroy, *In Public Houses: Drink and the Revolution of Authority in Colonial Massachusetts* (Chapel Hill, N.C., 1995).

tion of Christiana Campbell's Tavern, were managed by men. Women only rarely operated taverns described as genteel places with good entertainment.[41]

Women's placement in the hierarchical ordering of New England society made them inherently less qualified than men to operate taverns. While early American society expected women to serve men, and this function constituted an important part of the tavern proprietor's duties, women were also obligated to obey men. Like all proprietors of public houses, female tavern keepers were responsible for what transpired inside and for governing the conduct of their male patrons. Leaders feared that this situation—women ruling men—would subvert the order Puritans were obligated to protect. Moreover, it was assumed that women were incapable of commanding men to behave properly and that their houses would become the sites of great disorders. Issuing licenses to women for selling liquor out-of-doors limited their responsibilities; in that setting they constituted no more of a threat to the Puritan order than women who were shopkeepers or seamstresses.[42]

Since "qualified" publicans were by definition male, women labored under considerable disadvantage in their quest for licenses. To balance the pressure against licensing women, officials might achieve a compromise by placing men in supervisory roles over them. When the Boston officials approved Widow Franke's petition for a license to keep a tavern, they did so "provided yt Samuell Bosworth keepe ye house or some other carefull & suffitient man to manage it." Something convinced the selectmen that it was in their best interest to issue a license to Widow Franke, yet they were unsure that she could be entrusted with the responsibility. Male oversight was the only way to ensure good order in Widow Franke's house.[43] The Boston selectmen granted Goody (Goodwife) Upshall's petition for a license to "draw beer" in 1663 with the caveat that she commit "the trust and care" of the business "to some able honest man, whom the Towne men shall approve of." Like many women licensed to serve alcoholic beverages in early America, Goody Upshall acquired the license that had been granted to her husband. Usually this occurred after the husband's death, but not in Upshall's case, and the selectmen may have felt that she especially needed supervision because of her husband's behavior. Nicholas Upshall's troubles began in 1656 when he was fined twenty-five pounds and banished from Massachusetts for having Quaker sympathies. When he returned to Boston, he was immediately jailed; and though his wife's petition to the government for his release was successful, he was again admonished to leave Boston for Dorchester, where he was confined to the house of his brother-in-law, John Capen. Goody Upshall received her first license to draw beer in the year during which Nicholas was banished. In hysterical reaction to the Quaker presence in Boston, the selectmen may have feared that she would abuse her position as a tavern proprietor by serving heretical views along with her punch.[44]

The selectmen may have been willing to take the risk and issue Franke and Upshall licenses because otherwise both would have been unable to earn a living and would have required town support. Their decision proved to be a good one at least in the case of Upshall. She sold beer until her death in 1675, and no records exist to suggest that her house was the site of disorder nor is there any indication that she required public assistance.

John Carnes's route to a tavern license casts further doubt on how seriously the selectmen weighed impeccability of character and flawlessness of credentials in those they recommended as tavern proprietors. Carnes's career as a minister began quite auspiciously. By the time he was 23, he was invited to preach at Cambridge and in that same year, 1746, was ordained at the First Congregational Church in Stoneham.[45] Only four years into his ministry in Stoneham, his compensation had dropped from 240 pounds to 28 pounds. If that was not a sufficient indication that his congregants were unhappy with his performance, the parsonage they had been constructing remained unfinished, its lands were too meager to support a horse and two cows, and when Carnes complained, the congregants responded by cutting his salary further.

Carnes's problem appears to have been primarily one of style: "His talents were small and his manners displeasing but his simplicity had no vice in it. . . .

We used often to laugh at Carnes, but there was many a worse man in our wicked world."[46] Carnes slowly came to realize that he was no longer welcome at Stoneham and in 1757 he began a series of moves. He stayed briefly in Lynn and in Wrentham, worked for a Rehoboth, Massachusetts, congregation and finally settled in Boston. In August 1766 he applied for a license to operate a tavern out of his rented house in South Boston. The selectmen rejected his petition, but two years later, they reversed their decision.[47] Perhaps they considered that Carnes's Harvard degree was more emblematic of his character than was his failed ministerial career. They did not, however, have sufficient faith in him to grant him a tavern license. He was allowed to sell liquor only out-of-doors, at his house in Orange Street.

Only rarely did the Boston selectmen indicate why they had denied licenses to particular individuals. The selectmen labeled Samuel Moale as someone who was not "of a sober conversation," and they deemed John Sale as incapable of "keeping good rule in His House." Samuel Kendall came very close to receiving a license due to his perseverance. After four unsuccessful petitions, the General Court was poised to issue Kendall a license during their October 1705 session unless they heard otherwise from the selectmen. As a recent arrival to Boston, Kendall's character was scrutinized by the selectmen with some care to insure that he was an upstanding citizen and a likely candidate for a license. The selectmen discovered that he had recently been convicted of "Keeping bad orders in his House" and they concluded that since this was likely to occur again, he was "not a Sutable person to be admitted to keep a Tavern in this Town." The selectmen held firm to their decision even though Kendall had moved into a house that had previously been a tavern and he had support from its former proprietor. Kendall must have raised their suspicions, because most petitions representing the continuation of an ongoing establishment were approved.[48] To determine Mary Clapham's fitness for a license in 1758, the selectmen visited her house, after which they ruled to disallow her petition. They explained that she, "in the year past upon good Information given them, had been guilty of Misrule &c." Clapham requested that the court reconsider her application. She claimed that the selectmen's accusations were without foundation, that they had failed to identify specific allegations, and that they appeared motivated less by the nature of her business than by their desire to ruin her and propel her family into poverty.[49]

Clapham lost her appeal. However, the case record offers convincing evidence that Clatham's character was not the overriding issue commanding the selectmen's attention. The exchange between the selectmen and the court descended into a confrontation over who had jurisdiction in these matters, rather than a deliberation about what attributes made Clapham inadequate to operate a public house. The selectmen, although asked to, were never compelled to articulate the nature of Clapham's misrule. Rather, they raised their hackles at the mere thought that their judgment had been questioned. They were obligated by the law, they proclaimed, to report any license holder who did not keep "good Order & good rules in their Houses," and they had the power based on the law "to decide the Question, as to the fitness or unfitness of Persons to have their Licenses renewed." It was an insult to their integrity, they protested, to be asked to specify precisely the behavior in question, and they had "never heard of a Precedent to make Selectmen Accountable for their Judgments." Nor, they wrote, could they find anywhere a law to "Countenance Such a procedure." While protecting their turf, they made it impossible for Clapham to counter the accusations hurled against her; as a result, she lost the legal right to pursue her livelihood.[50]

Although the Boston selectmen guarded their authority with a vengeance, they did on occasion reconsider and reverse their licensing decisions. At their August 20, 1767, meeting, even though they had initially refused to renew the licenses of Richard Sylvester, Hezekiah Usher, Dorothy Turner, and John Stibbins, they overturned their judgment and issued licenses to all of them. The selectmen explained neither what had precipitated the rejections nor what had changed their minds.[51]

When women applied for licenses in the middle colonies or New England, they were usually motivated by an immediate and extreme economic need. At least half of the women licensed in Plymouth County, Massachusetts, took over the licenses of their deceased husbands. Joseph Barstow was licensed to operate a tavern in Hanover, Plymouth County, in 1727; from 1728 through 1731 the license was issued to his widow, Mary. Of the forty-eight women licensed between 1743 and 1774 in Chester County Pennsylvania, thirty were widows asking for the ability to continue their husband's tavern trade. Some of these women operated taverns for a fairly long period of time; Mary Briant ran her Plymouth Township tavern for eight years after the death of her husband, Jonathan, in

1730. Most women had their licenses renewed for fewer than four years. While men kept a license on average for just under seven years (6.9), their widows averaged less than half that amount of time (3.2 years). Women who obtained licenses on their own held them, on average, for less than three years.[52] In part, these data may reflect women's marital status; if a widow remarried, she was likely to give up the license altogether or transfer it to her new husband. Anne Bowcock fits this profile. Her husband Henry had operated a tavern in Williamsburg, Virginia, from 1716 until his death in 1730. The newly widowed Anne received his license, but when she married Henry Wetherburn, he claimed the business as proprietor.[53] This arrangement suited the preferences of the magistrates for male proprietors of taverns.

Alice Guest's story, while it conforms to the pattern of women widowed young who sought a license to sell liquors as a means to survive after the death of their husbands, has some unique features and displays her business ingenuity. George and Alice Guest emigrated from England to Philadelphia in 1683. George Guest listed his trade as "whitesmith," a tinsmith; but he petitioned William Penn in November 1683 for a warrant to establish a brickworks on some land located on the Delaware River between Front Street and the Delaware, bounded to the north by what would become Chestnut Street and to the south by Crooked Billet Alley. The land was among the worst possible, a steep bank, but it gave him proximity to the city's docks and wharves.

When George died in 1685, Alice applied for a license to operate a tavern in the cave she occupied in the bank of the river. That she lived in a cave implies that her economic resources were limited. Her lengthy stay on this site, however, indicates a different aspect of her circumstances. Her business grew gradually until by the end of her career, she was quite successful. In the cave, she was ideally positioned to provide tavern services to the increasingly large numbers of immigrants pouring into the colony by ship and to the men engaged in the sea trades—merchants, mariners, chandlers, and ship carpenters. In her first year of operation she amassed sufficient funds to post a bond on her business. Her prosperity apparently continued; when the city of Philadelphia moved to evict all of the cave dwellers, she, along with a few others, was exempted, because her property had achieved a certain value. By this time, Alice Guest's financial situation offered her a choice about the location of her tavern, and her decision to remain in the cave may reveal that her establishment had a solid reputation with a regular clientele. The cave might have given her tavern a distinctive atmosphere, a unique rock interior that set it apart from other public houses. By the time of her death, in 1693, she had received a patent to the land, built a structure to house her tavern, erected a wharf out from her river front, along which she constructed warehouses and a dwelling, and she had acquired another residence.[54]

Rachel Draper used the same strategy after she too was widowed. Draper's husband, a tailor, died in 1763 leaving her with three small children to support, the younger two about 2 and 4 years old. She petitioned the Philadelphia court to open a dram shop and asked that, in addition to providing food and beverages, she be approved to take in boarders. Her request was approved and by 1770, a city constable recorded that Draper resided in High Street Ward and that her household included one lodger. Draper never achieved the economic success of Alice Guest; indeed she operated her dram shop out of a house she rented. She was, however, able to support her family without having to ask for public assistance.[55]

Women proprietors in the South present a different profile than their counterparts in the North. Most women who sold drink or operated taverns in Boston, Philadelphia, and New York were either single or widowed. In Charleston, while some women inherited the business from their deceased husbands, far more of the city's female publicans were married. In 1767, Henry Fulcker, a Charleston "Vitner and Hoster" applied for sole trader status for his wife Hester. This agreement entitled her to keep any profits she earned from her tavern and protected her from any debts incurred by her husband. The document suggests that their businesses operated separately. However, given his occupation, it is likely that Hester procured her wine from Henry. Two other Charlestonians, Anne Bishop and her husband, John, were licensed to operate a tavern for six years, from 1767 to 1773. Anne held the license for the first three years, her husband for the second three. The same was the case for George and Margaret Calhoun. She was issued a license for two years for their tavern on King Street; George was licensed for one year in 1771.[56]

The number of tavern licenses held by married women was sufficiently high in Charleston that magistrates expressed concern about the undo influence exerted upon the female proprietors by their husbands. Colonial officials apparently assumed that women merely acted as their husbands' agents. In particular, there was concern about one category of "unfit persons" who were licensed— "constables' and watchmen's wives." The Grand Jury predicted a conflict of interest if the wives of constables and watchmen operated taverns. Rather than working to suppress the evils of drink and to discourage the frequenting of the public house, as was the duty of these officials, they might, motivated by profit, be inclined to encourage this behavior.[57]

A combination of factors helps to explain why married women held tavern licenses in Charleston. A portion of the South Carolina population was among the wealthiest in North America, and colonial lawmakers designed laws to guard that wealth, including specific acts to protect women. They established a liberal standard for feme covert businesswomen, who were allowed to separate their earnings from their husbands'. Prenuptial agreements were honored, and a high proportion of women made such contracts, to protect the property they brought with them into marriage. The nature of sole trader status in South Carolina contrasts dramatically when compared with Pennsylvania, the only other colony that enacted feme sole statutes. Pennsylvania limited the status "to women whose husbands did not support them." For female residents of South Carolina, sole trader status was available to any woman. The high proportion of married women who held tavern licenses demonstrates the colony's strong commitment to the rights of married women. South Carolina wives were actively engaged in family businesses and achieved a measure of autonomy long before women in other colonies did.[58] (Figure 14, in the next chapter, shows the proportion of female to male tavern keepers in Charleston in the mid-1700s.)

Vagaries and Inconsistencies

It is difficult to determine what criteria magistrates used to determine whether an individual qualified for a tavern license. Violating the law did not necessarily give one a negative character rating. Tavern keepers convicted of committing a crime retained their license after their first offence, assuming they could pay the fine. A second offense, however, was supposed to result in loss of the license. James Cole, a Plymouth Colony resident, appeared before the Plymouth court for selling wine without a license and for tolerating various disorders in his house. The judges prohibited Cole from drawing "any wine or strong water until the next General court" and subsequently fined him. The General Court evinced a short memory, for in January 1645, Cole was issued a license to operate one of the two ordinaries in Plymouth, and he did so for almost three decades.[59]

James Cole's career as a tavern keeper and his ability to operate a public drinking house after being accused and convicted of both selling liquor without a license and operating a disorderly house suggests that he held some privileged position in Plymouth. The circumstances surrounding his first license were unusual. Two people petitioned to operate ordinaries and even though the court noted that Cole's house was "inconveniently" located for travelers, he was issued a license. In addition, his license limited him to the sale of wine and he was ordered to buy the remaining wine stores from John Done, the other licensed innkeeper in the town of Plymouth. Finally, Cole's personal finances were also distinctive. The court agreed to give him money toward repairing his house so that it could be "fitted as an ordinary."[60]

Cole experienced no further interruptions in his licensure, although he appeared regularly before the court to defend himself against a series of infractions. In all but one accusation, the court found him guilty. He was fined, along with his wife Mary, for "selling strong liquors to an Indian," for "suffer[ing] divers persons afternamed to stay drinking on the Lords day . . . during the time of public worship." He was found guilty of drunkenness, of entertaining various townsmen contrary to law, of selling wine to Indians, and of "suffering Richard Dwelley to bee drunk in his house." Yet, even with this long litany of complaints, the court never again sought to revoke Cole's license. The magistrates were sufficiently sanguine about Cole's qualities as a publican that his son inherited the license. But his son, too, needed special consideration. The court abated his excise in June 1670 "in regard that he is a new beginner in keeping the ordinary at Plymouth."[61]

A few common threads indicate why some individuals who were found guilty of multiple offenses continued to receive licenses while others, who had similar records, had their applications denied. The applicant's status and a perceived need for a tavern in a particular locale carried considerable weight. Robert Rowse was licensed to keep a tavern in Charles City County, Virginia in 1656. The court meted out a severe punishment in 1659 when he was found guilty of selling drink to and "trucking with" an indentured servant. He was fined as well as whipped "upon his bare shoulders." At the next court session, Rowse was reissued his license to operate an ordinary and to sell drink. Rowse may have been an important resident of the county and thus able to get away with breaking the law and still have his license renewed. More likely, the justices were less interested in the transgression and more concerned with maintaining sufficient numbers of drinking establishments for their after-court hours. Jean Marot, whose tavern in Williamsburg, Virginia, operated from 1705 to 1717, was found guilty of failing to answer a warrant and, on two separate occasions, of "Selling Liquors at Higher Rates than is Set." After each trip to the court, twice in 1710 and once in 1713, he admitted he was at fault and agreed to pay a fine. The same court that sentenced him for over charging and contempt renewed his license. Marot's favor with the justices was likely based on his position within Virginia society and his close association with William Byrd, II, one of Virginia's leading citizens. Soon after Marot arrived in Virginia, he worked for Byrd as a secretary, and afterwards, from 1707 to 1709, he served in Williamsburg as a constable. Byrd was a frequent patron at Marot's establishment. He dined there on occasion but more frequently dropped in at various hours of the day or night to converse with friends, enjoy light refreshment, and play games. Virginia justices were unlikely to revoke the license of a public house keeper with close ties to Byrd.[62]

Selling liquor without a license appears to have been a common problem in Philadelphia, but the results for those convicted were not uniform. Character was not judged on some absolute scale but was complicated by issues of class. In 1683, Griffiths Jones was convicted of selling spirituous liquors without a license. This would not be worthy of mention except that at the time of his conviction Jones was a friend of colonial proprietor William Penn, was an officer of the Free Society of Traders (the joint stock company responsible for the economic development of the colony), was a justice in a county court, and his position in society was not altered by his operating a tavern without a license.[63] Griffiths Jones's status in society protected him from losing any of his leadership positions. While the relationship of tavern keeping to class left a faint trace in the early colonial period, differential treatment of upper-and lower-class tavern keepers became a prominent theme during the eighteenth century in the port cities.

The earliest licensing policies in the townships of Chester County, Pennsylvania reveal little rhyme or reason. At the turn of the eighteenth century, the court accused and found guilty Elizabeth Musgrove, George Oldfield, John Hoskins, Widow Cornish, William Cleaton, John Test, and Thomas Withers for selling liquor without a license. The court informed them that they could apply for a license, and when they did so each was recommended. In one of these decisions, the court offered some explanation for why it would license an individual who had broken the law: while John Test was selling drink illegally he had stocked up on alcoholic beverages; by awarding him a license, the court enabled him to sell his stores legally.[64]

Even when local residents banded together to speak against a publican, it was no guarantee that the officials would heed their recommendations about licensing. Residents of New Garden, London Grove, and Marlborough townships in Chester County asked that Sarah Baldwin's license not be renewed. Baldwin's establishment inspired a great many abuses. Her house caused "great murmuring and uneasiness in the neighborhood, for she entertains or detaines frequently great companies of children, hirelings, and servants, and other unthoughtful people about her house." In addition, excessive drinking was accompanied by singing. These infractions were deemed especially egregious on the first day of the week, the day reserved for Quaker worship. Not heeding her neighbors' objections, the court approved Baldwin's petition for a license. Similarly, the "heads of the presbyterian congregation" in Chester County petitioned in August of 1771 that Robert Darlington should not have his license renewed. They reported that on the Sabbath Day during their worship unlawful games were practiced and good order was not observed at his tavern. Not only did the county officials not heed the Presbyterians' request, they approved Darlington's license renewal during the same month in which they had received the complaint.[65]

Contrast these cases with the story of Adam Archer who, in 1730 received a license to operate a tavern in Chester County. Three years later, before his annual request for renewal had reached the court, the citizens of Ridley accused him of operating the worst sort of establishment. At his inn, on the road between Chester and Darby, according to "diverse inhabitants of the township," he kept a disorderly house. He suffered "many of the Sweads and neighbors servants and other loose idle persons to drink to an excess using unlawful exercise and sports frequently on the first day of the week." The court was not swayed by Archer's claim that he was much oppressed by travelers who demanded "victuals, drink, lodging and other accommodations to the great damage and perplexity of your petitioner," nor by a statement in his support signed by his father. It denied his renewal. One year later another petition against Archer was presented to the court. In it, Ridley inhabitants commended the court for setting aside Archer's license and rejoiced in how quiet and peaceful their neighborhood had been since the tavern had closed. They urged that the court allow no tavern there, and the court agreed. However, the next February, the court granted Archer a license to sell beer and cider, out-of-doors.[66]

The courts of New Amsterdam showed the same inconsistencies when awarding tavern licenses. Nicholas Terhaer was convicted of selling liquor to Indians on Sunday during the sermon, allowing an "uproar in his house," and striking Harmen de Kuyper in the face. As part of his sentence, Terhaer had to cease tapping any wine or beer. Two months later Terhaer presented his first request to have his license reinstated. On his fourth attempt he was successful. After he paid his fine, his license was returned under the provision of good behavior.

Sometimes courts managed some creative revenue gathering with their sentences. Piere Pia was accused of tapping for five people on a Sunday. The New Amsterdam court fined him thirty guilders as punishment for his crime, and then charged him an additional thirty guilders so that he could retain his right to tap for "one year and six weeks."[67]

Although the New York courts moved swiftly against tavern keepers who kept disorderly houses, licensing practices remained just as inconsistent under British rule. In August 1712, a New York court ordered John Webb to cease keeping an ale or tippling house, and Webb was committed to the custody of the sheriff until he and his wife could post bond for "entertaining and trading with Negro slaves." The court also charged Webb with allowing "divers suspected persons of evil conversation" to drink, swear, and play "at unlawful games," and it fined him three shillings four pence and court fees. But Webb must not have tweaked the ire of the magistrates too much, because by May of the following year the court had reinstated his license. His neighbors, who no doubt had pined at the loss of their local watering hole, rushed forward to vouch for his "orderly house," and two justices, who also may have frequented his establishment, guaranteed that his behavior would be impeccable in the future.[68]

Although persistence was not among the character attributes considered for prospective tavern keepers, badgering officials proved a useful technique for acquiring a license. Mary Stevens of Birmingham, Pennsylvania, started petitioning for a tavern license in 1731 and on her third attempt it was granted. The content of her requests did not change appreciably. In her first application she stated that she lived "upon the great road from Philadelphia to Nottingham in a convenient place for a public inn." In her successful petition, she gave her location as the "great road from Chester to Nottingham."[69] Perhaps the initial rejections reflected the justices' fear that she sought to attract the local Chester County population rather than travelers. William Robinson's dogged behavior also resulted in a license. His attempt to renew his license in 1734 was rejected because he was "now judicated" at the New Castle court for an assault. A year later Robinson petitioned for a recommendation to the governor, claiming that he had gone to considerable expense to equip his house to provide entertainment for travelers. He was aware that he was accused "for some misdemeanor" but asked to meet his accuser face to face. No determination of this petition was made. Three months later Robinson's petition was before the court again. He had been caught selling liquors without a license "for which he begs leave to express his real sorrow and concern" and he hoped that this would not in any way interfere with the courts' ability to recommend him for a license. Again there was no determination nor was there any decision four months later when he applied once again. Robinson tried one more time, claiming that he had "a considerable quantity of licker now on his hands." Robinson gave up temporarily in 1735 and moved to a new location, in Chester. He tried unsuccessfully to get a license there in 1737 and 1738. Finally, in 1739, the court relented and allowed him to operate a tavern in Chester.[70]

Taverns were intended for the convenience of travelers. Thus, in order to qualify for a license, potential proprietors were expected to meet two of the criteria for a license—a convenient location and a well-equipped house. When groups of citizens wished to persuade the court to deny a license, their complaints sometimes referred to these requirements. In Byberry Township, Philadelphia County, Richard Carver's neighbors felt compelled to write against his petition for a license. In 1746, they argued to the Court of Quarter Sessions that Carver was not appropriate to be a tavern keeper. In addition to claiming that he did not have the "conveniences of Either Dwelling house or Stables Suitable to Entertain Travelers if any Should Chance to offer," they pointed out that his house was extremely inconveniently located. He lived on a rarely traveled road and would attract "Idle Persons, Servants and Negroes." If allowed to open a tavern, great injury would descend upon the neighborhood where, the petition noted, three taverns already existed. It may be that the residents of Byberry were particularly vigilant. They petitioned the court again in 1755 to prevent Jacob Burskark from opening a tavern in the little house he had erected. This time they objected because Burskark's small house lacked a stables and outhouses and had no "Conveniences suitable to entertain travellers." Thus, he too would attract idle persons exclusively.[71] The court's willingness to issue licenses in these cases is puzzling. Carver's tavern was on a road with little traffic and close to three other public houses; neither house was well equipped to entertain strangers or their horses. Perhaps the magistrates did not take seriously their charge to see that taverns functioned as havens for travelers. They may have decided that these two houses would be adequate places for local residents. And the concerned citizens of Byberry may have being trying to prevent Carver and Burskark from receiving licenses in order to prevent additional competition for the existing taverns.

Sometimes, petitions by concerned citizens succeeded in their mission. In 1770, the inhabitants of West Nantmell, Chester County petitioned the court to refrain from renewing John Graham's license. Graham for a number of years had had a license to retail spirituous liquors at the west end of the township. But, the petitioners argued, he allowed "divers irregularities to be committed such as drunkenness, fighting, horseracing and the frequent entertaining of servants on the sabbath." These practices, the petitioners claimed, hurt many "unhappy women and young children whose husbands & father spend their time and money days and nights together at the place." This scenario struck a responsive chord. When John Graham requested that his tavern license be renewed, it was "disallowed for misbehavior."[72]

The capriciousness with which magistrates awarded licenses can be difficult to comprehend. In his petition for licensure, John Stacey stated that he had lost an eye, was ill, unable to earn a living by his labor, and that he, with his family, were living in "supreme poverty." But his request was to no avail, and not because the court did not believe him; the decision contains a written notation that the petitioner had "gone blind." Mary Moore, whose petition opened this chapter, urged the authorities to award her a license because, having tended to her ailing husband who subsequently died, she was stuck with a great medical debt as a result of his illness. Now a widow and without any means of support, her petition included the fact that her house had previously served as a stage stop. The court took the opposite position from that which it had taken on so many other licensing requests; it seems to have determined that supporting her on poor relief was preferable to issuing her a license. Even with these reasons and without any action by neighbors to block her license, and despite the common practice of issuing licenses for houses that had served as public houses previously, the court disallowed her petition.[73]

*   *   *

ANOMALIES in licensing practices seem to have been as commonplace in urban as in nonurban areas, in the sectarian as well as nonsectarian colonies, as baffling in the eighteenth-century examples as in the seventeenth-century ones. Over the course of the eighteenth century, a tension existed between the stated goals and the process. The specified criteria in licensing law were replaced by unspecified and random standards. Perseverance or badgering of officials substituted for character. Prime location mitigated against the effects of a previous court record. Greed overrode conflict of interest. Poverty, a qualifying category that included a substantial number of women, replaced the ideal of sobriety and honesty in proprietors, but inconsistently.

The most salient characteristic of licensing practices in the eighteenth century was its arbitrariness. Some individuals who had been prosecuted for violating tavern and drinking laws were denied licenses; others acquired them. A number of individuals who were convicted of selling drink without a license petitioned to sell legally; some were approved and others denied. Some repeat offenders were granted licenses while others were not.[74] Furthermore, this seemingly random pattern of administration implies that while colonial officials professed concern about tavern density and the character of those who operated public houses, their declaration lacked conviction.

By the eighteenth century, colonial officials seem no longer to believe in this ideal. Perhaps, they considered it fruitless to control licensing, giving in to what John Adams described as a bifurcation that had developed in tavern culture. At one extreme, more elite establishments opened, run by proprietors with impeccable credentials. On the opposite end of the spectrum were publicans who operated low-end establishments implicated in a culture in which transgression of the law was frequent. Honest, sober persons of high moral reputation had no desire to run or patronize these taverns, and officials were helpless in their attempts to close them down completely.

The analysis of tavern licenses also reveals the gendered nature of tavern keeping. Taverns operated by women were located primarily in the cities and towns, and these houses tended to be of lesser quality. Licenses for inns went more often to men, while women were relegated to selling liquor out-of-doors. Because women were thought incapable of keeping good order in their houses, they were likely to have men placed in supervisory capacities over them. Operating an ordinary was not high on women's list of desirable occupations, and they were more likely to apply for licenses based on severe financial need. Women applied for the license vacated by their deceased husband. Once licensed women remained in the business for fewer years than did men. Finally, as the perspective from inside the tavern discloses, women proprietors engaged their clientele differently than did their male counterparts.

Too Many Taverns?:
"Little better than Nurseries of
Vice and Debauchery"

We Present, as a great grievance, that granting of too great a number of Li-
cences for retailing Spirituous Liquors in Charlestown, whereby the morals
of our Slaves are debauched, frequent thefts ensue and the trade sufers,
by sailors being concealed, encouraged to neglect and desert their duty,
and other disorders arise.[1]

*M*eeting in January 1720, the grand jury of Charleston issued another of
their regular complaints that there were too many houses licensed to
sell drink. They believed that licensing laws should control how many taverns existed and who operated them. Legislators had designed the laws to limit the
number of taverns in an area and to designate who could be trusted, so that "disorders" would not arise and the availability of labor would not suffer.

Colonial authorities stated specifically that, in addition to selecting proper
proprietors and filling colonial coffers, licensing procedures were responsible for
controlling the number of taverns. Colonial leaders were responsible for achieving and maintaining a balance between a sufficient number of taverns to accommodate travelers and too many public houses, which, it was thought, would
lure folks into drink and idleness. Assemblies and city councils determined how

many taverns were desirable in a specific locale. In Massachusetts and Virginia, for example, the general courts ascertained how many licenses should be allowed based to a large extent on location of the population and distribution of tavern locations. The Massachusetts legislature assumed that port cities and towns had greater demand for taverns, since they were "havens for 'strangers and travellers.'" Agricultural areas required only one tavern, regardless of the population. The terminology of the law also distinguished between the more respectable drinking establishments and those on the water front. The former—inns and wine bars—drew their patrons from the elite ranks of society, while the latter—public houses and ordinaries—elicited suspicion from the lawmakers about the clientele and their drinking behaviors. Lawmakers exerted control by the type of license they issued, as well as the number, striking a balance between taverns and the retail trade in alcoholic beverages.[2]

While the standards were clear, the implementation was inconsistent. An analysis of the physical distribution of taverns and of the character of the individuals granted licenses reveals that there were deviations from the lawmakers' intentions almost from the moment the licensing process started. Colonial leaders regularly called for a diminution in the number of taverns. For brief intervals, courts responded by issuing fewer licenses, but soon afterward the numbers were restored, so that each of the major port cities boasted similar proportions of taverns to population.

It is important to keep in mind that this analysis of tavern density is based upon tavern licenses, yet not everyone who sold drink or operated a public house did so legally. In Boston in 1681, the General Court launched a campaign to reduce the number of licenses issued. The result was an increase in unlicensed establishments. George Monk, one of the proprietors who retained his license, petitioned the Assembly along with four other tavern keepers, complaining about the illegal sellers. In effect, the number of taverns remained constant although the proportion that were licensed declined.[3] The Rhode Island Assembly hinted at this problem when in 1765 they passed a law chastising "evil minded persons" who "set up signs for houses of public entertainment, and selling of strong liquors, without taking any license from the town council." The lawmakers lamented the damage done to the honest tavern keeper who took out a license and bemoaned the grim reality that these fraudulent proprietors tended to "keep disorderly houses, and suffer gaming, hard drinking, and many other indecent and irregular practices."[4] Indeed, operating a tippling house or selling alcoholic beverages without a license were among the most common violations of tavern-related law. Gauging the number of places selling liquor based only on licensed houses necessarily results in an undercount.

Tavern Density in Port Cities

Civic and clerical leaders in the colonies preached that controlling tavern density was critical to maintaining an orderly society. In the major port cities, they periodically expressed their anxiety about the proliferation of public houses and insisted that the numbers be reduced. Yet, residents in these port cities never had to search very far for a welcoming public house that could provide conversation and a stiff drink. The cities were packed with taverns (see Table 6.1).

Only two years after the founding of Pennsylvania, William Penn raised his first complaints about the disorders caused by the presence of too many taverns in Philadelphia, and he requested that their numbers be reduced. Of the eight licensed tavern keepers, seven were allowed to continue and one was ordered to "seek some other way for a livelihood." In 1693, one estimate placed the number of drink sellers at twenty—twelve licensed and eight individuals who were prosecuted for operating taverns without a license.

During the first half of the eighteenth century, the number of public houses rose steadily. In 1721, ninety-four ordinaries could be identified in the Quaker capital, representing an extraordinarily high ratio of one for every fifty-four city residents. Although the proportion of taverns to population did not vary much, the Philadelphia Grand Jury, in 1744, complained about the number of public houses and the threat they posed. These, they said, were "little better than Nurseries of Vice and Debauchery, and tend very much to encrease the Number of our Poor." Indeed, the section of town was labeled, Hell Town. To remedy this condition, a way was sought to diminish the number of public houses.[5] The proportion of taverns declined by midcentury, but the resolve to limit the debauchery did not last long. By the mid-1750s, the number of taverns maintained a steady per capita ratio of, on average, one public house for every 130 residents.[6]

The maps of Philadelphia (Figures 9, 10, and 11) display the licensed tav-

TABLE 6.1
Proportion of Drink Sellers to Population in Colonial Port Cities

	Years	Number of Licenses	Proportion of Licenses to Total Population
Philadelphia	1693	20	1/105
	1721	94	1/54
	1756	111	1/134
	1759	134	1/127
	1762	133	1/128
	1763	150	1/113
	1772	164	1/133
Boston	1681	24	1/240
	1696	74	1/100
	1722	134	1/94
	1737	174	1/93
	1752	162	1/97
	1758	135	1/116
	1765	134	1/123
New Amsterdam/New York	1663	18	1/90
	1693	24	1/125
	1722	78	1/91
	1759	287	1/55
Charleston	1762	101	1/96
	1770	102	1/112
	1772	101	1/112

SOURCES: David Conroy, *In Public Houses: Drink and the Revolution of Authority in Colonial Massachusetts* (Chapel Hill, N.C., 1995), 58, 59, 67, 80, 116–17, 142–43. Peter Thompson, Licenses for Marriages, Taverns, Peddlers, Secretary's Office, Ledger A, Historical Society of Pennsylvania, AM 2014; Mayor's Court, City of Philadelphia (Proportions of the population for Philadelphia were derived using the population figures in Gary B. Nash, *The Urban Crucible: Social Change, Political Consciousness, and the Origins of the American Revolution* [Cambridge, Mass., 1979], Appendix, Table 13, 407–8. I used the figure 17,060 for the population of Philadelphia in 1760.) *South Carolina Gazette,* April 17 to April 24, 1762; May 7, 1772, supplement. (Population figures for Charleston are from Peter A. Coclanis, *The Shadow of a Dream: Economic Life and Death in the South Carolina Low Country, 1670–1920* [New York 1989], 114, Table 4-3.

erns in the city for three successive fifteen-year periods in the eighteenth century. Two key points stand out. First, taverns originally clustered by the water and then gradually moved throughout the city. In addition, while taverns existed throughout the city, particular sections were densely populated with drinking establishments. Through the middle of the century they remained numerous along the waterfront, where public houses attracted maritime workers and accommodated recent arrivals to the port city. As the city grew and the population moved west, newer taverns appeared away from the Delaware River. By the middle of the eighteenth century, taverns were densely situated within a three block long swath, north to south, which extended from the river west. Scattered regions in the middle of the city were intensely populated with taverns. In 1770, ten li-

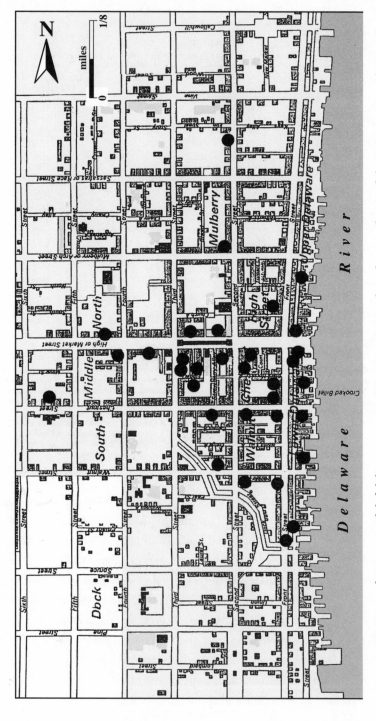

FIGURE 9. Licensed Taverns in Philadelphia, 1735–1750. Most taverns were along the waterfront and the main commercial street. Base map from the *Pennsylvania Gazette*, Malvern, Pa., Accessible Archives, 1991–. Adaptation by Langevin Geographic.

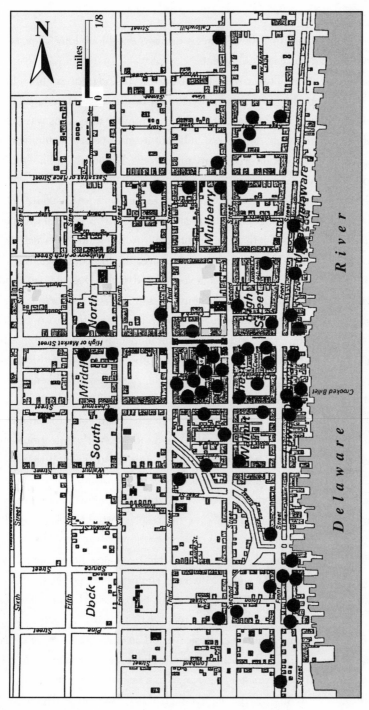

FIGURE 10. Licensed Taverns in Philadelphia, 1750–1765. The number of taverns of the waterfront and nearby blocks increased and other clusters of public houses developed. Base map from the *Pennsylvania Gazette*, Malvern, Pa., Accessible Archives, 1991–. Adaptation by Langevin Geographic.

censed houses operated in Elbow Lane, a narrow, one-block long alley, and Strawberry Lane, a two-block long street.[7]

A similar distribution of taverns existed in Boston. In 1681, for example, the General Court, responding to the cry that too many taverns existed, reduced the number. By the end of the century, however, the number of taverns was on a steady incline. Beginning in 1696, the number of licenses issued maintained a fairly steady relationship of taverns to city inhabitants, about one public house for every one hundred inhabitants.[8]

The volume of drink sellers had grown so large in part because the court, with the encouragement of the selectmen, had issued licenses to virtually all who petitioned. Ironically, throughout the seventeenth century, when Boston's small size enabled the selectmen to exert the most control over the lives of the city's residents, petitions for licenses were almost never refused. Gyles Dyer, who in 1679 was convicted of selling liquor without a license, was then granted a license. Even with the intense monitoring of individual behavior, from 1634 to 1701 only two individuals did not receive the selectmen's recommendation. Martin Stibbin was forbidden to brew and sell beer any more; two months later, however, this decision was reversed. The only other person the selectmen denied a license was William Morris. For him they were determined to "positively forbid it."[9]

At the turn of the century, Boston's leaders expressed their concern about the number of licensed establishments and called for a reduction. The selectmen accomplished this by recommending that more petitions be rejected than approved. They advised against granting licenses to certain individuals and refused to recommend renewals for others. As a result of this effort, a small dip occurred in the number of licenses issued. However, the resolve lasted less than twenty years. After 1718, the selectmen reversed the proportion and approved more applications than they disallowed. The result was that many new licenses were issued and taverns appeared throughout the city. The density of public houses is most striking when compared to the number of taxpayers. The 134 licenses issued in 1722 translated into one liquor retailer or tavern keeper for every twenty-two Boston taxpayers. By 1737, Boston could boast one licensee for every eighteen taxpayers. At midcentury, the number of licenses proportionate to the population remained approximately the same, one tavern or retailer for every seventeen taxable residents, but the population had begun a gradual decline and

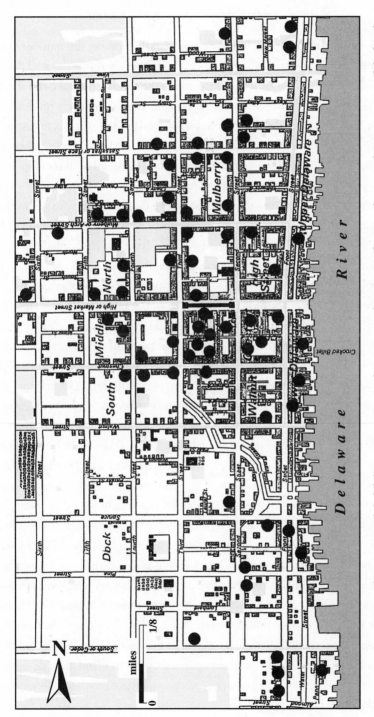

FIGURE 11. Licensed Taverns in Philadelphia, 1765–1780. As the city's population spread outward, taverns became more widely distributed. Base map from the *Pennsylvania Gazette*, Malvern, Pa., Accessible Archives, 1991–. Adaptation by Langevin Geographic.

so had the number of licenses. Toward the end of the decade, the number of licenses fell further. However, the population had declined further as well.[10]

The selectmen apparently worked to resolve the tension between the stated goal, to reduce the number of taverns in Boston, and the reality, a gradual increase in the number of drinking houses in proportion to residents, by issuing fewer licenses for taverns and more for retailers-out-of-doors. The numbers of licenses for inns remained somewhat constant while the number of retailers-out-of-doors grew steadily.[11] Altering the proportion of retailers to innkeepers may have worked to control tavern density, but determined drinkers who wished for the conpanionship of the public house had only to walk a little farther to locate one, and everyone else had easy access to alcohol from the city's retailers.

Granting of a tavern license to a new individual did not mean creation of an additional public house when a business was transferred to a new proprietor. In 1675, Thomas Bill was approved for a license in the place of Widow Upshall, "who latelie departed this life." Ten years later, the selectmen gave their consent when Daniel Turell, Jr., applied to keep a public house of entertainment in the place previously operated by Thomas Bill. Bill and his wife had decided to "lay downe that imploymt," due to their advancing years. In 1756, Samuel Ross requested a license "to retail strong liquors in small quantity." In his application, he reassured the selectmen that by issuing him a license, "it will be no addition to such Houses," for he had taken over a house that had been a licensed tavern for many years and whose proprietor had died. Ross himself had not been a tavern keeper before. He had apprenticed to a gunsmith and while he was testing small arms on the expedition against Cape Breton, one of the guns split. The injury was so severe that his hand had to be amputated. Although this accident disabled him and he could no longer practice the occupation for which he was trained, he, like others, turned to tavern keeping as an alternative occupation.[12] A Mr. Sever told a similar story. In 1763 he bought a house, near the town fortifications, that had been a tavern and applied to continue the business. He too was approved. When Mrs. Silense Torrey first applied for a tavern license, the selectmen took no action. When she appeared before them and explained that she was asking to continue the business operated by her husband, then deceased, which meant that the actual number of taverns would not increase, she was recommended for a license.[13]

A sense of the density of licensed drink sellers can be gleaned by examining a map of licenses for taverns and retailers. Figure 12 displays licenses approved for Boston in 1718.[14] They were clustered in two ways—in the areas of densest population and along the waterfront. Taverns were likely to be found where shops and residences were concentrated. Since walking was the most common form of transportation, thirsty city residents went to their neighborhood bars. They might stop in on their way home from work or leave their residences to find a drink and companionship. Living spaces were cramped in early America. Unmarried men rented a single room; most families had little more than two rooms. Taverns offered men a place to which they could escape the confines of their crowded quarters or the screams of their children.

The northern portion of the city housed the city's shipbuilders. According to Boston Town Records of 1742, shipbuilding employed the largest number of tradesmen in the city, as well as the ship carpenters who worked in the yards and the countless carters and hucksters who transported supplies. The north-end taverns offered these Bostonians easy access to imbibing after work, before and after cargo deliveries, or when the winter weather halted labor.[15] Mariners and recent arrivals by sea could easily find drink and food at these waterfront establishments. Once the seafarer had placed a wobbly foot on land, he could propel himself into a public house with little additional effort. The harbor acted as a magnet for taverns also because the location served the city's merchants so well. From a dockside tavern they could keep tabs on their cargoes and the activities on their wharves and in their warehouses and transact business with ships' captains or meet easily with each other over a friendly glass.[16]

Figure 13, which displays the distribution of licenses in Boston eighteen years later, reveals a remarkable constancy in the arrangement of drink sellers. They continued to be bunched in the most populated sections. The city's center and northern section maintained a high density of people and public houses. Taverns and retailers were so packed along the waterfront that it would have been difficult to avoid drinking establishments when stepping off a boat in Boston. Figure 13 also hints at the city's future growth to the south along the main southern thoroughfare out of the city toward Dorchester.

Also visible by comparing Figures 12 and 13 is the decline in taverns and increase in the number of licenses issued to retailers. Because the General Court

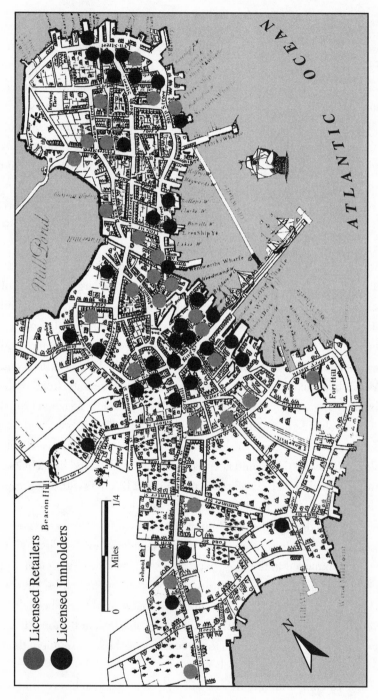

Licensed Retailers

Licensed Innholders

FIGURE 12. Licensed Taverns in Boston, 1718. Drink sellers were clustered along the waterfront and in areas of densest population. Base map: "Map of the Town of Boston in New England by Captain John Bonner, 1722," courtesy of the Massachusetts Historical Society. Adaptation by Langevin Geographic.

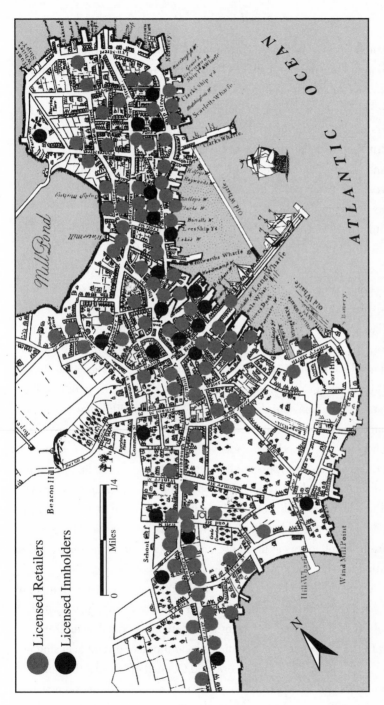

Licensed Retailers

Licensed Innholders

FIGURE 13. Licensed Taverns in Boston, 1736. Compared with 1718 (see figure 12), many more people were licensed to sell alcohol, but they continued to be found along the waterfront and in areas of highest population density. They had also increased along the main route out of town. Base map: "Map of the Town of Boston in New England by Captain John Bonner, 1722," courtesy of the Massachusetts Historical Society. Adaptation by Langevin Geographic.

was concerned with the increased consumption of hard liquor, they attempted, in 1712, to alter consumption patterns by reducing the number of taverns and banning the sale of spirituous liquors in them. Rum did not suddenly become unavailable, however. According to David Conroy, close to half of Boston's tavern keepers paid no attention to the law, continuing to sell hard liquor.[17] If so many tavern keepers failed to observe the law, it is likely that retailers behaved similarly and ignored the requirement. This suggests that little distinction existed between the two types of licenses. Retailers and taverns served the same range of beverages in their houses.

It is ironic that the General Court moved to reduce the number of public houses in Boston but in the end produced an opposite effect to the one they apparently desired. As Figure 13 demonstrates, the number of places from which Bostonians could procure a drink exploded. And while the city's selectmen attempted to differentiate between publicans and retailers, relegating women and laboring-class men most often to the trade out-of-doors while issuing tavern licenses to others, the differences in the license may reveal very little about what transpired inside. One distinction did become increasingly apparent in Boston by the mid-eighteenth century. Status played an increasing part in differentiating the character, location, and clientele of public houses. While taverns and retailers located on the waterfront continued to cater to the laboring classes, the finer establishments reserved for society's elite moved into the city center.[18]

One of the articulated purposes of licensing in Boston was to limit the number of public houses, so that city neighborhoods would not contain too many taverns. Yet, the selectmen could not have been paying attention to density as a criterion when they recommended that John Mulloy receive a license. Mulloy asked for a license to retail liquors at his house on the neck even though he stated in his application that his house was "over against the George Tavern."[19]

In New Amsterdam, the leaders also voiced their dismay with the number of houses licensed to sell drink; yet the city, from its earliest days, may have been the colonial city best endowed with taverns. Dutch policy added an entirely new dimension to the discrepancy between desire and practice. The licensing law voted on in 1654 by the Director General and Council of New Netherland and the Burgomasters and Schepens of New Amsterdam allowed that no new taprooms, taverns, or inns could be opened unless the request received unanimous approval from the director and council. It also stipulated that any public house already in existence would be allowed to remain open for the next four years. Current tapsters and tavern keepers had to put their names on a list, and they were forbidden from transferring their businesses without the consent of the director and council.[20] Even though this licensing law was on the books, it included no mechanisms for enforcement, so nothing prevented any resident of Manhattan Island from trading beer or alcohol or from consuming limitless quantities. In effect, no license was required for a person to sell drink.

Since the Dutch were inclined toward heavy drinking, it is not surprising that the Dutch West India Company established a brewery as one of its first enterprises. The company sold its beer, imported wine, and brandies in quantity and, in order to bolster business, urged residents to sell drink from their homes. This did inspire concern in some quarters. In 1626, Governor Keift, proclaiming "that nearly the just fourth of the city of New Amsterdam" were "Brandy shops, Tobacco, or Beer houses," expressed a fear that the proliferation of these houses would work toward the neglect of the "more honorable Trades and occupations," along with the corruption of "the Common people and the Company's servants." Other complaints emphasized that the number of establishments selling drink interfered with religious practices. In a letter sent from new to old Amsterdam, the writer whined that although this particular congregation had about 170 members, most were more interested in drink than religion; "They are led by seventeen tap-houses here." Population estimates for early New Amsterdam are hard to find. If the 1642–43 population estimate of a Father Jogue is accurate, four hundred men lived in and around the city, and one grog shop existed for every twenty-four men.[21] A sense of the Dutch colonists' devotion to drinking and the public house can be gleaned from the history of New Amsterdam's Stadt Herbergh, or City Tavern. By the 1640s, travel in and out of the city had become sufficiently heavy that the governor urged that a special tavern be erected to house the city's visitors, in order to ease the burden of caring for strangers that was being placed on the port's residents. As a result, a large stone house was built, the most expensive building constructed to that point in the city; even though a new and substantial church was built soon after, the City Tavern far exceeded it in terms of cost.[22]

Residents of New Amsterdam in the 1640s successfully maintained Old World drinking habits in their New World context. A minister who was in the city only temporarily admonished the Dutch East India Company's directors; he had found the inhabitants "very ignorant in regard to true religion, and very much given to drink. . . . What bad fruits result therefrom, your Reverences will easily understand." The minister recommended that the company close all but three or four taverns if they wished to prevent further offenses to good order.[23]

New Amsterdam's leaders made no effort to reduce the quantity of taverns. In addition to places licensed to sell liquor to locals and travelers, the early tradition of residents selling liquors from their homes continued. Also, landlords who rented rooms or ran boarding houses were not required to purchase licenses in order to retail drink.[24] New Amsterdam residents with dry throats had an easy job of finding a public house.[25] English rule in New York maintained the tradition of abundance (Table 6.1). It is difficult to imagine how New York, even with its steady stream of travelers, sustained so many public houses. A serious thirst and the desire for the revenue generated by tavern license fees must have been the primary motivations for the high number of public houses.[26]

Tavern density in Charleston, South Carolina, more than kept pace with its northern counterparts.[27] City residents and visitors had a variety of establishments from which to choose, since justices awarded three types of licenses—half licenses (for selling drink out-of-doors), full licenses (to serve indoors), and full licenses combined with a billiard table license. For example, in 1762, the city licensed thirty-seven individuals to sell liquor as a carry-out trade; of the sixty-four proprietors who ran actual taverns, ten businesses included a billiard table. Throughout the decades preceding the American Revolution, the proportion of drink sellers in Charleston relative to population remained constant and comparable to other North American port cities. On the eve of the Revolution, one estimate claims, "about one in thirteen of all the dwellings in Charleston was a licensed tipling house." By imagining the number of illegal establishments also selling drink, one can see that Charleston's landscape offered easy access to public houses and other sources of liquor.[28]

As in the northern seaports, the first taverns in Charleston to open their doors were along the water, located near the finger piers into the Cooper River, on the city's east side. These small, rough public houses were a welcome sight for seamen, whose first task when they reached shore was to find companionship

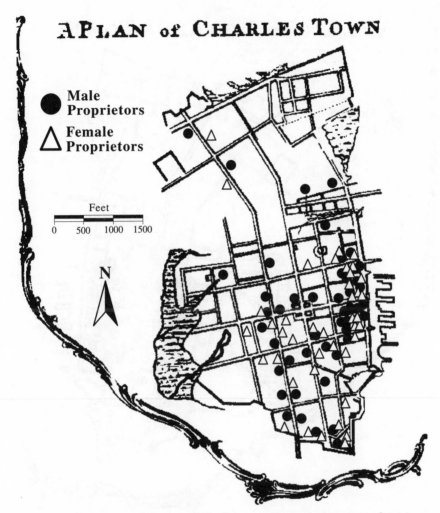

FIGURE 14. Licensed Taverns in Charleston, 1762. (Note: Locations of taverns are approximate.) Base map adapted from "A Map of the Province of South Carolina," by James Cook (London, 1773), courtesy of the Charleston County Library. Adaptation by Langevin Geographic.

and a stiff drink. By the turn of the seventeenth century, the sites of public houses had begun to spread gradually inland. By the second half of the eighteenth century, the space along the river was being filled in with the warehouses and counting houses associated with the colony's growing trade, and taverns were

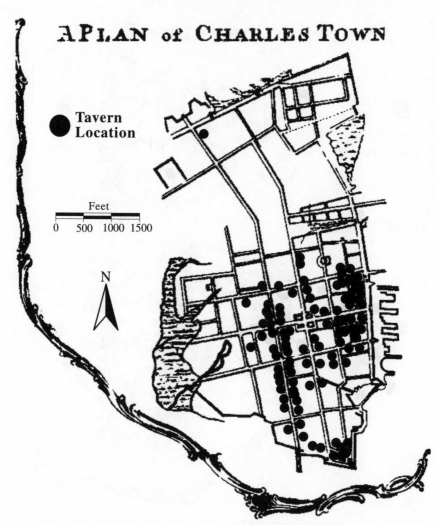

FIGURE 15. Licensed Taverns in Charleston, 1768. (Note: Locations of taverns are approximate.) Base map adapted from "A Map of the Province of South Carolina," by James Cook (London, 1773), courtesy of the Charleston County Library. Adaptation by Langevin Geographic.

clustered along the waterfront, within the most densely settled neighborhoods, and on both sides of the city's main street. When the Pink House Tavern opened about 1712 on what today is Chalmer's Street, about five blocks from the Cooper River, it was likely the only tavern within a number of blocks. By the middle of the eighteenth century, it was one of a number of houses associated with a debauched Charleston night life and was situated within a dense cluster of public houses.[29]

Figures 14 and 15 plot the distribution of Charleston's taverns. (Figure 14 also illustrates the large proportion of female proprietors in Charleston.) As the city developed, houses and businesses filled in the spaces between the Cooper River and the Ashley River on the west side of town. Taverns followed the same pattern. However, taverns increasingly clustered on the city's eastern shore and the same density was duplicated in the center of town on King Street. Given this distribution, it seems questionable that density governed the magistrates' decisions about who should be licensed to operate a public house.

Tavern Density in Towns and Rural Areas

By the eighteenth century, residents of agricultural and port towns, had the same access to taverns as the residents of the major port cities. The ubiquity of the drinking establishments of the time confirms how central these sites were for colonial sociability. Although attempts to control the number of drink sellers surfaced periodically, only feeble attempts were made to limit such licenses, and these efforts were usually short lived. Proximity to the water enhanced the need for taverns as did growing populations. Again, the licensing process appears to have been arbitrary and it does not reflect any systematic effort to control tavern density. The southern colonies, in most jurisdictions, lacked standardized administrative mechanisms for issuing and recording licenses. As a result, even if colonial leaders had wished to control the number of drinking houses, the task stretched beyond their capability.

Guarding against there being too many taverns was not the only density issue. Officials were sometimes also called upon to determine if particular locations had enough taverns to satisfy the needs of locals and travelers. For example, in 1672 in Massachusetts, because the town of Roxbury was "destitute of an ordinary," the selectmen recommended to the Suffolk County Court that it allow Samuel Rubbles to "keep a house of publique entertainment." In 1679, the Suffolk County Court went so far as to place the Dorchester selectmen "under penalty" because the town was without a tavern. The court ordered the selectmen "to nominate and present some fit person unto the next county court for their approbation to keep a house for publique entertainment." The court would not suffer a town to be without a tavern.[30]

During the first fifty years or so after Massachusetts was founded, the Bay Colony towns had only a single tavern. The quarterly Courts of Essex County contain records of only scattered licenses issued through the 1650s, and, except for Lynn and Salem, most towns appear to have had only one licensed house. The number of licensed taverns grew steadily, however. In 1678, four people sought new licenses in Salem, a town that already had at least fourteen ordinaries and public houses, some of which were licensed and others not. "Giving warning agst ye sine of drunkennes & ye excessive number of drinking howses in this place," a Salem watchman urged the court to refuse a license to Edward Bridges, who had recently been accused of drunkenness and abusive language toward the tithingmen.[31] The justices did not heed the limits they themselves had set on the number of taverns in the county's towns. In 1680, they allotted twenty-six licenses, to be distributed among the seventeen towns of the county; they issued thirty-seven licenses, surpassing the allocation in seven of the seventeen towns. As a whole, Essex County averaged one tavern for every 219 people, a drier place than the major port cities. Salem town, on the other hand, averaged one tavern for every 80 persons, a slightly higher proportion of drinking houses than the larger ports. The demand for public houses was greatest along the Salem-to-Marblehead waterfront and in the neighboring communities of Lynn and Salem Village.[32]

The court records suggest that by 1683 the number of licenses issued for Essex County had fallen. In that year, licenses in the county were down to twenty-seven. The Salem selectmen had begun to make a conscious effort to limit the number of drinking establishments. They noted that they had recommended Samuel Beadle for a license due to special circumstances, and as a result were forced to turn down William Stevens's license renewal. The Salem selectmen appear to have been committed to reducing the temptations of drink, and they did so in part by limiting the number of taverns.[33]

Residents of Plymouth County had easy access to taverns, especially in the towns. Plymouth Township had the densest tavern census of any township in the county. In 1690, for example, among an estimated town population of 775, seven individuals were licensed to sell alcoholic beverages. This trend of increasing numbers continued. From 1719 to 1745, ten of the fourteen towns in the county had more than one person licensed to sell liquor.[34] By the time of the next Massachusetts census, in 1765, Abbington, Pembroke, Plimton, and Scituate had comparable tavern densities to that of Boston. Kingston and Plymouth had one licensee for each 95 and 94 inhabitants, respectively, a slightly higher drink-seller density than Boston.[35]

Middlesex County, Massachusetts, supported very few taverns at the turn of the seventeenth century. However, they seem to have joined the trend toward increasing numbers of inns. In 1701, thirty-three taverns and five retailers plied their trade in the county. Although one-third of the towns had only one licensed house, Charlestown had at least five. From 1720 to 1740, the number of licenses issued increased dramatically; eight of the thirty-four towns had five or more public houses. The numbers continued to climb, so that by 1770 more than half of the then thirty-seven towns had five or more taverns.[36]

In July 1762, the Court of General Sessions of the Peace began an attempt to assess the quality as well as the number of taverns in the county. It appointed a committee to visit taverns and retailers. They rated three specific aspects: how well the lodging and provisions suited "the entertainment of travelers," the quality of the keepers, and the density of taverns in each town. The committee did its job and reported back to the court the following month. They suggested, for example, that, for the town of Dedham, the court refuse to renew the licenses of William Ellis, Jonathan Lewis, and Ephriam Colbern. The reason given was that they "are situated so near to other and better taverns there that they are needless for travellers." For the town of Walpole, they recommended denying a license to Charles Dupee, "whose house is within a mile and a half from Ezekiel Robins." They were not persuaded to recommend license renewal for proprietor Preserved Hall of Wrenthem, either, even though they noted that she was conveniently located in the center of town. An argument in her favor was that she was only a quarter of a mile from Man's tavern and hers might prove necessary on those rare occasions when Man's, "a large well furnished house[,] can't entertain all . . . which has sometimes been the case." Uriah Morse, an innholder from Medway, refused to allow the committee entry into his house. When told their business, he "replied that ye court took too much upon them." Morse had "declined our viewing his accomodations within doors (which we believe to be very scanty)." The last innholder to receive the committee's disapproval was Nathaniel Richards of Roxbury, whose house, they told the court, was badly located and ill suited for the trade. The committee urged that at least seven of the thrity-five licensed inns in the towns of Suffolk County be closed. This would have been a significant reduction in the number of taverns. The court's response, however, speaks to the tension between stated goals and practice. That same year, each of the taverns singled out for closure in the committee's report was relicensed.[37]

The committee's report provides clear evidence of the criteria deemed essential for the proper operation of the liquor trade. Inns should not be too close to one another, each house was to be well furnished, and the proprietors were to be of good character. The committee may have been responding also to issues of respectabililty. The taverns they marked for closure likely attracted a lower-class clientele, the type of drinker colonial leaders wished to discourage from frequenting public houses. Only certain proprietors earned their trust, and this was based in part on whom they entertained.

Through the seventeenth century in Massachusetts, the number of licensed houses remained proportionally small to the growing population. One of the most efficient means of controlling the sins related to drinking and the tavern was to limit the number of licensed houses. By the eighteenth century, the assumption that too many public houses would lead society inevitably into decline and decay had lost its edge. A space had opened between the intent of licensing law and its practice.

In Rowan County, North Carolina, deviations from licensing laws appear in the lack of administrative attention rather than in failing to control the number of taverns. Indeed, the county's tavern density cannot be calculated because of the scantiness of the record. Rowan County was established in 1753. The licensing records from the Minutes of the Court of Pleas and Quarter Sessions show that, for the twenty-one-year period 1753 through 1774, 129 petitioners held the 209 licenses. The yearly variation in number of licenses suggests that either the clerks did not systematically record all of the licenses granted or that county officials did not take the licensing laws terribly seriously. For example, while nine licenses were issued during the county's first year, a rough proportion of one tavern for every 444 people, and fifteen in 1754, only six were recorded the following year. Then the number jumps to sixteen in 1756 and falls again to eight in 1757; and according to the court records, only one license was issued in the county in both 1759 and 1760. The conclusion that the records are spotty, rather than that the county lacked for licensed tavern keepers, is supported by the case of George Bruner. He obtained a license in 1757, is missing from the list in 1758, and reappears in 1759. George Magoune is off then on the lists from 1764 to 1768.[38] The haphazard nature of either licensing or record keeping in Rowan County makes it impossible to determine tavern density and the lax administering of the license laws suggests the great likelihood that many drink sellers operated illegally.

The lists of licenses and bonds from Perquimans County, North Carolina, exhibit the same arbitrary record for renewals. From 1753 to 1766, the number of individuals who paid a bond for a license jumped up and down. Names appear and disappear, then reappear; and while it is possible that these individuals ceased to operate during the years they are missing from the lists, it is unlikely. A recorded bond exists for Jonathan Phelps in 1753. He is not listed in 1754 but appears regularly from 1755 until 1759, when he disappears from the list of tavern keepers in Perquimans County. Similarly, Cornelius Mullin paid his bond for a license in 1754, is not listed in 1755, did pay in 1756 and 1757. In 1758, his widow, Mary Mullin, apparently took over the business. Perhaps more revealing is the case of William Coles. Although he was issued a license to operate a tavern in 1774, he appears on no other list. However, in 1767 he had appeared in court as the plaintiff to collect money owed him for alcoholic beverages, products that he should have sold only with a license to operate a tavern.[39]

Alexander and John Lowrance's legacy highlights official attitudes toward licensing law. In 1755, Alexander Lowrance opened a tavern on his farm along Beaverdam Creek, ten miles west of Salisbury, North Carolina. He operated the tavern continuously until his death in 1762, when his son John assumed responsibility for both the farm and the tavern. No record exists anywhere of a license or a bond for either Alexander or John for the entire colonial period.[40]

The Moravians in North Carolina wished to limit the number of taverns within their communities, and they did so by a most unusual method. They decreed that only one tavern could operate in any Moravian settlement, and rather than entrust the business to a single proprietor, the congregation owned the establishment communally. They hired the tavern keeper whom they considered best qualified to operate the business and leased the building to that person. At times, this was a husband and wife; at others it was a single man. While serving as tavern proprietors, the landlords were forbidden to engage in any other enterprise; and for their labor they received room, board, and a small salary. If the venture was profitable they would receive one-third of the proceeds. This arrangement severely hampered the tavern keeper's ability to make decisions and to take actions necessary to the smooth operation of the business. The proprietor of the Salem tavern had to petition the congregation before he could build a new stable at the tavern. The congregation kept a close watch over the business, and if they found any fault with their proprietorship, the church could remove the landlord.[41] Moravians successfully limited the number of taverns in their communities. They appear, however, to have been motivated by their desire for a profitable venture rather than a need to control the number of taverns.

In many towns, taverns were more popular than churches. In 1755, when Salisbury, North Carolina was a town of seven or eight houses, four were taverns or inns. The extent of popularity of taverns and the perceived need by Rowan County settlers are clear from the number of requests to keep taverns; the county court was bombarded with petitions from many a resident who wished to "keep Ordinary att his Plantation." The Reverend Charles Woodmason lamented that in the competition between the church and tavern for souls, drinking houses were winning. He remarked that public houses drew "more Company of a Saturday, than in the Church on Sunday." Competing however was futile, since the magistrates were aware of the abuses—"Most of them being Store or Tavern Keepers."[42] Woodmason offered one plausible explanation for the divergence between tavern law, which prohibited town and county officials from obtaining licenses, and practice. When the magistrates operated the taverns, a huge gap appeared between the intent of the law and the interest of the law enforcers.

Tavern densities were quite low throughout the colonial period in Chester County, located in the southeastern portion of Pennsylvania. The placement of these public houses suggests that county officials took seriously the understanding that taverns were intended for the use of travelers. Travelers could probably locate a convenient house on their route, but residents would have had to venture some distance from their homes. In 1700, four individuals in the county were licensed to operate a public house, a ratio of one for every ninety-seven tax-payers. By 1717, the number of taverns had increased to nine, or one tavern for every ninety-one taxpayers. By 1730, the number of taverns per capita had declined. The Chester County Court issued at least thirty-five licenses to serve 1,791 taxpayers, or one drinking establishment for fifty-one heads of household. By 1769, the trend was reversing itself. Seventy tavern licenses were issued in Chester County, offering one public house for every sixty-one taxpayers.[43]

The inhabitants of Middletown, in Chester County, hoped to reduce the number of taverns in their midst, but county officials were not bound by the same motivation. Town residents requested specifically that the court not renew Peter Tregoe's license in 1733, because there were "already besides . . . two taverns or inns for the publick entertainment of strangers and travelers." One was situated on the road to Chester, the other was on the road to Philadelphia. The inspired complainers pointed out that with that density of taverns, Tregoe's could be reduced to a "tippling house to harbour idle and disorderly person." Almost as an afterthought, the petitioners noted that Tregoe's tavern was very near the place they had reserved for "our meeting together in a publick manner to worship." The court appeared unimpressed. While they refused to renew Tregoe's license in August 1733, he posted bond in early September, suggesting that he was indeed approved as a proprietor of a house of entertainment.[44]

Licensing Practice

By the eighteenth century, officials were paying less and less attention to identifying ideal publicans and controlling tavern density and appear to have unofficially substituted other licensing criteria. An analysis of Chester County, Pennsylvania, licenses confirms this shift. From 1700 to 1736, successful license petitions in Chester County fell into three distinct categories. By far the most common were petitioners who claimed prime location. Of the ninety-seven successful petitions presented to the Court of Quarter Sessions for recommendation to the governor, forty-six (47.4%) argued that their convenient location on major roads made them worthy candidates. Joseph Cloud claimed, in 1720, that many of his neighbors and others who traveled "the back roads" had urged him to keep a public house of entertainment. The Court of Quarter Sessions concurred. Similarly, in 1722, William Barns of Kennett appealed to the "great concerns" of travelers along the road linking the area to Maryland and Conestoga, Pennsylvania. The result was the "great necessity of establishing a public house." On occasion, the court received a petition that complained of the inconvenience suffered by an entire town because it lacked a convenient tavern. In 1727, the inhabitants of the town of Uwchlan, for example, grumbled that their residences were "fifty miles and upwards distant from Chester and no house of publick entertainment [was] erected in all spaces or distances." As a result, they were "often belated in our carriges and journeys and like to suffer extreamly."[45]

Jacob Wesler provided the most dramatic evidence for the centrality of location as a criterion for a license. Wesler resided in Schuylkill Township on the road from West Chester to Evansburgh in Montgomery County. He explained that a public house of entertainment was greatly needed on this road, since it was well traveled. Included with his petition was a statement signed by twelve presumably upstanding Schuylkill residents confirming their want of a tavern. Most unusual, eight days later the court received a map, presumably drawn by Wesler, detailing his location in relationship to the region's road system and another statement signed by five men, including Wesler, testifying to the accuracy of this drawing. The court rewarded Wesler's diligence and persuasiveness by approving him for a license.[46]

The second most common argument presented to the Chester County court was that the applicant proposed to assume an existing business. The petitioner would therefore not be increasing the density of taverns. The thirty applications during 1700–1736 that employed this argument (30.9%) stressed the petitioner's suitability for a license because he or she had taken over a house that was previously operated as a tavern. In 1731, David Cowpland of Chester took over the farm where "Ruth Hoskins lately dwelt which hath been a house of entertainment." Cowpland received a license. In 1732, Michael Atkinson of Radnor informed the court that he had just rented the house of David Evans, a former tavern keeper. Atkinson's had made previous attempts to obtain the court's approval and failed. When his petition represented no new tavern, the court ruled favorably on his request.[47] The audacious petition of Mathais Kyrlen (sometimes Kerlin) spoke directly to the court's stated intention to control tavern density. He reviewed various distresses caused by the presence of too many taverns in the town, and he suggested that the court limit the number of taverns in Concord to one, his. The court concurred, and for the next four years, at least, he had the only license to operate a tavern in the town.[48]

Insolvency and/or advanced age was the third most common reason petitioners cited for why they deserved a license. They claimed that a tavern license was their only hope for keeping the family off of the public dole. During the period 1700–1736, thirteen Chester Countians cited their impoverished state, infirmity, or old age in their claim that they could carry on no other trade (13.4%). Five of these thirteen noted that their location forced them to care for visitors and that this burden added to their already perilous economic condition. In 1724, John Rice of Chester argued that he and his wife were "both ancient and almost past their labour" so that they were unable to earn a living by any other means. In addition, they were constantly burdened with travelers and had "taken in several to lodge." Yet because they had no license they could not give them adequate accommodations nor could "they receive any satisfaction." Another petitioner, Elizabeth Rankin, lamented to the justices that she was a poor widow living on "the Kings Road, which leads from Brandywine to Conestoga." She was "much encumbered with travelers passing and repassing the road to the great damage and detriment of your petitioner." In 1731, Edward Thomas of Radnor found himself in a similar predicament. His house was near St. David's Church and he was "obliged to entertain many people that come to worship at the sd church and being but a poor man [he was] not able to bear that burden."[49]

The Chester County petitions confirm how difficult it is to ascertain what criteria justices applied to determine who would receive a license. Even though the vast majority of successful petitions related the desirability of their public house to the institutional guidelines governing public houses, the attempt to decipher the justices's bases for granting licenses remains confounded, since the petitions they rejected represented the same three categories as those that succeeded— well located, assuming the proprietorship of a recently vacated tavern, and age, infirmity, or poverty. James Patton, from Londonderry, did not receive the court's approval even though he described his house as situated on the main road leading to Lancaster County, and the closest public house was more than twenty miles away. Patrick Montgomery, from Hallowfield, received a license, having purchased a house that had been a "house of entertainment" for many years, but William Robinson left court without a license even though he had kept the Spread Eagle tavern for many years and neither he nor his patrons had appeared in court on any tavern- or drinking-related charges. George Wood, from Derby, cited his infirmities and inability to care for his family as the reasons he wanted a license; Barbara Custard, from Coventry, explained her need based on her widowhood and having to maintain "her poor fatherless children." Wood was licensed, Custard was not. There is no question that the justices in Chester County kept tabs on the number of taverns in the county; the proportion of taverns to population remained fairly constant throughout the colonial period. What is less clear, though, is how they decided between seemingly identical claims for licenses. Perhaps the justices's use of location was extremely straightforward and based upon making sure that ample public houses dotted their routes home or provided them with quality accommodations on their travel to the next circuit court. It is equally possible that some decisions were based on personal relationships and the justices were more inclined to award a license to their brother-in-law or neighbor than to a stranger.[50]

❖   ❖   ❖

PHILADELPHIA MERCHANT Charles Thomson's complaint to Benjamin Franklin that tavern licensing law was more about collecting revenue than regulating taverns was an astute comment on the divergence between the stated objectives of licensing and its practice. Although fee collection was not the only place in which the system veered from its goals, Thomson correctly assessed the seemingly arbitrary licensing process that only sometimes worked to control the number of taverns or quality of the keepers. Thomson's observation concerned Pennsylvania laws, but the colonies shared a tradition of articulating a standard from which they consistently deviated.

Whether by intention or by accidental consequence, licensing officials seem, in regions for which there exist sufficient records, to have achieved a proportion of drinking houses to population that varied little over time or place, regardless of changes in numbers of taverns. When the number of taverns in Boston dipped during the mid-eighteenth century, it mirrored a decline in the city's population. No thirsty soul, in a city or port town at least, had to search very far for an alcoholic beverage and drinking companions. This suggests that those responsible for issuing licenses interpreted their role less as a charge to limit accessibility than to guarantee their citizenry sufficient accessibility. Licensing officials operated from the premise that colonists expected to have a local tavern, even though the law specified that public houses were in the business of accommodating travelers not the locals. Petitioners in turn knew how important it was to claim that their house was situated in a "convenient location," but this phrase had multiple meanings. Some petitioners made the case that they were well situated for strangers, since their houses were located on a main road or in an area of a port city known to attract visitors. But potential publicans also invoked convenient location on behalf of their neighbors, who expected to be close to a public house. Because officials periodically voiced their concerns about too many taverns and occasionally cited this as a reason to reject a petition, aspiring proprietors sometimes employed convenient location by arguing that no other public house was close by. It is difficult to imagine that officials paid much attention to the spacial arrangement of taverns, because public houses clustered tightly in the major port cities, sometimes being next door to each other. Urban thirsts clearly demanded a high tavern density, and no policies or ideologies interfered seriously with the supply.

The Tavern Degenerate:
"Rendezvous of the very Dreggs
of the People"

It is notorious, that Ordinaries are now, in a great Measure, perverted from
their original Intention and proper Use; viz. the Reception, Accommodation, and Refreshment of the weary and benighted Traveller; which ends
they least serve or answer and are become the common Receptacle and
Rendezvous of the very Dreggs of the People; even of the most lazy and
dissolute that are to be found in their respective Neighbourhoods, where
not only Time and Money are, vainly and unprofitably, squandered away,
but (what is yet worse) where prohibited and unlawful Games, Sports, and
Pastimes are used, followed, and practised, almost without any Intermis-
sion; namely cards, dice, Horse-Racing, and cock-fighting, together with
Vices and Enormities of every other kind.[1]

*T*he anonymous Virginia clergyman who in 1751 penned this complaint
about the local tavern scene listed exactly the societal ills colonial leaders had sought to prevent. Taverns were supposed to accommodate travelers,
but, as he noted, they had been "perverted" from their proper use and had descended into decadence. His lament appears to be aimed at a particular segment
of society—those least able to spare the time or money and for whom abusing
drink inexorably led to other and greater vices.

Accommodation on the Road

For the travelers who depended upon taverns for their lodging and meals, finding a suitable house was like a game of chance in which the odds were most often stacked against them. James Clitherall, whose journey took him from his home in Charleston, South Carolina, to Philadelphia, complained bitterly about the taverns he encountered. At one of them he was resigned to ingratiation in order to secure services, even though he described it as "by far the worst House we visited. . . . We obliged to be on our very Best behavior for we were given to understand that ourselves & Horses would get nothing to eat."[2] When Ebenezer Hazard stopped at Smith's tavern in New Jersey on his trip through New England and New York, he encountered "as vile a house as I would ever wish to be in: about twenty drunken men in the house, cursing swearing and fighting in great abundance: an old man called his son a dog. . . . Smith did have a good stable and our horses were well taken care of." A few days later, Hazard stopped at Caleb Merrit's, which he judged to be a good clean house, although the bedroom was cold, and "the sheets not well aired." Again Hazard noted that his horse had the better end of the bargain.[3] A merchant named Anthony Stoddard, on his travels from Boston to Vermont, lamented how ill-prepared he was because he had virtually no way of gaining advance knowledge about the quality of the accommodations along his route. He discovered only too late about the mediocre facilities he was forced to hire. In two public houses it was the food that he found so awful, since it consisted exclusively of bacon and eggs. Stoddard ranked one house, which had only a few bugs, as "pretty good lodging," even though it was "very noisey most part of the night with partying, dancing, fireing guns &c on account of a training day & a wedding which disturbed our rest."[4] Philip Fithian described a tavern where he stayed one night in Port Tobacco, Maryland: "For my company all the night in my Room I had Bugs in every part of my Bed—& in the next Room several noisy Fellows playing at Billiards."[5]

Travelers often had little choice about where to stay, which put them at the mercy of the unpredictable roadside accommodations. Nicholas Cresswell, an English traveler, wandered through the colonies for three years, from 1774 to 1777, filling his diary with vivid, humorous descriptions of the meaner sorts of taverns. His literary efforts enabled him to highlight the inferior nature of taverns in the colonies as compared to public houses in Britain. In Annapolis, Maryland, he breakfasted at Rollins', "a Public House, but in this Country called Ordinaries, and indeed they have not their name for nothing, for they are ordinary enough." He complained that it made no difference where he ate or which meal of the day it was, for he was always served bacon or chicken. "If I still continue in this way [I] shall be grown over with Bristles or Feathers."[6]

Rural taverns could be even worse than those in towns. An account by William Logan, president of the governor's council of Pennsylvania, gives us a palpable sense of rural houses he encountered on his trip from Pennsylvania to Georgia. At Skidmore's tavern he "Lodged on a tolerable Good Bed" in "a very nasty room." Dinner the next day was broth made from recently killed fowls, "but everything was so nasty that One might have picked the Dirt off." In Bath, North Carolina, when rain prevented him from going on, he stopped at a tavern that was "by far the worse we have met with; there being a stinking ordinary Bed, an Earthen floor & many air holes."[7]

James Birket fashioned himself a keen observer of early American customs and habits from his year-long journey through the colonies. The tavern keepers he encountered shared the trait of indifference. In Rhode Island, he stopped at "One Mother Stacks, who I thought realy very Slack in her Attendance." All she supplied was a candle in a house that was so dark "we could Scarce See Another." What was worse, she offered them nothing for supper. However, he and his traveling companions rummaged around and found food aplenty, so that they made out a "Handsome supper & Liquor." He only wished they could have done as well with the "very Indifferent" beds. Birket was hard pressed to find good words to describe publicans. The best he could say about Captain Bradock's, in New London, Connecticut, was that the keeper was polite and had good manners "when Compared with the rude lay drones of this part of the world." Frustrated with again not being offered food and drink, Birket chalked a message on the table, perhaps to remind the proprietor of his duties to his patrons:

Wee can't pretend to Poetry
His Brains are dull whose Throat is Dry,
Wee Little else can say or think
But give us victuals and some Drink.[8]

One traveler, William Ellery, recorded the set of rituals he adopted to protect himself from the repugnant tavern services he expected to encounter. Rule number one was "Search [the bed] first before you enter." Ellery described one occasion in which this practice yielded an enormous, bloated bed bug, which he sacrificed, using the candle blaze, to the "God of Impurity." This, according to Ellery, was in a "good house."[9]

Favorable assessments of roadside accommodation, although few, also exist. John Penn reported on a number of quite agreeable taverns on his tour through Pennsylvania and Delaware. He found Whitman's tavern "worthy of a respectable country town." There he "dined heartily upon catfish, which the river plentifully affords." However, Penn's judgment did seem to be clouded by the proprietor's political views. He was the only tavern keeper whose name had not appeared on a petition written against the proprietary estate. Penn also discovered a good tavern in Newport, a town close to Wilmington, Delaware. Here he found "proper entertainment for horse and man." He liked the place even though while there he watched "two rustics completely drunk and by degrees becoming less and less intelligible."[10]

Although foreign travelers were not amused by having to stay in dirty and noisy taverns that failed to provide adequate food, they mustered even more hostility for the practice of sharing beds. European visitors equated the habit of bed sharing with the worst characteristics of American life. One, James Birket, described being forced by heavy rains and darkness to find shelter before reaching Horseneck, near Stamford, Connecticut, with his traveling party. The tavern keeper, "an Illnaturd old fellow" was reluctant to give him a room, and then he "wanted a barefooted fellow who we afterwards understood to be [the keeper's wife's] Son to Sleep with one of us but we one & all refused the favour." The French traveler Moreau de St. Mery criticized all manner of American accommodations, including how the lack of curtains on beds or windows in any inn meant that during the long summer days the fatigued traveler was sure to be awakened at the crack of dawn by the sun streaming into his room. But the very worst aspect of American taverns was the habit of sharing beds. For him, this practice was "untidy" and "unhealthy." According to the Scottish traveler Thomas Cather, American "guests pig together two and three in a bed." When he insisted on having a bed to himself, the landlords thought him quite unreasonable. St.

Mery and Cather evoked images of pigs and feared threats to their health. St. Mery was incredulous upon discovery that people who did not know each other were "admitted to the same room. . . . Even while one traveler is asleep, another often enters to share his bed." Americans, he observed, considered this custom "perfectly natural"; and he went on to reflect, "I cannot help but rebel at the nonsensical belief that such customs are a proof of liberty."[11]

Colonial travelers fully expected to join strangers in a bed or be awakened as newcomers arrived. Private sleeping spaces in public houses were so rare that a historian cites a case of a woman traveler who expressed discomfort at having a room at an inn all to herself.[12] Colonists described sleeping arrangements matter-of-factly; they might remark on the idiosyncracies of their sleeping partners, their manners or snoring habits, but they did not question the practice or expectation that they would sleep in a bed with one or more strangers. A distasteful example is provided in an account by James Clitheral, who somewhere in North Carolina stayed the night at Major Berkely's tavern, "by far the worst House we visited. . . . we passed the night very disagreeably & caught bad colds. In the morning our greasy landlord (who wanted to sleep with Me & entertained Me with his adventures when he went to subdue the Scopholites . . .) charged us an enormous Price for the worst of Accommodation." David Sewall, a Harvard undergraduate, kept a journal of his travels with a Harvard tutor, Mr. Flynt. Of the tavern in Marblehead he said, "we were cordially entertained, and at bedtime we were introduced to a chamber where was only one bed." Mr. Flynt iterated that Sewall would be "keeping well to his own side." Alexander Hamilton reported that early on in his travels he lodged at a ferry house; "my landlord, his wife, daughters, and I lay all in one room." On his way back to Annapolis, Hamilton stayed in a public house in Newcastle, Maryland, where he shared the room with "a certain Irish teague and one Gilpin, a dweller in Maryland." Hamilton had a bed to himself; the other two shared. Hamilton and Gilpin conversed while in bed before they went to sleep and then had their slumbers disturbed by the Irish teague "who made a hideous noise in coming to bed, and as he tossed and turned, kept still ejaculating either an ohon or sweet Jesus."[13]

Sharing accommodations was the custom in every colony and was not limited to those from a particular socioeconomic status. When colonial leader William Byrd and his party surveyed the boundary line between Virginia and North Carolina, they camped most nights, because taverns were so scarce. On one evening, however, they stopped at a private house. His traveling group and the family lodged in a single room; "nine persons, who all pigged lovingly together," as he put it. The group split up the next night. Three of his companions stayed at another private house, where the owner let them have his bed. The three of them "nestled together in one cotton sheet and one of brown Osnaburgs, made still browner by two months' copious perspiration." Edgecomb County, North Carolina, established a tavern rate schedule that included different costs "for a bed where more than one in a bed [or] any person requiring a bed to himself." The latter arrangement cost twice as much.[14]

The practice of putting strangers in beds together remained in American public houses until well after the Revolution and persisted as a source of irritation to visitors from abroad. Francisco de Miranda, a Portuguese visitor to the United States in 1783–84, found this particular custom to be among the most unpleasant he encountered in America and endlessly argued with tavern keepers about it. In a small North Carolina town, which contained only one public house, the proprietor intended that de Miranda would share a "terrible bed" with a Mr. Tucker, a fellow traveler, from Boston. De Miranda was adamant that this bed was suitable for only a single person. The landlady gave in to his pleading by "thrust[ing] two other guests into another small bed in the very room that had been set aside" for de Miranda and Tucker. In New London, Connecticut, de Miranda was relieved that the landlord had merely put "another guest in my room; thank God he was not put in my bed, according to the custom of the country!"[15]

The quality of accommodation at roadside taverns in early America ran a wide gamut. Travelers might encounter a public house with good provisions for humans and horses along with passable entertainments. They were just as likely, however, to stumble into houses in which the conditions made their skin crawl—monotonous diets served in filthy conditions and beds that contained the evidence of their previous occupants and commonly had six-legged occupants. Since the threshold for tolerance of dirt was quite high in early America—a time before regular laundering and bathing constituted normative behavior—the taverns that elicited negative comment must have been quite awful. The variation in services also suggests that while colonial statutes were designed to regulate tavern conditions, nothing motivated colonial officials to enforce these laws. Colonists traveled at their own risk.

Sociability and Conversation

Elite male travelers longed for good public houses. They assumed that they deserved decent fare for themselves and their horses and they expected suitable entertainment. They sought tavern sociability that would provide them with the opportunity to encounter men much like themselves who, with the aid of ample quantities of drink, were eager to explore ideas through conversation. Dr. Alexander Hamilton was one of a number of diarists whose writings offer insight into this tavern phenomenon. Hamilton was a physician who received his medical degree from the University of Edinburgh. His older brother John, also a doctor, had emigrated to Annapolis, Maryland, and established a lucrative practice; Alexander followed him in the winter of 1738. Six years later, following an illness, he journeyed from Maryland to Maine and back in an attempt to restore his health. In his detailed journal, he joins other elite men who expressed a common goal—to locate a tavern that would provide them with genteel entertainments. The pages of his diary drip with sardonic descriptions of how most taverns fell far short of what he, as an elite man, merited. Most public houses were indeed ordinary and frustrating approximations of an imagined space where men like Hamilton were forced to rub elbows, drink, and talk with those well beneath them in terms of education and status.[16]

Hamilton's stay at Waghorn's Sign of the Cart and Horse in New York turned into a lesson in frustration. Hamilton negotiated the terms of his lodging, arranged to buy horses for future travel, and secured goods. He detested the scene he encountered in the public room. It was midday and a group of drinkers was gathered around William Jameson, the High Sheriff of New York. Hamilton observed that those assembled were transfixed by Jameson's story telling—the combination of wit and vulgarity. Hamilton found himself incapable of concentrating on the tale; he could only stare at the man's face. He had a "homely carbuncle kind of a countenance with a hideous knob of a nose, he screwd it into a hundred different forms while he spoke and gave such a strong emphasis to his words that he merely spit in one's face att three or four foot's distance." His mouth was constantly full of spit "by the force of the liquor which he drank and the fumes of the tobacco that he smoaked." According to Hamilton's standards, the High Sheriff was as coarse as he was drunk and as ugly as he was common. The scene was made far more depressing for Hamilton because the crowd was so captivated by the sheriff.[17]

While elite men like Hamilton might have been frustrated in their attempts to find taverns and drinking companions that befit their stations in life, they could depend upon the locals to include them in their tavern entertainments. When Hamilton arrived in Trenton, New Jersey, he "put up" at Eliah Bond's tavern. Two gentlemen came in and invited him to join them; they "supped upon cold gammon and a sallet." Hamilton criticized their rambling conversation, although he appreciated the considerable time and effort they put into explaining New Jersey politics. After that "the discourse turned to religion and then to physick." Hamilton's experience was typical of the upper-class traveler. In towns in which he knew no one, he expected and received an invitation to join the locals. He may have considered them unworthy, but he was asked to participate in their drinking, eating, talking, or other entertainments.[18]

No matter where James Birket stayed on his journey or how foreign his surroundings appeared to him, the tavern provided him with companionship and a semblance of familiarity. In Portsmouth, New Hampshire, Birket lodged at the Widow Slaton's, "the best tavern for Strangers in town." He was there from August 16 through August 31, 1750, and listed his dining companions for each night in his diary. He recorded the same experiences in Boston. With the exception of the day he arrived, September 5, Birket did not dine alone in the city. William Gregory, a Virginia merchant, had no sooner arrived in Philadelphia than he was invited to dine with a Mr. Bell, described by Gregory as a gentleman, "in company with two others."[19]

During his stay in New York City, Hamilton presented himself and one of his letters of introduction and was soon invited to join a group of gentlemen for supper. After they finished eating, they settled in to drink. For Hamilton, this best summed up life in New York: "They filled bumpers att each round of toasting. I drank only three—to the King, and the governors of New Jersey and New York." Two or three of the company voiced their deep philosophical musings that the most sociable quality of a man was to "be able to pour down seas of liquor and remain unconquered while others sunk under the table." Hamilton's commentary reveals that these men did not measure up to his standards. They were incapable of sustaining a decent conversation, let alone a discourse on philosophy. He claimed that he did not agree with the views espoused, although he refused to share his own opinions publicly. He chose instead to leave the group early, around ten o'clock. This was Hamilton's rendition of the events. Another possible interpretation is that he could not get a word into the conversation and he crept away in silence. Even though he had consumed only three bumpers, he was "pritty well flushed."[20]

William Black, the Virginia representative to the treaty meeting with the Iroquois, claimed that the benefit derived from taverns was not to be found in the food and drink but in the conversations. It was to his and others great benefit that the focus was almost always on political topics. He professed that an hour spent in discussion in a tavern yielded more information about people and places than a week of observation. The advantages of "Polite Company" were numerous, he said; they assisted understanding in a person "who might otherwise [have] his Sight Limited to the Length of his Nose."[21]

Hamilton agreed with Black. At the end of his journey to and from Maine, Hamilton summarized what he had learned about the colonies as the result of his travels. He offered general observations about the density of the populations, governments, the quality of the air, and the relative physical size of the people. In his judgment, the "politeness and humanity" of the colonists was alike everywhere except in the "great towns where the inhabitants are more civilized, especially in Boston." He admitted that he learned quite a lot from walking the streets. However, most of his conversations and contact with people occurred in taverns. And these public houses shared a remarkable similarity no matter where he was. "Polite company" everywhere, he ventured, conformed to the same set of rules, and for Hamilton, this was an essential ingredient in being "civilized."[22]

Hamilton also concurred with Black's assessment that political discourse ranked among the most common forms of tavern conversation. At a tavern in Darby, near Philadelphia, Hamilton and his traveling companion "were entertained with an elegant dispute between a young Quaker and the boatswain of a privateer concerning the lawfullness of using arms against an enemy." The argument became quite heated, and Hamilton, in his most imperious tone, predicted that they would not reach a conclusion. At another stop, the local doctor talked to him about the miserable condition of the local governing assembly. It was "chiefly composed of mechanicks and ignorant wretches, obstinate to the last degree." In this situation Hamilton no doubt found comfort and companionship and appreciated the doctor's sentiments about the base nature of the assemblymen. In his journal he confessed to feeling more like the recipient of a lecture from the doctor than a participant in an intellectual discourse. By Hamilton's standards, even this fellow did not quite measure up.[23]

European travelers expressed genuine surprise at the level of political discourse that took place inside colonial taverns and the degree of emotion displayed in the course of the debates. A French visitor dined in a tavern not far from Annapolis, "in a large Company, the Conversation Continually on the Stamp Dutys. I was realy surprised to here the people talk so freely." It was the same the next night. "After dinner as the botle was going round the Conversat'n fell on the Stamps, and as the wine operated the rage against the proceedings of the parlement augment." The discussion became so agitated that someone declared that the citizenry should take up arms. Even the magistrate present, who throughout the proceedings had done his best to temper the intensity of feeling, agreed that he too might be required to defend "his liberty and property, upon which he had a huza from the Company." Politics combined with drink was a sure formula for increasing the political temperature.[24]

Tavern conversation afforded local residents the opportunity to inquire about the origins, goals, class, and religious persuasion of all strangers. Hamilton often referred to how completely he was scrutinized by landlords or their families and how he put up with a barrage of questions he thought impertinent from people he took to be beneath him and without the entitlement to ask them. Andrew Burnaby, on a visit to the colonies from his home in England, claimed that when he went into an ordinary in Massachusetts, every individual in the proprietor's family directed a question or two at him "relative to his history; and that, till each was satisfied, and they had conferred and compared together their information, there was no possibility of procuring any refreshment." Burnaby concocted a prepared speech detailing his identity in order to preempt the interrogation and increase his chances of quicker service. Travelers were at the mercy of such inquisitive tavern keepers.[25]

Josiah Quincy, in his travels from Boston to South Carolina in 1773, success-fully located well-appointed taverns by relying on the advice of folks he met on route. Through the rituals of drinking and the language of class he was able to connect with other gentlemen. "I toast all the friends, Sir. Each gent gave his toast round in succession."[26] The Marquis de Chastellux had a very different opinion of this custom. He complained of the tiresome rituals required of drinkers in the better American taverns. When he visited Philadelphia in the early 1780s, he described at length what he referred to as an absurd and bar-barous practice—with the first drink and at the start of the meal he had to call out each person's name to inform that man that he was drinking to his health. He likened the situation to an actor in a comedy who is dying of thirst yet must take the time to enquire after or "catch the eye of the five and twenty persons" be-fore taking the first swallow.[27]

By the mid-eighteenth century, when the well-heeled traveler happened upon a high-quality establishment in a city, he encountered scenes that were filled with strangers yet were familiar and comfortable. They were entreated to join with the locals, to participate in the drinking and conversation. Locals bombarded strangers with questions determined to gain information about where they had come from, why they were there, the nature of their business, and how long they might stay. In some regions, like New England, proprietors had a legal obliga-tion to know who was in their houses, so that the presence of any visitors who planned to remain in their tavern for more than a few days could be reported to the authorities. Elsewhere the interrogation was motivated by a desire for in-formation and news about places and events outside the locals' experience. It was also the time that travelers presented their identity, an identity that was based on their outward appearance as well as their familiarity with the rituals of tavern sociability, the drinking and conversation inside the tavern.

The Tavern as Gendered Space

In a letter penned to the *New England Courant*, Benjamin Franklin reminded readers about the vice of drunkenness and pointed out the value of moderate drinking: a "little Liquor" combined with "much Study and Experience," he claimed, were required in order for some men to become accomplished orators;

the moderate use of liquor endowed the bumbler with fluency and warmth. Intelligent, informed talk was valued and practiced by men in Franklin's station. The tavern was an important site of conversation, and the relationship of drinking to conversation contributed to sustaining the gendered nature of tavern culture. Franklin was quite sure that "my own Sex are generally the most eloquent because the most passionate . . . 'that they could talk whole Hours together upon any thing; but it must be owned to the Honour of the other Sex, that there are many among them who can talk whole Hours together on Nothing.'"[28]

Jacob Hiltzheimer, a lesser government official in Pennsylvania, engaged in a wide range of social events that took place both inside and outside the tavern. Away from the tavern his wife more often than not accompanied him. They attended weddings and funerals, dined at the homes of friends and family, entertained visitors at their home, and appeared at plays. On the many occasions when Hiltzheimer socialized in the tavern, his wife was not present. He could often be found in a tavern day or night, drinking with friends, celebrating special events, or meeting with business associates. He "got decently drunk" to celebrate the approaching marriage of a friend, although "the groom could not be accused of the same fault." He drank punch with Levi Hollingsworth to mark his recent marriage and with Henry Keppele to commemorate the birth of Keppele's son. Some trips to the tavern required no special excuse; on January 14, 1767, he "spent the evening at John Biddle's" with three gentlemen. Two days after his "wife gave birth to a son" Hiltzheimer spent the evening at Mrs. Gray's drinking punch.[29] Hiltzheimer also regularly dined at the tavern, with various informal gatherings of men. At times these meals preceded events, like the breakfast at Mrs. Gray's with five gentlemen before they set out to go fox hunting.[30] Hiltzheimer spent considerable social time with his wife; when he went inside the tavern, however, he did so without her. That space was reserved for his engagements with men.

Captain Francis Goelet worked the Boston to London sea route. By day, Goelet loaded and prepared his ship for its return voyage; at night he transformed into a frenetic socializer and drinker. Unlike many drinkers who remained planted in a single seat for hours, Goelet moved around the city from tavern to tavern. On one layover, his second night in Boston, Goelet joined a group of "abt 40 Gentlemen" in a tavern. They dined elegantly, drank extensive toasts, and "Sang a Number of Songs, and [were] Exceeding Merry until 3 a Clock in the Morning." The group he was with walked in the direction of his lodging, past the Boston Commons, where they encountered a group of "Country Young Men and Women with a Violin at A Tavern Danceing and Makeing Merry." When Goelet and his group pushed their way into the space, the "Young Women Fled, we took Posession of the Room." A fiddler was present; so was a "Keg of Sugard Dram," which, according to Goelet, contributed greatly to their merriment. They left the tavern and proceeded to Mr. Jacob Wendells' establishment, where they were "obliged to Drink Punch and Wine." The party broke up about five o'clock in the morning, and Goelet went off to bed. The following night he began his entertainments anew.[31] He went to a "Turtle Frolick with a Compy of Gentn and Ladies" (presumably a frolic with human companions while dining on turtle). They danced "Several Minuits and country Dances and [were] very Merry," and about dusk the men escorted the women to their homes and regrouped in a tavern for the evening's drinking. On another occasion, he "Drank Plentifully Toasted the Ladies Singing &c. Abt Dusk the Evening returned to Boston," and spent the remainder of the night playing cards with "some Ladies." Goelet was invited to dine at the home of Mr. Thomas Leachmore, the Surveyor General, and found there a gathering of men and several women. After he left the dinner he retired with his male friends to a tavern. Goelet lived a busy social life while in Boston. When the occasions took place outside the tavern, they included women; when inside the public house, it was only men.[32]

Account books confirm the gendered nature of tavern sociability. The Lowrence Tavern in Rowan County, North Carolina, sold liquor—by the drink and as a carry out trade—and exchanged a wide variety of goods—tobacco, paper, flints, shot powder, medicines, nails, tools, cloth, buttons, and leather goods. In the eleven years before the American Revolution, 195 individuals had accounts with the Lowrences. Only seven were women, and all of those appear to have been unmarried. Two were listed as widows, a third was referred to as Granny Cathy, and three others must have been recently widowed, since they replaced a male customer with the same surname.[33]

These seven women conducted their business with the Lowrences very differently than did their male counterparts. Men rarely went to the tavern just to pick up the supplies they needed. Usually, they tended to their business and spent some time in the tavern over a pint or a bowl of punch. In contrast, the women did not order anything to be consumed on the premises, nor did any of them purchase liquor in any quantity smaller than a quart. Women were clearly not part of the public culture of drink. If they bought liquor, they carted it off to the privacy of their homes.

Of all of the people with whom tavern keepers Robert and Lydia Moulder, of Chichester, Pennsylvania, had accounts, only two were women. Neither was charged for drink on the premises. Rachel Pedrick carried home wine, spirits, butter, and a small cash loan; Catherine Lawrence purchased six pounds of beef. Similarly, of 221 customers of John Wilson's merchandise business and tavern, only 6 women were listed has having accounts with him. They purchased a huge variety of goods—salt, gloves, nails, beef, sugar, rope, linen, buttons, butter, and more. Of the three women who purchased liquor, none did so in small quantity. Thus, it is highly unlikely that they stayed on the premises to imbibe. In an account book from an anonymous tavern in Salem, Massachusetts, from the early decades of the eighteenth century, not a single woman is listed as a customer.[34] Women are completely absent from Mary Cranch's account book as well.[35]

A business advice article in the *Boston Gazette* portrayed women's exclusion from the tavern as an advantage to employers. The author advocated apprenticing women to the retail trades, because it would ultimately lower overall expenses and increase profits. "Men generally transact all Business of this kind in Taverns and Coffee houses, at a great additional Expence, and the Loss of Much time . . . while Women, upon the Conclusion of a Bargain, have no Inducement to make a longer Stay, but go directly Home, and follow their Affairs."[36]

Respectable women in the colonial period entered public houses rarely and in restricted contexts. Their limited relationship to taverns as patrons is not meant to imply that women did not drink alcoholic beverages. Rather, they drank as they generally lived, in the private rather than the public realm. Even the notion of drunkenness was gendered. The condition was read differently if the culprit was a man or a woman. Female drunkenness exacted a toll on women's reputations that was not comparable with the same behavior in men.[37] In depositions taken in September 1626, Roger Dilke and his friend Thomas Dellamaior described the events that had occurred around nine or ten at night when they were returning to their lodging. They saw Goodwife Ffysher and Mr. Sotherne walking ahead of them. Dilke testified that "good wiefe Ffysher did reele and stagger as she wente, and that shee stumbled and fell uppon a Cow or by a Cow or an ewe or some such beste." Goodwife Ffysher's companion tried to grab her arm to steady her but her antics had already been witnessed. Dellamaior deposed that "it was greate shame to see a man drunke, But more shame to see a woman in that case."[38]

Over a hundred years later, drunkenness in women still left an indelible blemish. Late one spring night at around eleven o'clock, on William Black's walk back to his lodgings from his night's entertainments, he "was met by a Woman tolerably well dress'd, and seem'd a good likely Person to Appearance but very much in Liquor. . . . I had curiosity enough to turn her round to have a better view; on which I made the Discovery of her being in a Condition, which of all others, least becomes the Sex."[39] Black, Dilke, and Dellamaior represent the shared attitude of early Americans: public drinking and drunkenness were masculine and the consequences of being drunk were weighed differently if the person reeling and staggering was a man or a woman.

The experiences of women travelers exposes further the gendered nature of the tavern space. Although women occasionally stopped overnight in taverns, they stayed in them only reluctantly, after they had exhausted the possibility of other lodging. When women were in a traveling party, landlords on occasion made some effort to reduce the awkwardness of the sleeping arrangements, and sometimes homeowners came to their rescue. James Clitherall was escorting two women on a venture from Charleston, South Carolina, to Philadelphia in 1776. In one town along the way, a gentleman, "seeing the Poorness & noisiness of the tavern [and] having two spare beds in his house, kindly invited the ladies to partake of them." All Clitherall himself received from the same gentleman was an invitation to dine. He had to return for the night to his own, unsatisfactory, lodging at Adamson's tavern, where he found "so much drinking and gaming, fighting & swearing . . . that I found it impossible to continue there." He moved to Fagan's tavern, where to his delight there were clean sheets and no noise.[40]

Sarah Knight, whose four-month journey to New York from her home in Boston began in October 1704, also preferred lodging in private homes rather than taverns. Her guide escorted her as far as Dedham, Massachusetts, where he expected that she would catch the western post. However, it never appeared.

She adamantly refused to lodge at the local tavern, though she entered it briefly to inquire whether any of the group assembled would accompany her to Billings' tavern twelve miles down the road. She received no response. She interpreted their unwillingness to be of assistance as a reluctance to cease drinking even for a moment; "they being tyed by the Lippss to a pewter engine."[41]

"Madam Knight" secured a guide eventually, and her arrival late that night at Billings' tavern caused quite a stir. The proprietor's eldest daughter bombarded her with questions. The landlord's daughter confessed that she had never seen "a woman on the Rode so Dreadfull late, in all the days of my versall life." The sleeping arrangement offered was unappealing to Knight: "a parlour in a litle back Lento, wch was almost fill'd wth the bedsted." Knight "was forced to climb on a chair to gitt up to ye wretched bed that lay on it."[42]

Madam Knight was unable to avoid taverns altogether and lodged in them at other points in her journey. Unlike male travelers, she tended to overhear conversations rather than participate in them. At Mr. Havens', a rather good tavern, she reported that this house, despite being "neet and handsome," afforded her no rest. She was disturbed all night by "the Clamor of some of the Town topers in the next room, Who were entred into a strong debate." The intensity of the argument increased until opinions were punctuated by "Roreing voice and Thundering blows with the fist of wickedness on the Table." Knight wished the debater "tongue tyed" in her effort to sleep. She calmed herself by writing a poem and recalling a story told to her by a friend who was similarly disturbed all night in a country inn where four drinkers were "contriving how to bring a triangle into a Square." The only respite from the discussion was as they called for another "gill."[43]

If women partook of tavern services, proprietors and patrons assumed they were wives, servers, or prostitutes. Charlotte Brown, a matron of the English General Hospital in America, traveled to Philadelphia with her colleague Mr. Cherrington in 1756. At each tavern, the proprietors and patrons presumed, not surprisingly, that they were husband and wife. Charlotte Brown had a difficult time persuading them otherwise. In the first tavern, she refused the landlord's offer that she and Mr. Cherrington share one bed and she tried in vain to persuade them to give her a room of her own. At the Indian King in Philadelphia, Brown endured stares from all of "the People of the House," while those assembled debated whether she was Mr. Cherrington's wife or mistress. When her role was revealed, Brown reported, "they treated me with much more Respect." In order to conduct her business, Brown moved out of the tavern into the city's hospital. Her business required that she meet with both men and women. She would have been too exposed at the tavern, opening herself up to all sorts of misinterpretation about the nature of her business. Women did venture inside the tavern. However, respectable women preferred to avoid the discomfort and the risk to their reputations of being seen there.[44]

The gendered nature of the space was further revealed when women were present as proprietors or when they worked in the tavern alongside their husbands or fathers. It appears that women working in the tavern did not, like their male counterparts, participate in the sociability of the house. They were there to serve and not to be seen or heard. According to Dr. Alexander Hamilton, women had no place in the lofty conversations of men. In Annapolis, Hamilton and the tavern keeper Mr. Hart "conversed like a couple of virtuosos." Hart's wife, also present, did not participate in the conversation, a situation Hamilton relished. "He is blessed with silent women, but her muteness is owing to a defect in her hearing. . . . It is well I have thus accounted for it; else such a character in the sex would appear quite out of nature." Hamilton in fact lauded the gendered nature of "polite society." "There is polite conversation here among the better sort, among whom there is no scarcity of men of learning and good sense." However, he noted, the "ladies, for the most part, keep att home and seldom appear in the streets . . . Except att churches or meetings."[45]

A Dangerous Mingling

The earliest taverns included a mix of classes, although they quickly developed distinguishing characteristics and specialized clienteles. City taverns were the first to be differentiated by class. The first taverns in every port city were built along the waterfront. Gradually, as more public houses were erected toward the middle of towns, those clustered around the water became the sites for laboring-class socializing while the new establishments toward town centers attracted middling-class and elite clientele. By the middle of the eighteenth century, the tavern culture in the major port cities accentuated the gaping distance between those on the top of the economic ladder and the rest of society. The culture of drink practiced by proprietors and patrons of lower-end establishments was not only different in character from that of middle-class or elite houses; it challenged the traditional ordering of society by providing a place where various disenfranchised elements of society could mingle.[46]

Early in the history of New Amsterdam, taverns catered to particular clienteles: Farmers who traveled into the city congregated at Sergeant Litschoe's tavern. The White Horse tavern, opened in 1641 by Philip Geraerdy, was a small place, just eighteen by twenty-five feet, and contained only a single door and window, which likely opened into the kitchen, dining room, parlor, and taproom. It attracted servants and soldiers, "bumptious young fellows from all parts of Northern Europe, who caroused and brawled at the tavern when off duty." The White Horse witnessed its share of disorder when the drinking turned violent.[47] Inside the Blue Dove might be a mixture of apprentices, soldiers, and sailors. One particular night in the mid-seventeenth century, the night watchman was called to the Blue Dove to stop a brawl. The place was "badly battered." The watchman escaped, but without his sword. When asked, during his testimony about the event, to name those present, he named a hatter, a servant, and a number of soldiers and sailors.[48]

Sections of New Amsterdam, and later New York, earned a reputation for having rough houses, characterized by rowdy mobs, frequent violence, and hard drinking. Montayne's tavern was the "House where all the Riotous Liberty Boys met in 1765 and 1766." It was center stage during the Golden Hill and Nassau Street riots in 1770. Although less well known than a contemporary event, the Boston Massacre, the Golden Hill and Nassau Street riots had similar origins. The tensions in New York were related to the quartering of a large number of British troops in the city. Montayne's tavern was situated near the liberty pole, the site of much of the street action. A group of the British soldiers attempted to blow up the liberty pole but failed. In their embarrassment at their failure, the troops stormed the tavern. Once at the tavern they turned violent, shattering windows and smashing pottery and furniture. Among Montayne's patrons were those who had the most to lose economically in the competition with soldiers, who searched for temporary jobs to supplement their meagre army pay; for those colonists the liberty pole held much meaning.[49]

At the moment of the troops' attack, the tavern represented the mood of defiance within New York City. It remained a focal point. On the five-year anniversary of the repeal of the Stamp Act, newspaper reports claimed, thirty-five toasts were drunk there in celebration. Five years later the anniversary was marked at Montagne's with a mere twenty-nine toasts. Taverns like Montagne's also housed the city's prostitutes. These taverns, referred to as "receptacles for loose and disorderly persons," were well situated to cater to the soldiers quartered nearby. In 1760, "Mr. Pearson, a Mate belonging to his Majesty's Ship the Mercury, now in this Harbour, having been in Company with a lewd Woman . . . , got his Pocket picked of his Money." He suspected that the other women in the house had assisted in the robbery. On a Tuesday night in October 1766, between eleven and twelve o'clock, "a number of soldiers with bayonets went to Several houses in the Fields where they were very noisy and abusive, to the great disturbance and terror of the inhabitants. This was occasioned, it is said, by ill treatment, which some of the Soldiers had received the night before at one of those infamous houses."[50] In 1768, Fanny Bambridge, an apparently well-known New York prostitute, was found dead at a tavern; the coroner ruled an overdose of alcohol. As further indication of how violent these taverns could be, a report from the early 1770s claimed that a woman was murdered for refusing to bed with a customer in Dower's tavern. The proprietor of the house, Mary Harvey, left, after providing wine to a male customer, leaving him in the company of a woman, Christian Taylor. Taylor reported that the man had "set her on fire" by lighting her petticoats with a candle because she "refused to let him lie with her, he having threatened before, that if she would not, he would either stab or burn her to Death."[51]

Although these taverns contributed greatly to the violence and rowdiness of New York, officials were fundamentally unperturbed. However, when the tavern gatherings included both whites and blacks, New York's leaders took notice. The activities and alliances that occurred in certain taverns complicate our notions of race, status, and gender relations of the time. The stories of the 1712 and 1741 New York slave conspiracies are beyond the scope of this work. Germane, however, is the role played by the tavern in the events leading up to and during the revolts, as well as the involvement of tavern keepers in a series of related illegal activities. The 1712 uprising began on the night of New Year's Day. "A group of slaves" gathered in a tavern, "determined to strike against New York city in an effort of liberation and destruction." Little is known about the collaboration of the tavern keeper except that he welcomed slaves into his house and served them willingly and regularly. The conspirators were comfortable there and used the tavern space to plan the events of the next twelve days. The participants in these gatherings violated a number of New York laws. Tavern keepers could not legally serve slaves liquor nor allow them access to a public house without the express permission of their master. Slaves were forbidden to gather in groups, had their movements within the city restricted, were bound by a strict curfew, and were to limit their contact with free persons.[52]

More is known about the centrality of the tavern in the events leading up to the 1741 slave uprising. Daniel Horsmanden, one of the state supreme court justices involved in the postconspiracy trials, published an account of the 1741 slave conspiracy. In his efforts to convince readers that an organized conspiracy had taken place, "that the negroes were rising," Horsmanden mixed trial testimony with liberal doses of his interpretation and defense of his actions on the bench, but he accurately identified an unmistakable, and for him disturbing, alliance of blacks and whites. Horsmanden's portrayal describes a city divided along the lines of color and class, a configuration that he sought to maintain. What transpired in low-end taverns threatened to upset this racialized arrangement. Several people testified at the conspiracy trials that tavern keeper John Hughson had entertained twenty to thirty slaves at his alehouse and that on more than one occasion constables had had to be called to break up a party. A slave named Cuffee, hanged for his participation in the conspiracy, testified that a club was to meet at "Hughson's in the Easter hollidays, but that the d —— d constables hindered them." Another tavern owner, John Romme, was similarly implicated. One witness described a scene in Romme's tavern, "where she saw in company, together with said Romme and his wife, ten or eleven negroes, all in one room." In their July 23, 1741, session, the supreme court convicted and punished ten additional tavern keepers for keeping "a disorderly house, entertaining negroes, etc." Slaves would frequent city taverns "in the evenings, and . . . stay often late in the night, drinking and playing at dice."[53] Horsmanden's subtext called attention to how the plot was realized within an alliance of blacks and whites, and with the participation of women.[54]

Horsmanden devoted considerable space in his chronicle to the story of Margaret "Peg" Kerry, a white Irish woman, and John Gwin, also known as Ceasar, a black slave. Margaret Kerry lived at John Hughson's tavern, located on the waterfront on the west side of Manhattan. John Gwin paid her board and often spent the night with her. He entered her chamber by climbing through a window Kerry left open. In Horsmanden's telling, Kerry was a prostitute. However, no evidence exists to support that claim. More likely, Horsmanden was incapable of imagining a love relationship between a white woman and a black man. "She pretended to be married;" Horsmanden believed that it could only have been an illicit relationship. The idea of marriage between a black man and white woman apparently so repulsed Horsmanden that at one point he slipped and referred to Margaret Kerry as "Negro Peg." This constellation was more tolerable; sex between a black man and white woman was not.[55]

Horsmanden's knowledge of Gwin and Kerry's relationship contributed to his fears. This love connection revealed solidarity on the personal level but also reflected a far broader alliance. Since many illicit connections—fencing stolen goods, lovers meeting in the night, plots to free the slaves—took place in the multiracial waterfront taverns on the margins of New York society, it is little wonder that the only tavern-related crimes city officials prosecuted involved the illegal gatherings of whites and blacks. These taverns posed a thorny problem for New York's leaders who worked to prevent the "cabals" of poor whites and blacks before plans could be formed and executed. Horsmanden ordered "diligent inquiry into the economy and behaviour of all the mean ale-houses and tipling house within this city" with particular attention to those where "negroes, and the scum and dregs of white people [were] in conjunction." According to Horsmanden, these sites encouraged the worst sorts of behavior but most importantly provided space for the "most loose, debased and abandoned wretches among us to cabal and confederate together." Horsmanden's negative reaction to the racial fluidity of the low-end tavern hit its mark directly. "Negroes, the scum, and dregs of white people" did gather there, armed with a shared work experience and the "insurrectionary connections" aimed at turning the social order upside down.[56]

Dr. Alexander Hamilton's recounting of an event in Newtown, Maryland, in 1744 offers a different perspective on the ways race, gender, and class were marked within tavern culture, in the entertainment offered. After dinner one afternoon, Hamilton watched "the tricks of a female baboon in the yard." He expressed surprise at the size of the coterie of attendants and handlers for this baboon and claimed she received better care than members of the upper class in Newton. The baboon "was very fond of the compliments and company of the men and boys but expressed in her gestures an utter aversion att women and girls, especially negroes of that sex." Hamilton left nothing to the reader's imagination. He reminded us that the baboon too was "of a black complexion." He proclaimed his amazement that the black baboon demonstrated no affinity toward persons of color. Hamilton supplied the explanation for this behavior and a clear sense of his attitudes. He attributed class status to the baboon, referring to her as "this lady" and equating her attendants with servants. "This lady" behaved as a lady should: her gender assumed an attraction to men. Women were not the object of a well-bred woman's affections. Her class drew her to other people of quality. For Hamilton, as a member of a racialized society, *quality* meant white. Color and gender lines were so clearly drawn in eighteenth-century America that Hamilton assumed a trained baboon would not threaten the distinctions.[57]

Philadelphia's leaders also feared the disorders that could result from multitudes of people gathering in the tavern. Tavern keeper John Simes was presented before the court for keeping a disorderly house. According to the Grand Jury, Simes's tavern was the site, on December 26, 1701, of a "disturbing" event that was liable "to propagate the throne of wickedness amongst us." On that Boxing Day, Simes allowed and encouraged customers John Smith and Edward James to "dance and revel." This disorder would have been sufficient for official sanctions, because dancing in taverns was forbidden in Philadelphia; but it was compounded by the fact that both men were dressed in women's clothing and they were in the company of two women, Sarah Stivee and Dorothy Canterill, who were dressed in men's clothing. The only place where the day after Christmas was associated with this type of costuming was the West Indies. In its English versions, Boxing Day was for filling boxes of alms primarily for the poor. In Nassau, however, the day's festivities included a parade and festival incorporating elements of Mardi Gras and ancient African tribal rituals.[58] Whatever the origin of the Philadelphia revelers' activities, it is not by accident that this subversive behavior took place in a space that was by its very nature involved with various forms of resistance that often included rubbing up against the norms of the dominant culture. Simes was charged with keeping a disorderly house. He contested the charge and brought tailor John Williams with him to his hearing. It is unclear if Williams was consulted in his position as tailor to alter the costumes worn by the four revelers. He did supply a ten-pound bond for Simes's appearance in court. Simes survived this court appearance with his license intact.[59]

This eighteenth-century example of cultural inversion could imply a wide range of potential behaviors, it opens the possibility that the revelers were parodying social codes and were engaged in a form of subversion and resistance aimed directly at society's rigid gender roles.[60] The laboring classes residing in the northern American port cities shared a socioeconomic ethos. Pushed increasingly toward the economic margins, they turned toward strategies that enabled them to survive. The events in Simes's tavern reveal a particular moment in which members of the laboring class transgressed a number of boundaries. The raucous mixtures of men and women and the gatherings of individuals from different ethnicities constituted the regular fare of these lower-end public houses.

Philadelphia leaders continued to voice their concerns over gatherings that mixed race and gender. Beginning in 1732, the Philadelphia Common Council complained on a regular basis that "the frequent and tumultuous Meetings of the Negro Slaves, especially on Sundays," contributed greatly to the city's disorders. Drafts of laws were presented periodically to control these behaviors, and they began to mention not only the gatherings of slaves but also of "Mullato's & Indian Servants." In 1741, the Council ruled that in order to address the complaints that "great numbers of Negroes & other Set there [near the court house] with Milk pails & other things late at night," the Constables of the city would be allowed to ask these persons to disburse half an hour after sunset. If they failed to do so, they would be required to appear before the Council.[61]

The 1744 Philadelphia Grand Jury blamed a cluster of taverns situated in "Hell Town" as the cause of the city's disorders. Because so many taverns were concentrated in a small geographic space, they impoverished one another. In order to survive economically, tavern keepers enticed "even negroes" to drink in their establishments. Situated north of Arch Street between the Delaware River and Third Street, Hell Town harbored the city's under classes. It was also home to many of the city's transient mariners and a magnet to the apprentices, servants, and slaves when they gathered for their "evening pleasure." Situated in the middle of this section was the "Three Jolly Irishman," reputed to be one of the toughest taverns in the port town. Men gathered there to consume large quantities of drink and to gamble at a variety of games—cards, dice, bull baiting, cockfights, and boxing matches. It was there that traveling shows displayed their offerings; for a small payment, tavern patrons could view leopards, trained pigs, and camels.[62] Participants in these low-end tavern entertainments represented a mixture of races, and these were the only sorts of taverns where women were regularly included. The women who frequented them drank, danced, talked, engaged in illicit sex, and were involved in illegal trading networks. They violated the law and society's sensibilities.[63] The city's constables were charged with maintaining order in the city. Faced with the threats to the social order that these taverns housed, they did not hesitate to send to the workhouse "people of both sexes, who could give no good account of themselves, being found in a disorderly house."[64]

By the middle of the eighteenth century, laboring-class Philadelphians, like their New Yorker counterparts, were involved in a tavern culture that was separate from those of elite and middling society. There had developed a subversive economy in which servants and working-class people exchanged stolen goods. They drank together, made plans, hid their stolen items, and sold them. Hannah Gooding, the Philadelphia tavern keeper mentioned earlier, serves as an example. She had her license pulled for drinking-law violations, but the court was probably more concerned with her involvement in the underground economic network. She fenced stolen goods received from members of the city's servant class.[65]

The most notorious incident in Philadelphia involving a tavern and an illegal trading network erupted in the winter of 1750. The city was "alarmed by the unusual Frequency of Robberies, Thefts and burglaries." Stores and houses were being broken into. Clothing, jewelry, handkerchiefs, silver spoons, a tea chest, "among other things," had been taken.[66] The five people, men and women, most directly involved in the thefts were all from Philadelphia's lower orders and lived in the area of Water Street. Although no one linked their activities to anything that resembled a slave conspiracy, the cast of characters involved represented diverse ethnic groups and both free and unfree. Elizabeth Robinson was suspected of wrong doing when it was discovered that she had sold some goods at suspiciously low prices to an indentured servant. Robinson was an Englishwoman who had been shipped to Maryland as a convict servant. John Crow, the servant who was caught with the goods, was an Irish Catholic indentured to a Philadelphia brewer. Francis and Mary McCoy, husband and wife, also played a key role in the thefts. They were Irish Protestants who had lived in Philadelphia for a number of years. Also accused, but later released because he gave evidence against his fellow defendants, was Joseph Cooper, indentured to a "Turner in Town." John Morrison apparently orchestrated the events. At the time of these robberies he was about 24 years old, an Irish Catholic who had come to the colonies as an indentured servant about ten years before.[67]

The McCoys, Crow, and Robinson were arrested and held in the jail. Morrison was picked up somewhat later at his usual haunt, Stinson's Tavern in Water Street. The Stinsons admitted that they knew Morrison well, and Mr. Stinson was sentenced to be "burnt in the Hand and his Goods being forfeited were seiz'd by the Sheriff" for his involvement with the pilfered items. Once the thieves were captured, the court heard their confessions. Morrison provided a litany of thefts. They spoke of misspending their time, their delight in "Strong Drink, even to Excess," and how drink provided for them the energy to commit new sins. The members of the "gang"—John Morrison, Elizabeth Robinson, Francis McCoy, and John Crow—"receiv'd Sentence of DEATH"; Mary McCoy was released, since it was assumed that her participation had been coerced by her husband.[68]

Patrons of low-end taverns in New England challenged elite society as well, and were distasteful to them. In 1760, young John Adams found himself away from his usual haunts in Boston, meeting friends at Thayer's tavern in Weymouth, Massachusetts. The place was packed with people: "Negroes with a fiddle, young fellows and girls dancing in the chamber as if they would kick the floor thru . . . fiddling and dancing of both sexes and all ages, in the lower room, singing, dancing, fiddling, drinking flip and toddy, and drams." Although a scene that might appeal to many, Adams expressed great disdain for this experience. In this tavern, he was forced to rub elbows with, drink with, and shout over the noise of a greater variety of the people of Massachusetts than was his habit.[69]

The taverns of Salem and Marblehead, Massachusetts, were a mixture of legal and illegal houses. In Salem, a substantial proportion of the clientele was fishermen and sailors. Their presence was bolstered substantially by "farmers, artisans, housewives, church members, and even an occasional clergyman." Marblehead's taverngoers were somewhat different. There the patrons were "the often-transient, relatively poor, and predominantly young, male fishing population."[70] In the working-class taverns and illegal houses in Marblehead and Salem, patrons spent their time in ways "deemed improper in the larger society." Commonly men and women participated in dancing, fiddling, and gambling at cards and dice, and assaulted the rules for both physical and verbal conduct. The court records of Marblehead are suspiciously silent even though the population was notorious for drunken, unruly behavior. One reason for the low incidence of indictments was that the selectmen knew the dangers of entering this world. "Nither Constable grandjuryman nor Ti[t]hingman can com Nere them to prvent . . . Disorders." While the officials of Salem received more support than Marblehead's officals for their attempts to curb these behaviors, tithingmen and constables in Salem were often abused when they entered taverns to quell disturbances.[71]

Boston contained a wide range of public houses, including ones frequented by laborers, people of color, and women. The diary of Robert Love, a city clerk ordered by the selectmen to warn undesirable people out of the city of Boston, offers a tantalizing glimpse of gatherings of such taverngoers. Love noted, for instance, that Pennelape Whinkake, an Indian woman, had come into the city in October 1765, from Newport, Rhode Island. She first lodged with an unnamed tavern keeper but then began residing with Robert McCurday "near the windmill upon the neck at the South End." The link with McCurday and the south end is highly revealing. A large proportion of those warned out of the city of Boston had resided in the rooms of taverns, boarding houses, or private residences in Boston's south end. At about the same time that Love warned Whinkake, he also gave legal notice to Deborah Jennins. She had entered Boston from Ebintown; Love described her as well as an Indian woman who lodged at Robert McCurday's. About Jennins Love noted, "[She] keeps company with a Pacience Peck a mulatto woman that is often with gentlemen negros."[72]

It is unclear what all these individuals were doing at McCurday's. Did they reside with him because they labored for him as servants? Or did they work out of McCurday's as prostitutes? If so, were their primary clients the free black men of the city, a notable issue for the white men of Boston? Or is it, as Love suggests, that these Indian women and black men were "keeping company," that, living on the physical and social margins of Boston society, they found each other at McCurday's?

The southern urban environment also afforded blacks access to a tavern culture that heightened white anxiety. When in 1693 the governor complained about the city's disorderly houses where "strong liquors" were sold; he included among his list of their patrons the lower orders of whites and "Great numbers of Negroes . . . knowing they can have drinck . . . for mony or what else they bring." The Grand Council of South Carolina summoned Charleston's constables before them in 1702 to chastise them for not enforcing the "negro act" and for "Suffering Caballs of negroes" at a tavern called the Rat Trap. Given the number of references to these sorts of behaviors, the problems associated with the tavern escalated during the eighteenth century. A newspaper advertisement claimed that a runaway slave had been seen in a tavern; a mistress claimed that her slave had lost his wages "either by Gaming or spend[ing] among the lettle Punch-Houses"; the grand jury identified twelve houses that retailed "liquors to Negroes"; a butcher threatened to prosecute anyone who sold alcohol to his slave. During the 1770s, a series of grand jury presentments to the court warned about the dangers to society from dram shops and tippling houses that entertained "negroes and other disorderly persons" or enticed the youth into "corruption of the morals and loss of service to their masters." The grand jury recommended that a law be passed "that the selling of rum and other spirits to Negroes may be limited from sun rise to sun set." Because these establishments were open early in the morning and did not close until late at night, "Negroes" could become intoxicated early in the day and be of no use to their "owners." The late night hours encouraged "rioting through the streets." Complaints about servant and slave access to drinking establishments continued on the eve of the Revolution. A slave was advertised for sale because he was "too frequently getting to the Dram-Shops (these too numerous Pests that are a Scandal to this Town, and bid fair to ruin every Black Servant in it)." A "Stranger" reported that the city's dram shops were open at all times of the day and night, were crowded with "negroes," and were even equipped "with private passages for them to enter by."[73]

It is difficult to establish a relationship between Indians and the tavern. A very flimsy historical record inhibits our observation of Indians inside the tavern. Their invisibility in the sources derives from two impulses. Indians' presence inside the tavern went unrecorded because selling alcohol to Indians was illegal. Both the tavern keeper who sold the drink and the Indian who purchased it had powerful incentives to avoid keeping a written record of these illegal transactions. During the 1741 conspiracy trial in New York, "Wan, Indian man of Mr. Lowe," testified before the grand jury that he and John, "a free Indian, late of Cornelius Cosine," had gone together to John Hughson's tavern. There they each drank a mug of beer and paid for it. Hughson had stopped Wan as he was leaving to remind him that "a law was made to sell no liquor to slaves." He asked that they tell no one about their time in his tavern and they swore their silence. Countless examples exist in the unofficial record that convey the ease with which Indians could obtain alcohol, especially rum. Traders complained that if they refused Indians liquor, the Indians would find other traders to supply them.[74]

The analysis of alcohol-related prosecutions throughout the colonies reveals that selling drink to Indians played a significant role in the illegal activity related to alcohol. Tavern keepers were the most commonly prosecuted for these violations, and these men and women paid the price of a fine or the loss of their licenses. It is reasonable to assume that the transactions took place if not inside at least at public houses. Some of this illegal drink trade enabled Indians to carry the alcohol away and to use it as they wished. In other cases, it was consumed on the premises. William Beeckman, in a complaint to Peter Stuyvesant in 1660, directly linked Indians' access to alcohol with taverns: he saw "many drunken savages daily and I am told, that they sit drinking publicly in some taverns." Robert Love's records of the people he warned out of Boston offers evidence that Indians were present in the "meaner" sort of taverns in that city. James Logan, secretary to the Pennsylvania proprietor, blamed "low end establishments" for supplying Philadelphia Indians with alcohol.[75]

In addition, colonists essentially did not "see" Indians, although they lived and worked near them. With very few exceptions, journal writers and diarists failed to mention Indians, not because they were absent but because Indians did not warrant discussion any more than did other parts of the landscape. When Benjamin Bullivant stopped for a night in Newport, Rhode Island in 1697, he observed 3 Indians in the stocks who had been caught drunk on the Lord's day. They were to remain there until they were sober. Bullivant also "tooke notice of sundry sober Indians both men and women cleanly clothed, Quaker fashion, very observant at the meeting."[76] Dr. Hamilton's journal is also unusual in that he observed and mentioned Indians throughout his colonial travels; he "could not help but run into" them. He passed Indians on the road, he sat near them in a Boston church, and George Ningret, a Narragansett "King," treated him to a glass of wine.[77] Except for traders and treaty negotiators, Indians are missing from the pages of most colonial travel journals and diaries. Bullivant and Hamilton may have kept more accurate and more careful reports because they were relative newcomers to the colonies. Everything they witnessed and everyone with whom they interacted merited their attention, and this included their frequent encounters with Indians. Similarly, Gottlieb Mittleberger, who traveled from Germany to Pennsylvania in 1750, remarked that Indians "living close to the Europeans are frequently to be seen." He was also struck by their participation in Philadelphia trade: "Every fall they [Indians] come to Philadelphia in huge numbers, bringing with them various baskets which they can weave neatly and beautifully, many hides, as well as precious furs."[78]

Further clues reveal that Indians gathered at specific taverns and expected to meet friends there. The Narragansett, who lived in and around the towns of the colony of Rhode Island, patronized taverns. In 1753, Christopher Fowler, licensed to operate a tavern in South Kingston, was accused of "Entertaining Indeons, Negros &c." Joshua Gardner received a license in 1760 on the condition "that he Entertain no Indian or Black people on ye day Calld Fair [market] day at his House on any pretence whatever." When the Rhode Island General Assembly passed laws in 1704 and again in 1750 to prohibit Indian and black servants from frequenting taverns, they intended to stop an ongoing activity. It became illegal to sell liquor "to any Indian, Mulatto or Negro Servant or Slave." These laws notwithstanding, the Narragansett, free and slave, knew where they could go to drink, to relax, or to celebrate with their friends. Proof of this is in the writings of Joseph Fish, a Puritan pastor and a missionary to the Narragansett. He traveled regularly from his home in Connecticut to Narragansett settlements in Rhode Island. The record of his expenses reveals that he spent time eating and drinking with representatives of the Narragansett in a public house.[79]

Indians were also visible as patrons of public houses on the western fringes of the colonies and in the many trading posts established to do business with them. Vernon's tavern in Easton, Pennsylvania, was apparently a popular spot visited regularly by local Indians. German Geiger, who lived in South Carolina and established a trading network, was reputedly "supplying the traders with goods and serving food and drink to passing Indians."[80] Andrew Montour, an Indian guide and interpreter for the English, was detained in Carlisle, Pennsylvania, because of an outstanding debt to a tavern keeper. Montour had a reputation as a heavy drinker. His bill intimates that at least some of his drinking took place inside a public house.[81]

The historical record contains frustratingly few examples of Indians inside ordinaries, being entertained together or drinking alongside white or black companions. This lapse exposes the broad range of Euro-American hypocrisy. Colonists' representations of Indian drinking behavior and their expressed attitudes toward drinking reveal that the styles of drinking practiced by the two groups were not nearly as different as whites might have wished. And under self-serving circumstances, white colonists did join with Indians to drink. Most indicative of Indians' presence in taverns is that over time a substantial number of tavern keepers were indicted for serving alcohol to Indians.[82]

❈   ❈   ❈

FROM THE EARLIEST colonial period, many taverns catered to particular clienteles, and as the eighteenth century progressed, increasing numbers of public houses served society's elite exclusively. Upper-class men, especially in cities and port towns, frequented public houses that provided good entertainment and ample refreshment. Their rituals were inclusive, bonding each to the other, while also exclusive, reserving the space for them alone. Public houses located along the cities' wharves attracted their patrons from the middling and laboring classes. These taverngoers also shared a particular tavern culture, and their activities had similar effects of drawing some participants together while excluding others. This helps to explain why upper-class male travelers settled easily into the tavern routine in unfamiliar places while upper-class female travelers had to be prepared for an unwelcome environment and did their best to avoid staying in taverns.

A coherent alehouse culture did exist separated from polite society by at least issues of status. During a Sunday morning service a man wanted "a pot of beer and a cake" at an unlicensed house. He explained that "he scorned to go hear old Higginson [the Salem pastor] for he was an oppressor of the poor." A constable who sought to collect a delinquent ministerial rate in a tavern provoked "a rage." While the town's officials were offended by the behavior of taverngoers, the patrons seemed quite clear about the motivations for their actions. As Daniel Vickers suggests, "for men reminded daily of their subordinate status, the heavy consumption of cider and flip, and the tavern life which accompanied it, provided a realm of sociability in which they might set the rules."[83]

Conclusion

Early Americans used taverns for a variety of activities, all of which they lubricated generously with drink. Puritans refreshed themselves during the interval between the morning and evening service or scurried inside to shake the chill from their bones after a winter's sermon in an unheated meeting house. Virginia legislators drifted back and forth between the capitol and the tavern all day long; at night, they drank and caroused, generating sufficient noise that overnight guests could not sleep. The judges in Essex County, Massachusetts, efficiently eliminated the need to go back and forth by holding the court in the tavern; they effected a seamless transition from business to pleasure by replacing court documents with punch bowls. Colonial militias practiced on the village green and then retired to the local tavern to quench their thirst and relive their feats. Taverns assumed many forms, but regardless of their size or the quality of their food and drink, they played a central role in colonists' lives.

No matter what impulses established the formal criteria for regulating drink and tavern behavior in the American colonies, authorities during the mid-to-late eighteenth century administered policies in a manner that resembled randomness. Colonists who put thoughts to paper on the subject seemed to agree that undisciplined drinking—especially public drunkenness—could bring the ruin of humanity. But declining rates of prosecution for drunkenness suggest that those responsible for enforcing the drinking and tavern laws no longer shared the values that these laws represented. Authorities hauled the habitual drunkard before the bench or admonished individuals for selling liquor to Indians, but only rarely. Laments about the dangers of overdrinking—not surprisingly loudest and most frequent in the sectarian colonies—spurred criticism but had virtually no sustained effect on either containing the number of taverns or the consumption of alcohol. In the major port towns, the ratio of taverns to population remained virtually constant throughout the colonial period. In rural areas, tavern density also kept pace with population growth. Judges most consistently brought the force of law to bear on the proprietors and patrons of disorderly houses, especially those frequented by the laboring classes. Even so, legal authorities were motivated far less by anxieties about drinking than by fears of slave conspiracy, Indian hostility, or the subversion of male supremacy.

The reasons for official ambivalence lay with practice and necessity, both of which outweighed theory and doctrine in a rapidly growing and much-dispersed society: Taverns offered travelers necessary services and provided locals with entertainment. Spirituous liquors supplemented monotonous diets. Most important, the social act of drinking played a key role in the lives of colonists. William Penn's first plan for Pennsylvania had imagined the colony without taverns and drink, but advisors to Penn and potential immigrants reacted so strongly against it that he jettisoned the idea almost immediately. From the founding of the Massachusetts Bay Colony, settlers appeared on both sides of the debate to defend or attack drinking and the tavern. The dialogue ebbed and flowed, shriller when Puritans fell victim to Indian wars or located other threats to their way of life and certainly louder when hard liquor became the drink of choice. Anti-tavern sentiment grew muffled, however, when New England returned to a state of calm. Despite periodic attacks on the public house and drinking behavior by both religious and secular leaders, the tavern maintained its privileged place within the colonies and thrived everywhere.

Indeed, examining drinking and taverns from a broad perspective, in all the British mainland colonies, makes readily apparent the ways in which sociability inside taverns transcended distinct regional cultures. Local customs contributed little to tavern culture. Differences among colonial taverns were owed mostly to the type of patronage, whose mixed picture again illustrated the distance between law and lived experience. Taverns offered the laboring class a place for sociability, a venue their typically cramped living spaces did not supply. Inside a public house, they could join with friends, co-workers, and neighbors and drink together—generally heedless of laws whose authors aimed to control their behavior and thus maintain social order. Authorities objected without effect when whites and blacks, free and unfree, congregated together—just as they failed to bar prostitutes from hiring rooms in public houses and proprietors from dealing in stolen goods. City leaders paid particular attention if they sensed that taverns harbored the organizers of radical political activities, such as a revolt against the institution of slavery or a march against tax stamps. Impervious to reform by enactment, taverns played an integral role in the lives of the middling and laboring classes and fueled the elite critique of popular culture.

Most taverns drew from all ranks of society, but all ranks were no more equal there than anywhere else. Gentlemen could venture into any tavern they chose, associating with the laboring classes unavoidably, consorting with prostitutes gladly. Over the course of the eighteenth century, merchants and lawyers in large port cities developed one or more taverns that they identified as exclusively their own. The compiler (named as, but not proven to be, Tom Paine) of a 1796 volume devoted to jests and "patriotic bon mots," revealed this raw truth when he reported an exchange between two men. One of them extolled the perfection of American law, claiming that it was equally open to the poor and the rich. "So is the London Tavern," his companion retorted sarcastically.[1] Law gave only the illusion of equal access, just as the London tavern posed as a public house while in fact catering to the better sort of clientele.

Finally, colonial taverns offer an interesting window onto gender relations in early America. In some social rituals of the colonial gentry—teas, assemblies, balls—men and women joined together. Jacob Hiltzheimer's wife accompanied him on a range of social activities in Philadelphia. Goelet's nightly social whirl in Boston included mixed-gender and highly ritualized events. When, by contrast, Hiltzheimer or Goelet walked into the tavern, he entered a distinctly male preserve where he fully expected to be away from wife and homely concerns, where he could meet, talk, work, or relax, answering only to other men. These gatherings included various permutations of allies and rivals, friends and colleagues, neighbors and strangers, but not women of repute.

A curious kind of public space, the tavern blurred public with private. Any adult seeking food, drink, or a bed for the night, or who wanted drinking partners, the latest news, or idle conversation presumably had access to the colonial tavern, and thus we today may think of them as public. Yet tavern culture also contained elements of the private in the sense of their being concealed or secret. When thus segregated by sex, elite men often attended to matters of great import, and an unquestioned legitimacy hovered over these gatherings, a legitimacy sanctioned foremost by the participants themselves. They assembled for a variety of reasons: to participate in rituals of drink, promote business, debate the value of a text, display intellect or fluency, or fashion policy. They voiced their individual and collective opinions on topics ranging from local gossip to imperial politics. But only they were privy to these exchanges, which did not necessarily require secret handshakes, special hats, or oaths of allegiance. Women, unfree laborers, people of color, and the free laboring classes might be conscious of these gatherings but would not likely know what had happened in them unless the gathering resulted in a new policy or a call to political action. Tavern assemblies of elite white men evoked the image of the formal public as a universe of adult free white men. As the place where they usually occurred, the tavern supported gender, status, and race hierarchies within early American society, ultimately sustaining the privilege of well-born white males.

After the Revolution, elites channeled their effort to segregate public drinking by economic status into a new architectural shape, the hotel. Gentlemanly disdain for most tavern accommodations and George Washington's widely reported presidential tours of 1789–91 may have combined to encourage the new architectural form. Washington intended to learn as much as he possibly could about the new nation from his travels, and he hoped to bring unity to a country still reeling from the fight over the ratification of the Constitution. He dreaded the lack of amenities and inconsistent services in public houses and contemplated staying in private homes. He feared, however, that this gesture would send the wrong message. Using private lodging might be interpreted as bestowing favoritism on friends or family. He opted throughout his journey to lodge in taverns, and while he succeeded in conveying a sense of an American identity, his experiences also highlighted the unpredictable availability of comfortable or suitable accommodations.[2]

The first hotels, designed and built in the 1790s, signaled a dramatic departure from even elegant colonial public houses like the City Tavern in Philadelphia or the Raleigh Tavern in Williamsburg, whose public spaces may have been fashionable and comfortable but whose sleeping quarters remained cramped and lacking in privacy. Hotels, rivaling the largest structures in the country in size and cost, contrasted with the tavern in more than scale, for they featured private sleeping quarters. The New York City Hotel, built in 1794, contained 137 rooms. The bar, ballroom, public parlors, offices, and library filled the high-ceilinged main and second stories; overnight guests lodged in the remaining rooms above.[3]

Innovations in hotel policy helped further to define public drinking spaces by status and succeeded in creating a more finely graded separation of drinkers by class. During the colonial period, authorities required that tavern keepers charge uniform rates for all goods and services. The gradual decline of state-determined price schedules for food and drink after the Revolution enabled hotels to price the working classes out of their establishments. The hotel also assumed a place as the site of proper drinking. Visitors to the hotel bar by definition imbibed properly; their marginal contemporaries drank in taverns and saloons. Supporters of temperance and prohibition in the nineteenth century devoted themselves to shutting the doors of the saloon and tippling house, bypassing hotels. Drinkers in hotel bars, like their predecessors in exclusive colonial taverns, escaped criticism because they set the standard for public drinking.[4]

The hotel ushered in a new form of gendered space as well by welcoming women. Whether initially they were tolerated at the bar remains unclear. They did participate in celebratory dinners, which included alcoholic beverages, with greater regularity than did their colonial sisters. By the middle of the nineteenth century, pictorial advertisements for at least one New York hotel included bonneted women standing at the bar. A Utica, New York, hotel boasted two receiving rooms for ladies to be used for washing away the dust from their travels. Women's deportment books prescribed proper hotel behavior. Not all functions included women. Fraternal clubs and dinners for military leaders continued to be all-male affairs. In the best hotels the after-dinner parlors remained segregated by sex. Sensibilities, however, had clearly shifted from a time in which respectable women did not dare enter the colonial elite tavern to an era in which hotel proprietors promoted the presence of women.[5]

As a public space, the hotel claimed to be available and open to all. Yet, like the elite eighteenth-century public house, it beckoned to a particular clientele, those gentlemen who could afford to pay its prices.[6] For those in the new re-public for whom the American Revolution pledged a leveling and democratiz-ing of society, the emergence of the hotel offered another indicator that the promise of the Revolution was to be deferred. Colonial taverns and the hotels that developed from elite taverns manifested an American society that main-tained segregation in public by race, gender, and class.

Introduction

1. Throughout this work, the terms *status* and *class* are used interchangeably, alone or combined with a modifier—artisan or laboring, lower, middle, upper, or elite—in order to situate individuals within the social and economic hierarchy. This is not to imply that classes, in the Marxist, postindustrial sense, existed in early America. Individuals did, however, belong to particular groups based on their occupations, wealth, and education. While I share Richard Bushman's perception that the elite was separate from the rest of society, the laboring class carved its own tavern niche. Richard Bushman, *The Refinement of America: Persons, Houses, Cities* (New York, 1992).

2. Increase Mather, "Wo to Drunkards" (Cambridge, Mass., 1673), cited in Mark E. Lender and James Kirby Martin, *Drinking in America: A History* (New York, 1982), 1; "Silence Dogood, No. 12," *The Papers of Benjamin Franklin*, ed. Leonard W. Labaree (New Haven, 1959–), 1:39–40. On the vices of drunkenness see also "Nothing more like a Fool than a drunken man," *The Papers of Benjamin Franklin*, 2:173. As the pastor of the First Church of Salem warned, "drunkards are excluded from the kingdom of heaven." *The Records of the First Church of Salem Massachusetts, 1629–1736*, ed. Richard D. Pierce (Salem, Mass., 1974), 101.

3. Quoted in Louis P. Masur, *Rites of Execution: Capital Punishment and the Transformation of American Culture, 1776–1865* (New York, 1989), 90–91.

4. W. J. Rorabaugh, *The Alcoholic Republic: An American Tradition* (Oxford, 1979), 7–10.

5. Ibid., 5–7.

6. *Pennsylvania Gazette*, August 8, 1771; Rorabaugh, *The Alcoholic Republic*, 97–98. Edwin Powers, *Crime and Punishment in Early Massachusetts, 1620–1692: A Documentary History* (Boston, 1966), 370–71. For a Frenchman's view about the unhealthy character of water in colonial Virginia see Durand of Dauphiné, *A Huguenot Exile in Virginia . . .* (The Hague, 1687; New York, 1934), 129.

7. Rorabaugh, *The Alcoholic Republic*, 25; "William Logan's Journal of a Journey to Georgia, 1745," *Pennsylvania Magazine of History and Biography* 36 (1912), 5–6; see the recipe in the *Pennsylvania Gazette* for "Cordial Elixir of the Stomach," July 5, 1764.

Records of Plymouth Colony Laws, 1623–1682 (Boston, 1861; reprint, New York, 1968), 137 (June 1662). See also Bruce Daniels, *Puritans at Play: Leisure and Recreation in Colonial New England* (New York, 1995), 141–42; Adrian Wilson, *The Making of Man-Midwifery: Childbirth in England, 1660–1770* (Cambridge, Mass., 1995), 28. According to John Allen Krout, who studied the early temperance movement, colonial parents gave alcohol "to children for many of the minor ills of childhood, and its wholesomeness for those in health, it appeared, was only surpassed by its healing properties in case of disease." *The Origins of Prohibition* (New York, 1925), 38.

8. *The Journal of Nicholas Cresswell, 1774–1777,* (Port Washington, N.Y., 1924), 52. For physicians to prescribe increasing alcohol intake was not unusual. Mary Fisher wrote to Benjamin Franklin that her husband was ill. "His Physicians have obliged him to drink a greater Quantity of generous Wine than before he was used to." *Papers of Benjamin Franklin,* 8:120. Franklin himself described putting "Bark finely powdered into a bottle of Wine" if he "felt any feverish Indisposition" (11:537). In a letter written to Franklin, the Boston lawyer Benjamin Kent described a root used by Indians which, if steeped in Madeira, was the cure for gout (13:49–50).

9. The word *public* had two distinct connotations in colonial America. On the one hand *public* meant, "open to general observation, sight, or cognizance . . . manifest, not concealed." In the second meaning, *public* was used to evoke the content of earlier terms, like *commonweal*; and to this end it was often combined with other words—"those which are in the public trust," or "publick spirit," or "publick good." The distinction between public and private may be found, for example, when leaders admonished their flock to place the good of the people above their private desires. In the second meaning, *public* referred to "of or pertaining to the people as a whole." In both, public was differentiated from private. In the first, all that can be known to everyone resides in the public sphere but that which is unknown might "privately lurk and [be] Obscure." If the second meaning is divided further into the formal and informal public, these subsets enhance our understanding of how gender operated in the public sphere. The origins of the word lie in its Latin roots meaning "adult men" or "male population." The formal public, composed of state, church, and authority, was a universe of adult, free white men. The informal public, however, was less exclusive and "encompassed women of all ages, younger men, and even indentured servants or slaves." Mary Beth Norton, *Founding Mothers and Fathers: Gendered Power and the Forming of American Society* (New York, 1996), 19–23.

See Thomas Brennan, *Public Drinking and Popular Culture in Eighteenth-Century Paris* (Princeton, 1988); Peter Clark, *The English Alehouse: A Social History, 1200–1830* (London, 1983); David Joshua Pittman and Charles R. Snyder, *Society, Culture, and Drinking Patterns* (Carbondale, Ill., 1962); Michael Marrus, "Social Drinking in the *Belle Epoque,*" *Journal of Social History* 7 (1974), 115–41; James S. Roberts, *Drink, Temperance, and the Working Class in Nineteenth-Century Germany* (Boston, 1984); Keith Wrightson, "Alehouses, Order, and Reformation in Rural England, 1590–1660," in *Popular Culture and Class Conflict, 1590–1914: Explorations in the History of Labour and Leisure,* ed. Eileen Yeo and Stephen Yeo (Brighton, England, 1981), 1–27.

Although studies of the consumption of alcohol, the history of specific taverns, the reformers' impulses beginning in the late eighteenth century, and, most recently, taverns and drinking in Massachusetts and Philadelphia have expanded our knowledge, public drinking and the role played by taverns in the social life of early America have remained largely hidden. Elise Lathrop, *Early American Inns and Taverns* (New York, 1926; reissued 1977); Donna-Belle Garvin and James L. Garvin, *On the Road North of Boston: New Hampshire Taverns and Turnpikes, 1700–1900* (Concord, N.H., 1988); and Kym S. Rice, *Early American Taverns: For the Entertainment of Friends and Strangers* (Chicago, 1983). The two recent exceptions are David W. Conroy, *In Public Houses: Drink and the Revolution of Authority in Colonial Massachusetts* (Chapel Hill, N.C., 1995) and Peter Thompson, *Rum Punch and Revolution: Taverngoing and Public Life in Eighteenth-Century Philadelphia* (Philadelphia, 1999). In addition see Richard P. Gildrie, *The Profane, the Civil, and the Godly: The Reformation of Manners in Orthodox New England, 1679–1749* (University Park, Pa., 1994), esp. 63–83.

10. Conroy, *In Public Houses*, 6–7, 11, 83; and Thompson, *Rum Punch and Revolution*, 11–20.

11. Peter Mancall suggests that Conroy fails to define what he means by public space. "The Art of Getting Drunk," *Reviews in American History* 24 (1996), 386–87. Thompson does find the hints of a public sphere with the creation of such establishments as the City Tavern. It was, in part, founded with exclusion in mind and "altered the context of public political discussion in ways that suggest Habermasian themes." *Rum Punch and Revolution*, 17–19.

12. This book does not assess the tavern as a business or explore how much or how little tavern keepers earned or the financial risks involved in operating a tavern. It does not attempt to chronicle each political meeting and political action plotted within a tavern or claim to document all of the activities that occurred within taverns. Nor does this study claim to be geographically all-inclusive; no mention is made of the West Indies, which deserve a study of their own. Also, linking the cultural legacy of New France and New Spain to colonial British drinking proved to be too elusive.

13. "From the earliest times the fundamental characteristic of an inn has been its public nature." Joseph Henry Beale, Jr., *The Laws of Innkeepers and Hotels including other Public Houses, Theatres, Sleeping Cars* (Boston, 1906), 10.

14. See for example, Preston W. Edsall, *Journal of the Courts of Common Right and Chancery of East New Jersey, 1683–1702* (Philadelphia, 1937), December 1683, 124–25; Increase Mather, "Wo to Drunkards"; Rorabaugh, *The Alcoholic Republic*, 25.

15. This study employs Richard Bushman's definition of elites—"the most sharply defined social class in the colonies," who "were set off from the middling and lower sorts by their wealth, education and authority in government." *The Refinement of America*, xv; Brennan, *Public Drinking and Popular Culture*, 8.

16. Clifford Geertz, *The Interpretation of Cultures: Selected Essays* (New York, 1973), 17.

Chapter One / Dutch and English Origins

1. Daniel Fisher, "The Fisher History," *Some Prominent Virginia Families*, 4 vols., ed. Louise Pecquet du Bellet (Lynchburg: Va., 1907), 2:790–91.

2. This section depends upon Simon Schama, *The Embarrassment of Riches: An Interpretation of Dutch Culture in the Golden Age* (New York, 1987), 188–95, and the travel diaries he cites. For a traveler's view of Holland's water, marshes, and unhealthy air, see *The Travels of Peter Mundy*, 5 vols. (Hakluyt Society, 1925; reprinted, Lessing-Druckerei, Germany, 1967), 4:66, 74–75. For Mundy's reference to the Amsterdam Tun, see 78–79.

3. Schama, *Embarrassment of Riches*, 190.

4. Ibid.

5. Ibid., 191. Amsterdam's population in the seventeenth century is estimated at about 150,000. Oliver A. Rink, *Holland on the Hudson: An Economic and Social History of the Dutch in New York* (Ithaca, N.Y., 1986), 17.

6. This comes from a meeting between Sir William Brereton and an English minister, Mr. Peters. Sir William Brereton, *Travels in Holland, the United Provinces England Scotland and Ireland* (London, 1844), 10, 13, 22; Schama, *Embarrassment of Riches*, 191–92.

7. In 1590, 180 brewers operated in Amsterdam alone. Ibid., 191–93. Brereton confirms that the taxes on beer and wine were high and earned the city of Amsterdam "great revenues, to maintain the wars to the States." *Travels in Holland*, 65.

8. Schama, *Embarrassment of Riches*, 197–200.

9. Peter Clark, *The English Alehouse: A Social History, 1200–1830* (London, 1983), ix. "The Lawes of Drinking, 1617" is not attributed. Ibid., following p. 176. I disagree with his reading of the painting. Clark describes the bottom panel as depicting the "ruder pleasures of the London alehouse."

10. "The Gin Drinkers, 1736," can be found in ibid. following p. 176. John Brewer wrote that after the Glorious Revolution the alehouse was contrasted negatively with the coffee house. Decorum prevailed in the latter but not the former. *The Pleasures of the Imagination: English Culture in the Eighteenth Century* (New York, 1997), 38.

11. Quoted in Clark, *The English Alehouse*, 169; Sidney Webb and Beatrice Webb, *The History of Liquor Licensing in England Principally from 1700 to 1830* (London, 1903), 5–7.

12. The word *tippling* implies immoderate drinking. Clark, *The English Alehouse*, 169–71; Webb and Webb, *History of Liquor Licensing in England*, 7–11.

13. Peter Clark, "The Migrant in Kentish Towns, 1580–1640," in *Crisis and Order in English Towns, 1500–1700: Essays in Urban History*, ed. Peter Clark and Paul Slack (London, 1972), 139–40.

14. In his analysis of St. Aldate's parish, Peter Clark reports that the urban economy was unable to deal with the massive, escalating poverty and rising demographic pressure. The number of poor in the parish who received relief tripled between the late 1570s and the 1630s. The worst years were the 1620s, when an estimated 40% of the parish was des-

titute. "The hard core of traditional impotent poor" was joined by the laboring poor, those unable to secure steady work or keep up with rising food costs. Many tramped or became vagrants. Peter Clark, "'The Ramoth-Gilead of the Good': Urban Change and Political Radicalism at Gloucester, 1540–1640," in *The English Commonwealth, 1547–1640: Essays in Politics and Society Presented to Joel Hurstfield,* ed. Peter Clark, Alan G. R. Smith, and Nicholas Tyacke (Leicester, England, 1979), 174–75; see also Clark and Slack, *Crisis and Order in English Towns.*

15. Clark, "The Ramoth-Gilead of the Good," 175; see also A. L. Beier, *Masterless Men: The Vagrancy Problem in England, 1560–1640* (London, 1985), 43, 80–82.

16. Clark, *The English Alehouse,* 172; Webb and Webb, *History of Liquor Licensing in England,* 11–12.

17. Keepers were to be punished if they allowed drunkards and alehouse-haunters in their houses. Any convicted tipplers too poor to pay a fine were to be whipped; for subsequent offenses they were to be incarcerated. Clark, *The English Alehouse,* 174–75.

18. Quoted in Paul Slack, "Poverty and Politics in Salisbury, 1597–1666," in *Crisis and Order In English Towns,* 182.

19. Clark, *The English Alehouse,* 225–29.

20. Ibid., 256–58.

21. Elites' fears that the bills that controlled social conduct might be applied to them came from their distrust of justices of the peace. Enforcement of these laws empowered two justices to act out of sessions and the possibility that they might "act out of malice or ill will, passion or self-interest" and that they would disregard the social class of someone in the "exercise of their authority." Joan Kent, "Attitudes of Members of the House of Commons to the Regulation of 'Personal Conduct' in Late Elizabethan and Early Stuart England," *Bulletin of the Institute of Historical Research* 46 (1973), 48–52.

22. There is some evidence that the attempt to control the number of taverns was taken seriously. A 1623 report to the Privy Council from the mayor and aldermen of Ripon in York County claimed that they had followed directions and discovered that the number of alehouses in their town was "great"; "we have reduced them to half the number." Webb and Webb, *History of Liquor Licensing in England,* 12. David Shields, however, notes that no restrictions limited a tavern patron's stay in London and that elsewhere the closing times "were something of a joke." In Hogarth's *Morning,* the clientele of Tom King's Coffeehouse are leaving at the same time the maids are on their way to sunrise church services. *Civil Tongues and Polite Letters in British America* (Chapel Hill, N.C., 1997), 62–63.

23. Richard P. Gildrie, *The Profane, the Civil, and the Godly: The Reformation of Manners in Orthodox New England, 1679–1749* (University Park, Pa., 1994), 45.

24. For an excellent discussion of the gradual separation of the classes and the distinctive drinking characteristics of the upper classes, see Peter Thompson, "'The Friendly Glass': Drink and Gentility in Colonial Philadelphia," *Pennsylvania Magazine of History and Biography* 113 (October 1989), 549–73. Also Rhys Isaac, *The Transformation of Virginia, 1740–1790* (Chapel Hill, N.C., 1982), 94–98. David Conroy argues that taverns

attracted a specific clientele long before the Revolution. His conclusion is based on the interior appointments rather than any evidence of who was inside. *In Public Houses: Drink and the Revolution of Authority in Colonial Massachusetts* (Chapel Hill, N.C., 1995), 99–156.

25. See, for example, "An Act for encouragement of ordinary keepers," April 1662, *Archives of Maryland: Proceedings and Acts of the General Assembly of Maryland* (Baltimore, 1883), 1:447–48.

26. *The State Records of North Carolina*, comp. and ed. Walter Clark, vol. XXIII, *Laws 1715–1776* (Goldsboro, N.C., 1904), 182–85; and *The Statutes at Large of Pennsylvania*, comp. James T. Mitchell and Henry Flanders (Harrisburg, Pa., 1896), February 28, 1710–11, II:357–59; *The Colonial Laws of New York, from the Year 1664 to the Revolution*, 5 vols. (Albany, 1894), vol. I, *Duke of York's Laws, 1665–1675*, 39; and *The Acts and Resolves, Public and Private, of the Province of the Massachusetts Bay: To Which are Prefixed the Charters of the Province. With Historical and Explanatory Notes, and an Appendix.*, 21 vols. (Boston, 1869–1922), 1: (1693–94) 154, (1698) 330.

27. The counties include Albany, Tryon, Dutchess, Ulster, Orange, West Chester, Richmond, Kings, and Queens. *Colonial Laws of New York*, V: (1773) 583–84.

28. Patricia Ann Gibbs, "Taverns in Tidewater Virginia, 1700–1774," (M.A. thesis, College of William and Mary, 1968), 54–55.

29. *Archives of Maryland*, II: May–June 1674, 346–47.

30. *The Statutes at Large; Being a Collection of all the Laws of Virginia From the First Session of the Legislature, in the Year 1619*, [comp.] William Waller Hening, 18 vols. (New York, 1809–23), II: (February 1676–77) 393–94. Rhys Issac argues that only the gentry could afford the luxury of horse transportation. *Transformation of Virginia*, 53.

31. See, for example, *Statutes at Large of Pennsylvania*, II: (1705–6) 221–22, (1710–11) 357–59.

32. *The Records of the Governor and Company of Massachusetts Bay in New England*, ed. Nathaniel B. Shurtleff, 5 vols. (Boston, 1853–54), I: (6 June 1637) 199, (12 March 1637–38) 221, (22 May 1639) 258, and passim. *A Report of the Record Commissioners of the City of Boston, Containing the Boston Records From 1660 to 1701* (Boston, 1881), 109; Conroy, *In Public Houses*, 58–64, 74; and *Records and Files of the Quarterly Courts of Essex County, Massachusetts* (Salem, Mass., 1911), vol. 7, November 1678 session: 136; *Acts and Resolves of Massachusetts Bay*, II:302, 307. See also, *New Hampshire Court Records, 1640–1692, Court Papers, 1652–1668*, State Papers Series, vol. 40, ed. Otis G. Hammond (published by the State of New Hampshire, 1943), 12, 50, 51, 140, 141, passim. Innkeepers in Plymouth Colony were required to provide bedding and convenient pasturing for horses. They were to maintain a good stock of beer and charge a specified amount for it. *The Laws of the Pilgrims: A Facsimile Edition of The Book of General Laws of the Inhabitants of the Jurisdiction of New-Plymouth, 1672 and 1685* (Wilmington, Del., 1977), 34–36.

33. See, for example, for Massachusetts Bay, *Records of the Governor and Company of the Massachusetts Bay*, I: (3 September 1634) 126; *The State Records of North Car-*

olina, XXIII: (1741) 83; *Archives of Maryland,* II: (April–May 1666) 148; *Statutes at Large of Pennsylvania,* III: (May 31, 1718) 198–99; Virginia General Assembly, 1639, "Notes from Council and General Court Records," Conway Robinson, *Virginia Magazine of History and Biography* 14 (1906–7): 189, also *Statutes at Large of Virginia* III:395–400, VI:71–76.

34. Court of Common Pleas, Edgecomb County, March 1759, North Carolina State Archives, Raleigh.

35. Hampshire County Court, Mass., February 11, 1761, HM27095, Huntington Library, San Marino Calif.; and Court of Common Pleas, Rowan County, January 1756, North Carolina State Archives, Raleigh.

36. Craven County, June 1741, North Carolina State Archives, Raleigh. Hampshire County Court, Mass., February 11, 1761.

37. *Archives of Maryland,* II: (May–June 1674) 407–8.

38. See, for example, *State Records of North Carolina,* XXIII: (1741) 182, sec. IX; and *Statutes at Large of Virginia,* III: (October 1705) 395–401. Massachusetts lawmakers were the only ones to try to outlaw the sale of tobacco for both public and private use. They admitted that the law failed to achieve its goal. In 1638, one could smoke only while journeying or during mealtime. Smoking was permitted in common victualing houses, but the smoker was forced to light up in a private room and could only continue to smoke if no one complained. *Records of the Governor and Company of Massachusetts Bay,* I: (1634) 126, (1638), 241.

39. As Kathleen Brown notes, a universal spirit of hospitality facilitated travel and Virginia's dispersed settlement negated the need for inns. Kathleen M. Brown, *Good Wives, Nasty Wenches and Anxious Patriots: Gender, Race, and Power in Colonial Virginia* (Chapel Hill, N.C., 1996), 268.

40. *Statutes at Large of Virginia,* II: (September 1663) 192. See, for example, Timothy Breen, *Tobacco Culture* (Princeton, N.J., 1985).

41. "Report of the Journey of Francis Louis Michel from Berne, Switzerland, to Virginia, October 2, 1701–December 1, 1702," trans. and ed. William J. Hinke, *Virginia Magazine of History and Biography* 24 (1916): 1–43, 113–41, 275–88. Durand of Dauphiné concurred with this view. On his travels through Virginia he noted, "there are no inns but everywhere I went I was welcome. They cordially gave me to eat & to drink of whatever they had." *A Huguenot Exile in Virginia . . .* (The Hague, 1687; New York, 1934), 136.

42. *Records of the Governor of the Massachusetts Bay,* I: (5 November 1639) 279–80.

43. *Report of the Record Commissioners of the City of Boston, Containing the Records of Boston Selectmen, 1764–1768* (Boston, 1887), 20:172.

44. Gibbs, "Taverns in Tidewater Virginia," 22–23. William Stith, "Journal of the Meetings of the President and Masters of William and Mary College," *William and Mary Quarterly,* 1st ser., 2 (1983): 55; 14 (1906): 244. The law was first passed in 1721. *Acts and Resolves of Massachusetts Bay* II: (1721–22) 232–33, (1726–27), 385–86.

45. Yasuhide Kawashima, *Puritan Justice and the Indian: White Man's Law in Massachusetts, 1630–1763* (Middletown, Conn., 1986), 83–84; The law was passed in 1694.

254 Notes to Pages 23–26

Acts and Resolves of Massachusetts Bay, I:154; 4:204, 308, and 497. Lorenzo Greene, *The Negro in Colonial New England, 1670–1776* (New York, 1942), 135–36.

46. *Minutes of the Common Council of the City of New York, 1675–1776, In Eight Volumes* (New York, 1905), I: (22 March 1680) 85–86, (25th April 1691) 223–24.

47. Innkeepers could have their doors closed permanently if they ignored the law. See, for example, *Statutes at Large of Virginia*, III:395–400; VI:25, 71–76; *Statutes at Large of Pennsylvania*, III: (August 26, 1721) 248–51; *Records of the Governor and Company of Massachusetts Bay*, IV:59–60; David W. Conroy, "The Culture and Politics of Drink in Colonial and Revolutionary Massachusetts, 1681–1790" (Ph.D. diss., University of Connecticut, 1987), 46; *The Statutes at Large of South Carolina*, ed. Thomas Cooper, 10 vols. (Columbia, S.C., 1836–41), III: (December 11, 1717) 18; *Acts and laws, of His Majesties colony of Connecticut in New-England* (New Lond, Conn., 1715), 123–24; *State Records of North Carolina*, XXIII: (1741) 182–85; and *Colonial Laws of New York*, II: (1737) 952–55.

48. For one of the best descriptions of the legal status of married women, see Laurel Thatcher Ulrich, *Good Wives: Image and Reality in the Lives of Women in Northern New England, 1650–1750* (New York, 1980), 6–7, 38, 94, 240. Carole Shammas, "The Female Social Structure of Philadelphia in 1775," *Pennsylvania Magazine of History and Biography* 107 (January 1983): 69–83.

49. *Statutes at Large of Pennsylvania*, II: (January 12, 1705) 185.

50. *Statutes at Large of Virginia*, III: (April 1691) 74. The Massachusetts law prescribed whipping for any "Baud, Whore, or vile Person" who kept a "Whore-House or Brothel House." Edwin Powers, *Crime and Punishment in Early Massachusetts, 1620–1692: A Documentary History* (Boston, 1966), 172.

51. Peter Mancall, *Deadly Medicine: Indians and Alcohol in Early America* (Ithaca, 1995), 107.

52. Mancall, *Deadly Medicine*, 109; *Statutes at Large of Virginia*, III:468, V:273, VII:117, VIII:116.

53. *Statutes at Large of South Carolina*, II:67, 108–9, 309. The law was repeated in 1710. Mancall, *Deadly Medicine*, 109. See also, *Journals of the Commons House of Assembly of South Carolina for the four sessions of 1693*, ed. A. J. Salley, Jr. (Columbia, S.C., 1907), (September 12, 1693) 27.

54. Mancall, *Deadly Medicine*, 58–59.

55. In 1679, Jasper Danckaerts traveled throughout the colonies in search of a site on which to establish a community for a group of Labadists who wished to emigrate from Holland. He was distressed to find drunken Indians; the Labadists did not drink. When Danckaerts asked an Indian who had lived on Long Island how they had procured the alcohol, the Indian admitted that he wished he did not drink. But, he added, "my heart is so inclined that it causes me to do it, although I know it is wrong." *Journal of Jasper Danckaerts, 1679–1680*, ed. Bartlett B. James and J. Franklin Jameson (New York, 1913), 77. *The Discoveries of John Lederer in three several Marches from Virginia, to the West of Carolina . . . Begun in March 1669, and ended in September 1670 . . .*, comp. and trans.,

William Talbot Baronet (London, 1672), 26–27; and Mancall, *Deadly Medicine*, 49–50. For additional examples of traders abusing alcohol in their dealings with Indians see Peter Mancall, *Valley of Opportunity: Economic Culture along the Upper Susquehanna, 1700–1800* (Ithaca, N.Y., 1991), 60–64.

56. John Bartram, Lewis Evans, and Conrad Weiser, *A Journey from Pennsylvania to Onondaga in 1743* (Barre, Mass., 1973), 33; "Journal of James Kenny, 1761–1763," *Pennsylvania Magazine of History and Biography*, 37 (1913): 14, 16, 23, 38, 157; for Kenny's comments on the law and the sale of rum to Indians see 28, 44, 47. Only one Indian has been identified as a proprietor of a public house. Not surprisingly, his tavern was on the margins of colonial society. George White Eyes, a Delaware leader, operated a tavern, although it appears as though it was not his primary occupation. White Eyes, according to Richard White, in 1766, "kept a tavern at Big Beaver Creek," which was about twenty-five miles from Fort Pitt, in addition to his labors as a trader. Richard White, *The Middle Ground: Indians, Empires, and Republics in the Great Lakes Region, 1650–1815* (Cambridge, England, 1991), 360–61. *Journals of Charles Beatty, 1762–1769*, ed. Guy S. Klett (University Park, Pa., 1962), 46.

57. *Journal of the Grand Council of South Carolina*, ed. A. S. Salley, Jr., 2 vols. (Columbia, S.C., 1907), II: (20 August 1692) 56.

58. A 1715 law prohibited strangers from trading with Indians. *The Earliest Printed Laws of North Carolina, 1669–1751*, ed. John D. Cushing (Wilmington, Del., 1977), 2:2. Evidence of the attempts to pass a law to prevent the sale of alcohol to Indians can be found in *Colonial Records of North Carolina*, comp. and ed. William L. Saunders, 10 vols. (Goldsboro, N.C., 1886–1890), 1:231; 4:507; 5:583, 902; 6:616–17; Mancall, *Deadly Medicine*, 109.

59. *Colonial Records of North Carolina*, 5:142–43, 581; Mancall, *Deadly Medicine*, 117–18.

60. *Calender of Historical Manuscripts in the Office of the Secretary of State, Albany, N.Y.*, ed. E. B. O'Callaghan (Albany, N.Y., 1865), IV: (June 18, 1643) 169, (November 21, 1645) 239, (July 1, 1647) 297.

61. Ibid., IV: (July 1, 1647) 297; *The Records of New Amsterdam from 1653 to 1674*, ed. Berthold Fernow, 2 vols. (Baltimore, 1976), I: (May 13, 1648) 9, (December 31, 1655) 24–25; II: (October 26, 1656) 205.

62. *Records of New Amsterdam*, II:51; I. N. Phelps Stokes, *The Iconography of Manhattan Island, 1498–1909*, 6 vols. (New York, 1915–1928), IV:55.

63. *Calendar of Historical Manuscripts*, XVI: (August 28, 1654) 55; VIII: (September 13, 1656) 147. The ordinance against the sale of liquor to Indians was repeated, VIII: (October 26, 1656) 248 and IX: (July 21, 1660) 349. Oratan, chief of the Hackingkeshacky, and Mattano, "another chief." X: (March 30, 1662) 95; X: (July 19, 1663) 223.

64. *Colonial Laws of New York* I: (1709) 657–58, 685–86, (1711) 740–41, 751, (1712) 755, (1716) 888, III: (1755) 1096, IV: (1756) 93. *Minutes of the Common Council of New York*, I: (22 March 1680) 85–86, (25 April 1691) 223–24. Mancall, *Deadly Medicine*, 106–7.

65. *Records of Plymouth Colony Laws, 1623–1682*, (1636): 52, (1662): 140, (1664): 209.

66. Ibid., (1664): 215, (1667): 218, (1673): 234, (1677): 243, (1683): 253; *Laws of the Pilgrims*, (1685): 40.

67. Yasuhide Kawashima argues that permission from the governor would allow an individual to trade alcohol with Indians. Governors in every colony seemed to be able to subvert the laws. However, I do think the laws forbade the sale. The index to the *Records of the Governor and Company of Massachusetts Bay*, I:438, has an entry under Indians, "sale of strong water to, forbidden." *Records of the Court of Assistants of the Colony of Massachusetts Bay, 1630–1692*, 3 vols. (Boston, 1901–28), II: (July 2, 1633) 33. A number of individuals were brought before the court for selling to Indians without a license. I do not conclude from this, however, that it was possible to sell to Indians with a license. *Records of the Court of Assistants*, II: (6th Day 4th Mo, 1637) 68; (1st 4th Mo, 1641) 105, 106; *Records of the Governor and Company of Massachusetts Bay*, I: (1633) 106; and Kawashima, *Puritan Justice and the Indian*, 79–80. Mancall, *Deadly Medicine*, 103–5.

68. *Records of the Governor and Company of Massachusetts Bay*, II:85; III:258, 369; Kawashima, *Puritan Justice and the Indian*, 80.

69. *Records of the Governor and Company of Massachusetts Bay*, III: (May 6, 1657) 425–26. This law was virtually repeated in 1694 and remained in force through the colonial period. Kawashima, *Puritan Justice and the Indian*, 80–84; The fine in 1694 was ten pounds. *Acts and Resolves of Massachusetts Bay*, I:154; IV:204, 308, and 497. Greene, *The Negro in Colonial New England*, 135–36.

70. *Records of the Colony of Rhode Island and Providence Plantations, in New England*, ed. John Russell Bartlett, 10 vols. (Providence, R.I., 1856–65), I: (May 22, 1649) 149, 219; (August 31, 1654) 279; (May 25, 1655) 307; (1656) 338; (1659) 413–14. Mancall, *Deadly Medicine*, 105–6.

71. *Records of the Colony of Rhode Island*, II: (September 4, 1666) 174; (May 7, 1673) 486–87; (August 13, 1673) 488; (September 2, 1673) 500–503; (October 29, 1673) 509; (January 22, 1677) 560–61.

72. Ibid., IV: (May 2, 1718) 233, (June 3, 1729) 425.

73. Bruce C. Daniels, *Puritans at Play: Leisure and Recreation in Colonial New England* (New York, 1995), 109–11. David Hall notes that the Massachusetts General Court complained about "dancing in ordinaries . . . upon marriage of some persons." It argues that while they attempted to prohibit the practice, it was likely futile. *Worlds of Wonder, Days of Judgment: Popular Religious Belief in Early New England* (New York, 1989), 210.

74. James Merrell offers another explanation. The impulse to outlaw Indian dancing emerged because Euro-Americans and Indians lived in close proximity to each other. By the late colonial period, colonial leaders assumed that Indians would be regulated by provincial law. James H. Merrell, "Some Thoughts on Colonial Historians and American Indians," *William and Mary Quarterly*, 3d ser., 46 (1989): 116. Richard White's argument in *The Middle Ground* about the role of colonial law in Indians' lives is complex. Among the many points he makes, however, is that Indians could not understand why they should adhere to colonial laws when it appeared as if colonists did not. This is not to deny that

many Indians were engaged in complex economic relationships with colonists and were "thus pulled into the Euro-American world by the economic necessity of working as day laborers in nearby towns." For a recent discussion of the proximity of people, see Ruth Wallis Herndon and Ella Wilcox Sekatau, "The Right to a Name: The Narragansett People and Rhode Island Officials in the Revolutionary Era," in *King Philip's War: Presence and Persistence in Indian New England*, ed. Colin G. Calloway (Hanover, N.H., 1997), 114–43.

75. *Records of the Colony of Rhode Island*, III: (January 4, 1703/4) 492–93; IV: (October 27, 1708) 47.

76. *Journal of the Courts of Common Right and Chancery of East New Jersey, 1683–1702*, ed. Preston W. Edsall (Philadelphia, 1937), 125. For a thorough review of the legislation regulating alcohol and Indians see Mancall, *Deadly Medicine*, 103–10.

77. *Minutes of the Provincial Council of Pennsylvania, Colonial Records of Pennsylvania*, 10 vols. (Philadelphia, 1852), I: (8th of the 2d Mo., 1684) 105, (10th of the 3d month, 1684) 105, (17th of the 3d Mo., 1684) 109. Votes of the Assembly, *Pennsylvania Archives*, 8th ser., I: (10th day of the 3d month, 1684) 51. Mancall, *Deadly Medicine*, 107.

78. *Statutes at Large of Pennsylvania*, II: (October 28, 1701) 168–70. Wilbur Jacobs argued that traders used rum to rob Indians of their trade items. "Unsavory Sidelights on the Colonial Fur Trade," *New York History*, 34 (1953): 135–48.

79. *Statutes at Large of Pennsylvania*, III: (May 22, 1722) 310–13; VI: (April 2, 1763) 283–93. Jersey lawmakers also forbade the sale of rum, brandy, wine, or strong drink to slaves. They assumed that slaves could not have accumulated the funds sufficient to purchase drink in any legitimate way, so the law also forbade the buying, selling, or bartering with slaves for drink "or other goods or commodities." *Journal of the Courts of East New Jersey*, 125.

80. Daniel K. Richter, *The Ordeal of the Longhouse: The Peoples of the Iroquois League in the Era of European Colonization* (Chapel Hill, N.C., 1992), 86. Calvin Martin concurs with Richter's assessment of the ways in which alcohol as a trade item was incorporated into Micmac culture. "With liquor (rum and brandy were the usual fare) he could achieve spiritual ecstasy and a socially acceptable moral laxity." *Keepers of the Game: Indian-Animal Relationships and the Fur Trade* (Berkeley, Calif., 1978), 154. In a conversation with Monte Kugel, she could not think of a single historical example of an Indian people in eastern North America who held intoxicated persons responsible for their behavior.

81. The Guale Indians of Georgia used a drink made from cassina to effect a similar purging. Mancall, *Deadly Medicine*, 64–69.

82. Richter, *Ordeal of the Longhouse*, 85–86.

83. *Journal of Jasper Danckaerts*, 77; John Bartram, Lewis Evans, and Conrad Weiser, *A Journey from Pennsylvania to Onondaga in 1743* (Barre, Mass., 1973), 35.

84. For the best treatment of Indian drinking patterns and the perceptions by whites of these patterns see Mancall, *Deadly Medicine*, esp. chap. 1.

85. *Minutes of the Provincial Council of Pennsylvania*, IV:86–87; Thompson, "The Friendly Glass," 567; Mancall, *Deadly Medicine*, 46–47.

86. "The Journal of James Kenny, 1761–1763," ed. John W. Jordan, *Pennsylvania Magazine of History and Biography*, 37 (1913): 17. Kenny's sympathies are clear from a late entry in his journal in which he complained that the English nations could have been far more helpful to Indians. Instead, those English who knew Indian languages were "most Men of Base principles." The Indians were usually far "better & honester Men . . . then Most English People," 182.

87. Quoted in Mancall, *Deadly Medicine*, 73; "The Journal of Conrad Weiser, esqr., Indian Interpreter, to the Ohio," *Early Western Travels, 1748–1846*, ed. Reuben Gold Thwaites (New York, 1966), 28; "Journal of James Kenny," 192; *North Carolina Colonial and State Records* (Raleigh, N.C., 1886–1907), V:360. See also the "Journal of Thomas Bosomworth, extract of Journal and Proceedings as Agent to and in the Creek Nation, July 1752," in *Documents Relating to Indian Affairs, May 21, 1750–August 7, 1754*, ed. William L. McDowell, Jr. (Columbia, S.C., 1958), 270, 282, 289.

88. Witham Marshe, "Journal of the Treaty at Lancaster in 1744, with the Six Nations," annotated by William Egle, microfilm.

89. *Pennsylvania Gazette*, March 10, 1757.

90. Patrick Gordon, 14 August 1732, in "Order to Tavern-Keepers in re: Indians," Society Collection, case 2, box 18, Historical Society of Pennsylvania; James Logan quoted in Thompson, "The Friendly Glass," 567; Maurice C. Jones, *A Red Rose from the Olden Times . . .* (Philadelphia, 1872), 24–25.

91. *The Journal of the Commons House of Assembly, May 18, 1741–July 10, 1742*, ed. J. H. Easterby (Columbia, S.C., 1953), 377. Other tavern keepers, in addition to Mrs. Russell, presented accounts for sundries and rooms provided to Indians. *The Journal of the Commons House of Assembly, September 14, 1742–January 27, 1744*, ed. J. H. Easterby (Columbia, S.C., 1954), 248; "Journal of Isaac Norris, During a Trip to Albany in 1745, and an Account of a Treaty Held There in October of that Year," *Pennsylvania Magazine of History and Biography* 27 (1903), 23. The bills for Mrs. Russell's tavern were in 1742, 1746, and 1750 and ranged from eleven to twenty-five pounds. Robert L. Meriwether, *The Expansion of South Carolina, 1729–1765* (Kingsport, Tenn., 1940), 43.

92. Gary B. Nash, *The Urban Crucible: Social Change, Political Consciousness, and the Origins of the American Revolution* (Cambridge, Mass., 1979), 64; *Statutes at Large of Virginia*, III: (October 1705) 395–401; IV: (May 1722) 107–10.

93. *The Earliest Printed Laws of South Carolina, 1692–1734*, ed. John D. Cushing (Wilmington, Del., 1978), (March 16, 1695–96), 121–22; (December 23, 1703) 171.

94. *Statutes at Large of South Carolina*, III: (17 May 1751), 735; Journal of the Grand Council of South Carolina, (May 1, 1749–50) 421, South Carolina State Archives.

95. *Proceedings of the County Court of Charles County, 1658–1666 and Manor Court of St. Clement's Manor 1659–1672, Archives of Maryland, Court Series*, ed. J. Hall Pleasants (Baltimore, 1936), LIII: (April 1662) 447–48; *Proceedings of the County Courts of Kent (1648–1676), Talbot (1665–1668), and Somerset (1665–1668) Counties, Archives of Maryland, Court Series*, ed. J. Hall Pleasants (Baltimore, 1937), LIV: (January 25, 1676) 340. At the next court, held March 28, 1676, Andrews again brought suit, for the same

amount, before a jury; again, he lost (*Archives of Maryland, Court Series*, LIV:340). *State Records of North Carolina*, XXIII: (1766) 725–28.

96. *Acts and Resolves of Massachusetts Bay, 1715–1741*, II: (1720–21) 194–95; *Statutes at Large of Pennsylvania*, III: (August 26, 1721) 248–51; *Colonial Laws of New York*, II: (1737) 952–55; (1741) 166, 756–59.

97. *Statutes at Large of Virginia*, I: (October 1644) 287, (February 1644–45) 295, (November 1647) 350; II: (October 1666) 234; III: (October 1705) 400; IV: (August 1734) 428. The argument that the society operated on credit is found in Timothy Breen, *Tobacco Culture*.

98. *Virginia Gazette*, November 26, 1772, quoted in Arthur P. Scott, *Criminal Law in Colonial Virginia* (Chicago, 1930), 257–58.

99. Gibbs, "Taverns in Tidewater Virginia," 26–28; and *Journals of the House of Burgesses of Virginia, 1742–1747*, ed. Henry R. McIlwaine, 13 vols. (Richmond, 1905–19), VII:81, 94, 202, 330; *Statutes at Large of Virginia*, X: (1774) 145–47.

100. The total debt owed Kryder was almost one thousand pounds. Inventory of Martin Kryder, 1773, Philadelphia City Archives; The total owed from Connor's tavern business was £529.13.7; with his dry goods business included the total debt was £933.15.1. Wills and Administrations file #816, "A List of debts due to the estate of James Connor Late of Sadsburry in the County of Chester Province of Pennsylvania Tavern Keeper Drawn out of his books . . 1742," Chester County Archives; Allan Kulikoff, *Tobacco and Slaves: The Development of Southern Cultures in the Chesapeake, 1680–1800* (Chapel Hill, N.C., 1986), 223–24.

101. *Colonial Laws of New York*, (1695), 345–46, (1700) 438–39, (1709) 680–81, (1715) 866–67. *Proceedings of the Common Council of the City of New York* (New York, 1871), (28 January 1675) 28–29; *Minutes of the Common Council of New York*, I: (15 January 1675–76) 11–12.

102. *Statutes at Large of Virginia*, II: (September 1663) 192, (October 1666) 234; III: (April 1691) 44–46, (October 1705) 395–401.

103. What follows relies on Marcus Rediker's superb *Between the Devil and the Deep Blue Sea: Merchant Seamen, Pirates, and the Anglo-American Maritime World, 1700–1750* (Cambridge, Mass., 1987), esp. chap. 3. Quotation is from 116.

104. Ibid., 116–46, esp. 124. Furthermore, the largest category of merchant worker, common tars, or able seaman, experienced a decline in their real wages over the course of the eighteenth century. In a period, 1700–50, when urban colonial workers experienced stability or even a slight increase in real wages, the overall picture of seaman was of stagnant or falling wages. See also W. Jeffrey Bolster, *Black Jacks: African American Seamen in the Age of Sail* (Cambridge, Mass., 1997), 86.

105. Nash, *The Urban Crucible*, 64; Rediker, *Between the Devil and the Deep Blue Sea*, 147.

106. Rediker, *Between the Devil and the Deep Blue Sea*, 147.

107. Robert J. Steinfeld, *The Invention of Free Labor: The Employment Relation in English and American Law and Culture, 1350–1870* (Chapel Hill, N.C., 1991), 3–6, 44–46.

Chapter Two / Inside the Tavern

1. *The Life and Errors of John Dunton, Late Citizen of London . . .* , 2 vols. (London, 1705; reprint New York, 1969), 1:126–27.

2. Richard L. Bushman, *The Refinement of America: Persons, Houses, Cities* (New York, 1992), 161; *The Papers of William Penn: 1685–1700*, ed. Richard and Mary Dunn (Philadelphia, 1986), vol. 3: "[William Penn] to the Provincial Council," c. June 1686, 96; "A Proclamation concerning the Caves of Philadelphia," 24 January 1687, 134.

3. Richard P. Gildrie, *The Profane, the Civil and the Godly: The Reformation of Manners in Orthodox New England, 1679–1749* (University Park, Pa., 1994), 65–66, 72.

4. Bushman, *Refinement of America*, 162. See also, David W. Conroy, *In Public Houses: Drink and the Revolution of Authority in Colonial Massachusetts* (Chapel Hill, N.C., 1995), 119–23.

5. J. Thomas Scharf and Thompson Westcott, *History of Philadelphia, 1609–1884*, 3 vols. (Philadelphia, 1884), I:120. Franklin entered Philadelphia in 1723. *The Autobiography of Benjamin Franklin* (New York, 1965), 32; Bushman, *Refinement of America*, 160, 162.

6. Richard Bushman observed that the "refinement of America" was etched in the shifting location of taverns. *Refinement of America*, 162–64.

7. Voluminous evidence supports the contention that rum drinking dominated. Besides Conroy, *In Public Houses*, 72–75; see W. J. Rorabaugh, *The Alcoholic Republic: An American Tradition* (Oxford, England, 1979), 29–30; Tavern Account Books, B1F11 P. English (1684–1750) Papers, Essex Institute, Salem, Mass. (account entries: brandy—2, rum—80, wine—21). Thomas Amory Account Book, Boston, 1720–1728, Massachusetts Historical Society. Joseph Wise and Benjamin Dolbeare, Boston merchants, bought and sold a wide variety of products. Rum dominated their liquor trade. "Journal to the ledger in company with Joseph Wise and Benjamin Dolbeare begun the 1st July 1 1735 Boston New England [to August 26, 1742] volumes I–VIII," Dolbeare Family Papers, vol. I, Massachusetts Historical Society (receipt entries: rum—44, cider—6, beer—5, gin—2, spirits—4, port—1. Her accounts cover the years 1767–1770. Jane Cazneau, Receipts, 1767–1770, Massachusetts Historical Society. "Journal of Benjamin Mifflin on a Tour from Philadelphia to Delaware and Maryland, July 26 to August 14, 1762," ed. Victor Hugo Paltsits, *Bulletin of the New York Public Library*, 39 (1935), 428. Accounts and memoranda of a general merchandise business, tavern, and legal matters, 1772–1782. John Wilson, Guilford County, Robert Wilson Papers, 1772–1888, Southern Historical Collection, Manuscripts Department, Wilson Library, University of North Carolina at Chapel Hill. Just before the Revolution, Nicholas Cresswell reported that in Virginia "Madeira wine and punch made with Jamaica rum Is their chief Drink." "Journal of a French Traveller in the Colonies, 1765," *American Historical Review* 26 (1921): 736, 741–42.

8. Bushman, *Refinement of America*, 160, 162; Rorabaugh, *The Alcoholic Republic*, 29.

9. *The Diary of Samuel Sewall, 1674–1708*, ed. M. Halsey Thomas, 2 vols. (New York,

1973), I:xxvii, II:741–43; "Some Indictments by the Grand Jury of Philadelphia," *Pennsylvania Magazine of History and Biography* 22 (1898), 497–98.

10. Peter Mancall, *Deadly Medicine: Indians and Alcohol in Early America* (Ithaca, 1995), 21–22; and Richard Sennett, *Flesh and Stone: The Body and the City in Western Civilization* (New York, 1996), 19–21.

11. "Philadelphia Society Before the Revolution: Extracts from the Letters of Alexander Mackraby to Sir Philip Francis," *Pennsylvania Magazine of History and Biography* 11 (1887), 277.

12. John D. R. Platt, *The City Tavern: Independence National Historic Park, Philadelphia, Pennsylvania* (Denver, Colo., 1973), 2, 43–44; Peter Thompson, *Rum Punch and Revolution: Taverngoing and Public Life in Eighteenth-Century Philadelphia* (Philadelphia, 1999), 149–51. The term *entertainment* was used in a variety of ways. Commonly it referred to the food and drink. When William Black was describing a tavern, he noted that the "Entertainment was very Grand, and consisted of many dishes Substantial as well as curious." "The Journal of William Black," *Pennsylvania Magazine of History and Biography* 1 (1877), 246. The usage also included our current definition—that they were entertained by some performance, discussion, or lecture. The word might also refer to the service in general. In Boston entertaining described lodging a person who was not a legal inhabitant of the city. Individuals were fined if they did not inform the selectmen that they had out-of-towners in their house, even if the visitors were relatives. See for example, *Report of the Record Commissioners, Boston Town Records, 1660 to 1701* (Boston, 1872–1906), 7:147–48.

13. "A Glance at New York in 1697: The Travel Diary of Dr. Benjamin Bullivant," ed. Wayne Andrews, *The New York Historical Society Quarterly* 40 (1956): 67; Kym Rice, *Early American Taverns: For the Entertainment of Friends and Strangers* (New York, 1983), 102; "Biographical Sketch of Waightstill Avery," *North Carolina University Magazine* 4 (1885): 249.

14. *Records and Files of the Quarterly Court of Essex County, Massachusetts, 1636–1691*, ed. George F. Dow and Marty Thrasher, 9 vols. Salem, Mass., 1911–21, 1975, VII, 271–72; VIII, 285–86; IX, 29; Gildrie, *The Profane, the Civil, and the Godly*, 42.

15. *Pennsylvania Gazette*, June 19, 1766, August 11, 1768, November 17, 1768. The August advertisement for the sale of the Moulder tavern claims that it had 100 acres of land with about 600 trees. The advertisement in November reduced the amounts to 80 acres and 300 trees.

16. Robert and Lydia Moulder, Tavern Accounts, 1760–1817, Amb 58763, Historical Society of Pennsylvania.

17. "The Fisher History," *Some Prominent Virginia Families*, ed. Louise P. duBellet, 4 vols. (Lynchburg, Va., 1907) 2:788. There are many examples of successful receipts of mail. *Diary of Joshua Hempstead of New London, Connecticut covering a period of forty-seven years from September, 1711 to November, 1758 . . .* (New London, Conn., 1901), 526. Many examples exist as well for individuals who posted or received mail at specific

262 Notes to Pages 57–59

taverns. See, for example, Harold E. Davis, *The Fledgling Province: Social and Cultural Life in Colonial Georgia, 1733–1776* (Chapel Hill, N.C., 1976), 56. Advertisements also appeared in local newspapers assuring their readers that mail would be handled with great care. See, for example, *South Carolina Gazette,* June 4, 1761.

18. Platt, *The City Tavern,* 65; *Boston Newsletter,* March 29–April 5, 1708, June 4–11, 1711, June 15–22, 1713, March 7–14, 1715, May 19–26, 1726, June 23–30, 1726, December 12–19, 1734, May 14–21, 1741, January 4, 1744, March 1, 29, April 19, June 21, July 5, July 26, August 16, October 18, November 29, February 21, 1744 and October 9–16, 1735; Scharf and Westcott, *History of Philadelphia,* II:865; *Virginia Gazette,* March 20, 1752; Maurice C. Jones, *A Red Rose From the Olden Time . . .* (Philadelphia, 1872), 26–27; Adelaide L. Fries, *Records of the Moravians in North Carolina,* 8 vols. (Raleigh, N.C., 1922), 2:728.

19. *Gentleman's Progress: The Itinerarium of Dr. Alexander Hamilton, 1744,* ed. Carl Bridenbaugh (Chapel Hill, N.C., 1948), 84; *Boston Newsletter,* May 5–12, 1737. Carl Bridenbaugh, *Cities in the Wilderness: The First Century of Urban Life in America, 1625–1742* (London, 1938), 431. This particular lecture included a description of fire emitting from the face and hands of a boy suspended horizontally. "The Journal of William Black," *Pennsylvania Magazine of History and Biography* 1 (1877), 246; "Journal of Mr. Ballantine, New England clergyman, April 9, 1764," John H. Lockwood, *Westfied and Its Historic Influences, 1669–1919* (Springfield, Mass., 1922), I:408; *Gentleman's Progress,* 154. For other examples of curiosities to be viewed at the tavern see, I. N. Phelps Stokes, *The Iconography of Manhattan Island, 1498–1909,* 6 vols. (New York, reprinted 1967), 4:787, 797.

20. *A Report of the Record Commissioners of the City of Boston, Selectmen's Minutes, 1764–1768* (Boston, 1877), 111.

21. Individuals who traveled on business often followed the same routes and stayed in the same establishments. The same taverns appear over and over again in the diary of Benjamin Lynde, a judge who rode the circuit of the Massachusetts superior court. *The Diaries of Benjamin Lynde and of Benjamin Lynde, Jr., with an Appendix* (Boston, 1880); *The Diary of Colonel Landon Carter of Sabine Hall, 1752–1778,* 2 vols., ed. Jack P. Greene (Charlottesville, Va., 1965), II: 937–38; Allan Kulikoff, *Tobacco and Slaves: The Development of Southern Cultures in the Chesapeake, 1680–1800* (Chapel Hill, N.C., 1986), 221–22.

22. *The Records of New Amsterdam from 1653 to 1674,* I:325.

23. Account books must be used with some caution, since it is almost impossible to determine whether they record daily transactions or are credit ledgers. If the former, they provide the day-to-day activities of tavern life. If the latter, they merely represent those patrons who owed the proprietor money. The following analysis is based on the assumption that these account books refer to the tavern's total clientele.

24. *Pennsylvania Gazette,* September 19, 1734, April 30, 1741; John Shewbart Journal, Coates-Reynell Collection, Historical Society of Pennsylvania. The account book yields only an impression of the number of names, because Shewbart did not always pro-

vide a first name; occasionally he omits a last name. When he lists Samuel Carpenter and then Carpenter without a first name, I counted this as one individual. Also, when he notes Thomas Bond and Doctor Bond, this too was recorded as a single individual.

25. John Shewbart Journal. It is unclear why Shewbart's trade varied over time. In the years for which there is complete data over the entire year, the frequencies are as follows:

Year	Frequency
1737	1,383
1738	984
1739	442
1740	727
1741	381

It is possible that Hudson would have continued to come in except that Shewbart moved. The small number of entries for 1741 may also reflect the shift in location.

26. Eighty-one individuals were identified on the 1754 or 1756 tax lists. Hannah Benner Roach, "Taxables in Chestnut, Middle and South Wards, Philadelphia: 1754," *Pennsylvania Genealogical Magazine* 21 (1959): 159–96; Hannah Benner Roach, "Taxables in the City of Philadelphia, 1756," *Pennsylvania Genealogical Magazine* 22 (1961): 3–41. I traced individuals using a computer printout prepared by Billy G. Smith for the year 1756. Almost all of Shewbart's customers who were traced to the tax list patronized his tavern in its location at the old London Coffee House in Chestnut Ward.

27. The *Pennsylvania Gazette* referred to Shewbart's tavern interchangeably as the London Tavern or the London Coffee House. They are the same place. *Pennsylvania Gazette,* August 22, 1734.

28. At the time of Kryder's death, approximately 175 people owed him money—a debt that totaled more than 1000 pounds. If this long list of debtors represents his customers, identifying them offers information about the nature of his clientele. Of 108 patrons who could be traced to his ward accounting for less than half of the total debtors (46, or 42.6%). Inventory of the Estate of Martin Kryder, deceased, will 332, 1773. Billy G. Smith kindly gave me this document.

29. Kryder's customers were traced by the 1767, 1769, 1772, and 1774 tax lists and the 1775 Constable's Returns to the Assessor. Seventeen of his customers paid tax in Germantown. A similar attempt was made to trace the customers of Joseph Ogden, who operated the One Tun Tavern in Middle Ward at the northeast corner of Chestnut and Third. Ogden's accounts, however, include a high proportion of lodgers, suggesting that his ledger was a debit/credit account not a daily tab. Joseph Ogden Account Book, 1769–1771, Historical Society of Pennsylvania, Amb 431.

30. "Journal of Benjamin Mifflin on a Tour from Philadelphia to Delaware and Maryland, July 26 to August 14, 1762," ed. Victor Hugo Paltsits, *Bulletin of the New York Public Library* 39 (1935), 427.

31. Daniel B. Thorp, "Doing Business in the Backcountry: Retail Trade in Colonial Rowan County, North Carolina," *William and Mary Quarterly* 3d ser., 48 (1991): 392–94.

32. Accounts and memoranda of a general merchandise business, tavern, and legal matters, Guilford County, 1772–1782, John Wilson. Robert Wilson Papers, 1772–1888.

33. Kulikoff, *Tobacco and Slaves,* 223–24.

34. These data are from the year 1768, the most complete year in the ledger. Robert and Lydia Moulder, Tavern Accounts.

35. William Huey, another regular imbiber at the tavern, averaged just over three visits a month during the spring through the fall, but by November he too appeared only once a month. Arnold Hudson Ledger, Historical Society of Pennsylvania. The exact location of this tavern is unknown.

36. Thorp, "Doing Business in the Backcountry," 398–99.

37. This is based on an analysis of 3,746 visits to his ordinary. John Shewbart Journal.

38. December 10, 1748, Magistrates of City Court; *Pennsylvania Gazette,* November 17, 1750. *The Colonial Records of South Carolina: The Journal of the Common House of Assembly,* 14 vols. (Columbia, S.C., 1977), 10:188; 11:68, 92, 104, 214, 233; 12:96. *Hannah Logan's Courtship,* ed. Albert Cook Myers (Philadelphia, 1904), 263, 274–79. Jacob Hiltzheimer reported that the Amicable Fire Company met at the Widow Jenkin's. *Extracts from the Diary of Jacob Hiltzheimer, 1765–1798,* ed. Jacob Cox Parsons (Philadelphia, 1893), 20; Thompson, "'The Friendly Glass': Drinking and Gentility in Colonial Philadelphia," *Pennsylvania Magazine of History and Biography* 113 (1989): 562.

39. "Thomas Story in 1699 and 1704," *Two Centuries of Travel in Essex County Massachusetts: A Collection of Narratives and Observations Made by Travelers, 1605–1799,* ed. George Francis Dow (Topsfield, Mass., 1921), 50; *Pennsylvania Gazette,* December 5, 1749; and Thompson, *Rum Punch and Revolution,* 82.

40. Thompson, *Rum Punch and Revolution,* 98–99; "Some Account of the Fore Part of the Life of Elizabeth Ashbridge," ed. Daniel B. Shea, *Journeys in New Worlds: Early American Women's Narratives,* gen. ed. William L. Andrews (Madison, Wisc., 1990), 162–63. See also Andrew Sandoval-Strausz, "A Public House for a New Republic: The Architecture of Accommodation and the American State, 1789–1809," *Perspectives in Vernacular Architecture,* forthcoming), ms. 12.

41. "A Glance at New York in 1697," 64; *The Life and Errors of John Dunton,* I:126–27. See also Gildrie, *The Profane, the Civil, and the Godly,* 77.

42. Philip Alexander Bruce, *Social Life of Virginia in the Seventeenth Century* (Lynchburg, Va., 1927), 225–26.

43. "A Summer Jaunt in 1773," *Pennsylvania Magazine of History and Biography* 10 (1886), 205; "Journal of William Black," 240–41; Scharf and Westcott, *History of Philadelphia,* I:152. For the best overview of the sheer quantities of alcohol consumed by Americans see Rorabaugh, *The Alcoholic Republic*; and Mark Edward Lender and James Kirby Martin, *Drinking in America: A History* (New York, 1982).

44. *Gentleman's Progress,* 43, 88, 182–83.

45. *The Carolina Backcountry on the Eve of the Revolution: The Journal and Other Writings of Charles Woodmason, Anglican Itinerant,* ed. Richard J. Hooker (Chapel Hill,

N.C., 1953), 7, 30, 39. For more examples of Woodmason's descriptions of the widespread use of alcohol, see also, 52 and 56.

46. *Gentleman's Progress*, 6–7.

47. Ibid., 17, 43.

48. Durand of Dauphiné, *A Huguenot Exile in Virginia* . . . (New York, 1934, from the Hague Edition of 1687), 129, 137–39.

49. "William Gregory's Journal, from Fredericksburg, Va., To Philadelphia, 30th of September 1765, to 16th October, 1765," *William and Mary Quarterly*, 1st ser., 13 (1904–5): 228.

50. Thompson, "The Friendly Glass," 566.

51. Nancy L. Struna, *People of Prowess: Sport, Leisure, and Labor in Early America* (Urbana, Ill., 1996), 152.

52. "Abstracts from the Personal Account of Richard Neave, Jr.," *Pennsylvania Magazine of History and Biography* 30 (1906): 243.

53. *Pennsylvania Gazette*, July 24, 1732; "Extracts from Letters of Alexander Mackraby," 286.

54. "Journal of William Black, 1744," *Pennsylvania Magazine of History and Biography* 2 (1878): 45; "William Gregory's Journal," 228.

55. December 18, 1762. South Carolinians took the quality of their billiard tables seriously. See *South Carolina Gazette,* March 5, 1763.

56. Samuel Rowland Fisher, "Diary, Trip to Charleston, S.C. 25Th 11 mo, 1772 to 17th January 1773," January 1, 1773, Historical Society of Pennsylvania.

57. "Journal of a French Traveller in the Colonies, 1765," *American Historical Rreview* 26 (1921): 736, 741–42.

58. "A New Voyage to Georgia by a Young Gentleman, Giving an Account of his Travels to South Carolina and part of North Carolina," *Collections of the Georgia Historical Society* 2 (1842): 48–49.

59. "All-fours" got its name from the four chances involved. Each chance had the possibility of scoring one point. The game was later renamed "seven-up." *Journal and Letters of Philip Vickers Fithian: A Plantation Tutor of the Old Dominion, 1773–1774,* ed. Hunter Dickinson Farish (Charlottesville, Va., 1968), 104, 247.

60. *Gentleman's Progress*, 177, 178.

61. Bridenbaugh, *Cities in the Wilderness*, 431; Kulikoff, *Tobacco and Slaves*, 222.

62. Josiah Quincy Diary, (April 16, 20, 21, 22, 1773) 129–30, 137.

63. *Virginia Gazette*, February 27, 1752.

64. *Historical and Genealogical Miscellany: Early Settlers of New Jersey and their Descendants,* ed. John E. Stillwell (New York, 1914), III: (April 22, 1737) 368.

65. "Letter Book of Francis Jerdone," *William and Mary Quarterly*, 1st ser., 11 (1902–3): 153, 155.

66. Darrett B. Rutman and Anita H. Rutman, *A Place in Time: Middlesex County, Virginia, 1650–1750* (New York, 1984), 138–40.

67. Rutman and Rutman, *A Place in Time*.

68. Ibid., 140–42.

69. "Jockey Club," Alfred Stoddart Papers, Historical Society of Pennsylvania. This record is based in part on Hiltzheimer's diary, and according to Stoddart it offers one of the only records of racing. Even though he was a member of the city's elite, Hilztheimer could not join the club, since it would have been a conflict of interest. He kept the stable and was a horse dealer.

70. *Journal and Letters of Fithian*, 24–25, nn. 56 and 57.

71. Struna, *People of Prowess*, 150–51.

72. *Kelty* is a "term denoting the complete draining of a glas of liquor." *The Tuesday Club: A Shorter Edition of The History of the Ancient and Honorable Tuesday Club by Alexander Hamilton*, ed. Robert Micklus (Baltimore, 1995), xiii, 13. After considerable experience with forming and maintaining the Tuesday Club in Annapolis, Hamilton along with other club members formed a Freemason's Lodge. This was just another form of club for Hamilton, another way in which he could live his life as an "upright man." *The Tuesday Club*, x–xi.

73. *Gentleman's Progress*, xvi.

74. *Hannah Logan's Courtship*, 80; *Gentleman's Progress*, Maryland, June 1744, 21. Carl and Jessica Bridenbaugh estimate the existence of fifty clubs in Philadelphia. *Rebels and Gentlemen: Philadelphia in the Age of Franklin* (New York, 1942), 21–22. For the range of clubs in Georgia see Davis, *The Fledgling Province*, 171–74.

75. Josiah Quincy Diary, 8 February 1773–17 May 1773, Massachusetts Historical Society, March 12 and March 15. William Logan joined a club in George Town. "William Logan's Journal of a Journey to Georgia, 1745," *Pennsylvania Magazine of History and Biography* 36 (1912): 162, 174.

76. *Gentleman's Progress*, 6.

77. "Journal of William Black, 1744," ed. R. Alonzo Brock, *Pennsylvania Magazine of History and Biography* 1 (1877): 245–46; 2 (1878): 40–49.

78. *Gentleman's Progress*, 45, 79.

79. Ibid., 42–43.

80. "Journal of William Black," 409.

81. "Philadelphia Society Before the Revolution. Extracts from Letters of Alexander Mackraby to Sir Philip Francis, 1767–1770," *Pennsylvania Magazine of History and Biography* 11 (1887): 276–87, 491–94; and *Gentleman's Progress*, 137–38, 151.

82. *The Journal of John Fontaine an Irish Huguenot in Spain and Virginia, 1710–1719*, ed. Edward Porter Alexander (Williamsburg, Va., 1972), 114, 116, 117. For a wonderful depiction of the spirit and purpose of clubs see David Shields, *Civil Tongues and Polite Letters in British America* (Chapel Hill, N.C., 1997), 175–208.

83. John Brewer, *The Pleasures of the Imagination: English Culture in the Eighteenth Century* (New York, 1997), 39. See for example the announcement in the *Pennsylvania Gazette* that describes a meeting from the previous week of the St. John's Day Grand Lodge of Free and Accepted Masons held at the Sun Tavern in Water Street, June 19–26, 1732.

84. This newspaper exchange is likely a journalistic ploy rather than a real exchange. However, the complaint by Amy Prudence does highlight the "vile" nature of these gatherings. *American Weekly Mercury,* July 3d, 1729; Thompson, "The Friendly Glass," 556.

85. *American Weekly Mercury,* July 17, 1729; Thompson, *Rum Punch and Revolution,* fn 42, 229–30; "The Friendly Glass," 557.

86. Daniel Horsmanden, *The New York Conspiracy,* ed. Thomas J. Davis (Boston, 1971), May 12, 1741, 67n.

87. *Gentleman's Progress,* 6–7, 20, 21, 199.

88. Bridenbaugh and Bridenbaugh, *Rebels and Gentlemen,* 21–22.

Chapter Three / Preventing Drunkenness and Keeping Good Order in the Seventeenth Century

1. *Record of the Courts of Chester County, Pennsylvania, 1681–1697* (Colonial Society of Pennsylvania, 1910), (3d day of ye 2d weeke of ye 7th month, 1688), 130; (12th day of Sept., 1693) 295.

2. Douglas Greenberg notes that the colonies exhibited so much diversity, he doubts that the term *colonial society* is useful. "Crime, Law Enforcement, and Social Control in Colonial America, *American Journal of Legal History,* 26 (1982): 296.

3. Marylynn Salmon, "Notes and Documents: The Court Records of Philadelphia, Bucks, and Berks Counties in the Seventeenth and Eighteenth Centuries," *Pennsylvania Magazine of History and Biography,* 107 (1983): 253–54.

4. Bruce H. Mann, *Neighbors and Strangers: Law and Community in Early Connecticut* (Chapel Hill, N.C., 1987), 7. In 1707, the Pennsylvania Assembly separated criminal cases that involved capital punishment from lower court appeals by arranging for commissions of oyer and terminer to travel to any county on demand to hear capital cases. The provincial court continued to hear appeals. Salmon notes that the lines between all of the courts often blurred, since the same judges presided over all of the county courts. The records reflect this same spillage. The earliest docket for Philadelphia County, for example, contains records from both the court of quarter sessions and the court of common pleas. Salmon, "Notes and Documents," 253–55, 259. See also David Thomas Konig, *Law and Society in Puritan Massachusetts: Essex County, 1629–1692* (Chapel Hill, N.C., 1979), 35–36. For an analysis of the implementation of a county court system and the implications in Plymouth Colony see George D. Langdon, Jr., *Pilgrim Colony: A History of New Plymouth, 1620–1691* (New Haven, Conn., 1966), 201–10.

5. William E. Nelson, *Dispute and Conflict Resolution: Plymouth County, Massachusetts, 1725–1825* (Chapel Hill, N.C., 1981), 29–30.

6. *Records of the Court of Assistants of the Colony of Massachusetts Bay, 1630–1692,* ed. John Noble, 3 vols. (Boston, 1901–11), (19th of 7th mo., 1637) 71; (10th of 4th mo., 1643) 130; (10th of 4th mo., 1643) 130; (5th of 7th mo, 1643) 132; (5th of 10th mo., 1643) 136.

7. The word *drunk* apparently has more slang synonyms than any other word ap-

pearing in the *Dictionary of American Slang*. Harry Gene Levine, "The Vocabulary of Drunkenness," *Journal of Studies on Alcohol* 42 (1981): 1038–51. *Records and Files of the Quarterly Courts of Essex County Massachusetts* (Essex Institute, Salem, Mass., 1911), I: (17th day, 7th month, 1650) 194; *Plymouth Court Records, 1686–1859*, ed. David Thomas Konig (Wilmington, Del., 1978), December 1726, 83; *Records of the Court of Assistants*, (5th Day of the 4th Mo, 1638) 75. Edwin Powers, *Crime and Punishment in Early Massachusetts, 1620–1692: A Documentary History* (Boston, 1966), 384.

8. *Records and Files of Essex County*, I: (30th day, 4th mo., 1653) 286; *Records of Plymouth Colony Laws, 1623–1682* (Boston, 1861; reprint New York, 1968), July 1646: 50; *The Laws of the Pilgrims: A Facsimile Edition of The Book of General Laws of the Inhabitants of the Jurisdiction of New-Plymouth, 1672 and 1685* (Wilmington, Del., 1977) (1685): 25; *Colonial Justice in Western Massachusetts*, ed. Joseph H. Smith (Cambridge, Mass., 1961), January 12, 1661: 249, April 13, 1676: 287; and Mark Lender, "Drunkenness as an Offense in Early New England: A Study of 'Puritan' Attitudes," *Quarterly Journal of Studies on Alcohol* 34 (June 1973): 354–55.

9. *For the King and Both Houses of Parliament . . .* (London, 1660), 29. Carla Pestana kindly gave me this citation. Poems are quoted in Harry Gene Levine, "'The Good Creature of God and the Demon Rum': Colonial America and Nineteenth-Century Ideas about Alcohol, Crime, and Accidents," in *Alcohol and Disinhibition: Nature and Meaning of the Link*, ed. Robin Room and Gary Collins, NIAA Research Monograph, no. 12 (1983), 117–18.

10. *Minutes of the Provincial Council of Pennsylvania, Pennsylvania Colonial Records*, I: (9th of 4th month, 1683) 76. *The Colonial Laws of Massachusetts Reprinted from the edition of 1660, with the supplements to 1672. Containing also, The Body of Liberties of 1641* (Boston, 1889), 164. Lender, "Drunkenness as an Offense in Early New England," 354–55. New York law differentiated between stages of drunkenness. If someone approached the watch drunk, they would pay half the fine. If the person was abusive or "Quite Drunke," they owed the entire fine. *Minutes of the Common Council of the City of New York, 1675–1776*, 8 vols. (New York, 1905), I:8–9.

11. Levine, "The Good Creature of God," 114.

12. I take my cues from the superb study of Connecticut courts by Cornelia Hughes Dayton, *Women before the Bar: Gender, Law, and Society in Connecticut, 1639–1789* (Chapel Hill, N.C., 1995).

13. Mary Beth Norton, "Gender and Defamation in Seventeenth-Century Maryland," *William and Mary Quarterly* 44 (January 1987), 7.

14. Murders, duels, fights, and other forms of violent behavior were often played out in taverns For example, in 1763, in the Moravian-operated tavern in Bethabara, North Carolina, John Hall tried to settle his bill with counterfeit money. Hall reportedly hurled angry threats at the proprietor, Brother Loesch, who then had Hall "securely bound." Three days later another disturbance occurred in the tavern. Some travelers were arrested then released after Brother Loesch examined them. A few years later, a traveler refused to pay his entire bill and when challenged attacked one of the proprietors by placing a loaded gun "against his breast." A fight broke out "so that the blood flowed freely."

Records of the Moravians in North Carolina, ed. Adelaide L. Fries, 8 vols. (Raleigh, 1922), 1:271, 337. In 1771 in Charleston, South Carolina, a duel took place inside Mr. Holliday's tavern. A number of shots were fired and one man died as a result. *South Carolina Gazette,* August 22, 1771. See also Supplement to the *South Carolina Gazette,* and *Country Journal,* May 10, 1768.

15. In 1747, three young men were defendants in a libel suit brought by Stephen Howell. The young men were accused of attaching to the outer door of Samuel Cook's tavern in New Haven, a "Paper, Callender [or] Advertisement" proclaiming, in part, that Howell's character had been lost or taken away. To add insult to injury, they valued "his character or Reputation" at a measly four pounds and offered a piddling reward of "13 pence Halfpenny Sterling, hangmans Wages." The perpetrators had no doubt selected Cook's door to maximize the visibility of their message about Howell, since the tavern was frequented by "a great . . . Concourse of People." Dayton, *Women before the Bar,* 319, n 70.

16. Ibid., 3–4.

17. Most historians of early America agree that New England pursued prosecutions with far more vigor than other regions of the colonies did. See for example, Mary Beth Norton, *Founding Mothers and Fathers: Gendered Power and the Forming of American Society* (New York, 1996), 326–28. Puritans believed fervently that the community could function properly and carry out God's wishes only if everyone participated. The wrath of God was poised to descend upon an entire community if individuals were not vigilant in their efforts to suppress the sins of their neighbors. Thus, individuals and institutions supplemented the role of the courts and acted as agents of law enforcement. The churches handled a wide range of misdemeanors interpreted as crimes against morals or ecclesiastic discipline. As Emil Oberholzer observed, "disciplinary cases were the staples on the churches' agenda." Most, but not all, of these received independent hearings in the civil courts. Emil Oberholzer, Jr., *Delinquent Saints: Disciplinary Action in the Early Congregational Churches of Massachusetts* (New York, 1956), 31; and George Lee Haskins, *Law and Authority in Early Massachusetts: A Study in Tradition and Design* (New York, 1960), 28, 52, 88–90. For Connecticut, similar areas of crime were pursued both in church and court, but often a person disciplined in church was not hauled into court. This was true especially in the seventeenth century. Dayton, *Women before the Bar.*

18. *Records of the Colony of New Plymouth in New England,* ed. Nathaniel Shurtleff, 6 vols. (Boston, 1855–61), II: (4 November 1646) 171. See also *Acts and Laws of His Majesties Colony of Connecticut in New-England: Passed by the General Assembly* (Hartford, 1919), (1712) 177, (1715) 123–24, (1715) 203, (1723) 293; *The Public Records of the Colony of Connecticut,* transcribed by J. Hammond Trumbull, 15 vols. (Hartford, 1850–90), V: (May 1716) 562–63. Gail Sussman Marcus writes that New Haven magistrates, unlike those of Connecticut and Massachusetts, did not have the power to dispose of criminal cases without the courts. "'Due Execution of the Generall Rules of Righteousness': Criminal Procedure in New Haven Town and Colony, 1638–1658," in *Saints and Revolutionaries: Essays in Early American History,* ed. David Hall, John M. Murrin, and Thad W. Tate (New York, 1983), 103.

Drinking and tavern infractions were not the only ones handled informally. Carla Pestana describes a portion of William King's blasphemy case that occurred on the porch of the Plymouth magistrate, Bartholemew Gedney. "The Social World of Salem: William King's 1681 Blasphemy Trial," *American Quarterly* 41 (1989), 310.

Donna J. Spindel, "The Administration of Criminal Justice in North Carolina, 1720–1740," *American Journal of Legal History* 25 (1981), 37.

19. *The Diary of Samuel Sewall, 1674–1708,* ed. M. Halsey Thomas, 2 vols. (New York, 1973) I:154; and Louis B. Wright, *The Cultural Life of the American Colonies, 1607–1763* (New York, 1957), 178–79.

20. *Diary of Samuel Sewall,* I:xxvii, II:741–43; David W. Conroy, *In Public Houses: Drink and the Revolution of Authority in Colonial Massachusetts* (Chapel Hill, N.C., 1995), 57–58.

21. Albert Cook Myers, ed., *Hannah Logan's Courtship* (Philadelphia, 1904), 299.

22. Peter Mancall, "The Art of Getting Drunk," *Reviews in American History* 24 (1996): 386; Conroy, *In Public Houses,* 145.

23. *The Statutes at Large: Being a Collection of all of the Laws of Virginia From th First Session of the Legislature in the Year 1619,* ed. William Waller Hening, 18 vols. (New York, 1809–23) I: (November 20, 1606) 71.

24. "Proceedings of the First Assembly of Virginia, 1619," in *Collections of the New-York Historical Society,* ed. George Bancroft, 2d ser., III: (1857) 346; Arthur P. Scott, *Criminal Law in Colonial Virginia* (Chicago, 1930), 144; and *Statutes at Large of Virginia,* I: (March 1624) 126, (February 1632) 156, 167, (September 1632) 193–94, (March 1643) 240, (March 1646) 310, (March 1658) 433; Edmund Morgan, *American Slavery, American Freedom: The Ordeal of Colonial Virginia* (New York, 1975), 113.

25. *Statutes at Large of Virginia,* I:127.

26. The preamble to the 1662 law explained that "victualling houses" were necessary for the entertainment of "all persons as well as Strangers and others" and, most importantly, for providing comfortable sites for court meetings. *Archives of Maryland: Proceedings and Acts of the General Assembly of Maryland* (Baltimore, 1883), I: (16th March 1637) 20, (July–August 1642) 169, (September 1642) 193, (April 1650) 286, (October 1654) 342–43, (April 1658) 375, (April 1662) 447–48; "An Act for Encouraging of Ordinary Keepers," I: (September 1664) 537. In addition to requiring a license, the 1674 law stated that tavern keepers "shall not suffer any drinking nor gaming upon Sabbath day" and that credit could not exceed more than 400 pounds of tobacco annually. Idem, II: (May–June 1674) 346–47, 351, 407–8; (February 1675) 431, 434–35.

27. *Statutes at Large of Virginia,* I: (March 1623–24) "That whosoever shall absent himself from divine service any Sunday without an allowable excuse," 123; (October 1629) "It is ordered that there be an special care taken by all commanders and others that the people do repair to their churches on the Sabbath day," 144; (February 1631–32) "That the statutes for coming to church every Sunday and holidays be duly executed," 155; (September 1632) "Penalty for not attending church," 180; (March 1642–43) "profaning god's name, and his holy sabbaths," 240, and "for the better observation of the Sabbath," 261; (March 1657–58) "That the lord's day be kept holy and that no journeys be made except

in case of urgent necessity on that day, that no goods be laden in boats nor shooting in guns or the like tending to the profanation of that day," 434, and "Whereas it hath been the frequent practice of sheriffs and officers for their own ease and benefit to repair to the churches on sabbath days and other public meetings on purpose to serve executions warrants and other writs, by which means many times those duties are neglected by such who are in danger of arrests," 457; II: (March 1661–62) against "sabbath abusing," 51–52; (April 1691) against "sabbath abusing," 71–75; III: (October 1705) "Sunday may be kept holy," 358–62; (October 1705) "No tippling," 395–401.

28. *Archives of Maryland*, I: (July–August 1642) 159; (September 1642) 193; (April 1650) 286; (October 1654) 342–43; (April 1658) 375; (May–April 1661) 409; (April 1662) 447–48; (September 1664) 537; II: (April–May 1666) 148; (April–May 1669) 214–15. The protection of the Sabbath is in the May–June 1674 session, II: 346–47.

29. *Statutes at Large of Virginia*, I: (September 1632) 183.

30. "Proceedings of the first Assembly of Virginia, 1619," 346; *Statutes at Large of Virginia*, II: (September 1663) 206. For the first offense, the fine was increased to 500 pounds; misconduct a second time was a 1000 pound fine. II: (February 1676–77) 384; Scott, *Criminal Law in Colonial Virginia*, 256.

31. *Statutes at Large of Virginia*, II: (September 1668) Act IX, 268–69. Acts that set rates on liquor, to "moderate the rates of liquor sold," and to encourage the "productions of the country," were also explicit in their intent. For example, "for beer and cider being produced by the husbandry of this country and therefore fitter to be encouraged what profit they can make not exceeding 40 lbs tobacco or 4 s. per gallon." II: (October 1666) 234, (September 1667) 263, (September 1671) 287–88.

32. Ibid., III: (April 1691) Act XI, 71–75.

33. Ibid., VI: (October 1748) 73.

34. Kathleen Brown, *Good Wives, Nasty Wenches, and Anxious Patriarchs: Gender, Race, and Power in Colonial Virginia* (Chapel Hill, N.C., 1996), 91. Arthur P. Scott reached the same conclusion—prosecutions for drunkenness were rare and occurred primarily in conjunction with more serious crime. And drinking was universal. *Criminal Law in Colonial Virginia* (Chicago, 1930), 258–60. *Minutes of the Council and General Court of Colonial Virginia, 1622–1632, 1670–1676*, ed. H. R. McIlwaine (Richmond, 1924). Kathleen Brown reports that the General Court heard a wide variety of cases from 1623 to 1629, which may have given the court the impression that they were living "in a nest of rogues." Within this six-year period, the court prosecuted only eight cases of drunkenness. *Good Wives, Nasty Wenches, and Anxious Patriarchs*, 90, fn. 43.

35. James Slight is referred to as a yeoman. He was renting ground in Martin's Brandon for an annual rent of two Capons or two pullets a year. *Minutes of the Council and General Court of Colonial Virginia*, (4th day of July 1627) 151.

36. Ibid., (19th February 1626) 139–40, (5th March 1626) 141–42, (4th April 1627) 148.

37. Ibid., (6 March 1628) 190–92. A murder case involving alcohol was tried by the Richmond County court in December 1701. However, it played no discernible role. *Vir-*

ginia Colonial Abstracts, vol. 16, *Richmond County Records, 1692–1704* (Richmond, Va., n.d.), 84–91.

38. *Minutes of the Council and General Court of Colonial Virginia,* (21st August 1626) 108, (9th May 1625) 58.

39. Ibid., (30th November 1674) 34; Levine, "The Good Creature of God," 133–34. For a suggestive discussion of the "homosexual proclivities of seafarers" and the specific role played by the "boys who went to sea," see B. R. Burg, *Sodomy and the Pirate Tradition: English Sea Rovers in the Seventeenth-Century Caribbean* (New York, 1983, rev. 1995), 121–38.

40. *County Court Records of Accomack-Northampton, Virginia, 1632–1640,* ed. Susie M. Ames (Washington, D.C., 1954); and *County Court Records of Accomack-Northampton, Virginia, 1640–1645,* ed. Susie M. Ames (Charlottesville, Va., 1973). See also Elizabeth Stanton Haight, "Heirs of Tradition, Creators of Change: Law and Stability on Virginia's Eastern Shore, 1633 to 1663," (Ph.D. diss., University of Virginia, 1987), 321, Table 1.

41. Cole was convicted in 1674. The other case was heard in 1692. Levine, "The Good Creature of God," 139.

42. *Virginia Colonial Abstracts: Northumberland County Records, 1652–1655,* ed. Beverley Fleet, 3 vols. (Baltimore, 1988), I:331–400.

43. Ibid., 394; Levine, "The Good Creature of God," 132.

44. Northampton County Court Records, Virginia State Library, microfilm, reels 1 and 2, 1: (1679); *Virginia Colonial Abstracts, Northumberland County,* II: (September 1634); Levine, "The Good Creature of God," 133.

45. *Virginia Colonial Abstracts: Charles City County Court Orders,* (Richmond, Va., n.d.), III:222, 228, 230.

46. *Minutes of the General Council and Court of Colonial Virginia,* (9th May 1625) 58, (21st August 1626) 108. See also, Norton, *Founding Mothers and Fathers,* 326–28.

47. *Archives of Maryland LIII, Proceedings of the County Court of Charles County, 1658–1666 and Manor Court of St. Clement's Manor 1659–1672, Court Series,* ed. J. Hall Pleasants (Baltimore, Md., 1936) vol. 6; *Archives of Maryland LX, Proceedings of the County Court of Charles County, 1666–1674, Court Series,* 9, ed. J. Hall Pleasants (Baltimore, 1943); and *Archives of Maryland LIV: Proceedings of the County Courts of Kent (1648–1676), Talbot (1662–1674), and Somerset (1665–1668) Counties, Court Series,* 7, ed. J. Hall Pleasants (Baltimore, 1937). James Horn confirms these data. He found that drunkenness and being drunk in court constituted only 1.7% and 1.3% of all crimes and misdemeanors in Maryland from 1637–1675. *Adapting to a New World: English Society in the Seventeenth-Century Chesapeake* (Chapel Hill, N.C., 1996), 352–53, Table 33.

48. *The Earliest Printed Laws of South Carolina, 1692–1734,* ed. John D. Cushing (Wilmington, Del., 1978), 71, 109, 118, 231.

49. *Statutes at Large of South Carolina,* ed. Thomas Cooper (Columbia, S.C., 1837), II: (December 8, 1681) 68–69; *Journal of the Grand Council of South Carolina,* ed. A. S. Salley, Jr., 2 vols. (Columbia, S.C., 1907), II: (June 21, 1692) 31; and *Earliest Printed Laws of South Carolina,* Col. Nicholas Trott, 2 vols. (Wilmington, Del., 1978), I:(December 12, 1712) 298–302.

50. The fine was ten shillings for being drunk on the Sabbath, five shillings on the other days of the week. *The Earliest Printed Laws of North Carolina, 1669–1751*, ed. John D. Cushing (Wilmington, Del., 1977), 2:4.

51. *The State Records of North Carolina, Laws 1715–1776*, comp. and ed. Walter Clark (Goldsboro, N.C., 1904), XXIII: 182; The 1741 law was greatly enlarged and amended in 1758, 492–94. The rule about the Sabbath was reiterated in the 1766 law, idem, 725–28.

52. *The Records of New Amsterdam from 1653 to 1674 anno domini*, ed. Berthold Fernow, vol. 1, *1653–1655* (Baltimore, 1976), (May 1647) 1.

53. Ibid., (April 29, 1648) 8–9.

54. *Laws and Ordinances of New Netherland, 1653–1674*, comp. E. B. O'Callaghan (Albany, N.Y., 1868), 416.

55. Although the Duke of York's Laws did require all ale houses to be closed by nine at night, no specific mention of the Sabbath was made. *Colonial Laws of New York, 1664–1774*, 4 vols. (Albany, 1894), I:39.

56. The fine for the first offense was twenty-five guilders. It doubled for the second and doubled again for the third. Any person caught indulging on the Sabbath would be fined ten guilders "for Every such offence." *Proceedings of the Common Council of the City of New York* (New York, 1871), (November 1676) 70–71; and *Minutes of the Common Council of the City of New York*, 8 vols. (New York, 1905), I: (13th November 1676) 27.

57. *Proceedings of the Common Council of the City of New York*, (March 1683–84) 318, 319; *Minutes of the Common Council of the City of New York*, I: (15th March 1683–84) 133–34, IV: (18th November 1731) 79.

58. *Calendar of New York Colonial Manuscripts*, ed. E. B. O'Callaghan, 3 vols. (Albany, N.Y., 1865–66), I: (May 3, 1640) 71, (May 5, 1640) 13, (June 7, 1640) 72, (April 28, 1645) 94, (November 14, 1641) 77, (November 22, 1641) 78, September 24, 1641) 77.

59. Ibid., I: (April 1, 1660) 210, (April 26, 1660), (May 3, 1660) 210, (July 25, 1656) 170, (July 31, 1656) 171, (August 1, 1656), (August 3, 1656) 172.

60. Daniel Richter, *The Ordeal of the Longhouse: The Peoples of the Iroquois League in the Era of European Colonization* (Chapel Hill, N.C., 1992), 109.

61. *Records of New Amsterdam*, IV:205, II:73, I:286–87.

62. *Minutes of the Mayor's Court of New York, 1674–1675*, ed. Kenneth Scott (Baltimore, 1983), (22d December 1674) 8, (9th February 1675) 18–19, (9th February 1675) 20–21, (19th March 1675) 33; *Minutes of the Common Council of the City of New York*, I:85–86.

63. David Hall notes that being drunk was just one many possible excesses facing Puritans. *Worlds of Wonder, Days of Judgment: Popular Religious Belief in Early New England* (New York, 1989), 179. *Records of the Court of Assistants of the Colony of the Massachusetts Bay, 1630–1692*, II: (July 2, 1633) 33, and *Records of the Governor and Company of Massachusetts Bay in New England*, ed. Nathaniel B. Shurtleff, 5 vols. (Boston, 1853), I: (3 September 1634) 126, (4 March 1635) 140.

64. *Records of the Governor and Company of Massachusetts Bay*, I: (3 September 1634) 126, (2 November, 1637) 206, (20 November, 1637) 213–14, (6 September, 1638)

238, (22 May, 1639) 25, (5 November 1639) 279–80; II: (14 May 1645) 100, (4 November 1646) 171–73. David W. Conroy, *In Public Houses: Drink and the Revolution of Authority in Colonial Massachusetts* (Chapel Hill, N.C., 1995), 36.

65. *Records of the Governor and Company of Massachusetts Bay*, II: (4 November, 1646) 171; Conroy, *In Public Houses*, 37. See also *Acts and Laws of Connecticut Law Book* (1712) 177, (1715) 123–24, (1715) 203, (1723) 293; *The Public Records of the Colony of Connecticut*, transcr. J. Hammond Trumbull, 15 vols. (Hartford, 1850–90), IV: (May 1716) 562–63.

66. *The Colonial Laws of Massachusetts Reprinted from the edition of 1660, with the supplements to 1672. Containing also, The Body of Liberties of 1641* (Boston, 1889), 189.

67. *The Acts and Resolves, Public and Private, of the Province of the Massachusetts Bay, 1692–1714* (Boston, 1869), I: (1692), 58.

68. *Records of Plymouth Colony Laws*, 1636:17, 30, 52.

69. Ibid., 1646:50, 64; 1658:113–14; 1659:123–24; 1660:128; 1661:131; 1662:136, 137, 140; 1664:195–98; 1664:207; 1667:218; 1669:222–24; 1673:234–35; 1674:236; 1677:243–44; 1682:253, 257–58.

70. Ibid., 1662:137, 1664:207, 1674:236.

71. Langdon, *Pilgrim Colony*, 204, 208–9; *Laws of the Pilgrims*, 1685:57.

72. *Records of the Colony of Rhode Island and Providence Plantations, in New England* (Providence, R.I., 1856), I: (May 19–20, 1647) 160, 185, 186. For a description of Rhode Island's struggle for legitimacy, see Edwin Gaustad, *Liberty of Conscience: Roger Williams in America* (Grand Rapids, Mich., 1991).

73. In 1654, the commissioners of the four Rhode Island towns ordered each town to appoint or license one or two houses for the entertainment of strangers. To implement this requirement, the court would nominate and appoint two individuals until such time as the towns could select two. A law was also passed making it unlawful for any tavern keeper to "suffer any person to tipple after nine of ye clock at night, except they can give a satisfactorie reason to ye Constable or magistrate." The costs of transgressing this law fell more heavily on the tavern proprietor than on the drinker. In addition, the whole licensing structure softened considerably. In 1661, in response to a "great complaynt by reason that ther is no place or places for strangers to be entertained," anyone could retail liquor if they "keepe one bed at least, and victuals for the entertayning of strangers." *Records of the Colony of Rhode Island*, I: (1654) 274, 276, 279, 280; (May 25, 1655) 313; (March 17, 1656) 335; (May 21, 1661) 441. Laws were repeated: requiring licenses, II: (September 4, 1666) 174; III: (May 5, 1680) 89; IV: (February 3, 1729) 418; V: (October 1748) 260; VI: (October 1762) 343, (October 1765) 461; tavern keepers were not to suffer disorders, II: (April 11, 1671) 372; no liquor to be sold or drinking on Sundays, II: (September 2, 1673) 503–4; III: (May 7, 1679) 31; III: (December 14, 1687) 237; better preventing of drunkenness, IV: (May 1, 1721) 294.

74. The results of these efforts are examined more fully later. Conroy, *In Public Houses*, 39–41.

75. Ibid., 61–65.

76. *Laws of the Pilgrims*, 34–36.

77. For the first offense, a five-shilling fine or an hour in the stocks. For the second conviction, the violator was to pay ten shillings or sit in the stocks for two hours or be whipped. By the third offense the perpetrator was fined twenty shillings or whipped publicly and was to be incarcerated until he or she posted a bond against future violations. Ibid., 25–26.

78. The rates of prosecution were: for Virginia 13 cases in the ten-year period 1622–32, or 1.3 a year; for Plymouth from 1633 to 1691 158 cases, or 2.7 per year. The per capita rate does indicate a wide difference. The population of Plymouth in 1634 was less than half of that in Virginia, although accurate population statistics for Virginia are hard to find. Plymouth had a population of 1,800 in 1634, whereas Virginia's population totaled 4,914. Evarts Greene and Virginia Harrington, *American Population before the Federal Census of 1790* (New York, 1932), 8, 136. Edmund Morgan's estimates of the Virginia population are quite close to Greene and Harrington's. He reports 3,200 in 1632 and 5,200 in 1634. *American Slavery, American Freedom: The Ordeal of Colonial Virginia* (New York, 1975), 404. Michael Zuckerman pointed out the dramatic differences in rates of prosecution; his analysis appears throughout this chapter.

79. *Records of the Colony of New Plymouth*, I: (1638) 107; II: (1643) 66, (1648) 122, (1650) 156; III: (1651–52) 5, (1652–53) 22, (1657) 129, (1658–59), 159, (1661) 219; IV: (1665) 106; V: (1672) 88.

80. Ibid., III: (1656) 104, (1658) 150, (1659) 173, (1675) 182, (1660) 200, (1660–61) 206, 207, 212, 220; IV: (1662) 33, (1664) 51, 55, 66 (1665) 101, 106; V: (1668–69) 16–17, (1670) 39, (1673) 118, (1675) 169, 182; VI: (1678–79) 7, (1682) 97, (1684) 131. Powers, *Crime and Punishment*, 389–91.

81. *Records of the Colony of New Plymouth*, I: (3 September 1639) 132; III: (1660) 200; V: (1 March 1670) 31.

82. Helena Wall, *Fierce Communion: Family and Community in Early America* (Cambridge, Mass., 1990), 30–37.

83. *Records of the Court of Assistants*, II: (1636) 62. Powers, *Crime and Punishment*, 387.

84. *Records of the Court of Assistants*, II: (3 September 1633) 34–35; (4 March 1633/34) 41; *Records of the Governor and Company of Massachusetts Bay*, I: (1633) 107; (1634) 122. Powers, *Crime and Punishment*, 387–88.

85. *Boston Town Records*, 11 vols. (Boston, 1877–1906), VII:58–59; "Indian War Papers," comp. Charles W. Parsons, *New England Historical and Genealogical Register* 3 (1849): 165; "Soldiers in King Philip's War," comp. George M. Budge *New England Historical and Genealogical Register* 43 (1889): 275.

86. Kym S. Rice, *Early American Taverns: For the Entertainment of Friends and Strangers* (Chicago, 1983), 21, 31, 33–34, 104. Timothy J. Gilfoyle, *City of Eros: New York City, Prostitution, and the Commercialization of Sex* (New York, 1992), 164, 373 n 6.

87. *Records of the Suffolk County Court, 1671–1680*, Colonial Society of Massachusetts (January 30, 1672), 82–83.

88. Powers, *Crime and Punishment*, 201, 179; Haskins, *Law and Authority in Early Massachusetts*, 204–12.

89. *Records of the Suffolk County Court*, (January 30, 1671/2), 82–83; Powers, *Crime and Punishment*, 179–80.

90. Records of the Court of General Sessions of the Peace (Columbia Point, Mass.), July 18, 1707; April 14, 1707; July 1, 1707; October 7, 1707; July 31, 1710.

91. Ibid., July 1, 1707.

92. *Diary of Cotton Mather*, ed. Worthington Chauncey Ford, 2 vols. (reprint, New York, 1957), II: August 1713; "Diary of Lt. John Peebles, December 31, 1776," *William and Mary Quarterly*, 3d ser., 26 (1969), 441.

93. *The Papers of William Penn*, ed. Richard S. Dunn and Mary M. Dunn, 5 vols. (Philadelphia, 1981), II: 151. Penn's law to control taverns, written c. 23 March 1683, is on 206–7; *Minutes of the Provincial Council of Pennsylvania, Colonial Records*, 10 vols. (Philadelphia, 1852; AMS edition, 1968), I: (1683) 74, 75, (1684) 98.

94. Jean Soderlund, ed., *William Penn and the Founding of Pennsylvania, 1680–1684: A Documentary History* (Philadelphia, 1983), 206–7; David Shields, *Civil Tongues and Polite Letters in British America* (Chapel Hill, N.C., 1997), 62–63.

95. *The Statutes at Large of Pennsylvania*, comp. James T. Mitchell and Henry Flanders (Harrisburg, Pa., 1896), II: (January 12, 1706) 175–77.

Pennsylvania's eastern neighbor, East Jersey, fashioned its law from two sources: William Penn's "Laws Agreed upon in England" and the twenty-first and twenty-second chapters of Exodus. The General Assembly joined the consensus that "Brandy, rum and other strong liquors are in their kind (not abused but taken in moderation) creatures of God, and useful and beneficial to mankind." To control drinking, the assembly passed a considerable body of legislation. A special act in March 1683 established a five-shilling sterling fine for drunkenness, or six hours in the stocks for those who could not pay. In December 1683, because of the "great exorbitances and drunkenness . . . in this Province, occasioned by tolerating many persons in selling drink in private houses," the assembly passed a law that limited the sale of alcohol by the drink. Retailing liquor in quantities under a quart or wine, beer, or cider in amounts under a gallon required a license and a twenty-pound bond. In 1692, the law was altered slightly to apply to wine under a gallon and beer and cider under a barrel. The General Laws placed drunkenness within the category of offenses against God, and anyone found drunk would pay a fine of five shillings sterling or spend six hours in the stocks. *Journal of the Courts of Common Right and Chancery of East New Jersey, 1683–1702*, Preston W. Edsall, ed. (Philadelphia, 1937), 115, 124–25.

96. *Minutes of the Provincial Council of Pennsylvania*, I: (15th, 1st month, 1683) 60, (28th, 1st month, 1683) 68, (26th, 1st month, 1684) 98, (26th, 5th month, 1684) 117, (21st, 5th month, 1685) 147, (16th, 11th month, 1685) 167, (13th, 3rd month, 1690) 337, (30th, 5th month, 1690) 341–42. Peter Thompson, "A Social History of Philadelphia's Taverns, 1683–1800," (Ph.D. diss., University of Pennsylvania, 1989), 134.

97. *Minutes of the Provincial Council of Pennsylvania*, I: (15th, 1st month, 1683) 60, (28th, 1st month, 1683) 68, (26th, 1st month, 1684) 98.

98. Ibid., I: (26th, 5th month, 1684) 117, (21st, 5th month, 1685) 147.

99. *Records of the Courts of Quarter Sessions and Common Pleas of Bucks County, Pennsylvania, 1684–1700* (Meadville, Pa., 1943), (April 8, 1687) 77–78, (March 26, 1697) 321, (February 22, 1687) 75, 81.

100. *Records of the Courts of Chester County, Pennsylvania, 1681–1710*, transcribed by Dorothy Lapp, 2 vols. (Philadelphia, 1910–72).

101. Quoted in C. C. Pearson and J. Edwin Hendricks, *Liquor and Anti-Liquor in Virginia, 1619–1919* (Durham, N.C., 1967), 5.

102. Peter C. Hoffer and N. E. H. Hull, *Murdering Mothers: Infanticide in England and New England, 1558–1803* (New York, 1981), 34, 36–37.

103. David Flaherty, "Law and the Enforcement of Morals in Early America," *Perspectives in American History* 5 (1971), 208–11.

104. Ibid., 212–17; Scott, *Criminal Law in Colonial Virginia*, 279; William H. Seiler, "The Anglican Parish in Virginia," in *Seventeenth-Century America*, ed. James Morton Smith (Chapel Hill, N.C., 1959), 134.

Chapter Four / Eighteenth-Century Legislation and Prosecution

1. *Virginia Gazette*, July 18, 1766.

2. Ibid.

3. Edmund Morgan, *American Slavery, American Freedom: The Ordeal of Colonial Virginia* (New York, 1975), 111.

4. Fairfax County court minutes, 1763–1765, 2 vols., Huntington Library, San Marino, California.

5. *Criminal Proceedings in Colonial Virginia: Records of Fines, Examination of criminals, Trials of Slaves, etc., from March 1710 [1711] to [1754]* [Richmond County, Va., n.d.], ed. Peter Charles Hoffer and William B. Scott (Athens, Ga., 1984); *American Legal Records* 10: (August 1728), 110; (September 1728), 111.

6. *Virginia Colonial Abstracts: King and Queen County, Records Concerning 18th Century Persons*, ed. Beverly Fleet (Richmond, Va., 1940), 3:7, 18–26, 30.

7. Darrett B. Rutman and Anita H. Rutman, *A Place in Time: Middlesex County, Virginia, 1650–1750* (New York, 1984), 221–22.

8. *The Secret Diary of William Byrd of Westover, 1709–1712*, ed. Louis B. Wright and Marion Tinling (Richmond, Va., 1941), 1709: (March 4) 12, (June 7) 43, (October 28, 29) 98, (June 25) 52, (July 5) 57, (October 27) 98, (November 1) 101; 1710: (September 22) 135, (November 10) 256, (November 26) 263; 1711: (November 3) 432, (November 23) 442; 1712: (March 12) 400.

9. Ibid., 1710: (May 3) 173–74, (August 15) 218, (December 11) 270, (April 4) 324.

10. "Extracts from the Diary of Daniel Fisher, 1755," ed. Mrs. Conway Robinson Howard, *Pennsylvania Magazine of History and Biography* 17 (1893), 263–64.

11. *The Secret Diary of William Byrd*, ed. Wright and Tinling, 1710: (September 22) 234.

12. *Virginia Colonial Abstracts*, vol. 31, *Lower Norfolk County, 1651–1654*, ed. Bev-

erley Fleet (Richmond, 1948); Harry Gene Levine, "'The Good Creature of God and the Demon Rum': Colonial American and Nineteenth-Century Ideas about Alcohol, Crime, and Accidents," in *Alcohol and Disinhibition: Nature and Meaning of the Link*, ed. Robin Room and Gary Collins, NIAA Research Monograph no. 12 (1983), 118–19.

13. Northampton County Court Records, reels 1 and 2. Virginia State Library, microfilm; Levine, "The Good Creature of God," 116–17.

14. *Secret Diary of William Byrd*, (March 2, 1709) 11.

15. Some sense of the urgency can be determined by comparing the relative value of fines and penalties across colonies. This approach contains a number of pitfalls. First is the problem of comparing a fine in Virginia in 1626 with that of one in Massachusetts in another year. Furthermore, in Virginia, fines were meted out in both pounds of tobacco and Virginia currency. To add to the problem not all decisions included fines and in one series of convictions, the individuals were all fined "accordinge to the late Act of the Generall Assembly in that case made and provided." However no record of this act is extant. *Minutes of the Council and General Court of Colonial Virginia*, ed. H. R. McIlwaine (Richmond, 1924), August, 1626, 108.

16. The appearance of a small number of prosecutions in North Carolina is due in part to the spotty nature of the records. However, those courts for which there is a complete run of years also contain few cases.

17. *North Carolina Higher Court Minutes: The Colonial Records of North Carolina, 1709–1754*, 2d ser. (Raleigh, 1974–88): V, VI, VII, VIII; Criminal Court Papers, State Archives, Raleigh (Bertie, Edgecomb, and Pasquotank counties); Minutes of the Court of Common Pleas and Quarter Sessions, State Archives, Raleigh (Bertie, Chowan, Craven, Cumberland, Edgecomb, New Hanover, Pasquotank, Perquimans, Rowan, and Tyrrell counties).

18. Nine Charleston residents were convicted of selling liquor without a license. Court of General Sessions, Criminal Journal, 1769–1771, South Carolina State Archives, Columbia.

19. Douglas Greenberg failed to record the actual number of prosecutions for drunkenness he uncovered, but he indicated that the charge was infrequently invoked. *Crime and Law Enforcement in the Colony of New York, 1691–1776* (Ithaca, N.Y., 1974), 38–39; *Annals and Occurrences of New York City and State in the Olden Times . . .*, comp. John F. Watson (Philadelphia, 1846), 286. Although the clerk described this procedure as a punishment, it may also have been a technique devised to "cure" the drinker's taste for alcohol. If the drinker survived, he may have associated these forced liquids with drinking, thus diminishing his desire to imbibe. Or, the procedure may have been a formula designed to purge the body of the alcohol so that less was absorbed.

20. Minutes of the General Quarter Sessions for New York, (December 13, 1700) 56, 57.

21. *New York Weekly Mercury*, July 23, 1753.

22. "Patrick M'Robert's Tour Through Part of the North Provinces of America," ed. Carl Bridenbaugh, *Pennsylvania Magazine of History and Biography* 59 (1935), 142. For other indicators that prostitution was common in colonial New York see *New York Weekly*

Mercury, July 23, 1753, October 6, 1760, October 27, 1766; *New York Journal or General Advertiser,* October 23, 1766, May 13, 1773; *New York Gazette* (Weyman's), October 26, 1766, August 31 to September 7, 1767; *New York Post-Boy,* March 28, April 4, 1768.

23. *Annals of New York . . . ,* 298; and *New York Mercury,* October 27, 1766.

24. Roome was fined five pounds. Minutes of the General Quarter Sessions of the Peace for the City and County of New York, November 1702, May 1706. Peter, a Negro laborer in New York, "Commonly Called Peter the Doctor," was hauled before the Court of General Sessions in February 1715 for entertaining Negro slaves in his house, specifically "Sarah, the negro slave of William Walton." Joyce D. Goodfriend, *Before the Melting Pot: Society and Culture in Colonial New York City, 1664–1730* (Princeton, N.J., 1992), 117.

25. Minutes of the General Quarter Sessions of the Peace for the City and County of New York, May 1715. Douglas Greenberg also noted this connection between the disorderly house and slave conspiracies, but his interest was primarily the behavior of criminals rather than what this link implies about New York society or the tavern. Greenberg, *Crime and Law Enforcement in New York,* 52–53. See also Julius Goebel and T. Raymond Naughton, *Law Enforcement in Colonial New York* (New York, 1970), 100–101.

26. Forty percent of the defendants accused of operating disorderly houses were women. The court fined Peters forty shillings and Hutchins twenty shillings. The difference in the two women's fines is difficult to interpret. Neither woman had a previous charge or conviction. Hutchins, as a single woman, lived outside normative family structure and society would have labeled her, not Peters, as evil. Logically she should have suffered the larger penalty, since her status, as an unmarried woman, meant she had no man supervising her life and was the more likely troublemaker. The varying penalties may reflect the court's attempt to achieve balance between the seriousness of the crime and the perpetrator's ability to pay. Perhaps Peters received the stiffer fine because the court assumed that since she was married they could collect the fine from her husband if necessary. Minutes of the General Quarter Sessions for New York, November 1723, August 1724, November 1724, August 1728.

27. Ibid., November 1729, May 1730.

28. By the time the English seized New York, blacks accounted for twenty percent of the city's population. It is estimated that by 1698, "almost 35 percent of the [city's] heads of household owned slaves and five years later the percentage had increased to 41." Less than fifty years later, the proportion of blacks in New York's population remained steady at twenty-one percent but the number of households owning slaves climbed to approximately fifty percent. Goodfriend, *Before the Melting Pot,* chaps. 5, 6; and Marcus Rediker, "'The Outcasts of the Nations of the Earth': The New York Conspiracy of 1741 in Atlantic Perspective" (unpublished paper presented to the Richard Dunn Conference, University of Pennsylvania, May 16–18, 1996), 3, 7–10. Rediker's analysis is enormously insightful, and I am grateful for having had access to it in manuscript form. Gary B. Nash, *The Urban Crucible: Social Change, Political Consciousness, and the Origins of the American Revolution* (Cambridge, Mass., 1979), 14, 107.

29. Daniel Horsmanden, *A Journal of the Proceedings in the Detection of the Conspiracy formed by Some White People, in Conjunction with Negro and other Slaves, for*

Burning the city of New-York in America, and Murdering the Inhabitants (New York, 1744), 58, 59, 336.

30. The jury discharged Hyck because the New York Supreme Court had summoned him on a similar charge. Minutes of the General Quarter Sessions for New York, February 1735. Samuel McKee cites this case as February 1725 and gives the name as Henry Slyck. *Labor in Colonial New York* (Long Island, N.Y., 1935), 65. Horsmanden, *Journal of Detection of Conspiracy*, 39.

31. Horsmanden, *Journal of Detection of Conspiracy*, 67n, 60, 54, 57–59, 78, 135, 249.

32. Rediker, "Outcasts of the Nations," 10. McKee, *Labor in Colonial New York*, 68.

33. Horsmanden, *Journal of Detection of Conspiracy*, 14.

34. Ibid., xi, 37, 134, 167.

35. Ibid., xix.

36. Ibid., 168.

37. Horsmanden published the first edition of his journal in New York in 1744. He reported that twenty white people were indicted. Twenty-nine blacks were executed—thirteen by burning and sixteen by hanging. Four whites were hanged and more than "seventy blacks and seven whites" were banished from the colony. Ibid., 103, Appendix, vii.

38. Ibid., 140–41.

39. David W. Conroy, *In Public Houses: Drink and the Revolution of Authority in Colonial Massachusetts* (Chapel Hill, N.C., 1995), 60–61.

40. For Plymouth see George D. Langdon, Jr., *Pilgrim Colony: A History of New Plymouth, 1620–1691* (New Haven, Conn., 1966), 201–9. For Massachusetts, Conroy, *In Public Houses*, 60–61.

41. W. J. Rorabaugh, *The Alcoholic Republic: An American Tradition* (Oxford, 1979), 28–30.

42. Increase Mather, *Wo to Drunkards* (Cambridge, Mass., 1673), 3–4; Rorabaugh, *The Alcoholic Republic*, 30.

43. Increase Mather, *A sermon Occasioned by the Execution of a Man Found Guilty of Murder . . .* , 2d ed. (Boston, 1687), Early American Imprints, 1st ser., no. 432: 25–26. Conroy writes that people's consumption of increasing amounts of rum concerned ministers because it was more likely to create abusers and problem drinkers. I am more persuaded by the argument that with widespread use of rum, ministers and other leaders feared the loss of control over the patterns of drinking. *In Public Houses*, 61–86, 143–46.

44. Conroy, *In Public Houses*, 74; Cotton Mather, *Sober Considerations, on a growing Flood of Iniquity. Or, An Essay To Dry up a Fountain of, Confusion and every evil work . . .* (Boston, 1708), Early American Imprints, 1st ser., no. 1364: 2–3, 5, 15; Rorabaugh, *The Alcoholic Republic*, 30–31. Mather pondered, in 1710–11, whether he should write leaders in Connecticut to report on the "fearful Circumstances, into which the Love of rum, has brought several, even of their principal Ministers, and by Consequence very many of the miserable People." *Diary of Cotton Mather*, Massachusetts Historical Society Collections, 7th ser., (Boston, 1912), 8:51.

45. Mather, *Sober Considerations*, 14–18.

46. Benjamin Wadsworth, *An Essay to do good. By a disswasive from Tavern-haunting, and Excessive Drinking* (Boston, 1710), Early American Imprints, 1st ser., no. 1491, 2–3, 21–22.

47. Benjamin Wadsworth, *Vicious Courses, Procuring Poverty Describ'd and Condemn'd . . .* (Boston, 1719), 21. See also idem, *A Serious Address to those Who unnecessarily frequent the Tavern and Often Spend the Evening in Public Houses. By several Ministers . . .* (Boston, 1726), Early American Imprints, 1st ser., no. 2780. Conroy argues that Wadsworth ignored the "tensions and doubts inherent in the conduct of business that the exchange of drink helped to ease." It appears rather that Wadsworth knew precisely what these rituals were about; he did not approve and wished they were otherwise. *In Public Houses.* Conroy notes that the two Wadsworth sermons were three years apart instead of 19. This is because of a typo in which the first sermon is listed as 1716. (The citation is correct.) *In Public Houses,* 74–75, 76–77.

48. *The Indictment and Trial of Sir Richard Rum and Captain Whiskey; With additions and Improvements* (Philadelphia, 6th ed., 1796), Early American Imprints, 1st ser., no. 1184, 3, 4.

49. Ibid., 5–12.

50. Ibid., 13–18.

51. Ibid., 3, 24; Conroy, *In Public Houses,* 86.

52. Conroy, *In Public Houses,* 62–65. Conroy argues too that this law, while designed first to curb drunkenness, also had a monetary side. Local manufacture of rum started in the 1660s and it soon became an important item in the trade between Boston and England. An excise tax on liquors made it clear that domestically produced beverages were being encouraged.

53. *The Diary of Samuel Sewall, 1674–1708,* ed. M. Halsey Thomas, 2 vols. (New York, 1973), 1:xxvii; 2:741–43; Conroy, *In Public Houses,* 57–58.

54. *Plymouth Court Records, 1686–1859,* ed. David Thomas Konig, 16 vols. (Wilmington, Del., 1978–81). The per capita rate of prosecutions was extremely low; in 1690, Scituate, the largest town, had approximately 865 inhabitants; Plymouth County had a population of approximately 23,119 in 1765. The proportion of infractions in Plymouth County mirrored that of Plymouth colony. Drunkenness had the largest number (41), followed by selling without a license and selling liquor to Indians (36). About fifteen percent of the cases were for playing cards or for allowing cards to be played in a tavern.

55. *Records of the Suffolk County Court 1671–1680,* Colonial Society of Massachusetts (Boston, 1933), 29:1671–75, 30: 1675–80; Records of the Court of General Sessions of the Peace, 1712–1732, Massachusetts State Archives.

56. William E. Nelson, *Dispute and Conflict Resolution: Plymouth County, Massachusetts, 1725–1825* (Chapel Hill, N.C., 1981), 29–30, 54.

57. *Boston Town Records, 1716–1736,* 171; Records of the Court of General Sessions of the Peace, January 2, 1727, September 1725–October 1732.

58. "Extracts from Capt. Francis Goelet's Journal, Relative to Boston, Salem and Marblehead, &c., 1746–1750," *New England Historical and Genealogical Register* 24 (1870): 55.

59. Ibid., 61.

60. Goelet claimed that fiddlers were present, a detail confirmed elsewhere. The inventories of estate of two Boston tavern keepers each recorded that they owned a violin that was presumably a part of their regular entertainments. It was also "common practice to keep small instruments such as citterns in ordinaries for the entertainment of guests." Dancing was prohibited but the playing of musical instruments was not. Barbara Lambert, "Social Music, Musicians, and Their Musical Instruments in and Around Boston," *Music in Colonial Massachusetts, II,* Publications of the Colonial Society of Massachusetts no. 54 (Boston, 1985), 477–78.

61. I thank Ruth Herndon for generously sharing her Rhode Island data with me. Almost all of the actions regarding taverns in Rhode Island towns, from the mid eighteenth century to the Revolution, had to do with licensing.

62. "Philadelphia County Court of Quarter Sessions and Common Pleas, 1695," ed. Edwin Bronner, *Pennsylvania Magazine of History and Biography* 77 (1953), 457–80; Combined Common Pleas and Quarter Sessions Docket: March 1695, Historical Society of Pennsylvania (HSP), AM 30365; Court Papers, Philadelphia County, 1715–1790, HSP, AM 3093; Court Papers, Philadelphia County, 1749–1821, HSP, AM 3093; Docket Book of the Mayor's Court, City of Philadelphia, Pennsylvania, 1759–1764, microfilm, American Trial Court Record Series, Series I, 1957; Mayor's Court Docket from October sessions 1766 to January 1772, HSP, AM 30853; and *Minutes of the Common Council of Philadelphia, 1704–1776* (Philadelphia, 1847). Data for Philadelphia County are from "Docket Book of the Court of Quarter Sessions, Philadelphia County, Pennsylvania, 1763–1775," American Trial Court Record Series I, microfilm.

63. "Some Indictments by the Grand Jury of Philadelphia," *Pennsylvania Magazine of History and Biography,* 22 (1898), 497–98.

64. Ibid., 497; Peter Thompson, *Rum Punch and Revolution: Taverngoing and Public Life in Eighteenth-Century Philadelphia* (Philadelphia, 1999), 42.

65. Frances May Manges, "Women Shopkeepers, Tavernkeepers, and Artisans in Colonial Philadelphia," (Ph.D. diss., University of Pennsylvania, 1958), 79–80; G. S. Rowe, "Women's Crime and Criminal Administration in Pennsylvania, 1763–1790," *Pennsylvania Magazine of History and Biography* 109 (1985): 346–47.

66. Even though there were no prosecutions for drunkenness discovered in Philadelphia courts, Billy G. Smith reports that drunkenness accounted for more than a quarter (27%) of the postrevolutionary cases recorded in the Vagrancy Docket. I thank Billy for sharing his data with me.

67. Thompson, *Rum Punch and Revolution,* 42; "Some Indictments of the Grand Jury of Philadelphia," 497.

68. Jack D. Marietta argues that there was an inverse relationship between the concern over drunkenness demonstrated by officials in Pennsylvania and that shown by the Friends—while it declined among the colony's officials, it increased among the Friends. It is clear that the number of cases that came before the meeting increased over the course of the eighteenth century. What is less clear is whether Pennsylvania officials up-

held the laws of drunkenness before the Revolution. *The Reformation of American Quakerism, 1748–1783* (Philadelphia, 1984), 19, 105–6. See also Carl and Jessica Bridenbaugh, *Rebels and Gentlemen: Philadelphia in the Age of Franklin* (New York, 1965), 182.

69. Marietta, *Reformation of American Quakerism*, 19–21. The statistic about women is at best an estimate. Jack Marietta kindly gave me his data on individuals disciplined for drunkenness by the Quaker meetings. Of the 1,019 cases, only 31 are recognizable as women. However, in many cases the clerk of the meeting failed to record a first name.

70. Ibid., 20–21.

71. Rowe, "Women's Crime," 346.

72. The constables ordered into the workhouse "several people of both sexes, who could give no good account of themselves, being found in a disorderly house on Society Hill." Reported in *The New York Mercury*, Monday, July 23, 1753.

73. Thompson, *Rum Punch and Revolution*, 44; Philadelphia Court Records Taken by Patrick Robinson, 1685–1686, Historical Society of Pennsylvania.

74. An Account of the Robberies Committed by John Morrison, Philadelphia, 1750/1, Rosenbach Foundation copy, Evans Imprint Series, #6624.

75. The Chester Pennsylvania Monthly meeting for eastern Chester County, from 1700, the first year in which offences were specified, to the eve of the Revolution, heard 113 cases involving drunkenness; ten offenders were women. Chester (PA) Monthly Meeting. (Men's)—1686–1780 for eastern Chester county. Jean Soderlund kindly provided these data.

76. *Records of the Governor and Company of Massachusetts Bay*, ed. Nathaniel B. Shurtleff, 5 vols. (Boston, 1853–54), I: (1637) 213. In East Jersey, drunkenness was included in the "General Laws as an offence against God." "Brandy, rum and other strong liquors are in their kind (not abused but taken in moderation) creatures of God, and useful and beneficial to mankind." The object of the laws was to keep the creatures of God properly controlled. Preston W. Edsall, *Journal of the Courts of the Common Right and Chancery of East New Jersey, 1683–1702* (Philadelphia, 1937), 124.

77. *Journals of the House of Burgesses of Virginia*, ed. H. R. McIlwaine, 13 vols. (Richmond, 1905–15), II: (1659) 9; C. C. Pearson and J. Edwin Hendricks, *Liquor and Anti-Liquor in Virginia, 1619–1919* (Durham, N.C., 1967), 6.

78. David Flaherty, "Law and the Enforcement of Morals in Early America," *Perspectives in American History* 5 (1971), 225–28.

79. Ibid., 228–33.

80. Edwin Powers, *Crime and Punishment in Early Massachusetts, 1620–1692: A Documentary History* (Boston, 1966), 168.

Chapter Five / Licensing Criteria and Law in the Eighteenth Century

1. Chester County Tavern Petitions, Chester County Archives, West Chester, Pa., William Hartley, August 1740; Mary Moore, n.d. filed 1741.

2. For an example of the charge to the committee see Court of General Sessions of the Peace, Boston, July 19, 1762, James Otis Sr. papers, Massachusetts Historical Society.

3. In 1633, Massachusetts required all prospective drink sellers to petition the governor or deputy governor for permission. In 1639, as the population began to disperse, every town was to present to the General Court for approval "a man to be allowed to sell wine and strong water." If an individual wished only to sell cider, this permission could come from the local selectmen. With a revision to the law in the 1640s, the power to grant licenses rested with the quarter sessions courts. In 1681, selectmen were included in the process; they had to approve of the individual before he or she could be recommended to the quarter sessions court. At this point the selling of all alcoholic beverages required a license and licenses had to be renewed annually. This shift located the primary power for licensing in the local administrators. The licensing law was altered yet again in 1698. In an attempt to tighten procedures, justices reviewed license petitions only at the first session of the courts of general sessions. Thus, toward the end of the seventeenth century, in Massachusetts, the provincial government became "the first seat of approval" for licensing applications. David W. Conroy, *In Public Houses: Drink and the Revolution of Authority in Colonial Massachusetts* (Chapel Hill, N.C., 1995), 36–38, 63–64.

4. I thank Ruth Herndon for sharing her Rhode Island tavern data with me.

5. Votes of the Assembly, *Pennsylvania Archives,* 8th ser., (Philadelphia, 1931), I: (1682) 29; *The Statutes at Large of Pennsylvania,* comp. Gail McKnight Beckman (New York, 1976), I: (18 May 1699) 239–40. *The Statutes at Large of Pennsylvania,* comp. James T. Mitchell and Henry Flanders (Harrisburg, Pa., 1896), II: (November 27, 1700) 100–104.

6. Governor's Message, April 10, 1693, Miscellaneous Records of the Secretary of the Province, 1692–1700, 54, South Carolina Department of Archives and History, Columbia. Philip D. Morgan, "Black Life in Eighteenth-Century Charleston," *Perspectives in American History,* new ser. 1 (1984), 206–8.

7. *The Statutes at Large of South Carolina,* ed. Thomas Cooper (Columbia, S.C., 1837), II: (17 January 1694) 85–86.

8. North and South Carolina were established late, so some of their earliest laws concerning taverns and drinking were enacted in the eighteenth century. It seemed appropriate to include them in the earlier chronological discussion. Ibid.: (16 May 1703) 198–99, (4 January 1710) 336–38, (28 June 1711) 362–65.

9. *Journal of the Grand Council of South Carolina, August 25, 1671–June 24, 1680,* ed. A. S. Salley, Jr. (Columbia, S.C., 1907), 12, 17. In 1685, two types of liquor licenses were included in a list of fees to be collected by the governor. For five pounds the person was permitted to sell wine; for three pounds the licensee could retail punch or other liquors. *Statutes at Large of South Carolina,* II: (April 11, 1685) 3, II: (1694) 86–88. An early extortion case reveals the extent to which licensing fees could be abused. See *Journal of the Grand Council of South Carolina, April 11, 1692–September 26, 1692.* A. S. Salley, Jr. (Columbia, S.C., 1907), 40.

10. *Statutes at Large of South Carolina,* II: (28 June 1711) 364.

11. Fees were 40-shilling fine, 6-pound license fee with right to sell wine, 4-pound without, and bond of 7 shillings 6 pence. The law also required that a record be kept of the licenses issued. *The Earliest Printed Laws of South Carolina,* ed. John D. Cushing (Wilmington, Del., 1978), (June 28, 1711) 250–53.

12. *Statutes at Large of South Carolina,* III: (8 March 1741) 581–82.

13. Ibid., 581–85. The act also continued the 14-pound fee for the license, the quantities of liquor to be sold, the penalties for violating the act, and a provision that billiards not be played "after the sun hath been set one hour."

14. The governor received 120 pounds from fees. *The Journal of the Commons House of Assembly, January 19, 1748–June 29, 1748,* ed. J. H. Easterby (Columbia, S.C., 1951), 374.

15. *The Journal of the Commons House of Assembly, 23 April 1750–31 August 1751,* ed. R. Nicholas Olsberg, (Columbia, S.C., 1951), 357, 385, 386, 411, 409. *Statutes at Large of South Carolina,* III: 751–53.

16. *Archives of Maryland: Proceedings and Acts of the General Assembly of Maryland* (Baltimore, 1883), II: (May–June 1674) 346–47, 351, 407–8; (February 1675) 431, 434–35.
Arthur Scott argued that Virginia's licensing law followed the English example in that it was an attempt to prevent drunkenness and "its attendant disorders." He includes a whole range of abuses in addition to gambling, Sabbath breaking, tippling, and the unnecessary entertainment of servants, slaves, and seamen. I will discuss these issues as well. Scott and I disagree only on the matter of timing. Virginia law, I argue, does not begin addressing these concerns for more than seventy-five years after the colony was established. Indeed, Scott cites as his examples laws which begin in 1705. Arthur P. Scott, *Criminal Law in Colonial Virginia* (Chicago, 1930), 257–59. My argument seems to be more in line with the work of C. C. Pearson and J. Edwin Hendricks, *Liquor and Anti-Liquor in Virginia, 1619–1919* (Durham, N.C., 1967). However, they are most interested in the issue of drunkenness (see esp. 3–17). *The Statutes at Large . . . of Virginia,* ed. William Waller Hening (New York, 1823), I: (October 1644) 187, (March 1654–55) Act V, 411, (March 1658–59) Act XIV, 521–22.

17. *Archives of Maryland,* VII: (October–November 1678) 65–68; XIII: (November 14–December 8, 1688) 213–15. In 1692, lawmakers raised the price of the bond once more. In the capital, St. Mary's City, or within two miles of the city, proprietors had to pay 2,000 pounds of tobacco yearly. In the countryside the fee was 1,200 pounds. The cost differential declares that the greater danger to debauchery resided in the city, where the population was most dense. XIII: (1692) 488–91, 545–46; IX: (May 8–22, 1695) 174.

18. William Byrd II noted that a friend of his, Major Ben Robinson, survived because of his "industrious wife, who has kept him from sinking by the weight of gaming and idleness." Apparently Robinson reformed and no longer threatened his family's economic survival. *The Prose Work of William Byrd of Westover: Narratives of a Colonial Virginian,* ed. Louis B. Wright (Cambridge, Mass., 1966), 373.

19. Church wardens continued to be responsible for punishing the sin of drunken-

ness. *Statutes at Large of Virginia*, II: (March 1660–61) Act VI, 19–20; (March 1661–62) Act XIII, 50–51; and Scott, *Criminal Law in Colonial Virginia*, 256.

20. *Minutes of the Provincial Council of Pennsylvania, from the Organization to the Termination of the Proprietary Government*, Colonial Records of Pennsylvania (Harrisburg, 1838), II: 163.

21. City licenses cost three pounds as opposed to forty shillings outside Philadelphia. Ibid., 163, 546.

22. *The Papers of Benjamin Franklin*, ed. Leonard W. Labaree (New Haven, Conn., 1959–), XI: 521–22.

23. *Records of the Colony of Rhode Island and Providence Plantations, in New England*, 6 vols., (Providence, R.I., 1856), 4:64–65.

24. *Works of John Adams, Second President of the United States*, 10 vols. (Boston, 1856), II:84–85.

25. *Minutes of the Common Council of the City of New York, 1765–1776*, 8 vols. (New York, 1905), I: (12 September 1685) 368–69; *Abstracts of Minutes of the Court of Pleas and Quarter Sessions of Cumberland County, October 1755–January 1779*, ed. William C. Fields, 2 vols. (Fayetteville, N.C., 1977), I: Robert Love, (January 22, 1756) 4, (July 20, 1757) 22, (October 21, 1757) 27, (July 21, 1758) 40, (July 1759) 60, (November 1760) 75, (August 20, 1762) 116; Neil McNeil, (April 20, 1757) 19, (October 21, 1757) 27, (July 19, 1758) 37, (May 20, 1761) 86, (February 18, 1762) 105, (May 19, 1762) 109, (August 18, 1762) 114, (November 21, 1764) 165; William Dawson, (July 21, 1758) 40, (July 1759) 57, (February 21, 1761) 83; Hector McNeil, (January 1760) 66; Stephen Phillips, (January 19, 1759) 48, (January 1760) 65; William Bennerman, (February 18, 1763) 120, (February 19, 1763) 121, (May 18, 1763) 123, (May 16, 1764) 148; Minutes of the Court of Common Pleas and Quarter Sessions, Cumberland County, State Archives, Raleigh. *The Colonial Records of North Carolina*, ed. William L. Saunders, 10 vols. (Raleigh, 1886–90), IV: 951.

26. The law preventing proprietors from serving on juries was passed by the General Assembly in 1748. *Statutes at Large of Virginia*, V: 253, VIII: 325.

27. Peter Clark, *The English Alehouse: A Social History, 1200–1830* (London, 1983), 20–25.

28. Ibid., 28–30, 78–79.

29. Ibid., 79–80.

30. Ibid., 82–87.

31. Conroy, *In Public Houses*, 71, 80, 107–17. "Names of Persons Licensed in the County of Suffolk," James Otis Sr. papers, II, 1642–1747, box 1, Massachusetts Historical Society; *Report of the Record Commissioners of the City of Boston, Selectmen's Minutes, 1764–1768* (Boston, 1811); miscellaneous bound licenses 1761–1765, Massachusetts Historical Society.

32. *South Carolina Gazette*, April 24, 1762, April 9, 1763, May 11, 1767, May 9, 1768, April 9, 1768, April 18, 1771, May 7, 1772, April 8, 1774.

33. At first glance, it appears as if county officials issued licenses to two women in

Rowan County, North Carolina, from the county's inception to the eve of the American Revolution. Closer examination reveals that one women received a license but under different names. Elizabeth Gillespie was married to Robert, a Salisbury tavern keeper and storekeeper. He died in 1759. She was issued a license as Gillespie, presumably to carry on his tavern trade. In 1763, she married William Steel, who was also a Salisbury tavern keeper and merchant. A year after his subsequent death she received a new license, under Steel. *Abstracts of Minutes of the Court of Pleas and Quarter Sessions of Cumberland County,* I: 143; *Abstracts of the Minutes of the Court of Pleas and Quarter Sessions, Rowan County,* ed. Jo White Linn, 2 vols. (Salisbury, N.C., 1977–82); Johanna Miller Lewis, *Artisans in the North Carolina Backcountry* (Lexington, N.C., 1995), 107–8. The data for Orange County, North Carolina, follow the same pattern. From 1752 to 1766, 122 licenses were issued; three to women. *Abstracts of the Minutes of the Court of Pleas and Quarter Sessions of Orange County in the Province of North Carolina, September 1752 through August 1766,* Ruth Herndon Shields, comp. (Chapel Hill, N.C., 1966). In Perquimans County, North Carolina, from 1745 to 1774, Sarah Calloway and Mary Mullin were the only women licensed. Mary apparently assumed the business at the death of her husband Cornelius. Both women, however, received licenses for only one year. Court Records are organized by county. Minutes of the Court of Common Pleas and Quarter Sessions, State Archives, Raleigh.

34. *Plymouth Court Records, 1686–1859,* ed. David Thomas Konig, 3 vols. (Wilmington, Del., 1978); and *Records of the Court of General Sessions of the Peace, Worcester, Massachusetts, from 1731 to 1737,* ed. Franklin P. Rice (Worcester, Mass., 1882). From 1671 to 1677 no women received licenses in Suffolk County. In 1678, only one woman received a license; the court recorder noted that she was married. The data are: 1736, 16%; 1737, 13%. Twenty-five years later there was no appreciable difference. By 1762, women's share of the licenses remained low at 11%. "Names of Persons Licensed in the County of Suffolk," James Otis Sr. papers II, 1642–1747, box 1.

In Chester County, Pennsylvania the story was the same. The court reviewed approximately 591 petitions for licenses from 1736 to 1774; only 9% (53) of the licenses were issued to women. Tavern License Papers, Chester County Archives.

35. Forty of the women licensed (63.6%) resided in either the Northern Liberties or Southwark. These two townships accounted for more than a third of the licenses issued to the entire county (203 or 38.7%). Sharon V. Salinger, *"To Serve Well and Faithfully:" Labor and Indentured Servants Pennsylvania, 1682–1800* (Cambridge, Mass., 1987), 71; and Court of Quarter Sessions, Philadelphia County, Pennsylvania.

36. Richard P. Gildrie, *The Profane, the Civil, and the Godly: The Reformation of Manners in Orthodox New England, 1679–1749* (University Park, Pa., 1994), 65.

37. Daniel Scott Smith concluded that female heads of household were far more likely to live in cities than in rural areas. "Female Householding in Late Eighteenth-Century America and the Problem of Poverty," *Journal of Social History* 17 (1984): 83–107. Sharon V. Salinger and Charles Wetherell, "Wealth and Renting in Late Eighteenth-Century Philadelphia," *Journal of American History* 71, no. 4 (March 1985), 826–40. See also Ca-

role Shammas, "The Female Social Structure of Philadelphia in 1775," *Pennsylvania Magazine of History and Biography* 107 (1983), 72; and Carole Shammas, "The Space Problem in Early United States Cities," *William and Mary Quarterly* 57 (July 2000), 541.

38. Gildrie, *The Profane, the Civil, and the Godly*, 70. March was seeking an abatement, but the document does not reveal for what. He might have wanted out of the license. It is unclear whether the Nordens received a license. Photostats of Massachusetts Archives records, Massachusetts Historical Society, box #8.

39. Ibid., 72.

40. Boston, July 31, 1735, Otis papers II: 1642–1747, file 1734–35.

41. *Historic Philadelphia*, ed. Luther B. Eisenhart (Philadelphia, 1953), 7; Christiana Campbell's House History File, Colonial Williamsburg Foundation Library.

42. "Names of Persons Licensed in the County of Suffolk"; miscellaneous bound licenses, 1761–1765, Massachusetts Historical Society. Conroy, *In Public Houses*, 108–9.

43. *Record Commissioners of the City of Boston; Boston Records, 1660–1701*, Widow Franke, 110. In 1673, Mrs. Dorothy Jones was granted a license to sell wine, in addition to her initial license to sell coffee, as long as her husband acted as the principal. *Suffolk County Court Records*, XXIX:268.

44. Nicholas kept a tavern in Dorchester, beginning in 1636, and when he moved to Boston in 1641 he continued the trade there. He operated the Red Lyon Inn, among the oldest ordinaries in the city. We do not know whether his wife shared his Quaker leanings. Augustine Jones, "Nicholas Upsall," *New England Historical and Genealogical Register* 35 (1880): 21–31. Nicholas's devotion to Quaker beliefs is clear from his will, posted in 1666. "Abstracts of Early Wills," *New England Historical and Genealogical Register* 15 (1861): 250–51. *Boston Town Records, 1634–1660*, 154; *Boston Town Records, 1660–1701*, 2, 15, 25, 30, 35, 37, 48, 54, 60, 68, 76, 87, 95, 97. The records refer originally to Goodwife Upshall and in 1665 list her as Widow Upshall.

45. *Sibley's Harvard Graduates* (Cambridge, Mass., 1873–1975), XI:137–38.

46. Ibid., 138–39.

47. Ibid., 140–42.

48. *Selectmen's Minutes, 1701–1715*, 49. For examples of petitions approved because individuals were asking to operate existing taverns see, *Selectmen's Minutes, 1764–1768*, 55, 100, 105.

49. Ibid., *1754–1763*, 93.

50. Ibid., 94–95.

51. Ibid., *1764–1768*, 266.

52. *Plymouth Court Records, 1686–1859; Records of the Court of General Sessions of the Peace, Worcester, Massachusetts*; Tavern License Petitions, Chester County Archives.

53. Wetherburn Tavern House History, Colonial Williamsburg Foundation Library.

54. Peter Thompson, "A Social History of Philadelphia's Taverns, 1683–1800" (Ph.D. diss., University of Pennsylvania, 1989), 102; idem, *Rum Punch and Revolution: Taverngoing and Public Life in Eighteenth-Century Philadelphia*, (Philadelphia, 1999), 31. For evidence of Alice Guest's license see *Minutes of the Provincial Council* (16th day 11th

month, 1685) I:167. For the complaints about the conduct in the caves see J. Thomas Scharf and Thompson Westcott, *History of Philadelphia, 1609–1884,* 3 vols. (Philadelphia, 1884), I:120. See also *Minutes of the Provincial Council* (17th day 9th month, 1685) I:163.

55. Draper received a license in 1767, although it is unclear if this was her first license. "List of Public Housekeepers Recommended," July 1767, Mayor's Court Docket, Historical Society of Pennsylvania; "Constables' Returns to the Assessor, 1770."

56. Miscellaneous Records, Charleston County, 1765–1769, Charleston County Public Library; *South Carolina Gazette,* April 14, 1762, May 11, 1767, May 7, 1772.

57. Journal of the General Sessions Court, 1769–1776, South Carolina, South Carolina Archives, (21 May 1773) 252, (19th February 1774) 270.

58. Marylynn Salmon, *Women and the Law of Property* (Chapel Hill, N.C., 1986), 44–53; idem, "Women and Property in South Carolina: The Evidence from Marriage Settlements, 1730–1830," *William and Mary Quarterly* 39 (1982), 655–85. Salmon cites Mary Beth Norton's findings that before the Revolution wives played little of a role in family businesses. This relationship began to change by the end of the eighteenth century. Salmon, "Women and Property in South Carolina," 669.

59. *Records of the Colony of New Plymouth in New England,* ed. Nathaniel B. Shurtleff, 6 vols. (Boston, 1855), I: (5 May 1640) 153, (2 June 1640) 156, and (1 September 1640) 162; II: (1644–45) 79–80.

60. This is the only example of this form of assistance discovered in any of the New England records. *Records of the Colony of New Plymouth in New England,* II: (7 January 1645) 79–80; III: (7 June 1659) 166. Powers, *Crime and Punishment in Early Massachusetts,* 384.

61. *Records of the Colony of New Plymouth in New England.* Cole was acquitted of the charge of entertaining townsmen in his house, III: (5 October 1652) 17. He was fined or cautioned in all the other cases: I: (5 May 1640) 153, (1 September 1640) 162; III: (5 March 1661) 207; IV: (3 October 1665) 107; V: (2 March 1669) 15, (7 June 1670) 39, (5 June 1671) 61, (29 October 1671) 81; see also John Demos, *A Little Commonwealth: Family Life in Plymouth Colony* (New York, 1970), 89–90.

62. *Virginia Colonial Abstracts: Charles City County Court Orders,* (Richmond, Va., n.d.), X:55; XI:29, 38, 68. Shields' Tavern, House History, Colonial Williamsburg Foundation Library; and Patricia Ann Gibbs, "Taverns in Tidewater Virginia, 1700–1774," (M.A. thesis, College of William and Mary, 1968), 30.

63. For the first seventeen years of the colony, the Philadelphia courts prosecuted on average eight disorderly houses a year. "Presentments of the Grand Inquest of Philadelphia County, 1683," *Pennsylvania Magazine of History and Biography* 23 (1899), 403–5. Peter Thompson notes ironically that when Griffith Jones's tavern was demolished, Jones demanded compensation, even though he had been operating it without a license. *Rum Punch and Revolution,* 22.

64. *Records of the Courts of Chester County, Pennsylvania, 1697–1710* (Danboro, Pa., 1972), 17, 22, 70, 115, 129, 130, 133, 140.

65. Tavern License Papers, Chester County Archives.

66. To trace the petition history for Adam Archer see ibid., August 28, 1733, February 26, 1734, May 28, 1734, February 25, 1734, August 27, 1734. Archer tried on many more occasions to get a full license again; see for example August 31, 1736.

67. *The Records of New Amsterdam from 1653 to 1674*, ed. Berthold Fernow, 2 vols. (Baltimore, 1976), I:207–8, 228, 231, 240, 252; III:391.

68. Minutes of the General Quarter Sessions of the Peace for the City and County of New York, John Webb, August 1712, February 1712, May 1713.

69. Mary Stevens's license petitions can be found in Tavern License Papers, Chester County, August 31, 1731, February 29, 1731, May 1732. She posted bond on August 30, 1732.

70. For a history of William Robinson's attempts to procure a tavern license, see ibid., August 30, 1732, February court, 1734, November 26, 1734, February 1735, May 27, 1735, May, 1739, August 1737, February 1738, August 1741.

71. Court of Quarter Sessions, Philadelphia County, Society Miscellaneous Collections, box 4a, folder 2, Historical Society of Pennsylvania.

72. Tavern License Papers, Chester County Archives. Peter Thompson argues that the vagaries of the licensing process suggest that the magistrates did not use their licensing powers to promote any particular form of community or to control the nature of tavern keeping. Rather, he says, the process appears "contradictory" and the decisions "fundamentally illogical." Thompson does note that personal misfortunes, particularly among women, were frequently the cause for granting a license. Thompson, *Rum Punch and Revolution,* 37. David Conroy concludes that in contrast to the seemingly random ways in which Philadelphia justices issued licenses, the method in Massachusetts was far from arbitrary. The Court of General Sessions did deviate from the assembly's guidelines, but because they were responding to another set of concerns. Conroy uses the example of Elizabeth Hawksworth to highlight the tension between official policy and the needs of the poor. In 1704, the assembly had made it very clear that "justices and selectmen should not approve widows." In addition, Boston selectmen were under pressure from a 1712 act to issue fewer licenses and reduce the number of public houses. Hawksworth made four unsuccessful attempts to obtain a license before she was approved. Conroy, *In Public Houses,* 99–156. This scenario can also be interpreted as arbitrary, though. Perhaps the Court of General Sessions simply tired of Hawksworth's pleas. The court also claimed as its goal a reduction in the number of licenses. They did not, however, heed their own advice. Boston's licensed drink sellers increased steadily in number over the course of the eighteenth century; the proportion of women climbed as well.

73. Thompson, "Social History of Philadelphia's Taverns," 153–154; Miscellaneous Court Papers, 1732–44, Historical Society of Pennsylvania.; Robert Earle Graham, "Philadelphia Inns and Taverns, 1774–1780," (typescript, American Philosophical Society, 1952), 6. Tavern License Papers, Chester County Archives.

74. "Despite demands for reform of the English discretionary system, partially answered by codification of the criminal law in New England, the magistrates in the colonies continued to exercise great power in administration of the law." Peter C. Hoffer and N.

E. H. Hull, *Murdering Mothers: Infanticide in England and New England, 1558–1803* (New York, 1981), 193–94, fn4.

Chapter Six / Too Many Taverns?

1. Journal of the General Sessions Court, 1769–1776, 15 January 1770: 42–43, South Carolina, South Carolina Archives.

2. Richard P. Gildrie, *The Profane, the Civil, and the Godly: The Reformation of Manners in Orthodox New England, 1679–1749* (University Park, Pa., 1994), 65.

3. David W. Conroy, *In Public Houses: Drink and the Revolution of Authority in Colonial Massachusetts* (Chapel Hill, N.C., 1995), 58–59.

4. *Records of the Colony of Rhode Island*, 6: (October 1765) 460–61.

5. "Some Indictments by the Grand Jury of Philadelphia," *Pennsylvania Magazine of History and Biography* 22 (1898), 497–98.

6. J. Thomas Scharf and Thompson Westcott, *History of Philadelphia, 1609–1884*, 3 vols. (Philadelphia, 1884), I:120. The 1693 tax list includes 12 individuals who stated as their occupations inn holder or tavern keeper. But because the tax lists undercounted the number of taxpayers and did not include occupational information for everyone, 20 houses is likely a better estimate. Philadelphia's population is estimated at 2,200 individuals at the turn of the century. In 1720, the population was about 4,885, including 872 taxable persons. In 1756, 2,660 taxable residents were counted in Philadelphia for a population estimate of 14,895. For that year, Peter Thompson calculates this to be one tavern for every 130 persons: my figure is slightly higher. Thompson, "A Social History of Philadelphia's Taverns, 1683–1800" (Ph.D. diss., University of Pennsylvania, 1989), 133–36, 139, 232–35; Mayor's Court Docket from October Sessions 1766 to January 1772, Historical Society of Pennsylvania, AM30853. Gary Nash reports that the 1772 Philadelphia tax lists show 79 individuals who gave as their occupations tavern keeper or innkeeper. The list of occupations is incomplete, however, both because not all individuals listed an occupation and because the assessors failed to include everyone. For 1772 he reports 3,907 taxpayers and a population estimated at 21,880. Gary B. Nash, *The Urban Crucible: Social Change, Political Consciousness, and the Origins of the American Revolution* (Cambridge, Mass., 1979), 4, Appendix, Table 1, 388, Table 13, 407–8. John Watson reports 117 public houses in Philadelphia in 1756. *Annals of Philadelphia, and Pennsylvania in Olden Time . . .* (Philadelphia, 1857).

7. The tavern maps represent the most conservative picture. The maps were constructed using the Walter Brenner Tavern Listing found at the Historical Society of Pennsylvania in conjunction with licensing records. Then each tavern and landlord was searched in the *Pennsylvania Gazette* and Provincial Tax Records to determine the precise location of the inn. If the information from the Brenner document could not be verified in the *Gazette* or on the tax list, the tavern was not included on the map. The dates of the maps follow the CD-ROM version of the *Pennsylvania Gazette*, which at this point consists of three folios: 1735 to 1750, 1750 to 1765, and 1765 to 1780.

8. Conroy, *In Public Houses*, 58–59. The Boston population is based on the number of polls in 1687.

9. *Records of the Suffolk County Court, 1671–1680* (Boston, 1933), XXX:1064; *A Report of the Record Commissioners of the City of Boston, Boston Town Records, 1634–1660*, 91, 107, 112; *1660–1701*, 24. (Martin did not appear to have any more difficulty procuring his license.)

10. Conroy, *In Public Houses*, 67, 80, 116, 142–43. The figures for 1737 are my own; they differ only slightly from Conroy's and are derived from the same source, "Names of persons licensed in the county of Suffolk, 1737," James Otis Sr. papers II, box 1, Massachusetts Historical Society. My proportions also vary from those in Conroy's work because I used the population data in Nash, *Urban Crucible*, Appendix, Table 13, 407–8. No estimates for the Boston population exist for 1722. Nash reports 3,000 taxable residents for 1728 and a population of 12,650. In 1737, Boston's population was approximately 16,500 with 3,202 taxpayers. Conroy apparently used the population figures from the Boston Selectmen's Minutes for 1765. The proportion of taverns to patrons remained nearly constant—one license for every 116 Bostonians. By 1765, 134 public houses operated in Boston; using the population estimates for 1771, this yields one public house for every 123 residents. However, because the figures for Boston are so sketchy and it is unclear how reliable these data are, the fluctuations in the proportions of residents to public houses cannot be interpreted as significant. I agree with Conroy that while the selectmen claimed that they wished to reduce the number of public houses, they did not. However, Conroy does not convincingly link their reluctance to reduce the number of taverns with their concerns over the rising costs of poor relief. *A Report of the Record Commissioners of the City of Boston, Selectmen's Minutes, 1764–1768* (Boston, 1877), 170.

Michael Zuckerman computed the mean based on the numbers provided in the text. (The median is 127 for Philadelphia, 116 for Boston.)

11. Conroy, *In Public Houses*, 8–9, 116–17. Conroy explains this phenomenon differently. He credits Samuel Sewall with attempting to change drinking practices. Conroy also argues that the political elite were determined to demonstrate their "fitness for higher office" by controlling public behavior especially as it related to drinking. If more lofty considerations had governed this, Bostonians could have tinkered further with the laws. They did not claim that the laws were insufficient to govern taverns adequately. Names of Persons Licensed in the County of Suffolk, 1737, James Otis Sr. papers, II, 1642–1747, box 1, Massachusetts Historical Society.

12. *Boston Town Records, 1660–1701*, Thomas Bill, 97; Daniel Turrell, 178. Petition of Samuel Ross, July 29, 1756, James Otis Sr. papers, box 2, folder 1756. Numerous examples of this process exist. See, for example, Mrs. Simpson's application to the selectmen "for their approbation as an Innholder in the House where she now lives." She had recently taken over the house of her deceased brother, and he had maintained a tavern at that location for almost forty years. Similarly, Mrs. Sarah Ridgway came before the selectmen to request a tavern license, and her petition was approved without debate. Again, giving her a license did not increase the number of Boston taverns, because her husband

had received permission to operate an inn that same year. *Selectmen's Minutes, 1754–1763*, 165, 171–72.

13. *Selectmen's Minutes, 1754–1763*, 283; *1764–1768*, 191, 192.

14. Boston issued 91 licenses to sell alcoholic beverages in 1718. I was able to locate addresses for 66.

15. Annie H. Thwing, *Crooked and Narrow Streets of the Town of Boston, 1630–1822* (Detroit, 1970); Carl Bridenbaugh notes that Boston was losing its share of the ship-building industries to other port cities, in both New England and the middle colonies. The city, however, still "employed large numbers of hands" in the maritime industries. *Cities in Revolt: Urban Life in America, 1743–1776* (London, 1955), 73, 269. The possibility that taverns and their offerings lured men away from their wives and families was not lost on contemporaries. See, for example, *The Diary of Colonel Landon Carter of Sabine Hall, 1752–1778*, 2 vols. (Charlottesville, Va., 1965), II:870.

16. Richard L. Bushman, *The Refinement of America: Persons, Houses, Cities* (New York, 1992), 162.

17. Conroy, *In Public Houses*, 72–74.

18. Bushman is describing the differentiation of taverns by character, location, and clientele in New York and Philadelphia. It appears, however, that the same phenomenon took place in Boston. *Refinement of America*, 162. South Boston refers to the portion of the city south of Milk Street.

19. *Records of Boston Selectmen, 1764–1768*, 184.

20. *The Records of New Amsterdam from 1653 to 1674 Anno Domini*, ed. Berthold Fernow, 7 vols. (Baltimore, 1976), I:5–7.

21. Quoted in I. N. Phelps Stokes, *The Iconography of Manhattan Island, 1498–1909*, 6 vols. (New York, 1915), IV:27–28; *The Memorial History of the City of New-York from Its First Settlement to the Year 1892*, ed. James Grant Wilson, 5 vols. (New York, 1892), I:224; and W. Harrison Bayles, *Old Taverns of New York* (New York, 1915), 5.

22. Bayles, *Old Taverns of New York*, 6–7; Ellis Lawrence Raesly, *Portrait of New Netherland* (New York, 1945), 40.

23. Raesly, *Portrait of New Netherland*, 209.

24. Carl Bridenbaugh, *Cities in the Wilderness: The First Century of Urban Life in America, 1625–1742* (London, 1938, 1966), 111–12; *Memorial History of the City of New-York*, I:224.

25. By 1664, 315 of the residents of New Amsterdam were taxable, suggesting a ratio of one licensed house for every 18 adult males. The city's Common Council issued 24 licenses for the year 1680—approximately 1 public house for every 25 adult male taxpayers. Although the proportion of New York taverns was not quite the 25 percent of dwellings estimated by early governors, almost 13 percent of the city's taxpayers were issued licenses. In 1722, the treasurer reported that his accounts revealed that 78 licenses had been issued for that year. Approximately 1,429 individuals paid tax in the city, suggestion that there was 1 tavern for every 18 taxpayers. From March to August 1759, the New York Mayor's Court issued 287 tavern licenses. This calculates to one license for

every 55 residents or one tavern for better than 1 in 10 taxpayers. For the same period one year later, the city issued 273 licenses; from October 1764 through March 1766, 284 tavern keepers were licensed. *Records of New Amsterdam;* Joyce Goodfriend, *Before the Melting Pot: Society and Culture in Colonial New York City, 1664–1730* (Princeton, N.J., 1992), 14. Goodfriend's figures suggest that Carl Bridenbaugh's population estimates for New Amsterdam are high. Bridenbaugh placed the 1660 population at 2,400. It is difficult to reconcile the two sets of figures. Goodfriend's estimates on the number of taxable residents compared with Bridenbaugh's total population would require a very large household size, 7 persons per household. Bridenbaugh notes that his figures are at best approximations. *Cities in the Wilderness,* 6. Because the records are so spotty, it is virtually impossible to determine the gender ratio of licensees. The only woman shown in these records to have a license to tap was Lysbet Auckers, and she was charged with tapping beer for which she had not paid the excise. *Records of New Amsterdam,* IV: 265–66, 320.

The Dutch colonial court did try to avoid issuing a license if it would result in a conflict of interest. Their actions were not always consistent nor were they overly vigilant. Warner Wessels, who was either a distiller or a brewer, had his petition to sell drink by small measure denied because "according to the custom of the city," distillers and brewers were not allowed licenses to tap. Wessels managed to overcome this obstacle. Two years after his attempt to get a license, Wessels' mother Neeltie petitioned successfully "to follow the trade of an eating house and to bring in and tap out wine and beer." *Records of New Amsterdam,* I:266, II:233.

26. *Minutes of the Common Council of the City of New York,* 8 vols. (New York, 1905), I: (21st April 1680) 80–81. Population statistics for New York are also spotty. The first figure is calculated on 583 male taxpayers in 1695. Goodfriend, *Before the Melting Pot,* Table 4-1, 62. The number of licenses in 1722 was compared with 1,429 taxpayers in 1723. Gary Nash estimated 2,200 taxable persons in 1756 and 2,588 in 1771, and a total population of 15,680 in 1756 and 16,540 in 1771. To calculate the proportion of taverns, I assumed steady growth. Nash, *The Urban Crucible,* Appendix, Table 13, 405–8; Mayor's Office Tavern Keeper's Licence Book, 1756–1766, New York City, New-York Historical Society.

27. It is possible to calculate the number of taverns in Charleston beginning in 1762 when the *South Carolina Gazette* began to publish the list of licensees. *South Carolina Gazette,* April 17–24, 1762.

28. *South Carolina Gazette,* May 7, 1772, supplement. Population figures for Charleston are from Peter A. Coclanis, *The Shadow of a Dream: Economic Life and Death in the South Carolina Low Country, 1670–1920* (New York, 1989), 114 Table 4-3; Philip D. Morgan, "Black Life in Eighteenth-Century Charleston," *Perspectives in American History,* new ser. 1 (1984), 208.

29. John G. Leland, "Early Taverns in Charleston," in *Preservation Progress Newsletter* (printed by the Preservation Society of Charleston) 16 (May 1971), 1, Charleston County Public Library, vertical files.

30. Records of the Suffolk County Court, XXX:1159.

31. By 1675, at least thirty individuals received permission to sell alcoholic bever-

ages or operate a public house in Essex County. In 1678, the number more than doubled; 84 individuals were licensed. *Records and Files of the Quarterly Courts of Essex County, Massachusetts* (Salem, Mass., 1911), vols.1 and 6. The towns with more than one licensed house were Charlestown, Cambridge, and Woburn in Middlesex County; Plymouth and Scituate in Plymouth County; and Boston in Suffolk County. Conroy, *In Public Houses,* 31–32.

32. Richard P. Gildrie, "Taverns and Popular Culture in Essex County, Massachusetts, 1678–1686," *Essex Institute Historical Collections,* 124 (1988), 162–63. By the 1730s, the towns of Braintree, Wrentham, Weymouth, Stoughton, Roxbury, Cambridge, and Higham had at least five public houses each for populations that ranged from one thousand to two thousand inhabitants. This suggests that one legal public house existed for every two hundred to four hundred persons. Conroy, *In Public Houses,* 80–81.

33. *Records and Files of the Quarter Courts of Essex County,* 9: (June 1683) 65–66.

34. In 1690, the town of Plymouth, with an estimated population of 775, had seven individuals licensed to sell alcoholic beverages. *Plymouth Court Records, 1686–1859,* ed. David Thomas Konig, 3 vols. (Wilmington, Del., 1978).

35. A number of towns—Abbington, Pembroke, Plimton, and Scituate—had tavern densities comparable to Boston's. Kingston had one licensee for each 95 inhabitants; like Plymouth this was slightly denser than Boston. I was able to locate tavern license information for only 1764 and 1766. *Plymouth Court Records,* I:6, III:228–29.

36. Conroy, *In Public Houses,* 147–48.

37. James Otis Sr. papers II, Massachusetts Historical Society.

38. *Abstracts of the Minutes of the Court of Pleas and Quarter Sessions of Rowan County, North Carolina, 1753–1774,* ed. Jo White Linn (Salisbury, N.C., 1977, 1979), 2 vols.; Robert W. Ramsey, *Carolina Cradle: Settlement of the Northwest Carolina Frontier, 1747–1762* (Chapel Hill, N.C., 1964). The records for Cumberland County appear more even, but this is only because the same people had their licenses renewed. From 1756 to 1764 the court issued an average of 11.5 licenses a year. *Abstracts of the Minutes of the Court of Pleas and Quarter Sessions of Cumberland County,* ed. William C. Fields, 2 vols. (Fayetteville, N.C., 1978), vol. 1.

39. Perquimans County, North Carolina Court of Common Pleas, North Carolina State Archives, Raleigh, N.C.; Rowan County Civil Action Papers, 1755–1774, North Carolina State Library.

40. The ledger ends in 1796. Alexander and John Lowrance Ledger, Perkins Library, Duke University.

41. Mary Katherine Petlewski, "Taverns in Eighteenth-Century North Carolina" (M.A. thesis, University of North Carolina, 1972), 26; Elise Lathrop, *Early American Inns and Taverns* (New York, 1935, 1977), 226; *Records of the Moravians in North Carolina,* ed. Adelaide L. Fries, 8 vols. (Raleigh, N.C., 1922), I:160; II:707, 884, 901.

42. James H. Merrell, *The Indians' New World: Catawbas and Their Neighbors from European Contact through the Era of Removal* (New York, 1989), 178–79. *Abstracts of Minutes of Court of Pleas of Rowan County,* II: 56, 58, 60, 63, 64, 78, 86, 96, 99, 100, 103. 130, 138. Richard J. Hooker, ed., *The Carolina Backcountry on the Eve of the Revolution:*

The Journal and Other Writings of Charles Woodmason, Anglican Itinerant (Chapel Hill, N.C., 1953), 96–97; Robert L. Meriwether, *The Expansion of South Carolina, 1729–1765* (Kingsport, Tenn., 1940), 140.

43. *Tavern License Papers, Chester County* (Pennsylvania), vol. 1, 1700–1728, vol. 2, 1729–1736, Chester County Archives. I estimated the number of taxpayers in Chester County in 1700 at 389. This was calculated by assuming steady growth of 18.9 persons per year from 1693 to 1715. Similarly, the number of taxpayers for 1717 was determined by assuming steady growth from 1715 to 1730, or 74.7 taxpayers per year, yielding 819 taxpayers. No figures are available for the number of taxpayers in Chester County for 1769. However, in 1760, 4,290 individuals were taxed and the population declined slightly after that. James T. Lemon reports 257 taxpayers in 1693 and 1,670 in 1715. *The Best Poor Man's Country: A Geographic Study of Early Southeastern Pennsylvania* (Baltimore, 1972), 11.

44. Tavern License Papers, Chester County, August 28, 1733; November 27, 1733; and September 4, 1733.

45. Ibid., February 23, 1720; November 27, 1722; February 28, 1727.

46. Ibid., January 12 and 20, 1732.

47. Ibid., February 29, 1732; August 31, 1731.

48. Ibid., August 31, 1731.

49. Ibid.,November 24, 1724; May 1730; May 28, 1717.

50. The Chester County court denied almost one-quarter of the petitions (23%, 29 of 126). No town was listed for William Robinson. Ibid., May 31, 1737, February 28, 1738, August 1737, August 1739, August 1744.

Chapter Seven / The Tavern Degenerate

1. *Virginia Gazette,* April 11, 1751.

2. James Clitherall Diary, April 7–July 2, 1776 on a trip from Charleston, South Carolina to Philadelphia escorting Mrs. Arthur Middleton and Mrs. Edward Rutledge. #159, Southern Historical Collection, Wilson Library, Chapel Hill, North Carolina.

3. Ebenezer Hazard's Journal, January 13, 1772–March 18, 1773, Trip Through New England and New York, Hazard Family Papers, Historical Society of Pennsylvania.

4. Unbound travel journal kept by Anthony Stoddard, merchant of Boston, on his visit to his land, farms and tenants in Ashford, and Pomfret, Vermont, in May 1733, Massachusetts Historical Society.

5. *Journal and Letters of Philip Vickers Fithian, A Plantation Tutor of the Old Dominion, 1773–1774,* ed. Hunter Dickinson Farish (Charlottesville, Va., 1968). 109.

6. *The Journal of Nicholas Cresswell, 1774–1777* (New York, 1924), 20–22, 52.

7. "William Logan's Journal of a Journey to Georgia, 1745," *The Pennsylvania Magazine of History and Biography* 36 (1912): 210.

8. *Some Cursory Remarks made by James Birket in his Voyage to North America, 1750–1751* (New Haven, Conn., 1916), 25, 33. Descriptions of bad tavern experiences

are easy to locate. Robert Hale on a trip to Canada stopped in Exeter, New Hampshire. This was not a well-equipped tavern. It had very little food and they paid 1 shilling less than the bill, because the landlord had no change. "Journal of a Voyage to Nova Scotia Made in 1731 by Robert Hale of Beverly," *Historical Collections of the Essex Institute* 42 (1906), 239.

9. "Journal of Route and Occurrences in a Journey to Philadelphia from Dighton, Begun October 24th, 1778 by William Ellery," *Pennsylvania Magazine of History and Biography* 12 (1888): 196.

10. "John Penn's Journal of a Visit to Reading, Harrisburg, Carlisle, and Lancaster in 1788," *Pennsylvania Magazine of History and Biography* 3 (1879): 286–87, 295.

11. *Some Cursory Remarks made by James Birket*, 38; *Voyage to America: The Journals of Thomas Cather*, ed. Thomas Yoseloff (New York, 1961), 103; *Moreau St. Mery's American Journey (1793–1798)*, ed. Anna and Kenneth Roberts (Garden City, N.Y., 1947), 121–22.

12. Flaherty, *Privacy in Colonial New England*, 76–77.

13. A few days later Sewall commented, "We again slept in the same bed, together." Diary of David Sewall, *Massachusetts Historical Society Proceedings* 1st ser., 16 (1878): 7, 10; "James Clitherall Diary," 6; and *Gentleman's Progress: The Itinerarium of Dr. Alexander Hamilton,* ed. Carl Bridenbaugh (Chapel Hill, N.C., 1948), 9–10, 195.

14. Louis B. Wright, *The Prose Work of William of Westover: Narratives of a Colonial Virginian* (Cambridge, Mass., 1966), 318–19. also recorded "laying" together with "the Doctor." *The Secret Diary of William of Westover, 1709–1712*, ed. Louis B. Wright and Marion Tinling (Richmond, 1941), May 11, 1709. Minutes of the Court of Common Pleas and Quarter Sessions, Edgecomb County, March 1759, North Carolina State Archives, Raleigh.

15. *The New Democracy in America: Travels of Francisco de Miranda in the United States, 1783–1784*, transcribed Judson P. Wood, ed. John S. Ezell (Norman, Okla., 1963), 16–17, 126. Trying to locate when the practice of sharing beds ended goes way beyond this project. Clearly it is very much a class issue. In families that have little space, sons and daughters continue to share beds. The practice remained common through the nineteenth century. I suspect that the end of bed sharing among men occurred when men aspired to a masculine ideal and feared the taint of homosexuality. Michael Kimmel, *Manhood in America: A Cultural History* (New York, 1996).

16. Dr. Alexander Hamilton, *The Tuesday Club: A Shorter Edition of the History of the Ancient and Honorable Tuesday Club,* ed. Robert Micklus (Baltimore, 1995), xii–xiv; *Gentleman's Progress.*

17. *Gentleman's Progress,* 41–42.

18. According to the *Oxford English Dictionary, gammon* means "the ham or haunch of a swine;" *sallet* refers to a measure of wine. *Gentleman's Progress,* xi–xv, 30–31, 37, 42, 65, 91.

19. *Some Cursory Remarks made by James Birket*, 3–6, 15–20. See also *The Journal of John Fontaine: An Irish Huguenot Son in Spain and New York, 1710–1719,* ed. Edward

Porter Alexander (Williamsburg, Va., 1972), 110–22; "William Gregory's Journal, From Fredericksburg, Va., to Philadelphia, 30th of September, 1765 to 16th October, 1765, *William and Mary Quarterly,* 1st ser., 13 (1904–5): 228.

20. *Gentleman's Progress,* 43.

21. "Journal of William Black," *Pennsylvania Magazine of History and Biography* 1 (1877): 405.

22. *Gentleman's Progress,* 6–7, 20, 21, 199.

23. Ibid., 17, 31.

24. Ibid., 41–42.

25. Andrew Burnaby, *Travels Through the Middle Settlements in North-America, In the Years 1759 and 1760, With Observations upon the State of the Colonies* (1775; reprint, Ithaca, N.Y., 1960), 101–2.

26. Josiah Quincy Diary, 8 February 1773–17 May 1773, Massachusetts Historical Society, 7 March 1773.

27. Quoted in Peter Thompson, "'The Friendly Glass': Drink and Gentility in Colonial Philadelphia," *Pennsylvania Magazine of History and Biography* 113 (1989): 563. Thompson's article is devoted to articulating these behaviors among the upper classes.

28. "Silence Dogood, No. 12," Printed in *The New-England Courant,* September 10, 1722, *The Papers of Benjamin Franklin,* ed. Leonard W. Labaree (New Haven, 1959), I:39–41.

29. *Extracts from the Diary of Jacob Hiltzheimer, of Philadelphia. 1765–1798,* ed. Jacob Cox Parsons (Philadelphia, 1893), 12, 13, 14, 15, 17, 20.

30. Ibid., 9.

31. "Extracts from Capt. Francis Goelet's Journal, Relative to Boston, Salem and Marblehead, &c., 1746–1750," *New England Historical and Genealogical Register* 24 (1870): 53.

32. "Extracts from Capt. Francis Goelet's Journal," 53, 54.

33. Alexander and John Lowrence Ledger, Perkins Library, Duke University; Daniel B. Thorp, "Doing Business in the Backcountry: Retail Trade in Colonial Rowan County, North Carolina," *William and Mary Quarterly,* 3d ser., 48 (1991), 398.

34. Robert and Lydia Moulder Tavern Accounts; Tavern Account Books, B1F11 P. English Papers (1684–1750), vols. 7–9, Essex Institute Salem, Massachusetts.

35. Accounts and memoranda of a general merchandise business, tavern, and legal matters. John Wilson. Mary Cranch Account Book and Leaves, 1739–1769, J. Touzel (1727–1785) Papers B5F7, Essex Institute, Salem, Massachusetts.

36. *Boston Gazette,* March 17 to March 24, 1740, No. 1052.

37. See, for example, the cases of four women fined in Essex County for drunkenness, from 1636 to 1662, including Marie Hill who was "overcome with wine." *Records and Files of the Quarterly Courts of Essex County Massachusetts,* 8 vols. (Essex Institute, 1911), I:57, 157, 414; II:254.

38. *Minutes of the Council and General Court of Colonial Virginia 1622–1632, 1670–1676,* ed. H. R. McIlwaine (Richmond, 1924), September 1626, 115.

39. The ellipses at the end of this entry are Black's. "Journal of William Black," 416. Drunk women were described differently than men. "Went with Deacon Taylor & Shepard to talk with Martin —— wife, scandalously drunk." Journal of Mr. Ballantine, August 3, 1763 in John Lockwood, *Westfield and Its Historic Influences, 1669–1919* (Springfield, Mass., 1922), I:403.

40. "James Clitherall Diary, April 7–July 2, 1776 on a trip from Charleston, South Carolina to Philadelphia escorting Mrs. Arthur Middleton and Mrs. Edward Rutledge," Southern Historical Collection, #159, Wilson Library, University of North Carolina, Chapel Hill, 4. Catherine Phillips, on her trip to the south, did stay at taverns occasionally and rarely had a good word to say about them. However, she most often lodged in private homes or stayed outside. "We breakfasted at a miserable inn, about eight or ten miles on our way; where we met such a wicked set of company, who had spent the night there that we concluded it providential that we did not press forward to lodge there; respecting which we were considering before we pitched our tent." *Memoir of the Life of Catherine Phillips: to which are added some of her epistles* (London, 1797), 82.

For examples of eighteenth-century women travelers who most often stayed at private lodging, see *A Short Account of the Life and Religious Labours of Patience Brayton, Late of Swansey, in the State of Massachusetts* (New York, 1801). Similarly, Miss Sarah Eve seems never to have lodged in a public house. "Extracts from the Journal of Miss Sarah Eve," *Pennsylvania Magazine of History and Biography* 5 (1881): 19–36. Also, "Extracts from the Diary of Hannah Callender," *Pennsylvania Magazine of History and Biography* 12 (1888), 432–56.

41. *The Journal of Madam Knight* (Winship, N.Y., 1935), 27–28.

42. Ibid., 31. The term *versal*, according to the *Compact Edition of the Oxford English Dictionary*, was a colloquial abbreviation for universal or whole. I assume the daughter means whole or entire life. (Oxford, 1971), 3615.

43. *Journal of Madam Knight*, 38–39. For an example of a woman traveler who spent time in both public and private houses and who did on occasion drink in the tavern, see "A Ride Across Connecticut Before the Revolution," *Papers of the New Haven Colony Historical Society* 9 (New Haven, 1918), 161–69.

44. "The Journal of Charlotte Brown, Matron of the General Hospital with the English Forces in America, 1754–1756," *Colonial Captivities, Marches and Journeys*, ed. Isabel M. Calder (Port Washington, N.Y., 1935, reissued 1967), 188, 190–92; Peter Thompson, *Rum Punch and Revolution: Taverngoing and Public Life in Eighteenth-Century Philadelphia* (Philadelphia, 1999), 90; Sandoval-Strausz, "A Public House for the New Republic," ms. 12 .

45. *Gentleman's Progress*, 4, 31.

46. David Conroy argues that taverns contributed to a more open, less paternalistic society. I think the opposite more likely. *In Public Houses: Drink and the Revolution of Authority in Colonial Massachusetts* (Chapel Hill, N.C. , 1995), esp. ch. 5. See also Nancy L. Struna, *People of Prowess: Sport, Leisure, and Labor in Early America* (Urbana, Ill., 1996), fn 28, 245.

47. J. H. Innes, *New Amsterdam and Its People: Studies, Social and Topographical, of the Town under Dutch and Early English Rule* (New York, 1902), 9–11.

48. Ellis Lawrence Raesly, *Portrait of New Netherland* (New York, 1945), 159.

49. Lee R. Boyer, "Lobster Backs, Liberty Boys, and Laborers in the Streets: New York's Golden Hill and Nassau Street Riots," *The New-York Historical Society Quarterly* 57 (1973), 289–91.

50. Carl Abbott, "The Neighborhoods of New York, 1760–1775," *New York History* 55 (1974): 49–50; William Smith, *Historical Memoirs from 1 March, 1763, to 9 July, 1776* (New York, 1956), 102–3; *New York Gazette and Weekly Mercury*, March 26, 1770; *New York Gazette and Weekly Mercury*, March 20, 1775; *New York Mercury* October 6, 1760; *The New York Mercury*, October 27, 1766.

51. *The New York Journal; or the General Advertiser*, May 13, 1773; Bambridge, *New York Gazette; or the Weekly Post-Boy*, Monday, March 28, 1768; and Carl Bridenbaugh, *Cities in Revolt: Urban Life in America* (New York, 1955), 316.

52. Thomas Davis, "Slavery in Colonial New York City," (Ph.D. diss., Columbia University, 1974), 99.

53. Daniel Horsmanden, *The New York Conspiracy*, ed. Thomas J. Davis (Boston, 1971), 330, 68, 59, 61, 37, 61, 70.

54. Ibid., xii.

55. Ibid., 15; Rediker, "The Outcasts of the Nations of the Earth," 1.

56. Peter Linebaugh and Marcus Rediker, *The Many-Headed Hydra: Sailors, Slaves, Commoners, and the Hidden History o the Revolutionary Atlantic* (Boston, 2000), 174–83, 204–10; Horsmanden, *The New York Conspiracy*, 389, 411–12.

57. *Gentleman's Progress*, 11.

58. *Holidays, Festivals and Celebrations of the World Dictionary*, comp. Sue Ellen Thompson and Barbara W. Carlson (Detroit, Mich., 1994), 41, 162.

59. Simes was in court again two years later, this time because one of his patrons was accused of passing counterfeit coins in his tavern. He was found guilty. Peter Thompson, "A Social History of Philadelphia's Taverns, 1683–1800" (Ph.D. Diss., University of Pennsylvania, 1989), 114, 115; Scharf and Westcott describe the activities in Simes' house as a masquerade. J. Thomas Scharf and Thompson Westcott, *History of Philadelphia, 1609–1884*, 3 vols. (Philadelphia, 1884), I:157. Rituals in eighteenth-century England included cross-dressing as part of the custom. On Easter Monday in Middleton, "young men, 'grotesquely dress', some in female attire, who would go in companies led by a fidler." Christmas celebrations, in sixteenth- and seventeenth-century England also included "groups of mummers, cross-dress youth of both sexes." Barry Reay, *Popular Cultures in England, 1550–1750* (London, 1998), 135, 137.

60. Beth Fowkes Tobin, *Picturing Imperial Power: Colonial Subjects in Eighteenth-Century British Painting* (Durham, N.C., 1999), 21–23. There is an increasing literature on the theory of cross-dressing and the related dynamics of mimicry, masquerade, and parody that inhere in cross-dressing. See, for example, Vern L. Bullough and Bonnie Bullough, *Cross-Dressing, Sex, and Gender* (Philadelphia, 1993); Judith Butler, *Gender Trou-*

ble: Feminism and the Subversion of Identity (London, 1990); Marjorie Garber, *Vested Interests: Cross-Dressing and Cultural Authority* (New York, 1992); Anne McClintock, *Imperial Leather: Race, Gender and Sexuality in the Colonial Contest* (New York, 1995); Luce Irigaray, *This Sex Which Is Not One* (Ithaca, N.Y., 1985).

Alfred Young has compiled a listing of all of the colonial cross-dressing cases he could locate. Only the one cited here occurred inside a tavern. Young concludes that cases fit into several categories: attire for runaway servants, one incident for overtly sexual purposes, for women's participation in military activities, and at holidays (Shrove Tuesday, Christmas, Election Days, Commencement, Popes Day, and the one here, Boxing Day). Alfred F. Young, "Reports of Cross Dressing," March 26, 2000.

61. *Minutes of the Common Council of Philadelphia, 1704–1776* (Philadelphia, 1847): (April 17th, 1732) 314, (July 1738) 376, (August 1741) 405.

62. The name Hell Town was used in a "Presentment to the Grand Jury," January 3, 1744, *Pennsylvania Magazine of History and Biography* 22 (1898), 497–98; *The Papers of Benjamin Franklin* (New Haven, 1959), 3: 11. Billy G. Smith, *The "Lower Sort:" Philadelphia's Laboring People, 1750–1800* (Ithaca, N.Y., 1990), 21–26.

63. Peter Thompson questions whether the taverns in Mulberry Ward, the area the grand jury labeled as Hell Town, were properly identified. Thompson agrees that the taverns were most densely clustered here; however, he argues, they were among the most wealthy. Even if the grand jury incorrectly identified the socioeconomic position of the taverns in Mulberry Ward, they successfully conveyed the source of the fear in Philadelphia's elite and at the same time offered a glimpse into the activities inside many waterfront establishments. Thompson, "A Social History of Philadelphia's Taverns," 142.

64. Reported in the *New York Mercury*, Monday, July 23, 1753.

65. Thompson, *Rum Punch and Revolution*, 44; Philadelphia Court Record Taken by Patrick Robinson, 1685–1686, Historical Society of Pennsylvania.

66. "An Account of the Robberies Committed" by John Morrison, Philadelphia, 1751, Rosenbach Foundation Copy, Evans Imprint series, #6624.

67. Ibid.

68. Ibid. A similar event took place one year later. John Webster was captured and confined in jail after having committed a series of robberies in the vicinity of Philadelphia. He was discovered at a tavern with his female accomplice and their cache. *Pennsylvania Gazette*, December 10, 1751, December 24, 1751, January 21, 1752, April 23, 1752, May 7, 1752.

69. Quoted in Bruce C. Daniels, *Puritans and Play: Leisure and Recreation in Colonial New England* (New York, 1995), 159.

70. Richard P. Gildrie, "Taverns and Popular Culture in Essex County, Massachusetts," Essex Institute Historical Collections, 124 (1988), 164–69.

71. Ibid., 169–71.

72. The Robert Love Diary, April 5, 1766; April 22, 1766, Massachusetts Historical Society. Evidence in the Boston's Selectmen's Minutes confirms the mixing of races in Boston. "Jerusha Will an Indian Woman & Stranger who lay Dead at Humpreys a Negro

Mans house at the North end." *Report of the Record Commissioners of the City of Boston, Selectmen's Minutes, 1742–3 to 1753* (Boston, 1811), 17:37.

73. *Journals of the Commons House of Assembly of South Carolina for 1702,* ed. A. S. Salley (Columbia, S.C., 1932), 99; Journal of the General Sessions Court, 1769–1776, Court of Common Pleas, 19, April 1770, 64; 25, January 1771, 108; 20 January 1772, 170; 18 May 1775, 326; Philip D. Morgan, "Black Life in Eighteenth-Century Charleston," *Perspectives in American History* 1 (1984), 206–8.

74. Horsmanden, *The New York Conspiracy,* 194.

75. Mancall, *Deadly Medicine,* 44, 46. The number of laws prohibiting colonists from selling alcohol to Indians in every colony (see Chapter 2) strongly suggests that the practice was widespread. See for example 3 October 1731, Joseph Payne of Braintree who was indicted for keep bad orders in his house and selling drink to Indians. Records of the Court of General Sessions of the Peace, Massachusetts State Archives, Columbia Point. Or examine the 24 cases involving Indians in *Record of the Suffolk County Court, 1671–1680* (Boston, 1933), publications of the Colonial Society of Massachusetts, XXIX and XXX.

76. "A Journal with observations of my Travail from Boston in N.E. to N.Y., New Jersies & Philadelphia in Pennsylvania. A.D. 1697," Benjamin Bullivant, New York Historical Society.

77. *Gentleman's Progress,* xiii, 23, 34, 98, 103–4, 110, 112–14, 141, 162, 168, 172, 178. See also James H. Merrell, "Some Thoughts on Colonial Historians and American Indians," *William and Mary Quarterly,* 3d ser., 46 (1989): 116.

78. Gottlieb Mittelberger, *Journey to Pennsylvania* (Cambridge, Mass., 1960), 62–63. I thank James H. Merrell for alerting me to this reference (I worked from a different edition of the diary) and for giving generously of his time discussing, through cyberspace, the implications of so few diary entries about Indians.

79. This paragraph is based on Ruth Wallis Herndon and Ella Wilcox Sekatau, "The Right to a Name: The Narragansett People and Rhode Island Officials in the Revolutionary Era," in *After King Philip's War: Presence and Persistence in Indian New England,* ed. Colin G. Calloway (Hanover, N.H., 1997), 129. Fish noted: "Toby Shaddick, Ditto Another Indian . . . Entertaining, Danel. And Sachim. Victuals, Drink, Horses and My time." *Old Light on Separate Ways: The Narragansett Diary of Joseph Fish, 1765–1776,* ed. William S. Simmons and Cheryl L. Simmons, (Hanover, N.H., 1982), 19–20.

80. The reference to the Vernon tavern was provided by James H. Merrell. The manuscripts for these accounts are at the Historical Society of Pennsylvania. Merriwether, *The Expansion of South Carolina,* 63.

81. On the tavern debt see *The Papers of William Johnson,* 14 vols. (1951), 10:148; for specific references to Montour's drinking behavior see James H. Merrell, "'The Cast of His Countenance': Reading Andrew Montour," in *Through a Glass Darkly: Reflections on Personal Identity in Early America,* ed. Ronald Hoffman, et al. (Chapel Hill, 1997), 24.

82. The descriptions of Indians' imbibing took two seemingly contradictory forms. The first sought to highlight difference and thus magnified the divisions between the two

cultures. Thus, Indians were characterized in their drinking as "wild," "savage," and "frightening;" while colonists embodied "civilization" and "moderation." The second stressed shared manners, as if to deemphasize these differences. Here, for example, colonists and Indians joined together to toast the English king or colonial governor. In both cases, these representations served to affirm the dominance of the colonists over the Indians. In the first scenario the process is clearer. Colonists emerged as better, their style of drinking a confirmation of the natural, self-evident superiority of the dominant society. In the second case, what materialized was a successful example of the colonizer's project of assimilation, to convert the Indians to their customs. This "shared" behavior demonstrated the colonists' belief that the Indians already desired to take on these superior customs. For a discussion of assimilation goals and practices, see Tzvetan Todorov, *The Conquest of America: The Question of the Other,* trans. Richard Howard (New York, 1984), 42–44.

83. Gildrie, "Taverns and Popular Culture in Essex County," 171; Daniel Vickers, "Work and Life on the Fishing Periphery of Essex County, Massachusetts, 1630–1675," in *Seventeenth-Century New England,* ed. David D. Hall and David G. Allen (Charlottesville, Va., 1984), 113–14.

Conclusion

1. "Tom Paine's jests; being an entirely new and select collection of patriotic bon mots, repartees, anecdotes, epigrams, observations, &c. on political subjects. By Thomas Paine, and other supporters of the rights of man. To which is added, A tribute to the swinish multitude, being a choice collection of patriotic songs" (Philadelphia, 1796). Evans Imprint Series no. 30952.

2. This section owes a great deal to exchanges with Andrew Sandoval-Strausz. See also A. K. Sandoval-Strausz, "A Public House for a New Republic: The Architecture of Accommodation and the American State, 1789–1809," *Perspectives in Vernacular Architecture* (forthcoming).

3. Sandoval-Strausz, "A Public House for a New Republic."

4. A. K. Sandoval-Strausz, "For the Accommodation of Strangers: Urbanism, Space, Travel, and the American Hotel, 1789–1908," (Ph.D. diss., University of Chicago, 2001). Madelon Powers, *Faces Along the Bar: Lore and Order in the Workingman's Saloon, 1870–1920* (Chicago, 1998).

5. Miss Leslie, *The Behaviour Book: A Manual for Ladies* (Philadelphia, 1855), 101–47. Sandoval-Strausz, "For the Accommodation of Strangers."

6. While the social character of the first generation of hotels (those of the 1790s and first decade of the 1800s) was indeed very exclusionary, that aspect begins to fall away slightly in the Jacksonian period. Sandoval-Strausz, "A Public House for a New Republic."

Index